D0170717

The Time of the Gypsies

The Time of the Gypsies

MICHAEL STEWART

WestviewPress

A Division of HarperCollins*Publishers*

Studies in the Ethnographic Imagination

All photographs appear courtesy of the author unless otherwise credited.

Published in 1997 in the United States of America by Westview Press, 5500 Central Avenue, Boulder, Colorado 80301-2877, and in the United Kingdom by Westview Press, 12 Hid's Copse Road, Cumnor Hill, Oxford OX2 9JJ

A CIP catalog record for this book is available from the Library of Congress.
ISBN 0-8133-3198-6

The paper used in this publication meets the requirements of the American National Standard for Permanence of Paper for Printed Library Materials Z39.48-1984.

10   9   8   7   6   5   4   3   2

For Előd, Gergely, and Bálint

CONTENTS

TABLES AND ILLUSTRATIONS

Tables

Photos

FOREWORD

Maurice Bloch

THIS IS A STUDY OF HOW some of the most marginal and exploited people that exist can imagine themselves to be princes of the world.

During the past two hundred years the Gypsies of Eastern Europe have faced near enslavement by land owners, the physical and moral onslaught of the Nazi holocaust, the fundamental challenge to their central values from the Communist state, and the violent discrimination and dislocation caused by the return to capitalism. One would have thought that the challenge would be too great, that they would have suffered cultural annihilation.

In fact this has not been the case. The documentation and analysis of this success, partial though it is, is the subject matter of this important and original study.

The evocation of feasting Hungarian Gypsy men, a strong and confident group of "brothers" bound forever, in their imagination, in a world outside history and nation-states, forms the hub of this book. It bears witness to the ability of people to construct a representation of coherence through art and symbols. This representation is fragile and temporary. Nevertheless its joyful acting-out creates the lasting identity—as Gypsies—of those who evoke it.

This is what Durkheim meant when he saw ritual as a means by which people collectively create the moral order of society at the very moment when they believe most strongly that it originates from a transcendental beyond. What Durkheim forgot, however, and what this book never forgets, is that the experience of being outside history and beyond the exercise of earthly power is only an illusion.

This consciousness of the illusory nature of representation exists at two levels: analytic and phenomenological. Analytic because it is obvious that these fleeting images of autonomy and power can only be created with the raw materials that history at any given moment provides; they are mere interludes in the constant human struggle with the world as it is, and as it changes. Phenomenological because these festive and exultant representations are known by the actors themselves to be only one among many others that they feel able to control less well or not at all.

Michael Stewart has, therefore, undertaken two major tasks. First, he shows that the Gypsies cannot be understood in isolation from the wider society of which they have always formed a part. We need to take into account the changing attitudes and policies towards the Gypsies in the Austro-Hungarian empire, in Communist Europe and in post-Communist Hungary to comprehend their present condition. In doing this, he performs another unexpected service: He articulates a more profound understanding of the nature of these regimes themselves.

In particular, Stewart makes us aware of the great significance of the ways in which Eastern European peasants and Communist ideologues evaluated different forms of work and commerce. When they inform a subtle discourse about the Gypsies, these ostensibly crude ideas reveal themselves to be far more ambiguous and complex than they at first seem. Thus the study of non-Gypsy attitudes and beliefs about Gypsies becomes an alternative political and economic history of this part of Eastern Europe as a whole.

Foucault has argued that the study of discourses about marginal groups becomes a means of revealing in a new light the central tenets of those who hold power. The second major task that Stewart undertakes in this book is one that Foucault in his studies of prisoners or deviants notably failed to do. This task is to demonstrate how those whom power-holders consider to be marginal are central to themselves.

Stewart's achievement is to make us see the Gypsies from their point of view or, rather, from the many points of view they employ to cope with their situation. The Gypsies create new types of knowledge and forge new skills in a dialectic with the "center." In response to exclusion and exploitation they create their own subversive economic doctrines.

These creations are not, however, easily accomplished. They are often tentative and involve elements of unconvincing swagger. And they create their own legitimation of exploitation, particularly of women. Above all, they involve ignoring much of the reality of life; for example, the engagement of Gypsies in factory work under communism, or the brute fact that the ways in which non-Gypsies can finally be outsmarted are limited indeed and tend to provoke further humiliations.

Stewart carried out long-term field work with the Gypsies, speaking to them in their own language, in the multitude of contexts everyday life provides. He is, therefore, able to make explicit the implicit. The anthropologist is not a spokesperson for the people he or she studies, since one cannot and should not take away their right, when they are able to exercise it, of speaking for themselves. What the anthropologist can do is make meaningful to us the actions and reactions of those who only seem to be foreign until understanding is achieved. As Stewart shows so well, in spite of history and culture the Gypsies do, in the end, belong to our one shared social network. They are moved by emotions and beliefs similar to those that move us and everyone else.

An intimate knowledge of the meaning ordinary people give to and express through their lives is what historical studies almost entirely lack because, most of the time, historians can find no record of it. Because of the distance that exists between political scientists, sociologists, or economists and their subjects, they too are often unaware of these deep levels of data. The work of anthropologists such as Michael Stewart does not replace the contribution of these other disciplines but adds to them human depth and understanding.

This book is, therefore, not just an important anthropological account of a minority group in Hungary. It is also a valuable and unique contribution to the general study of the recent dramatic transformations that have occurred throughout Eastern Europe.

ACKNOWLEDGMENTS

I HAVE A DEBT TO THE ROM of Harangos that I cannot repay. Fieldwork is one of the great adventures, and I thank them for allowing me to go on that journey among them. I have protected the identities of everyone I know by altering names, conflating and separating persons, and disguising the town.

In Hungary I was helped, above all, by Judit Szegő, who came and lived with me and our one-month-old baby. She put up with the hardest aspects of the work. Havas Gábor, who then was one of the founder members of an illegal charity—illegal because under communism there was officially no need for charities—first took me to Rom communities, and more than anyone else he has kept reminding me of the place of the Harangos Rom in the wider picture of Hungarian Gypsies. Katalin Kovalcsik of the Zenetudományi Intézet taught me Romany, introduced me to Harangos, and shared her time and insights with me. Bodor Ágnes of the Társadalom Tudományi Intézet organized permission and funds for me to work in a factory in 1988. Lajos Boglár, Mihály Hoppál, Ildikó Kríza, and especially Mihály Sárkány of the Ethnographic Research Group provided assistance whenever I asked for it. Peter Szuhay of the Néprajzi Muzeum arranged for the reproduction of six of the photographs. Ágnes Mészáros, Endre Tálos, Ágnes Daróczi, József Bogdán, György Rostás-Farkas, Attila Balogh, Károly Bari, István Szentandrássy, Ágnes Diósi, Balogh Katalin, and the Spilák family provided much of the fun I had when I was not in Harangos.

In England the members of the London School of Economics thesis writing seminar, 1986–1987, are due my gratitude. Janet Carsten, in particular, has continued to read and suggest improvements to my work. Fenella Cannell provided some of those telling phrases that bring an argument into shape. The Economic and Social Research Council generously funded the Ph.D. research and dissertation writing. In Cambridge Corpus Christi College offered me a Junior Research Fellowship, and the Department of Anthropology there provided me with a new intellectual home for four years. Conversations with Keith Hart kept me believing in the wider relevance of this story. Tanya Schwarz provided much fun, and support, and encouragement. John Blake, formerly of Granada Television, produced a film about the Harangos Rom and by so doing launched me in new directions. The University of Paris X at Nanterre gave me a chance to put together an early version of this book.

Mike Kirkwood read my thesis anonymously and suggested the title of the book. Though there has since been a film of the same name, the reader will discover that there the similarity ends. Charles Stafford kindly read and criticized the manuscript at its penultimate stage. Chris Hann and Frances Pine, who have provided a constant flow of helpful and critical comments over the years since we were at Corpus together, put the commas in and removed, I hope, some of the most grating grammar. They also generously improved the substance and the structure of the argument. I hope they are not too appalled at the outcome. Cornelia Sorabji read two versions of this book, and the present structure of the argument is her suggestion.

There is, too, a special vote of thanks for Maurice Bloch, my supervisor, whose trust, whose uncomplaining acceptance of changes of direction, and whose vision of the whole open doors where others put up walls. Together with the other staff at the London School of Economics, he has provided the place where most of this work has been written. Sophie Day and Akis Papataxiarchis, colleagues at the school with whom I have organized a seminar on marginality and resistance, will recognize the influence of our discussions on the way I cast some of the argument.

There are some intellectual debts that cannot be tied to place or time. The influence of Patrick Williams's work throughout the text will be obvious to anyone who knows it. While I was listening to the Rom sing around me day by day, I read his book, and he made them sing in a way I can only envy. David Lan brought me into anthropology, visited me in the field, and has read this work at every stage. He has been an inspiration.

This book has been sheltered in various houses and to their owners— David Lan and Nicholas Wright in London and Toulouse, Janet Carsten in London, Anne-Marie Hardouin in Paris, the Langlois at Genissac, and Mellissa Llewelyn-Davies in London and Wales—many thanks. Cornelia Sorabji showed me how to stop living like a nomad. To her is due much more than thanks.

Michael Stewart

A NOTE ON THE TEXT

IN THE ABSENCE OF ANY internationally agreed on orthography for Romany, I have adopted a slightly simplified version of that currently used by the Musicological and Linguistics Institutes of the Hungarian Academy of Sciences.

Characters that may be unfamiliar are:

č as in *ch*urch
ś as in *sh*op
š indicates a rougher, alveopalatal *sh*
ź as in plea*s*ure
h after *k, p, t* indicates aspiration

In Romany there are two forms of the sound represented by *r* in the text. In the words Rom and its derivatives (Romni, *romanes*, etc.), *čoro*, *rodel, muro*, the *r* represents a more intensely trilled and usually uvular-ized rhotic than normal *r*. The same holds for the second *r* in *korkoro*. In technical texts this sound would normally be indicated with a macron over the *r*.

All Romany words not in direct quotes are given in the singular (and in the case of adjectives) masculine form unless otherwise stated. Following Fél and Hofer (1969), when I use such words in the plural I have added an English *s*.

The Communist Party of Hungary was known as such only until 1948, when it changed its name. The name changed again in 1956, but I have kept the simple, generic title throughout.

M.S.

1

INTRODUCTION: THE LOWEST OF THE LOW

Everywhere Gypsies are the lowest of the low. Why? Because they are different. Because they steal, are restless, roam, have the Evil Eye and that stunning beauty that makes us ugly to ourselves. Because their mere existence puts our values in question. Because they are all very well in operas and operettas, but in reality . . . they are anti-social, odd and don't fit in. "Torch them!" shout the skinheads.

Günter Grass, "Losses"

UNTIL 1989 IT WAS OFFICIAL COMMUNIST POLICY in Eastern Europe to absorb Gypsies into the "ruling" working class. But many Gypsies fought to maintain their separate identity. This book is about the refusal of one group of Gypsies, the Rom, to abandon their way of life and accept assimilation into the majority population. Forget romantic notions of the careless freedoms of caravans and campfires; these Gypsies' lives were hard and sometimes brutal. They dreamed of riches gained from gambling or lucky horse deals, but in reality they were poverty-stricken. They lived in semislums, ghettos in all but name, taken over from Hungarian peasants, and the law insisted that the Gypsies work, often for very low wages in industry or on collective farms. And yet despite their lowly position and all their suffering, they held onto an image of their own dignity and joy as Gypsies.

The people whom the reader will meet in this book are all Hungarian citizens, and their stories come from the time when that country, like the whole of Eastern Europe, was under Communist rule, but what they have to say concerns anyone who lives in the industrialized world. Ultimately, this is a story about the sources of cultural diversity in modern industrial society and of the fear and hatred that such social and cultural difference may give rise to. The heart of the book, based on a total of eighteen months' observation of daily life in a Gypsy settlement, describes the cultivation, celebration, and reinvention of cultural difference and diversity by a people deemed by its social superiors too stupid and uncivilized to have a culture at all. The other part of the story concerns the sometimes disastrous, sometimes comic, and sometimes sinister consequences of a well-intentioned policy of social engineering. Although the Hungarian attempt to impose a standardized vision of how an ethnic minority like the Gypsies should live was in some respects a specifically Communist project, in many other ways it illustrated a relation between social reformers and the people who were supposed to benefit from these reforms that could have been found anywhere in the "democratic" Western world.

Post-Communist Gypsies, or Roma

In April 1993 seventeen-year-old Magdalena Babicka stood on the stage of a newly renovated hotel in the Czech spa town of Karlovy Vary. Magdalena was one of the twelve finalists in a new, televised competition, Miss Czech-Slovakia. At one point in the evening, the master of ceremonies asked the girls, one by one, about their ambition. The options chosen by the other girls, air hostess, model, or even journalist, were not for Magdalena. "I want to become a public prosecutor," she announced, "so I can clean our town of its dark-skinned inhabitants." Magdalena, appearing for the first time on national television, looked around nervously for an instant, but the ripple of laughter in the invited audience turned into a burst of applause. Magdalena's "little joke" had worked. "You're a brave girl," the master of ceremonies told her. "Some newspapers won't like you for saying that, but those of us who don't live in your town have no idea how difficult things are."[1]

The next morning Magdalena found that she had turned herself into headline material across Europe. The BBC World Service broadcast an item about her, and newspapers across the Continent told the story of the "Czech beauty" who "wants to rid her town of Gypsies." For a few days in the Czech Republic, there was talk of prosecuting her, but the authorities decided to let the dust settle over the incident.

Magdalena had inadvertently set off a small international outcry, but back in her hometown the work for which she thought herself fitted was already being initiated. The impending separation of the Czech and Slovak Republics meant that all residents of the former Czechoslovakia had to acquire new papers and proof of citizenship. In the Second World

War, the Nazis had wiped out the Czech Gypsy population, so in 1993 many of those living in the Czech lands were still seen by Czechs as "immigrants" from Slovakia.[2] Their presence had long caused resentment among the tidy Czechs, and the redefinition of nationality provided a chance, to officials so minded, to encourage some of the troublesome and "antisocial" Gypsies to leave. Through a clever use of stalling, obfuscation, and bureaucratic intimidation, several families from Magdalena's hometown were being sent on their way by spring 1993. And despite the restraining influence of the media, alerted by Magdalena's outburst, by August 1995 conservative estimates suggested that 25,000 Czech Gypsies (out of a total population of 200,000) were now being excluded from citizenship and voting rights in the country where they lived and worked.[3]

But it was not just in the order-obsessed Czech Republic that Gypsies were discovering a harsh new reality. Gypsies have become the scapegoats of postcommunism throughout the region. In the Czech Republic, most of the petty and not so petty machinations that are worked against luckless Gypsy families have the seal of bureaucratic procedure stamped on them. Elsewhere in post-Communist Europe, the marks of oppression are different. Gypsy refugees from warring Yugoslavia have repeatedly claimed that they were the first sent into battle by their Croat and Serb commanders. In Romania in the first two years after the revolution, nearly two hundred Gypsy homes were burned to the ground in eleven separate incidents. Five individuals died in these attacks. There were countless other incidents of random beatings, some of them carried out with official connivance.[4] In Poland, and in Hungary, too, there have been lynchings and small-scale pogroms.[5] In the three years from 1993 through 1995, twenty-eight Gypsies were killed by skinheads in the Czech Republic.[6] In a more organized fashion throughout the region, revived fascist parties have targeted Gypsies rather than the former victims of the extreme right, the Jews.

Gypsy suffering has not been caused by racist violence alone. Having been the cheap labor of Warsaw Pact communism, Gypsies have often suffered most from the social and economic disintegration that has affected the whole region since 1989. In Hungary in 1994, 65 percent of Gypsy men were unemployed. The figure rose to an astonishing 90 percent in one of the northern counties, a former center of steel production. Incidents of terror and the objective hopelessness of the economic situation of most Gypsies in the new order have led inevitably to migration and flight. In Germany in 1993, estimates from Gypsy organizations suggested that there were more than 30,000 Romanian Gypsy asylum-seekers. So severe was the problem that special arrangements seem to have been made at that time between the Czech and German authorities not to allow Romanian Gypsies through their borders. And in early 1996 there were plans afoot in Warsaw to deport large numbers of those Gypsies unable to get any farther west than Poland.[7]

The history of persecution, suffering, and forced assimilation provokes two questions about the Gypsies. First, just what makes them so threatening to their host populations? And second, the central question that I try to answer in this book, given the hostility toward them, how and why do the Gypsies go on?

The problem is even more striking when seen in a deeper historical perspective. For as long as there have been Gypsies in Europe, they have suffered hostility, segregation, and misery. In preindustrial Europe, despite finding an occupational niche, especially in rural areas of Eastern Europe, where they provided crafts and services, the Gypsies were harried as they traveled and harassed when they settled. In the Czech lands in the sixteenth century, the Gypsies were forced to be executioners, in the Romanian provinces of Moldavia and Wallachia they were enslaved, and in the France of the Sun King they were tied into the galleys as oarsmen. In the late eighteenth century in Hungarian-administered Slovakia, some forty Gypsy men and women were executed for a supposed cannibal feast that was later proved to have never taken place. A novel solution to "the Gypsy problem" in the Austro-Hungarian Empire was adopted around this time by the "enlightened absolutist" rulers Maria Theresa and her son Joseph II: Gypsy children were to be forcibly adopted into peasant families and their parents declared "new Hungarians" or "new peasants." The policy failed in large part because the nobility objected to the loss of a source of cheap labor.[8] The rise of capitalism and democratic or quasidemocratic states reinforced, if anything, the marginal position of the Gypsies. From the late nineteenth century one finds in law books and local edicts across Europe traces of efforts to restrict the movement of the Gypsies and control the "nomad menace."[9]

Only very recently have a small number of Gypsies begun to respond to persecution by organizing political parties and social movements. Meetings of Gypsy intellectuals and political leaders have been held under the formal aegis of the International Romany Union, with representatives from twenty-six countries. Numerous less formal gatherings, known as the Romano Congresso (the Rom Conference), take place each year in Eastern Europe. But for the ordinary Gypsy in one of the unofficial ghettos on the edge of an Eastern European village or town, the maneuvers of Gypsy intellectuals on the national and international stages rarely mean much, at least as yet. Sometimes it seems that the Romany political parties spend more effort establishing their credibility among non-Gypsy authorities than among their own constituents. Even though in most countries these leaders have successfully argued that the Gypsies should be treated as an ethnic minority and have succeeded in changing some official practices—for instance, Gypsies are now normally referred to in the media as Roma, or some local version of this, rather than the derogatory local words for Gypsies, Zigeuner in German, Cigány in Hungarian, Tsigani in Romanian—the leaders' concerns remain very different from those of ordinary Gypsies. It is a telling statistic that in a recent survey of 10,000 Hungarian Gypsies, 90 percent of the respondents were unable to name a single Gypsy political party.[10]

To understand how ordinary Gypsies survive persecution and perpetuate their way of life, we have to turn away from the round-tables and international forums beloved of journalists and television reporters and toward the politics of daily life on and off the Gypsy settlements in Eastern Europe. It is in the repeated negotiation of identity and interest, in conflict with hostile non-Gypsies in towns such as the one I lived in, that the secret of Gypsy survival will be found.

Communists and Gypsies

Since the beginning of the Second World War, there have been two dramatic attempts to "solve the Gypsy problem" once and for all. Between 1941 and 1945, the Nazis exterminated some 500,000 Gypsies in an effort to eliminate their "degenerate" and "antisocial" way of life.[11] Between 1957 and 1989, a very different sort of campaign against the Gypsies was waged in Eastern Europe. No one was to be imprisoned, let alone killed. Indeed, repression and discrimination could not have been further from the thoughts of the early Communist reformers. But the desired end was surprisingly close to the fascist dream: The Gypsies were to disappear.

The task that Eastern European Communists set themselves in 1957 was indeed herculean—the social and cultural assimilation of millions of people who had suffered discrimination for centuries. But the Communists believed that history was on their side.[12] And then there was the desire to use the Gypsies as an example. What better proof could there be of the power of the Communist method of social transformation than the disappearance of the Gypsies? So throughout the Communist bloc, with the partial exception of Yugoslavia, the Gypsies were subject to a systematic assimilationist campaign. Czechoslovakia, Poland, the Soviet Union, Romania, and Hungary pursued almost identical policies.[13]

While in the capitalist West the Gypsy problem receded after the war, in the East two factors kept the Gypsies in the public and official eye. First was their demographic importance. Whereas the Gypsies made up a tiny proportion (0.1–0.3 percent) of the population in the West, across the Iron Curtain they formed up to 5 percent and were often, as in Hungary, the largest single ethnic group. Second was the fact that the mere existence of the Gypsies grated on the Communist ideological sensitivities. These are issues I return to in Chapter 6, but the reader may find it helpful to have the key elements highlighted here.

From the Communist point of view, Gypsies were the poorest of the poor. They often lived in hovels outside of the village to which they were attached, and in some highly visible places, such as the capital of Hungary, the Gypsies could still be found living in caves. Hardly any of them had any education, and as few had jobs. Faced with this deeply un-civilized legacy of the capitalist past, the authorities took what, to their minds, was a sympathetic approach. Although the "anarchic" and "un-productive" Gypsy way of life might have been a rational response to ex-treme social marginalization and poverty, Communist society could pro-vide a home for the Gypsies and so integrate them into "normal" life. In the past the Gypsies had been excluded from villages by Magyar peas-ants or only allowed to live beside the village carrion pit; they had sys-tematically been paid less than their Magyar landless neighbors for iden-tical work and had often found themselves paid in kind, not cash.[14] The Communists would put an end to such discrimination.

Crucially, however, the Gypsies were not to be allowed to "enter soci-ety" on their own terms. From the Communist point of view, there was a profound opposition between the Gypsy attitude toward wealth, work, and good housekeeping and the socialist one. Communist theoreticians argued that when capitalist industrialization had rendered the Gypsies' traditional skills (as foresters, trough and basket makers, petty black-smiths, and musicians) redundant, most of them had been reduced to scavenging and begging. Some had tried to surrender their way of life, but there were others who instead had turned to "hustling." From the of-ficial point of view, this "wheeling and dealing" was either a more de-veloped form of begging or, worse, active commercial exploitation. Either way, these Gypsies "lived off the labor of others." The Communists viewed the Gypsies as members of the lumpen proletariat and so as po-tential opponents of the socialist transformation of society.[15] The task, therefore, was to "raise" them into the working class by putting them to work in factories. There, the discipline, the organization, and the collec-tive spirit of the socialist production line would provide the Gypsies with a model not just for the time spent working but for all their lives. The val-ues of labor, thrift, and diligence would replace their old, feckless, and ir-responsible moral code. By finding their place in the proletariat, the Gypsies would find their place at the heart of social life; their age-old ex-clusion would cease, and so would their distinct identity and lifestyle.

I discuss these ideas at much greater length later, but it is important to understand from the outset that in many ways the Communist doctrine that labor was the sole legitimate source of value and that the profits of "trade" and "commerce" were morally illegitimate reproduced ideas that were already current among the mass of Hungarians. So in contrast to the numerous unpopular Communist policies, the effort "to put the Gypsies to gainful work" was a project that had widespread support in the population.

Ironically, however, far from merging into the working class, the Gypsies, and the "problems" associated with them, became more prominent as the assimilation campaign continued. By the time I began doing my research in 1984–1985, the "Gypsy question" had a public salience greater than at any time since the 1930s. There were two sources of this renewed anti-Gypsy feeling that I deal with in this book. First, there was a dramatic gap between the theory of social assimilation and the reality of increasing social differentiation. Non-Gypsies were being told by the Communists that much was being done to improve the Gypsies' lot and that the disappearance of the Gypsies might soon be expected. But there was very little evidence that this was the case. Ordinary Hungarians saw good money being thrown after bad as rehousing policies did not achieve their goals, schooling results failed to live up to expectations, and Gypsy communities carried on, some thriving. Second, the policy reproduced, in a new guise, old ideas about the Gypsies as "the other." As the social and economic system stumbled into crisis in the 1980s, so the otherness of Gypsies became more prominent and threatening. But this happened in surprising ways, for these were confusing times. One unexpected way in which the "Gypsies" erupted into political discourse was in a common rhetorical device for trashing the Communist Party and its apparatchiks: to describe them as people with a Gypsy mentality. The very people who were trying to get rid of the Gypsies were now popularly described as Gypsies themselves.

The fall of communism brought freedom of political expression for all hues of the political spectrum. Feelings that had formerly not been allowed public expression have surfaced and been intensified by the way Eastern Europe has been drawn into the world economy. But the ideas by which the Gypsies are judged have changed surprisingly little. Notions of honest labor, just prices, and reward for effort, which informed popular discussions of the economy under the Communists, still fuel the fear and loathing felt so widely toward the Gypsies. Nowadays, the wealth of the new robber baron capitalists appears to bear little relation to effort and diligence. And it is again the Gypsies who are the focus for the anger of people who feel excluded from the system. Those rare individual Gypsies who have succeeded in manipulating the new possibilities have brought down the wrath of their non-Gypsy neighbors. Often the success of these Gypsies is interpreted as the result of a cunning, simultaneous manipulation of both the market and the state benefit system—just as in the past the Gypsies were thought to benefit both from state handouts and from the semilegal trade sector. So although this book deals only with the period up to the fall of communism, in its pages the reader will find stories and experiences that are being repeated across Eastern Europe today. As Magdalena Babicka's mother told me: "I would very much like to see the day when honest work will be properly rewarded. I wouldn't have any worries then. So that those who do not want to work have a lower living standard than those who do. Today people like me live so close to those who live off social benefits. We have to install some sort of a legal order here." It is, then, at the rich Gypsies, as much as at the half-starved Gypsy pickpockets and thieves, that the ethnic cleansers now direct their fury.

Modernity and Diversity

It is an all-pervasive myth of the modern age that says our time is witnessing the replacement of cultural difference and diversity by a homogenized global culture. Like any good myth, this modern one is constantly being reinvented in apparently new guises. In the nineteenth century, Karl Marx argued that the spread of commodification would render all aspects of human existence quantifiable on a single (monetary) scale, that "everything solid melts into air."[16] Although Marx put his prediction in a radical context, his argument seems closely related to the liberal view, expounded most fully perhaps by Max Weber and George Simmel, that the rise of a modern nation-state based on standard bureaucratic and technical apparatuses would require a shared, uniform body of knowledge and culture.[17] Both the radical and the liberal visions were of a flattened social and cultural landscape. Fifty years later, postwar theories of mass or consumer society revived these ideas for boom-time capitalism, while in Eastern Europe official Communist ideology seemed to promote an analogous vision of modernity: the leveling of class, ethnic, and national differences to create a homogeneous and unitary society. At the same time, as if echoing Communist propaganda, Western Cold War mythology asserted that communism turned all its subjects into uniform little gray men. Uniting all these myths was the idea that the "imperatives" of machine production, market organization, bureaucratic power, global means of communication, unleashed forces of production, or some combination of these would ensure that when diverse peoples were brought into the same technological, social, and cultural space, difference and variation would be eliminated.

From the perspective of modernization theories, the existence of groups, such as the Gypsies, displaying striking cultural "difference" from the surrounding population appears to result from their lack of integration into the wider social order. This book argues the opposite point of view, starting from an argument made forty-five years ago by Claude Lévi-Strauss in an essay he wrote for UNESCO: "Besides those differences due to isolation, there are those (just as important) due to proximity, that is, the desire to differ to stand out, to be oneself. . . . Diversity," he said, "is less a function of the isolation of groups than of the relationships that unite them."[18] What this book shows is that, far from creating a world of little gray men, the Communists inadvertently provided a particularly fertile ground for preserving and elaborating cultural difference.

In developing this argument, I use three separable levels and styles of analysis. The book opens with some of the Gypsy characters who taught me much of what I know about the Gypsy way. Then, outside the settlement in the world of the factory, I take the opportunity to give a broader, macroperspective on features of the social landscape that impinged on the lives of the Gypsies. The Gypsies' view of the socialist factory and the socialist market, of the formation of government policy and its application by local government, was inherently limited. Hence, I adopt a new language and level of analysis in Chapters 5 and 6. Finally, in Chapters 9 through 12, to develop an understanding of the resilience of their way of life, I introduce a more structuralist perspective in interpreting Gypsy or Rom ideology, the ideas that inform Rom cultural activities. I make no bones about mixing levels of analysis and what seem to me appropriate literary styles in this fashion. Each of these corresponds to an aspect of the total social process. To listen only to the Rom's official account of themselves would be to succumb to a romantic view of "Gypsy freedom." To pay heed only to an objective, sociological view of the position of the Gypsies in the Hungarian division of labor would be to commit the converse error: to imagine that the Gypsies had no autonomy and merely reacted passively to their circumstances. It is in the lives of individuals, observed through fieldwork, that we can see how these two aspects of social life meet and how real people survive and surmount the contradictions they face. And so it is to them, ultimately, that I return. I hope that, by trying to integrate the three worlds of the Gypsies, their peasant neighbors, and the socialist state into a single study, I have given a more precise ethnographic sense than has been customary in earlier studies of the Gypsies and the wider context in which they found themselves.

The Local Setting and the Problem of Difference

In October 1984, together with my six-week-old son, Gergely, and his mother, Judit Szegő, I moved to the town of Harangos, two hours' drive from Budapest. There I spent the next fifteen months[19] in the settlement known locally as "The Third Class." The name, it turned out, referred not to its level of comfort or its reputation but to a technical classification of types of land around the town. Harangos, an agrotown situated just north of the great Hungarian plain, had more than 1,000 Gypsy inhabitants (according to a then recent, if unreliable, census). There is always something arbitrary about the choice of a fieldwork site, and Harangos happened to be the first place where I could envisage doing fieldwork in reasonably propitious circumstances. In particular this meant that the town was prosperous enough to afford plenty of employment opportunities in local factories for the Rom: They did not have to commute weekly to Budapest as did many Rom from poorer areas. The Rom themselves were therefore neither miserably impoverished nor so wealthy as to make fieldwork a tricky prospect: Our research relies, after all, on people's willingness to leave their doors open for us. But there was also a self-esteem and dignity among the Rom of the Third Class that attracted me. In other settlements I had visited with my ethnomusicologist guide we had been taken into the Gypsies' homes and seated on the smartest furniture. Here, the Rom gathered in a courtyard and sat us on the ground, "in the Gypsy way," as they would with one another. These were Gypsies who were not afraid of seeming "uncivilized"; they were too proud for that.

In contrast to what outsiders might expect, the Gypsies in Hungary historically did not form a single, homogeneous group. I chose to research among the Vlach Gypsy group, who alone of all Gypsies in Hungary call themselves Rom. Therefore when I talk of the Rom and Rom ways of doing things it is to them alone that I refer. To avoid confusion, I should say that there is no universally agreed on set of categories for classifying Gypsy groups. Hungarian scholars normally talk of three main groups of Gypsies. The so-called Hungarian Gypsies formed the majority, perhaps even 70 percent of the total, and were found throughout the country. These were, by and large, descendants of Gypsies whose ancestors had spoken the Carpathian dialect recorded by Archduke Franz Josef in his dictionary of 1893. One hundred years later, most of these spoke only Hungarian, though in a few communities where some independent economic activity had been sustained, their dialect of Romany was still spoken. Then there were the Boyash Gypsies, who made up some 10 percent of the total, living mostly in the southern counties where their ancestors had arrived from Romania and Serbia at the end of the nineteenth century. They spoke an eighteenth-century dialect of Romanian and were traditionally renowned as foresters and woodworkers, especially troughmakers. Finally, the Romany-speaking Gypsies of various subdialects —the Gypsies of the Third Class in Harangos spoke the Mašari dialect— accounted for some 20 percent of the population. Their ancestors had come in several waves of migration from Transylvania and the Romanian principalities during the nineteenth and early twentieth centuries, and they now lived dispersed throughout the country. They were especially numerous in the far eastern counties and around the major industrial towns. A majority were Vlach, that is to say, immigrants from the Romanian provinces of Moldavia and Wallachia at the turn of the last century; a minority were from other Transylvanian groups.[20] Ordinary Hungarians and officials alike thought these to be the "worst" of the Gypsies.

Linguistic and historical differences aside, from a sociological point of view none of these Gypsy "groups" formed a homogeneous population. Family organization and culture were varied, and consequently official policies did not have a uniform, across-the-board effect. The Hungarian Gypsies were mostly laborers in factories and building sites, but some were also traders selling fashionable clothes and other consumer goods. Boyash Gypsies were mostly employed as miners and agricultural laborers but also traded in wooden tools. Vlach Gypsies, too, were mostly proletarians, but they also managed to dominate the horse trade and, increasingly, the used-car market.[21]

The reader will discover that this last point was particularly important in shaping the experience of the Harangos Gypsies. Communist hostility and, later, ambivalence toward trade meant that the Gypsies who dealt on the market were particularly liable to repressive measures. But from the Rom point of view, as I demonstrate in Chapter 6, Communist practice merely repeated earlier non-Gypsy attitudes. In the interwar period, the Gypsies had been attacked by the Far Right in Hungary for their "do-nothing" lifestyle, and when the Nazis occupied the country and started deporting Gypsies, it was likewise because they "didn't work" and were "unproductive parasites."

The idea that ethnic minorities may take on the role of "intermediary" and play an especially prominent role in trade and markets is a very familiar one in social science.[22] But perhaps because we think that we know intuitively what a market is, surprisingly little has been written about how such groups actually think about their activity as traders. One of the more distinctive features, I believe, of this book is its attempt at a detailed ethnography of a market and the rich symbolism of trade for the Rom.[23]

The variation among Gypsy groups means that no single book could tell the story of all Hungarian Gypsies under communism. Given this diversity I would have been pursuing a mirage if I had hunted for an "average" Gypsy community. Nevertheless, I believe that in Harangos I found most of the issues that pitted Gypsies of all groups against ordinary Magyars and Communists elsewhere in Hungary. The particular way the Rom resisted assimilation may have been unique to them, but none of the other

Gypsy groups gave up its identity as a distinct group. And it was this that the Communists could neither stomach nor understand.[24]

A final word on difference: One of the ways that the Rom dealt with their position at the bottom of the social order was by elaborating a complex ideology of gender difference. This is a theme that occurs throughout the book and is discussed in detail in Chapters 4 and 12. Since Gypsy men tended to spend time together and women likewise, I was reliant on Judit Szegő for much of my information about women and their doings. At times I asked her to carry out particular tasks for me, such as interviewing women about shame and purity. Judit also did her own research on child development and worked for the Hungarian Academy of Sciences' Linguistics Institute collecting texts of baby talk and children's games. She has kindly made all these data available for me. There are, however, and perhaps inevitably, serious gaps in my knowledge. I know much less about how women talked with each other and behaved when there were no men present than I would like. I am particularly aware that I give no sense of a critical, alternative, or even subversive discourse, however fragmentary, among Gypsy women. I would stress, however, that though my book presents what may seem to be a male-centered view of Gypsy social life, that is how Gypsy men and women often represent their activities. Indeed one aim of this book is to explain how such a partial representation of life can seem acceptable and desirable much of the time to the Rom.

"Gaiety in the Face of Despair"

Gypsies are a part of our world and yet are distinct from the rest of us. They live in the world we know, yet they seem to offer an alternative way to be in our world. The Gypsy woman who appears on your doorstep selling clothespins may be poor and dressed in threadbare clothes, but most likely she will have a style, a panache, and a charm denied to most of the rest of us. It is no accident that the question everyone wants answered about the Gypsies concerns their origins, since we have difficulty in placing these outside-insiders, understanding where they come from. When they offer to tell our fortunes, Gypsies claim that they can speak directly to our innermost hopes and dreams, and yet at other times they display a nonchalant disregard for local ways. There is always an ambivalence in our feelings toward the Gypsies. By their difference, they remind us of our ordinariness, and though their unruliness may lift us out of ourselves, at other times we resent it. Alternately, we find them attractive and threatening. The woman who offers to bless you in the subway with a gift of heather might be the same lady of folklore who steals your children.

The sheer persistence of the Gypsies needs, I think, to be stressed. They do not have faith in a particular creed or book that might impart a sense of destiny and history to them or in religious leaders who might encourage them to remain firm in the face of adversity. Patrick Williams argued that there is no single "core" to Gypsy culture.[25] It reminds me of the Russian dolls in which progressively smaller dolls are hidden inside the largest one; however, with the Gypsies, each one of those dolls differs slightly from the next. So that even if the Gypsies have to abandon larger and more spectacular forms of their way of life for a period, they are often able to reinvent the larger pattern from the smaller section they have been able to hang on to. In Western Europe it is commonly thought that nomadism is an essential feature of the Gypsies. But in Eastern Europe, where most of the world's Gypsies live, far fewer than 1 percent of the Gypsies travel. Likewise, the rejection of wage labor by the Gypsies in Western Europe has been taken, by both themselves and their ethnographers, as a key marker of their identity.[26] But in Hungary and other Communist countries, nearly all the Gypsies work for wages. So the Gypsies can be sedentarized and proletarianized—they can give up what seem to be defining features of their identity—without that leading to their cultural extinction. Why?

Günter Grass talked of the Gypsies' "gaiety in the face of despair," and it is here, in the ways they defy adversity and the sheer inventiveness of their responses to life's challenges, that the secret of the Gypsies' survival and the fury they provoke in others can be found. In the chapters that follow, I show how the Gypsies transform their often harsh experience of the world into something that makes sense of and gives value to their suffering. The solution to the puzzle of the Gypsies, a people without a homeland but, unlike any other diaspora population, with no dream of a homeland, lies in unfamiliar territory. Their "Torah," the reader will discover, lies in their cultivated insouciance, their careful disregard and attentive disdain for the non-Gypsy way. The Gypsies take objects, representations, and practices—in Hungary, horses, cleanliness beliefs, market trading—that exist in the outside world, and they invert or subvert their meanings to their own ends. In this way, they create a specifically Rom sense of what it is to be human.

Part One

THE GYPSY WAY

2

GYPSY WORK

THIS BOOK DEALS WITH REPRESENTATIONS and misrepresentations. Both the Gypsy and non-Gypsy give a systematically distorted sense of the other. A good place to begin is with a basic source of misunderstanding—attitudes toward work and the acquisition of wealth—since it was around this issue that the Communist state focused its campaign to assimilate the Gypsies.

As far as most non-Gypsies were concerned, there were no more inveterate thieves and parasites than the Gypsies. Although most Magyars would have agreed that the Hungarian economy under Communist rule could not have functioned without widespread disregard of the regulations, without semilegal and sometimes fraudulent activities, the Gypsies were nonetheless held up as a particular example of lawlessness. Confusingly, the Gypsies themselves, in some contexts at least, seemed quite willing to accept the non-Gypsy stereotypes. By creating legends around these stereotypes and rhetorically celebrating economic cunning, the Gypsies cultivated an ethic that inverted prevailing non-Gypsy ideas about labor and the creation of value. It is this, their central ethic of nonproduction, that I explore here.

An Origin Story

Daily life on a Gypsy settlement could be uneventful, and I would often fill my days with making rounds of the households I had come to know, hearing their news, checking up on their latest livestock trades, delivering photographs from earlier visits, or just passing the time of day in the company of people other than my immediate hosts. On one such lazy afternoon some months after I had moved to Harangos, I called in at a small cottage on the edge of the settlement. A man called Zeleno lived there with his wife and three young children. Zeleno had always been

17

slightly suspicious of me and my activities in the settlement, and when I entered, rather than sitting with me as other men might, he busied himself with his nine-year-old daughter, Rebuš. However, after a short while he settled her down and told me I might like to listen in on the following story, a "true" story, he insisted:

Kana o Sunto Del ostilas djiv le gaźenge,	When Holy God gave out wheat to the *gaźos,*
akhardas vi le romen	he called the Rom as well
te del.	to give them some.
De le romenge nas gono,	But the Rom did not have a sack,
ke čore sas.	because they were poor.
Kana phende le roma le Suntone Devleske:	Then the Rom said to Holy God:
"Suntona Devla,	"Dear Holy God,
amenge de ande gaźenge gono!"	give us ours in the *gaźos'* sack!"
Taj o Sunto Del merilas o djiv	So Holy God poured the wheat
ande gaźenge gono.	into the *gaźos'* sack.
Pala kodo le gaźe	But afterward the *gaźos*
či kamel te den o djiv,	did not want to give wheat [to the Rom],
hiaba mangle le kodo.	even if the Rom asked for it.
Azir čoren le roma	That's why the Rom steal
Kathar le gaźe.	from the *gaźos.*

The story was meant, no doubt, to amuse Rebuš, but Zeleno had also told it for my benefit, as an example of a type of moral tale Gypsies called "true speech" that he knew I was keen to record. This one, like many such stories, dealt with Gypsy poverty and explained the origin of the Gypsies' deceitful attitude toward the non-Gypsies: The result of God's original distribution of wheat was that the *gaźos,* non-Gypsies, had become people with productive wealth who could exploit the poverty of the Gypsies and deny them what was rightfully theirs. As a result, the *gaźos* could now produce wealth by working on their land, while the Gypsies had been forced to get their daily bread by deceit.

Zeleno's story made me uncomfortable. Many Magyars believed that there was an epidemic of "Gypsy criminality" in Hungary, and some police forces even had special departments devoted to "Gypsy crime."[1] I saw one of my roles as an ethnographer as helping to dispel the prejudice that sustained the fear of the Gypsy. But Zeleno's story did nothing to expose such concoctions as the mythological products of a fevered, late-Communist imagination. Instead, this story was forcing to my attention something that I had been trying to avoid for some months. Early in summer 1985, a fellow anthropologist had visited. One day, through me, he questioned Marča, the old lady of the family with whom I lived, about how the Gypsies lived. In sign language, Marča told him that it was by cunning and trickery. What she did was show him the fingers of her right hand palming an imaginary object. This, I was told to tell him, was "Gypsy work" (*romani butji*)—going "round the back" and putting one's hand on goods by more or less devious means, including theft. Frequently after that, when he asked what someone had been doing, he was shown that same gesture. I knew, from living with Marča and her husband, that the amount of wealth that she and Šanko acquired through theft was minimal and that the rent I paid for myself and my family accounted for half of all the monthly income, yet here they were boasting of a lucrative larceny. Likewise, Zeleno, together with most of the men in the settlement, left home each day not as a predator on the undeserved wealth of the *gažos* but as a semiskilled worker in the factory that dominated the horizon outside the windows of his two-room house. There he worked alongside of, and as a subordinate to, a number of *gažos*, as an operative testing the quality of railway track, not as a thief. It is true that he had been involved in occasional cattle rustling and had even been imprisoned for this, but the money that his daughter Rebuš spent when her mother sent her to the shops for daily provisions came from banally legitimate sources.

My Gypsy "mother," Marča, had, of course, been playing on non-Gypsy stereotypes when talking to my friend, but as was so often the case with the Gypsies and the *gažos*, the outsiders' stereotype was not wholly false. Indeed, there was also something of which Marča was obviously proud in that gesture of palming. It was only later in my fieldwork, again as a result of something that Zeleno said, that I understood the pride and the broader metaphorical truth conveyed in Zeleno's origin story. The point was that, although the game of life was set up so that the *gažos* could exploit the weaknesses of the Gypsies, there were also activities in which the Gypsies could gain the upper hand and redress the balance. In these, the Gypsies got something for nothing, palmed objects that the *gažos* thought belonged to them. Participation in such activities, which went under the generic term of "Gypsy work," was what any self-respecting Gypsy man or woman aspired to.

The Free Lunch

In Harangos, Gypsies often talked about how "stupid" (*prosto*) or "foolish" (*dilo*) the *gažos* were and told me of ways that the "cunning" (*bužanglo*) Gypsies outwitted them. In all these activities, mythical and real, the point was to assert an attachment to wit, cunning, and the Gypsy way of doing things, that is (to borrow a peasant metaphor), harvesting wealth without having sown its seeds.[2] There was no strict boundary among scavenging, begging, or trading as forms of appropriation, nor was legality always of concern. The Rom were the ultimate *bricoleurs*, able to turn whatever was at hand—whether it was material items or rhetorical cunning during dealing—to some good use. The point was simply to get the goods of the *gażos* at a rate that appeared to benefit the Rom, that is, to realize the "free lunch" of which others only dreamed.[3]

For Zeleno and his family, there were several ways in which they were able to engage in such *romani butji*. Most of these involved scavenging raw or discarded material and selling it back at profit to the *gażos*. Like many women in the Third Class, Zeleno's wife, Morga, kept pigs, which she fed on bread scavenged from rubbish bins in nearby housing estates and sold later at a profit to the State Slaughtering Company. But this was not her only form of Gypsy work. Together with groups of women who themselves, or whose husbands, worked in the Railway Company and therefore had free rail travel, Morga would visit a huge industrial garbage dump outside Budapest to collect nylon thread discarded by a tire factory, as well as rubber gloves on occasion. The women later sold the nylon and gloves at markets to *gażo* viticulturists, who used the thread as twine for their vines. By not paying market taxes, these women could make some profit from every trip. Discarded book covers or even Pirelli calendars, also found on the industrial dumps, provided another form of "income"—these were used to decorate the Gypsies' homes. In Harangos Zeleno himself bought scrapped horse carts from peasants who no longer needed them. Using a homemade welding system cobbled together from spare parts acquired at work, and daringly running this off his home (non–heavy duty) electricity supply, he repaired and repainted the carts. He then sold them back to the "peasants." Most of the materials came as a gift from his sister, who specialized in scrap dealings, thereby reducing his costs, but as important to his success as that was his skill at placing his goods. A week's work at this endeavor produced the equivalent return of a month's factory earnings.

The Rom tried to provide feed for their horses too from Gypsy work. Throughout spring and summer Zeleno would go off with other men and cut grass from the roadside to feed his horse, and in the early autumn he could often be found with his brother-in-law out gathering unharvested agricultural produce on the fields of the collective farms. During this time of intensive gleaning, many Rom took several days off from their official jobs. As each day's parties of Gypsies went off to see what their luck would bring them, a festive atmosphere built up. Brandy was brought early in the morning to the settlement and bottles passed around freely among the different families before they set off in groups. Sugar beets for horses, fruit for immediate domestic consumption, and root vegetables for the winter were all garnered this way. Though most trips brought only petty returns, in 1985 the entire settlement, Zeleno's family included, found enough potatoes to last through the winter. And that same year, grapes were gleaned in such quantities that many individuals made more money in four days—selling the grapes to private wine makers—than they did in the whole month at the factory. In the winter carrion was occasionally given by peasants or even on rare occasions taken from state farms where a bribable official had been located. Although only a tiny portion of the meat that the Rom ate was acquired this way, there was a sense in which it was especially "Rom" to have eaten "dead meat" (*mulo mas*), and Rom from other families would ask me, in a part-teasing, part-serious tone, whether I ate this kind of food with my hosts.

Gypsies liked to spend much of their time when they were not at work for wages dealing with peasants and trying to gain an advantage over them in various trades. Whenever there was an opportunity to do so, it was taken with alacrity. Thus, every Friday morning when there was a particularly large market in Harangos, men would come "into town" from all the settlements to see "if something can be done." When I was doing research, I was often struck by the willingness of Gypsy men to convert their resources into almost any number of different assets. Cows, pigs, secondhand cars, horses, and gold could all pass through a man's hands, whichever would allow him to realize the arbitrage opportunities presented by different price levels. I use the term "market" here in a broad, modern sense, rather as the Rom talked. In fact, there was no special term for market in Romany: The phrase "he/she makes *foro*"—a word commonly translated in dictionaries as "market"—was used for any business conducted, any exchange in which money or other valuables were "turned around" (*bolel peske love*). *Foro* also referred to "the town," as when each morning some of the inhabitants of the Third Class would announce that they were going *ando foro*, "into the town." The sense of expectation as someone set off to that site of generalized dealing was almost tangible. And afterward, on the return of these traders to the settlement, everyone wanted to know "what had been done."

Sometimes the markets were far flung. At a time when the Gypsies could obtain only the "red" passports for travel within the socialist bloc, some men planned trips to Bulgaria to benefit from the advantageous street price of gold there. Then in the mid-1980s as travel restrictions eased for all Hungarian citizens, Istanbul became the focus of the men's travel plans, since sheepskin coats, denims, and gold were said to be well priced there. By 1987 the Rom had turned west to Vienna, where they bought, among other things, pornographic videos—still semi-illicit in Hungary—for resale to Magyar buyers at the workplace.

All these activities rested, it was said, on one's being "lucky" (*baxtalo*), on having gone out and tried one's luck in the non-Gypsy world.[4] In part

Children gamble: Getting into the spirit of Gypsy work. (I. Németh)

because of this, there was a feeling that *romani butji* ought to be engaged in collectively, that the opportunities ought to be shared. So whether scavenging on garbage dumps, visiting the houses of non-Gypsy clients, or just touring a local market, few Rom went alone; and where "helpers" had enabled a deal, profits were shared out equally.

In the context of *romani butji*, the horse market was just one moment in a continual effort to profit from the non-Gypsies; but more than any other aspect of Gypsy work, it was these trades that were rhetorically elaborated and celebrated. Just as the non-Gypsies and Rom seemed to agree that Gypsy economic activity was larded with a healthy helping of deceit, in relation to horses I found that both the *gažos* and Rom were keen to talk about one thing in particular: "Gypsy hookery and crookery" (*cigány csalafintaság*). Stories of crooked horse deals are, of course, one of the staples of the European folk imagination.[5] In Hungary there were also plenty of tales of a man drugging an animal by pouring fruit brandy in its ear so as to render a wild horse calmer or concealing the cracks in a horse's hoof with tar. But the favorite story of all time, in socialist Hungary as elsewhere, is of the man who could buy a horse, disguise it, and sell it back to its former owner for a profit. I must emphasize that these were *stories,* and in over a year of observation I only once witnessed a successful bit of trickery.[6] But in the context of the market, where all exchanges were supposed to be fair and even "equal," where, ideally, no one bought a horse for more than its value, these stories of trickery affirmed that the Gypsies were nonetheless getting something for nothing, an unearned profit from the *gaźos*. On close inspection, then, Gypsy crookery proved to be a concoction of fantasy and genuine cunning. This was especially true of a strange category of animals, of which the *gaźos* were unaware and through which the Rom reconstructed the nature of their activity as traders.

Gypsy Horses

On a trip one day to hunt for a horse to buy, I was told by the person I was transporting to stop at his uncle's house.[7] While our host went inside to find us refreshment, my passenger approached a horse standing in the yard. Irritated by her sluggish response to a command, he moved to strike the beast, but our host, returning just then, interrupted him. "Don't do that, boy! Don't strike her. She's Gypsy. Speak Romany to her!" Somewhat surprised, I later asked what gave this horse her special status. This one, I was told, had been raised by the Gypsies and understood Romany and thus, unlike with recalcitrant *gaźo* horses, one did not need to hit her to urge her on. Although I had never before noticed one, I soon discovered that this was not a unique or entirely rare sort of horse.

Some two years later while I was helping make a film for Granada Television, the proud owner of one such mare, Mokuš, explained how Romany horses came into the world. In most cases horses were bought by the Gypsies from peasants, who bred and raised them. The Gypsy horse, however, was bred and raised by the Rom. To do so, the Rom had to take a normal horse at birth, kill and then eat its mother, and finally introduce the foal to their house, where it would eat and sleep. For the first few months, the foal's owner would feed it by hand from a bottle. Now this horse would speak only Romany and would understand no Hungarian. Mokuš's wife, Terez, spoke to me about their own "Gypsy" mare:

> I really love her. I taught her Romany and to be with the children. She never bothers them or kicks them; she is really calm. The Rom asked for her, but we wouldn't sell her for any amount. They offered us 100,000 for her, but we wouldn't give her because we loved her. Have you ever seen such a beauti-

ful horse? You could never have seen such a beautiful animal either among the *gaźos* or among the Rom. She is young, only four years old, and she goes so easily in the cart. However much mud there is, she'd always take the cart through. That's why we really love her a lot.

On another occasion a man explained, "We love these horses like our own children; that is why we don't hit them."

All the horses that the Gypsies dealt in were used to make money off the peasants, but with Gypsy horses this occurred in a unique fashion because the horses never passed permanently into the *gaźos'* hands. One way that the Gypsies kept such a horse in circulation was to take it to market with a Gypsy seated on its back. Then passersby were asked to bet that they could answer the question "From whom does this horse come?" The answer given by the luckless passerby was, naturally, "its mother," and so the Gypsies won the bet, explaining that the horse came from them because they had reared it. A second "method" was explained to me by Zeleno:

> The Gypsies take her to the market, and when they show her off, they speak to her in Romany. She goes. They sell her to the peasant, but when he arrives home, he puts her into his cart, and the horse won't go at all. Then what does he do? He goes back to the Gypsy who sold him the horse. "Look, this horse doesn't go at all." And then the Gypsy takes her back from the peasant and gives him back his money. But less money, half the money he sold it for, because the horse won't go and the peasant wants to buy a different one now. Now, this is a really beautiful horse. . . . This is not some fairy story, Michael; this is the truth, reality. It is really true: Gypsy horses won't go for the peasants!

The Gypsy horse had been made part and parcel of the Gypsies themselves. They killed her mother and ate her in what one might describe as a sacrificial meal. Having destroyed and consumed the mother of the young horse, inevitably a *"gaźo* horse," they then took her progeny into their family. Thus, the young horse, cleansed of its past, grew up Gypsy and not *gaźo*. In deals with such animals, horses parted from the Gypsies only to be returned immediately as the *gaźos* had no use for them. Normally, the Rom bought *gaźo* horses, which they then sold back to the *gaźos*, hoping to make some profit in the exchange, but with these animals the Gypsies could represent magical exchanges in which, paradoxically, nothing was really given by the Gypsies.

The strange story of the Gypsy horse resolves, I believe, my original puzzle about the connection among scavenging, *romani butji*, and Zeleno's rhetorical celebration of thievishness. In all these forms of appropriation, the Rom showed their "cunning" and "intelligence" by taking what they found in the world around them and finding a market for it. What had come from the *gażo* went back to the *gażo* and in so doing allowed money to come to the Gypsies. Wealth was conjured from nothing by the mystery of *romani butji*. Just as David Ricardo and Marx talked of a religious fetishization of money by capitalist traders, on receiving money in a deal, a Rom might spit on it and say in Hungarian, "Your Father! Your Mother! Come here!" (*Apád! Anyád! Ide jöjjön!*).

From the Rom point of view, the essence of *romani butji* was that in exchanges with the *gażos*, the Gypsies could deny that they were giving anything and so transformed the real *exchange* relationship with their *gażo* trading partners into one of apparent exploitation. One particularly admired woman, Zeleno's sister as it happened, owned a permit to remove scrap from the official garbage dump. There she would stand each day sorting out scrap metal from a state-owned truck, lifting it onto her own cart and taking it down the hill to be paid for delivery by the state-owned Scrap Company: taking from one arm of the state in order to give to the other and reaping a profit! Another way to alter the moral value of exchanges with the *gażos* was to pilfer from them while dealing with them. By getting something without its owner's awareness, a Rom got it completely free of all taint of that person. It is for this reason that the story of a horse sold back to its owner unaware that he was buying back what he had earlier sold always recurred: Here the dealer was represented as living out the alchemical fantasy of money growing from money without giving anything of himself.[8] This was also the point behind Zeleno's story. By refusing to share the wheat, the *gażos* had in effect denied their relationship with the Gypsies, just as the Rom knew that in real life *gażos* might look the other way when passing a begging Gypsy woman in the street, or pay a Gypsy less than a Magyar for identical work, or merely turn their backs on a Gypsy coming into a bar. In return, Gypsies denied the relationship they had with the *gażos* and represented themselves as living like parasites on *gażo* backs. This was why in doing such work, the Rom said they felt *lașes*, a word commonly translated as "good." But the full meaning of *lașes* is only really apparent in contrast to the Rom description of working for a wage as *pares:* heavy. The weight of labor, of experience out in the *gażo* world when under obligation to serve others, was the opposite of Gypsy work; this was "light" and "easy" and made the Rom feel the same.

If the cultural logic of *romani butji* is perhaps a little clearer, my explanation raises two deeper puzzles, both of which derive from the fantastical nature of the idea of Gypsy work. In discussions of Gypsy work, the Rom often gave the impression that it was they who were supported by the peasants, but to an outside observer like myself, the opposite seemed more true. The Gypsies' fantasy was that they lived easily and luckily, whereas the reality was that they lived in grinding poverty and were subject to multiple disadvantages and repeated misfortunes. Indeed, it would be hard to imagine a group of people less blessed than the Rom were. The Gypsies had provided the cheap labor for generations of Hungarian peasants. Then as Communist industry expanded, the Gypsies had supplied the labor for the dirtiest and worst-paid jobs in the nationalized economy. In 1983, when one-third of Magyar families had cars, only 4 percent of Gypsies in the area around Harangos were so fortunate.[9] Many Gypsies were inadequately educated to cope with the bureaucratic structures that controlled their lives, badly fed, and often in poor health. For some of them, the closest they came to the fantasy of living from a permanent free lunch was the obsessive weekly purchase of a set of Lotto cards and the wait until the numbers were read out on the radio. The idea of *romani butji* did not really "fit" the observable facts of Gypsy life—a reality of which the Gypsies were, at times, as aware as anyone.

But it is also to an outsider, a little surprising that such a vision of the creation of wealth should be an ideal central to a way of life and a culture. We have very little information about Rom culture in the past, but from studies of Romany-speaking Gypsies in the United States, Paris, and north Italy, it seems fair to say that the ethic of Gypsy work is today a shared, and therefore quite possibly an ancestral, cultural characteristic.[10] Theoretically, the Rom could have rhetorically constructed trade as a service performed for the non-Gypsies, as other trading peoples have done. They could then have argued that they had put effort into acquiring knowledge about products and markets and were, in effect, selling information—a valuable commodity—and in so doing making a "social contribution" and performing an "economic task." Likewise, scavenging could have been represented as a "productive, socially beneficial" activity. But among themselves, the Rom happily reveled in an idea of commerce as living off an abundant world.[11] An occasional curse, "Let the *gaźo*s die if I lie," seemed to acknowledge a kind of dependence on the *gaźo*s—as the curse was explained to me, if the *gaźo*s were to die, what would become of the Rom?—but it was a dependence in which the Rom were the supposed beneficiaries. In the rest of this book, I try to explain these two paradoxes: how the Gypsies, who were really marginalized, thought of themselves as successful exploiters of the "foolish" non-Gypsies and how the Gypsies could perceive themselves as living lightly and easily in an uninterrupted free lunch.

3

A PLACE OF THEIR OWN

THANKS TO GYPSY WORK, the Rom could imagine that it was possible to live "well and lightly" (*laśes*) in the world. To them, it was obvious why their way of life persisted: Who would not choose to live so easily? But there was more to the self-definition of the Rom than *romani butji*. In this chapter I explore the way in which Gypsy communities were held together by an ethic of mutual support, and in the next chapter I turn to the male-centered rhetoric of relatedness that underlay Rom communal ethics. To set the scene, I provide thumbnail sketches of Gypsy settlements in Harangos and the way the Rom spent their time day by day. What I do not do, and this perhaps requires a word of explanation, is discuss the origins of the Rom as an "ethnic group."

Unlike other diaspora populations, which may cling to the idea of a place where they might one day be "at home," the Gypsies have been a nomad people with no homeland to dream of, no original territory to reclaim. What makes them so special is that they are quite happy in this condition. The same cannot be said for those who study the Gypsies. It is a curious fact that the aspect of the Gypsies that has most interested non-Gypsy observers, at least since the eighteenth century, is their obscure "origins." In 1753 a Hungarian theologian, István Wáli, discovered that the vocabulary of three Indian students from Malabar, whom he had met in Leiden, was comprehensible to native Gypsies. But it was only when H. M. Grellmann published his book *Die Zigeuner* (The Gypsies) in 1783 that Wáli's discovery became widely known.[1] Since that time, most reconstructions of the Gypsies' history have used the existence of several hundred Sanskrit-derived terms in modern Romany as evidence of an Indian origin. The differential presence of a handful of other terms from various parts of central Asia and the Middle East in the main Romany dialects is then used to plot a chronology of population movements.

27

Almost alone, English anthropologist Judith Okely has stood against this appealingly simple model, which suggests that the Gypsies exist today as outsiders who moved into European societies and have never been assimilated. Okely turned the model on its head and argued instead that Gypsies are "insiders" who grew apart from our societies at the time of the collapse of feudalism.[2] In one sense the evidence on which Okely rests her case is particular. Unlike most Gypsies and Rom in Eastern Europe, many of whom look "foreign" and some of whom have a distinctly southern Asian appearance, English Gypsies tend to look exactly like other English people. But even for Eastern European Gypsies, Okely's highly original suggestion points to two very important conclusions. First, talk of Indian origins unnecessarily exoticizes the Gypsies, and second, it ignores their own view of themselves. For the fact is that most nonintellectual Rom do not seem to care where their ancestors came from. In all the time I have spent in Harangos, I have never once heard a spontaneous conversation about the geographical or historical roots of their own people. And even when once the Rom engaged the topic in response to my questioning, this was clearly to humor me and did not reflect any interest of their own. Although the Rom were aware that the non-Gypsies had a fantastical hierarchy of "real Gypsies" and "miscegenated half-castes," in dealings with each other, the Rom showed little or no concern for their pedigree as "true" or "bastardized" Gypsies.

In Europe it has become one of those taken-for-granted "facts" that everyone nowadays has an "ethnic" identity in the sense of a more or less primordial, unchosen, traditional identity into which he or she was born. At times of crisis, when habitual ways of doing things no longer seem adequate, it is to this ethnic identity that people are thought to return. My extended experience in Hungary and shorter trips elsewhere in Eastern Europe have convinced me that, with the exception of the educated Gypsy intellectuals who run the Rom political parties, the Rom do not have an ethnic identity. For them, identity is constructed and constantly remade in the present in relations with significant others, not something inherited from the past.[3] For the Rom I knew in Harangos, the basis of their social cohesion lay neither in a dream of a future reunion of their people nor in a mythology of shared ancestry. By a kind of internal emigration, they created a place of their own in which they could feel at home, a social space composed according to their own ethic of relatedness. For the Rom, this was also another sort of distancing from the harsh reality of daily life on a settlement.[4]

Gypsy Settlements

For self-protection, the Rom in Western Europe have tended to disguise themselves or "pass" as members of other ethnic groups. In Paris, for instance, there is a large community of Rom who, by keeping residential concentration low, avoid being seen for what they are, "an organized community, a cohesive culture."[5] The same is true of the Rom in the United States, where most citizens do not even know that there are Gypsies in their country.[6] In Eastern Europe, by contrast, one sign of the weak structural position of the Rom is that it is never hard to find their communities. Here, in ghettolike concentrations inside ethnically homogeneous societies, there is no chance for the Rom to disappear.

The Third Class Settlement

The Third Class settlement, named after a classification of lands around the town of Harangos, lay beyond the maintained tarmac road, across the tracks of the railway line that ran along one side of the built-up area. Beyond was a mud track, and at the end of that lived the Gypsies. As far as most Magyar inhabitants of Harangos were concerned, the railway line marked the moral boundary of the civilized town. Only a few Magyars entered the Gypsy settlement, and even the police tended to come accompanied by armed soldiers.

There were advantages for the Rom in living so far out of town. The three factories that provided them with their main income lay close to the settlement. The porters at one factory took phone messages for residents of the settlement—their only phone link to the outside world. A bus route running nearby allowed easy access to the center of the town; and the very isolation of the place meant that potentially interfering *gažo* authorities had to make an effort to enforce regulations, track down truant children, or notice the carts laden with hay returning late at night.

I had seen settlements of Rom in the impoverished far east of Hungary, where the best house was a single-room mud hovel with a simple stick fence outside. Often there was no supply of piped water. These were the wastelands of Eastern European communism. But Harangos lay in the center of a prosperous wine-producing area, and the Rom there benefited from the reasonably high standard of living in the town. At the Third Class there was only one hovel, which sat on its own on the edge of the square. Most of the houses had plastered, newly painted walls; fruit trees grew in several gardens. There were pigsties in almost every yard and stables for horses, too. The impression of prosperity notwithstanding, no one could have said that the general appearance was "neat": None of the gardens was tended, a huge pile of scrap metal lay most days by the corner of one house, outside several stables dung heaps spread out, and few families seemed to care about the piles of unused materials and rubbish that accumulated in their courtyards.

On my first visit, having recently witnessed the poverty of eastern Hungary, the houses in the Third Class impressed me. But nothing had

Rom riddle: "When are people happy? When they're talking." (I. Németh)

prepared me for what I was to see at the house of Thulo, the man who had invited me to witness his eldest daughter's wedding the next day. Thulo, I was told when I arrived, was busy with his horses, cleaning them for display to his guests. As I was led into Thulo's yard, the first thing that impressed was the scale. Beside his long, brick house was a large, fully furnished room that seemed to have lost one of its side walls. This, it turned out, was a "summer kitchen": an open-air room for use in the warm summer months. Behind this I saw concrete sties for at least a dozen pigs (most other families had rickety wooden structures) and beyond them, a huge brick stable. Out of this a short, large-bellied man was leading two massive dapple-gray horses, each twice his size. At the back of the yard rose a haystack several meters high. Back near the entrance to the house, on the far side of the yard, a huge tent had been constructed, and boxes of beer were stacked in the shade under the awnings. Some young men appeared to be constructing a stage, where hired Magyar musicians would play the next day.

I was taken behind the tent to see the preparations for the feast. A pig lay, gutted and singed, in a pool of black blood, while another was being carved up into manageable portions in a wooden trough. The butcher appeared to be Magyar, and the Gypsies spoke to him in Hungarian. Then I was introduced to the short man I had seen leaving the stable: Thulo. He boasted to me that he would have one hundred chickens killed the next morning—for the soup alone—and promised twice as many guests. He knew that I had wanted to see a Gypsy wedding and told me that no other Rom in Harangos had ever held such a feast as he would for his daughter the next day. With that, he told his son to show me the house.

Thulo's house at that time had to accommodate only his four children and his wife. Later, when their son married, they would hope to bring the daughter-in-law into their home, at least until she had children; and later still they might expect some of their grandchildren to live with them— certainly they would never be left to live on their own. Various relatives might come to stay with them for a few weeks, but for close to twenty years Thulo and his wife would live, like most Rom, as a nuclear family.

The arrangement of Thulo's house was typical of most Gypsies in the Third Class, if distinctly a grander variation than the average. The kitchen, where during the winter the Rom spent their day indoors, was the first room into which we walked. There Thulo, his wife, and their two small children slept, their older son bedding down inside the house. The walls in the kitchen were plastered and painted in an outrageously gaudy pink over which yellow flowers had been lain on with a patterned roller to give a semblance of wallpaper. On the wall above the bed was a huge calendar nude, and in the adjacent corner was a picture of Mary with the infant Jesus.

Leading off this room was the hall, with fake-leather pouffes (ottomans) arranged around a coffee table. Normally members of the family took their shoes off in the kitchen before walking over the spotlessly clean carpet. On a shelf was a picture of (the illiterate) Thulo dressed in a student's gown, standing beside a case of books, with a couple clasped under his arm, keen, like so many Rom, to play on *gaźo* notions of status. Above that was a photo of him and his wife when "first married." In fact, they had married in "the Gypsy way" (*romanes*) long before they went to the registry office to collect a paper that allowed them to secure a loan from the bank as a "newly" married couple. In between they had this studio photo taken of themselves in "proper" Hungarian wedding dress. On the opposite wall was a picture of the Hungarian-born world champion horse-and-cart driver trotting leisurely through the Tyrolean countryside.

The hall led on to the "clean room" (*śukar soba*). This room (every house had one) was never used unless some *gaźo* came to spend the night or there was a death in the family and the corpse was laid out here. It was a shrine to Gypsy taste and style, constructed from shiny and glittering materials, fake silver, false gold, white steel: It "shines" (*phabol;* literally, burns), Thulo's son proudly told me. Shimmering against the whole of

Husband and wife in their "clean room," where gaźo guests are entertained and the dead are laid out.

the far wall was a mock-teak wall-to-wall cupboard, with every foot of shelf space used for display of porcelain "valuables" and fancy trinkets. Thick cream carpet padded the floor, and the sofa was covered in white animal skins. Gaudy, rose-patterned cloths and brand-new head scarves were carefully placed as covers on the furniture. On the central table, set as if waiting for a guest of honor, bouquets of plastic roses tumbled out of glass vases. A huge poster of the Tátra hills thick in snow ran the length and height of the remaining wall. And in the far corner there was what non-Gypsy women use as a dressing table with a mirror. The glass at the edge of the mirror was cut in a jagged design and had been draped in plastic flowers all around its edges.

Waiting to get permission to install a bathroom in this recently converted home, Thulo represented one extreme of a broad spectrum in the Third Class. At the other end was Źunga, who lived in a "shed" (*koliba*), as other Rom disparagingly called his home. Barely three paces long and not two high, its walls were made of mud bricks baked by Źunga and his wife. The space inside was tiny, but all of Źunga's family of five fitted in during the winter. Pictures covered the plaster that was missing on the walls. Saints jostled with nudes, and there were the same brochure images of foreign places that I had seen in Thulo's kitchen.[7] There was no electricity here, but there was a metal stove; and the tight space meant that no one ever felt cold. On one bed Źunga and his adult son slept, and on the other, his wife and daughters. Five paces across the patch of mud outside lived his parents-in-law, in what had once been a stable. Apart from two ripped and crooked beds, a cracked cupboard was the only furniture in the old people's home. In the context of such miserable poverty, it seemed odd to me, during my early days in the settlement, that the bedclothes in both houses were so carefully put away each morning in the cupboard.

Many of the Gypsies were a little ashamed if asked about Źunga. They pointed out that he had two grown daughters and a married son. "Where can the women wash?" or (more euphemistically) "Where can the women do this and that?" asked the other Rom. To be associated with the hovel style of living did no good for the reputation of the other Rom among the Magyar authorities. Źunga reminded everyone of a "past" that was supposed to have been got rid off under communism and that most residents of the Third Class had "risen above." But Źunga, I gradually learned, was no uncultured pauper who could not be bothered to live any better. He was, for instance, a renowned storyteller and wit. Around the fire that his sons lit most evenings outside his home, stories, songs, and talk passed among any people who cared to sit down. He was also one of the gastronomes of the Third Class and, as I was often told, could choose a finer bunch of wild mushrooms than any other man there. And despite the ambivalent feelings of other residents toward him, it was Źunga, with his "fine voice," who led Thulo's daughter's marriage procession around the Third Class.

One feature of the Third Class that the Rom liked was that as families grew and new couples needed space for their own young families, there was always room to improvise and expand a dwelling. For the wealthier, there was also sometimes a chance to buy a property being abandoned by elderly Magyars. Directly after marriage and in the long term, couples tended to live at the husband's parent's home, virilocally. Although a young couple often spent several years moving back and forth between each spouse's natal settlements, and sometimes "neutral" third homes, there was a marked tendency for brothers to end up living in the same town, if not always the same settlement. In the Third Class by my reckoning there were three such groups of brothers.[8] Given that most marriages were between first or second cousins, nearly everyone (male and female alike) counted each other as related. The only exceptions were the last seven families of Magyar descent who had come there before the war. The Third Class, comprising nearly forty plots of land, had originally been developed by Harangos's urban poor in the 1930s. It was only after 1945 that plots gradually passed into Gypsy hands, a process much accelerated during the 1970s and 1980s. But from the Gypsy point of view, the remaining Magyars did not count. They were not part of the Rom world any more than the Rom were an acknowledged part of the life of Harangos. One or two Rom men would talk of particular Magyars in the Third Class as "mates" *(haver)* and might have had a drink with them in town after payday, but I can count on the fingers of one hand the number of times I have seen one of these "neighbors" inside a Rom house.

The "Chicken Plot"

Apart from the more than 200 Gypsies who lived in the Third Class in huts and houses built around twenty-one courtyards, there were another 800 or so Gypsies in the town, 2.5 percent of its 40,000 inhabitants.[9] Three very wealthy Gypsy families lived in private houses in the center of town, and several dozen families lived in housing similar to, if less well positioned than, that of the Third Class.[10] But nearly one-third of the Gypsies lived in settlements set aside for Gypsies by the town council. The largest of these settlements, four rows of barrack flats originally built for miners, had been used in 1944 as a ghetto for the town's Jews before deportation. After the war Hungarians moved back, but during the late 1970s the Gypsies were rehoused there en masse. The Gypsies referred to this place either as "the Chicken Plot," a play on its actual Hungarian name, or, more pointedly, as "the ghetto." Just before I arrived in town, the council had walled in the ghetto so that tourists on the adjoining main road would not have their impression of the town spoiled by the living conditions of the wayward Gypsies.

The Chicken Plot had none of the attractions of the Third Class. On the plot the Rom had to live next door to Hungarian-speaking Gypsies, Romungros (that is, Gypsies who did not speak Romany), whom they despised. Here no one even bothered to maintain the level of tidiness acceptable in the Third Class. Many of the houses were derelict, their doors swinging dislocatedly on their hinges. Feces piled up in abandoned flats. Few of the inhabited houses there, except the renovated shop, were wholly intact. Gypsy families often squatted in the empty houses, and council officials claimed that many Gypsies avoided paying rent. One whole block of houses in the middle was occupied by resentful Magyar families who had lived there "before the Gypsies arrived" and felt that they had suffered the ultimate indignity of being made to live on a Gypsy settlement.[11] In contrast to the Third Class, where close relatives often tried to live near one another, here family ties made no difference to which apartment people lived in, since people were housed wherever the council deemed appropriate. The layout of the houses, too, constrained

The pavement runs out a long way before the road reaches the gypsy settlement.

people's lifestyles, since none had the partial privacy afforded by a courtyard. The lack of space, as well as urban regulations, made it impossible to keep pigs or other larger animals.

Because of the nature of the buildings, the way the settlement had come into being, and the consequent relations among the residents, the tone and intensity of social life in the Chicken Plot differed dramatically from those in the Third Class. This was noticeable both in the cycle of daily activities and at formal gatherings. Only in the Third Class did one see the creation of a community by the participation of most, and sometimes all, the men who lived there in the regular *mulatšago*, the "celebration."[12] The following incident illustrates the anomie so characteristic of life in the Chicken Plot:[13] Early one Sunday afternoon in April, Bangi and her brother Jozsi, two of the despised Romungros, were fighting. The latter had stolen 1,000 forints from Bangi and had used them to buy alcohol, which he had consumed.[14] Bangi, in desperation at her brother's behavior, had called the police, who now stood in the open space in front of the houses. There was great shouting, arguing, and chaotic noise. From a short distance, a group of other residents looked on. The mother of the two squabbling siblings sat alone on a stone, crying. At some point she claimed that she had taken the money herself. Now Bangi, facing her mother, cried out, "Destroy yourselves, the lot of you!"

The Communist authorities broke up traditional Gypsy settlements to rehouse them in slums. (Courtesy Néprajzi Muzeum; photo by Z. Hajtmanszki)

Jozsi put his hand on the police-car door handle and turned roughly to the policeman, asking sarcastically: "Shall I get in? It's alright; you can take me away."

The policeman stepped forward, shouting as Jozsi edged back toward the house: "Don't bother your head. Come 'ere, you trash! Jump into the car!"

Jozsi, replying to some imagined slur, said, "Did someone say my mother was a whore?"

The policeman fired back, "Who said that, you animal!?" He moved threateningly toward Jozsi, who retreated to his mother's house, boasting: "In '83 they came for me, six of them. I squashed them flat, all six."

"Don't worry. I'll deal with you on my own if I must," retorted the policeman. "I'll smash you apart with the truncheon. Just come out here. . . . It's only because of your mother that I'm not taking you in. You can thank her, trash!"

With this he returned to the car and started reversing up the mud. Jozsi, taking heart now, came out of the doorway and marched toward the car's hood, calling out with a fool's bravery, "Backward! Backward!" The policeman ignored him. A Rom women standing by commented: "It was her own brother. You shouldn't do things like that, turn your own brother in!" A Hungarian woman added: "He was only released a couple of weeks ago. It won't take long till he's back. Last time he beat his wife so bad. . . . He kicked her from here to there."

In the neighboring block a solitary old Hungarian man had passed away in his home. The policeman climbed out of his car again and broke down the door. Apparently the corpse stank. The man had died in his bed that same day or the previous one. An hour later there was still no sign of anyone coming to clean up.

Such scenes did not occur daily, but to the Rom of the Third Class, this kind of oppressive existence was associated with the barrack settlements. By contrast, consider the reaction to the death of the single Gypsy man in the Third Class, a man who had no blood relatives there or anywhere else in Harangos. He was a poor Rom who had been retired for several years because of ill health, during which time his wife provided the regular family income by working in a local factory. His family had no resources to pay for the wake each night (in all, several times the monthly wage of the wife) or for the funeral. The Rom of the Third Class raised the money from contributions from each household, attended his wake each night, and collectively buried their "brother."

Work

Beyond the very real differences in the quality of life on different Gypsy settlements there were some important continuities. Wherever the Rom lived, with very few exceptions, they were dependent on wage labor in the socialist sector of the economy. So from Monday through Friday, and for some on the occasional Communist Saturday, most men, and those women who were not on extended maternity leave,[15] worked eight-hour shifts in factories around town. The sexual division of work was also similar across Rom communities. Although men and women worked alongside each other at work, at home they had distinct spheres of activity.

When not at work, men often spent their time investigating fodder or animals for sale or completing small domestic tasks, such as cleaning the stables or shoeing a horse. Summer was a time of house building and decoration, and on weekends many men would spend some of the day engaged in some form of improvement on their own home or that of a neighbor.[16] But most commonly men spent their "free time" visiting relatives or just sitting around talking with one another. Often in the morning, first thing, they would visit an informal, private bar and drink two or three "shorts" of fruit brandy. On weekends and holidays, these visits tended to be longer. In winter in the evenings, they might visit some of the semilegal private bars on the edge of town. In summer they were more likely to lie around in the ditches in the Third Class or on the pavement in the Chicken Plot. Whenever there was money, beer would be brought to be shared. Quite often I caught myself wondering, in a slightly puritanical spirit, how men could spend so much time happily sitting around "without doing anything."

Almost all domestic labor was a woman's responsibility, from child care through cooking, washing, and decorating the house each spring. Before or after going to work for wages, a woman had to purchase food at the market (a good half hour's walk from the house), clean the house, and prepare food for her family, as well as look after the needs of her children. Sometimes she would be helped by her daughters, daughters-in-law, or younger sisters; groups of these young girls often toured the Third Class doing the housework in each of their mother's houses in turn. After all this, women of the Third Class were also expected to do the main work in looking after pigs.

Čaja, whose story I describe at length in Chapter 5, provides a good case study. She lived with three grandchildren (born during the first marriage of her eldest daughter), her own youngest adult daughter, the latter's husband, and their child. Čaja herself was out scavenging all day long. Her daughter, Minou, and eldest granddaughter, Čoli, both stayed at home most days looking after Minou's baby and Čoli's baby half-brother. Minou normally cooked and looked after the animals in the yard: Chickens and pigs had to be fed, and once or twice a week the pigsty was washed out. Minou also had to clean the whole house, a larger job than it sounds, since children were rarely forbidden any form of game, however messy, and adults used the floor as a rubbish bin, as if deliberately ignoring the fact that someone was going to have to clean up the mess afterward. One of the girls had to take the cart out twice a day and fill several large plastic containers with water to take to the cows, which were tethered one kilometer away on a piece of scrap land. In between all of this, Minou had to breast-feed her baby on demand, ensure that he was never left on his own, and, above all, give him plenty of practice in standing and talking.

Čoli's workload was in some ways even greater, since she also had duties at her mother's house. Her working day normally went on into the evening as she took part in milking the cows at the end of the day. Then, after sweeping up once more, she could rest until morning—that is, if she was not called to milk a cow in the middle of the night to give fresh milk to one of her younger brothers. He, she told me without any sign of resentment, got cow's milk on demand. Not all girls were so self-sacrificing. Some hung around the Chicken Plot or houses where an older sister lived, but they ran the risk of acquiring a damaging reputation for laziness and loose behavior if not seen to be so steadfastly devoted to the well-being of their kin and homes.

For an old woman, the burden of domestic tasks ought to have diminished. Grandchildren often lent a hand, but despite such help, most older women were active up to their last day. I knew, for instance, several grandmothers in their sixties who throughout winter 1984–1985 "did the bins"—that is, ran the gauntlet of official and unofficial hostility as they collected bread from garbage containers around the town for their families' pigs.

Although great value was put by the Rom on time spent talking to one another, when the men sat around in the ditches at dawn and again an hour or so before dusk and the women sat a few feet away, sewing, looking after their children, and chatting, there were normally more men present, and they stayed longer. Most evenings after sitting out together, men retired to their homes with their families to watch television. On Monday nights when there was no television in Hungary, men went into town to the cinemas. No Gypsy woman went to a cinema in the time I lived in the Third Class. They said that there was no point—they would have fallen asleep from exhaustion.

The Ethics of Communal Life

Even though the organization of work—both wage and domestic labor— was a shared feature of most Gypsies' lives, work in this sense was not something that the Rom talked about much. In fact, my discussion here is based entirely on observed behavior or on replies to questions I asked. The pattern I describe is something that I, as an outsider, believe is important. There were, however, shared aspects of their lives that the Rom did articulate and discuss at length without my prompting.

From the Rom point of view, there were two constants in life. First, wherever the Rom lived, they were surrounded by a majority of hostile and snobbish Magyars who considered the inhabitants of Gypsy settlements beyond the moral pale. Second, the only valid response of the Rom to *gaźo* hostility was to defend a certain quality of relationship with each other, summed up in the term *romanes*, "in the Gypsy way."

A State of Siege

The sense of being surrounded by a more powerful and often malicious population gave rise among the Rom to a sense of living in a "state of siege," a "ghetto."[17] The Rom were, naturally, well aware of the stigma of being what the Magyars called *Cigány* (Gypsy), and as far as they were concerned, there was not a world of difference among the *gaźo* visitor who was too "proud" to sit down, speak to, or eat with the Rom in their homes; the authorities who treated their children in school as educationally subnormal; and the doctors and nurses who addressed them with the gross, familiar *tu* form. None of these was willing to treat the Rom as equal human beings. A common complaint about the *gaźos* of Harangos, and elsewhere, was that they were proud or "big-headed" (*barimasko*). For the Rom, the truth of this belief was continually illustrated by the residential segregation of the Gypsies in Hungarian towns and villages. Once the Gypsies knew that my attitude was different from that of other *gaźos*, they asked me—to confirm what they anyway knew—whether I had been asked by the *gaźos* how I could stand life in the Third Class and if I was terrified for my life there. They knew that tradespeople, such as skilled builders, would enter the Gypsy settlement only with trepidation. Even those whose income depended on the Gypsies, such as the town veterinarian, abandoned all civility on entering the settlement. This man in particular, before bothering to say, "Good day" to his clients, would commonly call out, "Have you got any money?" In the town itself, the presence of Gypsies in public spaces seemed to cause offense to the more "respectable" citizens.[18]

The Rom were extremely sensitive to *gaźo* "pride," and they bitterly criticized *gaźo* visitors to the Third Class who were ill at ease in their company. Shyness, in this case, was no excuse. Rom heard *gaźo* colleagues at work talking of the "new world" in which there was no "prejudice," and in the media they heard that there was no racism in Hungary. From bitter experience, the Gypsies knew otherwise. Thulo, for instance, used to dress up as a non-Gypsy to do business with *gaźo* store owners, and when he had an important deal, he would encourage his Magyar friends to join him "so they don't think I'm a Gypsy." At other times the Rom would teasingly try to expose *gaźo* hypocrisy. Once during a boisterous hospital visit when some nurses complained rather roughly about our behavior, a man who rightly prided himself on his good *gaźo* connections called out to the nurses about our party, "Don't worry; we're just Italian!" This man seemed embarrassed to be treated like "any other Gypsy," and yet he wanted to suggest how differently we would have been treated had our ethnic identity been more acceptable to the Magyars.

Sometimes the Rom set out to prove to themselves how mean a *gaźo* was by asking for small gifts at the end of a transaction. While buying wine at a peasant house, one of a party of young men mentioned that he was so hungry that his stomach was hurting. When the wife of the vendor brought out a slice of bread with lard smeared on it, the boy complained that a cat would not satisfy itself on what had been offered. Far from being grateful, and much to my embarrassment, he appeared deliberately to insult her hospitality. The Rom felt no shame, knowing that in a converse situation a whole bowl of food would have been brought out by a Gypsy.

The sense that the Rom lived under siege did not just derive from pressure to conform to the dominant majority's style. In dealings with officials, whose obligation was to rise above such casual racism, the Rom also found that they had to deal with a quite brazen contempt. One of my "sisters," Bina, told me about an occasion some years before, when she had gone to ask for emergency social security after her husband had left her temporarily. She had dressed all her children up in their finest clothes so as not to look "shameful" but had then been humiliated by the officer, who scorned her claim to need cash while she dressed her kids so sumptuously. When she told me this, another woman chimed in with her account of a visit when she had taken along her barefoot children. Then the same officer had leaned over the desk and asked her why she had put shoes on herself before she had clothed her children. From experiences like this, the Rom knew that it was hard, if not impossible, to win with officialdom.

Because the *gaźo*s were powerful, as well as prejudiced, the world outside of the settlement could seem a threatening and dangerous place, particularly for male Gypsies "out there" on their own. At first I found it perplexing and irritating that the Rom felt a man could not be left alone in town by his fellows, and on occasion I found myself driving around with an increasingly frantic group of Rom to find a man and bring him home safely. Quite by accident, however, I, too, began to understand the emotional support that this kind of solicitousness provided. I had gone on a journey to the administrative seat of the region with some elderly Gypsies, and there we had gone our separate ways: I to research in the archives, my passengers to conclude a deal. I was much delayed, and the Gypsies, who had long finished their business, looked for me high and low in the town. When we did finally meet up, far from being irritated at my delay, as I had feared, they could only burst into tears with relief that I had not been arrested and carted off while in their care, as they had feared.

One particularly shocking incident brought home the underlying rationale for this kind of attentive care of one another. In the Third Class there lived a willful eight-year-old boy called Malats. Shortly after first going to school, he had, like most Gypsy children, been transferred to the school for the educationally subnormal, where he was indifferently treated and started missing classes. Soon he was on a list of "children in danger" and, thanks to his absences from school, given a probation officer. In summer 1985 just after the school year began, he was sent out from class early one day by his teacher on a supposedly innocent errand to buy food at the local shop. There a police car lay in wait to remove him "quietly" to a children's home on the authority of the Children's Welfare Department (*Gyámhatóság*). Another Gypsy child, coming late to school, saw Malats being dragged shrieking into the police car and ran back to tell Malats's mother. She, still in her nightdress, tore barefoot down the road to the school, where she set about his teacher in a fury, beating her to the ground. That night not only was Malats in solitary confinement in the children's home in Eger, but also his mother was in the local police station. In the end she was lucky only to receive a six-month sentence at the first trial and then to defeat the state prosecutor's appeal for a longer sentence. Malats, however, spent the next six years of his life in a children's home. It was, after all, the Harangos council's officially stated policy that keeping Gypsy children in homes was a means of assimilating them and "tearing" them from their parents' way of life.

This case touched me, since it involved close relatives of the family I lived with, and I still remember the sudden way that disaster struck that day and everything in this family's life fell apart. Although a lawyer was hired, no one in the settlement seriously believed that Malats's mother, a *Cigány*, would be acquitted of assaulting a teacher, whatever the provocation. Without a mother in the house, the recently married daughter had to be brought back home even though she was nearing the end of her first pregnancy; then the marriage of the next daughter was delayed, since all the savings of the father would be dissipated on the lawyer and prison visits. From one moment to the next, the socialist state was capable of disrupting a family's life and turning it around. It was then that I began to understand the constant insecurity and anxiety with which Gypsies lived.

Sometimes it was the community as a whole, not any one individual family, that seemed to be threatened. One such moment came in summer 1988 as the Communist system teetered on the brink of collapse. Strange rumors started circulating among Hungarian Gypsy communities about a skinhead revival. In the previous decade, racist anti-Gypsy graffiti had appeared in many parts of Hungary. Slogans such as "Gypsy-free Zone" had been sprayed on railway sidings and bus stops. But in the few cases of incitement to racial hatred that had been brought to trial by the authorities, the perpetrators had been severely punished. Now, in 1988, the belief spread among Gypsies in many parts of Hungary that the skin-heads were preparing to attack the settlements. On the railway platform beside the Third Class someone had spray-painted:

We'll be back
Dirty Gypsies
To shoot you down.
The skinheads.

A day or so later a Gypsy woman in Harangos thought she saw two skinheads getting into a car in the middle of town. Panic spread through-out the Third Class. That week a colleague of mine from the Academy of Sciences, quite unaware of what was going on, happened to visit and found that all two hundred Gypsies had spent the previous two nights huddled together in the houses in the center of the settlement, seeking protection in their numbers from what they feared was an impending as-sault. Many of the men, and all the women, had refused to go to work on the previous evening shift, having sought and been refused police pro-tection on the way home. For days after returning to work, the Rom all traveled together to and from the factories. In this case the threatened at-tacks never materialized; but the incident was a stark reminder of a fear that remained hidden most of the time.

One consequence of the siegelike conditions in which Gypsies lived was that the Third Class could come to seem like a safe "inside" in contrast to a dangerous, insecure "outside" world. At least once each week, this dis-tinction was reinforced by the organization of a *mulatšago* among the men when one of their number departed to or returned from hospital, the army, prison, or another kind of enforced stay among the *gaźos*. Even if such jour-neys occurred weekly—as they did with some men—the Rom were ex-pected to go and salute the departing or arriving fellow Rom and share a little food or drink together. In the hospital, army, and prison, the Gypsies moved as isolated, unprotected individuals among the *gaźos*. Such time outside therefore embodied the opposite of the ideal by which Gypsies tried to live inside their settlements, where they might be enclosed in a hos-tile world, but where they could speak their own language and treat each other with the respect and attention they deserved, giving and receiving the honor and esteem they were so conspicuously denied by the *gaźos*.

Idioms of Community and Identity: Romanes

In the first few months of my research as I asked about various acts and customs, I was often given the simple explanation: *romanes*, "it is the Gypsy way." It was *romanes* to sit on the floor and eat together from a bowl. It was *romanes* to smile and not complain too vigorously when one's "brother" went off with a bicycle one liked but did not really need. It was *romanes* to dress in style, eat particular foods in a certain way, drink some beers and not others. It was *romanes* for women to wear a scarf and apron, for men to keep a mustache and wear a hat. And it was *romanes* for everyone to be always open to the needs of brothers and sisters. *Romanes* was also trivial things, such as the way we warmed our hands around the fire in the cold winter mornings or the way a man salvaged old iron to make nails. At the other end of the scale of value, *romanes* stood for the crucial marker of identity, the Romany language, and, most important, *romanes* stood for the whole moral code elaborated around the idea of respecting those who lived in the Rom's state of siege.

Romanes as Language

Some two months after I had arrived in Harangos, I was traveling with some Gypsies to a nearby town, and they asked me how I would greet the Gypsies we were going to visit. Pleased with my accurate responses, although my general knowledge of Romany was still barely passable, my passengers complimented me warmly: "You can speak Romany now" (*žanes aba romanes*). I was being flattered and encouraged, I knew; but something more interesting was also being said. Because the Rom lived in a world in which a *gažo* meeting a Gypsy in public might well not bother to greet him at all, questions of politeness and respect occupied the Gypsies' imagination. Indeed, the correct use of greetings was emblematic of a willingness to engage in a relationship of mutual respect, especially at all formal public events and life crisis rituals.

At Christmas, New Year, and Easter, the men of each household went around greeting their relatives in other houses with elaborate wishes for health and luck. However highly formalized these greetings, they rarely failed to touch, since they were, in effect, an offer of renewed relationship. Once I saw a man cry when an old adversary whom he had raised as a child arrived unexpectedly on such a morning, knocking at the door and offering such a greeting.

Droboj tume, papo!	I wish you well, Grandfather.
Te train pe but Patradji	May you live for many Easter Sundays
maj feder sar akanak,	in a better state than now,
tumare šavorentsa khetane,	together with your sons,
tumare šejantsa khetane,	together with your daughters,
tumare grastentsa khetane,	together with your horses,
tumare neposa khetane.	together with your relatives.

T'aven tumenge maj but śavore.	May you have many grandchildren.
Te baron	May they grow up
te kerasa bijava lentsa.	so we can make weddings.
T'aven baxtale.	May they be lucky.
Šoha te na meren!	May they never die!
Te źutin tumen o Sunto	May Holy God
del taj e sunto Maria.	and Holy Mary help you.
T'aven Baxtale!	May you be lucky!

Then the recipient replied more briefly but in similar vein, concluding, as he kissed his visitor:

O Del te marel kon	May God strike anyone who gets cross
Xoljavel!	with another!

And the visitor butted in:

Te merel rögtön!	May he die right away!

And the host, to ensure understanding, affirmed:

Na-j Xolji kathe, muro śav!	There's no anger here, my son!

Romany was the language of celebration, but it was not just in formal settings that its use was required. The significance of Romany to its users was all the keener in Hungary because by 1985 Romany-speakers constituted only a minority (one in five) of all Gypsies. The other, Hungarian-speaking, Gypsies were called Romungro by the Rom. A century or so earlier many of these had spoken the Carpathian dialect of *romanes,* but in the intervening period they had almost entirely abandoned their own tongue.[19] The Rom in Harangos tended, in some respects, to conflate the Romungros and the *gaźos* because the Romungros, too, were said to be proud and ashamed to be associated with the Rom. But there was also a fierce note of scorn in the Rom's references to these erstwhile brothers, for most of the Romungros in Harangos lived in wretched poverty, having, as far as the Rom were concerned, surrendered their way of life and yet not found a place in Hungarian society. They provided an example to the Rom of what happened when one resigned one's language and culture—with it one gave up independence and self-respect and slid into a horrible half-world that was neither Rom nor *gaźo.*[20]

With the example of the Romungro in mind, Rom parents gave their children intensive verbal coaching in Romany. Despite the disadvantages felt in the first years at school when children had to learn Hungarian, mothers, elder sisters, and, to some extent, elder male relatives kept up a flow of patter, chat, and verbal play in Romany—exciting the child's interest in the language with stories, scenarios, and repeated questioning to elicit a verbal response.[21] In one case where a girl was being raised by a young Romungro woman who had separated from her Rom husband, his Rom grandparents talked of removing the child to teach her *romanes*.

By marking out those raised by Rom in opposition to the hostile outside world, Romany was a potent means of exclusion, of drawing a boundary that, for a people like the Rom, was otherwise all too hard to maintain. During various arguments that took place within earshot of neighboring *gaźos*, I felt that the Gypsies enjoyed placing the normally ever-so-superior Hungarians in the humiliating position of being unable to understand what was being discussed by the Gypsies. The Rom could have moved away or closed the gate on their prying neighbors, but they chose to allow the uncomprehending "audience" to remain in order to underline their distinctiveness. Likewise, on several occasions when dealing with "bad" *gaźos*, the Rom would ostentatiously speak Romany to each other, much to the *gaźos'* irritation; conversely, when dealing with a "good" (*laśo*) *gaźo*, the Rom would avoid Romany. The choice of which language to speak also, but more embarrassingly, arose with Rom one did not know. When at pilgrimages we met "stranger Rom" (*strejina rom*), the men would hesitate for a moment, uncertain about which language to speak in, and the tone would warm if their new friends agreed that they always spoke Romany with the Rom.

Romanes as the Gypsy Way, or a Life in Common

If I was to be accepted by the Gypsies as part of their community, even if only as a visitor, learning to live by *romanes* was my most urgent, and also most difficult, task. When I first moved to the Third Class with Judit Szegő and our son, Gergely, we tried for a while to maintain some of the trappings of our previous life in Budapest. We had a larder full of preserves and a shelf lined from one end to the other with spices, and we kept our refrigerator replete with fine foods. We rapidly acquired a reputation for having more food than we could possibly need and found ourselves being asked for all kinds of small items, a few eggs, some flour, a handful of paprika. We began to feel as if our generosity were being abused, but we resisted saying anything, believing that our gift-giving was repayment for the hospitality of the community. Nonetheless, we gradually stopped replacing items from the cupboard as they ran out. It was only then, as visitors simply stopped asking for things, that we realized how mistaken we had been. It was not that we were expected to provide a take-out service but rather that the generosity of anyone who hoarded anything would be tested by needy relatives and friends. Our sense of personal property as a means to exclude other people had misled us, since it had given us the impression that we were being subjected to a polite form of expropriation. Among the Rom, possession of consumable goods conferred the right to give away and lend as much as it did the right to possess exclusively.[22] Thus, when I first arrived in Harangos, a young man who was befriending me asked if I would give him my penknife. Still too much of a *gaźo*, I got out of the situation because I did not believe it could be reciprocated. But I was quite wrong; this kind of gesture, I later discovered, was what made men brothers.

The Rom liked to represent themselves as always being open to the needs of others, to behave as though one could assume this. One woman spoke to me as follows: "Rom help each other out [*źutin amen*]. If a Rom has lots of money and somebody else needs some, then he'll give it to him. If one Gypsy woman sees another who hasn't got anything to eat or cook, she says to the other one, 'Come to the shop with me, and we'll buy some food to eat.' They help each other out . . . unlike the *gaźos*. That's not the custom with them." This was a romanticized account of daily life, but there genuinely was an expectation that the Rom should help one another. Thus, I was corrected when I thanked people for small gifts and favors—in a ceremonial context one might say, "Be lucky" to someone who offered help, but otherwise the presumption to be maintained in public was that one had a right to expect such help from others.[23] To thank would have been to undermine this basic assumption.

As part of this ethic, in the Third Class there was a constant flow of goods and services between households. If a family lost one or more pigs through disease and the meat was edible, it would be shared out among the Gypsies without expectation of direct return. One family seemed never to buy a broom during the whole time I lived there. The main room in each house was normally swept out several times a day, but this family managed by borrowing brooms from neighbors. I often heard one neighbor in particular complain that the broom was never returned without being sent for, but she would not complain directly lest she be accused of being "stingy" (*bokhalo*; literally, hungry). Judit Szegő likewise found that her sewing machine, the only one in the settlement, was soon in constant use. Among the men, slightly different demands were made. Hay for the horses was always being asked for, and during the winter months I would often see poorer men crossing the settlement with a sack slung over their shoulders, returning home from the house of a wealthier relative. Indeed, throughout winter 1984–1985 there was one horse owner who never once bought fodder and kept his animal on his relative's resources. Offers of help concerned rather shoeing horses, breaking their kicking habits, and, above all, going to deal with the *gaźo*s.

Romanes also meant caring for other Gypsies as they suffered in the *gaźo* world. Once we drove past some Rom whose car had broken down on the roadside. Even though my passengers did not know them, I was told to stop. In answer to my questioning, the Gypsies simply said, "They are Rom" (*Rom-i*), no more, no less. This kind of solicitousness in time of trouble was even stronger within the community. Whenever, for instance, someone was ill, a large party of up to thirty or more people would leave the Third Class by train for the hospital in town. Hospitals were dangerous, dirty places where the Rom were inevitably isolated from their kin most of the time, but during official visiting hours, and much to the consternation of hospital staff, the Rom would reconstitute the settlement, bringing Gypsy food with them and sometimes smuggling in alcohol. During such collective visits, many of the taboos that governed polite speech and behavior in the formal *mulatšagos* were in force.[24]

But it was perhaps in respect to food and alcohol that the ethic of sharing was most visible in the Third Class from day to day.[25] Although most people ate in their own homes, every house prepared twice as much cooked food as it consumed in order to offer some to visitors. And each day I saw several pans of food passing from one house to another as small gifts of cooked food were circulated between a daughter and her mother's household or a mother and her daughter-in-law's house. The very organization of eating emphasized the ethos of sharing. Because there was no formal family gathering or set time to eat, food that was offered to a visitor seemed not to be the remains of a private family occasion but what the house provided for everyone who passed through it, to eat as and when he or she saw fit. Whereas hostile Hungarian commentators saw in these customs proof of a lack of elementary culture, they make more sense when seen as a means to avoid the exclusive association of the family meal.[26]

When food was served, it was placed in a bowl on the ground or on a stool in the middle of the room, and any men present were enjoined to sit down together around the food. The women would eat either at once from a different bowl or later from the same bowl. Partly because of the resistance of these Gypsies to assimilating Hungarian customs, many people made a special point of eating on the ground, *romanes*, as they said. (The occasional honored *gaźo* guests of mine, like myself on my first visits, were offered food on a table.) Since commensality was such an emotive sign of sharing, of being Gypsies together, if any Gypsy went into a yard or house where another was eating, he or she would be called to "come! Eat!" (*av! Xa!*). The offer would be repeated with astonishing persistence, since the Gypsies profoundly disliked eating while another sat by. The *gaźos*, however, just as they disliked conversing with the Gypsies, were notoriously unwilling to eat with the Gypsies. They feared that the food would be dirty and maybe that they might have to reciprocate by inviting the Gypsies to their own homes. So after my arrival, it was important for me to show that I was not "ashamed" (*či laźalpe*) in this way, and until I had established this, tiring though it was, I could not refuse food in the houses that I visited.[27]

The communal ethic I have just discussed was rooted in a vision or ideology of egalitarian relations sustained among the Rom themselves and eschewed by the *gaźos*. I try now to take the reader inside this ideology and to investigate the ways in which the Rom perceived that they related to one another as equals.

4

"WE ARE ALL BROTHERS HERE"

IN THIS CHAPTER I BEGIN TO EXPLORE the radical gender divisions that characterized Rom identity and community. My ultimate goal is to explain how for Gypsy men and women alike, male-gendered activities and relations provided an image of communal affairs. After all, it would have been quite possible theoretically for the Rom to define their community as a "family" or "kin group" in an ungendered fashion. Instead, they divided the world and used one-half of this severed image to imagine the whole. In this chapter, having established the nature of the ideological representation of "brotherhood," I then look at some of the contradictions it generated in the representation of relations established through marriage and relations within households. I begin to uncover a rather more tortured aspect of *romanes* than we saw in Chapter 3.

When the Gypsies of the Third Class talked about the people they shared their lives with, at times they referred to the *nepo*, "people" or "family" who lived in the settlement. It was more common, however, to hear about the "brothers" (*phrals*) who lived there. At the very outset of my stay in the Third Class, the old man in whose house I was to live explained that I would have nothing to fear, since "everyone's a brother here" (*sa phrala-j kathe*). "The brothers," I was told, "will protect you." Over the next fifteen months, it became apparent that for the Rom, it was because men were brothers that they helped one another and participated in joint activities together. In daily life one addressed other men not as brother but by their names or some other form of address, most commonly, "boy." Nonetheless, the brotherly way of conceiving communal relations was in some sense ever present, underlying other representations. For instance, when I began to inquire into men's and women's residential history, I was commonly told about the brothers who lived together in a settlement at any one time. These were not necessarily accurate historical accounts; they were more like mythical reconstructions of the recent past. But as such they revealed the model, the ideal of relations between those who live together.

The language of kinship and gender provides a way of talking about those aspects of our identity that we have not chosen, that we have been born into. It provides an image of relations in which we are both obligated and dependent. Gypsy talk of brotherhood provided a metaphor that linked ideas about male and female natures with an ideal of egalitarian, nonhierarchical social relations and with notions that trivialized ancestral identity in favor of identity achieved in the present. The power of the image of brotherhood derived from the way it strung together these complex ideas. At its most concrete, brotherhood referred to the individual (male) Gypsy's experience of growing up in an extended family and therefore seemed supremely self-obvious, but at its most abstract, the term referred to the ideal nature of relationships among humans. So it was not simply that "brotherhood" focused the community on men. Rather, this male-gendered relationship provided an image that could stand for communal relations in general, not just those of the men. Disentangling the symbolism behind this image is an essential task of this book, since the idea of communal relations as brotherly was one of the cruxes of the Rom's resistance to the Communist attempt to eliminate their way of life. To understand how the idea of brotherhood worked, we need to unpick its concealed knots and see how they were originally tied together. We must first untie the gender knot. How was it possible for all Gypsies to talk as though communal relations were brotherly, to privilege and culturally elaborate the activities of men in such a way?

A World Apparently Made of Men

If the idea of the community was as a brotherhood, inevitably one wonders, What about the sisters? At first sight the Romany term for "sister," *phenj*, seemed to be used like the term *phral*, as a way of being polite. To call a woman "my sister" (*muri phenj*) was to be affectionate and welcoming. Just as men would assure me of their sentimental attachment by ostentatiously talking of me as "our brother" (*amaro phral*), so women would talk of Judit Szegő as their sister, and they did the same to one another. However, there the similarity ended, since only the concept of *phral* was "extended" to refer to larger social groups and gatherings. The Rom might have felt great affection toward a sister or other woman, but there were few or no contexts in which this emotion could be publicly manifested in the way that brotherly sentiment was, *as a basis of a wider Rom social order*. It was for this reason, as well as a recognition of the norm of virilocal marriage, that women talked of "the brothers" when discussing a settlement as a whole. In representation of interhousehold relations, at least in their public aspect, the default, determinate position was the men's relations with one another.[1]

The use of male qualities in talk of communal concerns and socially integrative activity was part of a general male bias in Gypsy discourse rooted, in part, in the Romany language itself. Since the term *Rom* ambiguously meant both "male Gypsy" and "Gypsy" (and "human"), the assimilation of Gypsy affairs to male Gypsy affairs was constantly achieved linguistically without comment. Quite casually in the conversation of both men and women, male Gypsies and their activities came to be spoken of as if only they existed or mattered, as if they were the whole world of the Gypsies. Male prominence was also explicitly stressed in Gypsy discourse. Thus, shortly after a family lost its only son, one of five children, the child's grandmother told me in Hungarian that the worst thing about the loss was that this was her son's "only child" (*az egyetlen gyermeke*). Both this man and his mother loved the girls dearly and cared for their welfare, but there was something different about a son.

The "distortion" in discourse was to some extent reinforced by a striking preeminence, on the public stage at least, of Gypsy men vis-à-vis their women.[2] At all the formal moments of Gypsy life when large numbers of Rom were gathered together, especially christenings, funerals, and the much more frequent celebrations of departures and arrivals of relatives, it was men who took center stage, whose activities were deemed central to the successful performance of Rom behavior. The same was true of horse markets, one of the key encounters with non-Gypsy society, and for meetings of Gypsy men to discuss disputes between aggrieved Gypsy parties (*kris*). The task of Gypsy women on such occasions was respectfully to keep out of the men's way, to remain observers. Although some women did go to markets and trade, this was not talked about in the same way as horse deals, since the point of women's economic activity, what they were proud of, was supporting their households with minimal expenditure. Unlike the men, the women did not sing about their deals with the *gaźo*s.

The subordination of Gypsy women to their men was not simply a feature of the formal moments of social life. From birth onward a girl's social status was such that she was less able to be an unambiguous participant in Gypsy social life than a boy. The birth of a daughter might produce little reaction or even a hostile one from some fathers. One young man I knew cried when he heard that his wife had given birth to a daughter; he said that he could not bear to look at my baby son, since this gave him too much pain. Months later when in my presence his mother encouraged him to leave his wife, she reminded him that his wife had produced only a girl and not a son. Zeleno expressed a commonly held view: "You can't start anything with a girl. When she says she won't go to school because she is sick [that is, menstruating], what can one do? It's only with boys that you can start things."

Boys learned in early life to expect preeminence and priority over girls in all matters. Young boys were given much larger sums of money by their parents to buy sweets or gamble at cards; a father returning from abroad tended to bring more lavish presents for a son than a daughter; no boy was ever reprimanded in my sight for taking a toy or game from a girl, however wanton his disregard for her pleasure. All these privileges inevitably affected manner and deportment. At weddings when young Gypsies of both sexes danced all day, eight-year-old boys led girls twice their age with absolute confidence and authority. As young men, Gypsy boys discovered that they were free to travel as they wished, to visit the cinema and discos without restraint; not so, girls. Parents took pride in a daughter's ability to work hard or even more in her displays of shyness or shame, while they told stories of the exploits and affairs a son had conducted on the stage of the world. Thus, a friend could speak with warmth of his six-year-old daughter, who, he said, was too ashamed to wash in front of him and moments later strongly defend his married teenage son's philandering.

This differentiated pattern continued throughout adulthood. If a Gypsy husband and wife left the settlement together on foot, she walked behind him and carried any load on her back unaided by him. When a middle-aged couple set off to a funeral together, she carried him piggyback to avoid his shoes being splattered with mud. At home men ate first, washed first, and were given priority in most affairs. In economic matters, too, such as the fattening of pigs, despite the greater contribution of women, men had the control. In this process, so crucial for household survival and status improvement, the purchase of the animal was the man's task, whereas the actual fattening was assigned to the woman. The husband might build the sty in which pigs were kept, but until delivery day, while his wife and daughters scavenged, he hardly bothered with them. At the point of sale, listening to some men boasting about their good connections with the man on the weighing bridge who would bump the price up by "adding a few kilos" or putting the pigs in a better price class than they deserved, one might have believed that the whole business of making money from pigs depended on the men's contribution. The animals were delivered by the men, who left their wives at home, and it was the men who celebrated their earnings by going off drinking with their brothers.

Without a wife, a man would not have kept pigs, yet her labor did not give her a decisive say in what happened with the animals. A woman might complain if she felt that the fruits of her efforts were being frittered away by her husband, but it was hard for her to enforce her will against his.[3] I did see women criticizing men for not making a good enough horse deal with money from pigs they had raised—but only after the event. The recommended solution was, moreover, not to return the money to the wife but for the man to deal again. On one occasion a woman successfully reversed a swap made by her husband of pigs for a young cow by pointing out that her husband had been drunk when he made the swap. But to do this, the woman had to sit in her yard half-cursing, half-singing until the wife of the other man came over and personally returned the swapped animals. As she did so, she cursed the animals so they would bring no luck. The aggrieved wife was thus able to act only after the event and then only indirectly: She had to shout her curses into the air and was dealt with by the other wife, not the man who had made the deal.[4] For this "interference" the first woman was scorned by others in the settlement, and when the returned pigs died a few weeks later, several people pointed out to me that the curse had worked.

In comparison with Gypsy and Rom groups elsewhere in the world, the position of the Harangos Rom women is perhaps rather special, though not unique. In England, Traveler-Gypsy women play a key role in dealings with the non-Gypsy world, and they can sometimes bring the self-confidence they develop in relation to the world outside back into dealings with other Gypsies.[5] In the United States the Gypsy women's activities, especially as fortune-tellers and as mediators with welfare workers, also provides a basis on which their authority within the community grows. In Harangos there was no female equivalent of the horse market, no publicly salient moment when the Rom women took on the outside world. This may, in part, explain the relatively subordinate position of the women here in contrast to other Rom groups.[6] However, the general point remains true of Harangos and Rom communities elsewhere: There is a radical, gendered division of social affairs. Quite how this plays out to produce any particular distribution of power and authority in a community may depend on political and economic factors like those I just mentioned.[7] But what seems fairly constant is that, whereas women may be proud to feed their families and sustain their households each day, men's activities are aimed at spectacular, one-shot successes and the expenditure of the proceeds on conspicuous home improvements, horses, or celebration with other men.[8]

Gender discourse "uses attributes of the sexes to define qualities of social concern."[9] This discussion of the attributes of the Gypsy sexes begins to suggest some of the reasons that both Rom men and women conceived their community as being rooted in the brotherly relations of a group of men rather than in ungendered sibling or other kin relations. However, we are still far from understanding why femaleness was rendered so differently from maleness in terms of Rom values, why women and men were kept "apart" in this way, and what was it about "femaleness" that made it "impossible to start anything with girls." To answer these questions, we need to know much more about the Rom's relations with the world outside their communities. At this stage, to take the interpretation of the metaphor of brotherhood further, we need first to consider what "qualities of social concern" were being defined by the idea of brotherhood.

Brothers as Equals

Although in Christian Europe we are accustomed to thinking that brotherhood connotes equality, in the rural Hungarian (peasant) context "brother," like most other kinship terms, also connoted hierarchy, since brothers were always either "elder" or "younger," "superior" or "junior." To address an elder stranger in Hungarian as *bátyám* (my elder brother) was a politely affectionate way of being respectful, whereas to address the same man as *öcsém* (my younger brother) would have been rudely patronizing. In Romany, however, no such hierarchical nuances were available, for the concept of brother implied symmetry and identity.[10] To call someone *phral,* as all Gypsy men did one another, including complete strangers, was to display the respect of treating this other as an equal of oneself. There was no more honorable position to be offered by a Rom. And though the relation between brothers-in-law was always potentially hierarchical, since among the Hungarian Rom the gift of a woman could not be directly returned, in most contexts brothers-in-law preferred to address each other as brother. Such egalitarian values were found in quasi-ceremonial contexts in which men addressed each other as *phral,* as well as in everyday speech, when all men of whatever age could be and normally were addressed as "boy" (*šav*) and women likewise as "girl" (*šej*).

This symmetry in Gypsy relations was also given tangible form in a gesture that was particularly expressive of brotherly sentiment—the exchange of small personal possessions. In the Third Class I often witnessed such trading (*paruvel*) of clothing, jewelry, hats, knives, radios, watches, or music cassettes.[11] In such deals identical sorts of objects were exchanged along with, when necessary, a cash supplement to ensure fairness. The English term "swap" fairly captures the notion of the substitutability of both object and person for each other in the exchange—for what was being achieved was patently not a transfer of material wealth. Rather, the swap demonstrated that what was good enough for one brother was good enough for the other, and since the goods transferred were different, the swap also showed a degree of trust that one brother would not cheat, and thereby ridicule, the other. On one occasion I saw two elderly and rather distinguished Gypsy men agreeing during a drink at a bar to swap their boots, and then, as they struggled rather comically to fit on their new boots, they proudly announced to the world at large, with great smacking kisses on their lips, their brotherly feelings for each other. At other times if I asked why the men swapped, they responded with the simple statement "He is my brother" (*Phral-i mange*).

The notion that communal relations should be shaped by brotherly equality also produced a strong tendency toward the homogenization of activity in settlement life.[12] In the Third Class I was often surprised to find that on any one day the same food was being cooked in several households. Bowls of this identical food would then be circulated among close relatives. Although supplies on the markets were sometimes restricted, they were never so poor in prosperous Harangos that this was a matter of necessity. Likewise, men would religiously buy only one particular brand of beer, though there were other equivalent brews. Fashions passed across a settlement in this way, so when one boy bought a particular cassette, a few days later the same music would be heard in every house. One winter bantam ducks were all the rage to decorate people's courtyards; another year it was pigeons. One week a man bought some gravel to lay over the mud in his courtyard; the next week the yards of all the wealthier families in the Third Class were similarly covered. I could lay on the examples. In each case there may have been a nugget of "economic" sense in that, for instance, gravel may have been cheaper one year than another, but this could not explain the uniformity that the Gypsies sought to construct in their lifestyles. This homogenization, though partly a matter of keeping up with the Lakatoses, was also lived as another form of brotherhood, as a means for the Rom households—which were really of different economic standing thanks to the activities of their various members—to appear to live in the same way.

Relations between men, too, both within the immediate family and in broader groups, were shaped by the egalitarianism of the Gypsy idea of brotherhood. I was at first rather shocked by the casual way in which children treated their elders, often simply ignoring their requests. Parents who tried to order their children about were roundly castigated for their bossiness by other relatives. From the age of seven or eight, children, especially boys, were treated as increasingly autonomous moral agents. One might almost say that, whereas among the peasants the nature of brotherly relations was inflected by an element of paternal authority, among the Gypsies the filial relation was strongly tinted by an element of brotherly egalitarianism. It was not the case that elders were never respected. Rather, age conferred only a dubious legitimacy on their opinions. Men would tell me that the "old men" (*phuro rom*) should be carefully listened to and then would themselves proceed to ignore the old men, almost rudely it seemed, from my *gaźo* point of view. In this sense egalitarianism posited autonomy as a greater value than respect.

In fact, Gypsy children were generally treated with remarkable tolerance. When all the windows were broken in a house by a boisterous pair of children, a "good" mother might bewail her plight, curse, and even shout, but she would never punish them. Again, this contrasts with common Hungarian behavior: In most Magyar families the phrase "That's not allowed" (*nem szabad*) was a constant refrain. In all the time months in the Third Class, I hardly ever heard it used, and on each occasion there were *gaźos* around whom the Rom were trying to impress with their knowledge of supposedly "civilized" (*művelt*) manners.

Just as paternal authority was drastically restricted, so there was no other relation between men outside the family in which one man had the right to lead or in other ways stand over his brothers. This was especially apparent in the system of Gypsy justice known as the *kris*—a gathering of Gypsies, almost always men, though sometimes including an old woman, to adjudicate disputes between Rom over matters as diverse as compensation for divorce, accusations of theft, cheating at horse deals, and betrayal to *gaźo* authorities.[13] In the eighteen months I spent in Harangos in the 1980s, I witnessed six conflicts that went to *kris*, one of which took four successive *kris* meetings to be resolved. Rom justice relied entirely on the willingness of each Gypsy to acknowledge his moral ties with other Gypsies and so to consider their needs empathetically. The judgments given in *kris* were no more than the advice of one or more men whom no one was compelled to heed, since the men who gave their opinions did so as individuals, not as representatives of some abstract system or idea of justice. They stood for themselves, nothing more. If they had authority, it was entirely personal and found no support in a system of power relations or means of coercion, since they had no means, moral or otherwise, to enforce their decisions. Thus, the four *kris*es called to resolve a dispute about an accident did not go to "higher" authorities each time, but to different ones in new areas of the country. The final meeting was successfully concluded only when all parties were persuaded to agree to the suggestion of compensation.[14]

It is important to stress the informal nature of Gypsy equality: It was presumed that all men were equal, but this was given no formal recognition in office or status. In fact, in the settlement men were constantly in competition with one another to assert their equality, to deny that anyone else was a better man than oneself. The fragility of brotherly equality surfaced when men spoke together. To talk was to demand attention. To pay attention, to attend, was to respect and to honor. But the status of the listener in this situation was at best ambiguous, since his silence could be construed by others as a sign of weakness and passivity. When a Gypsy started to recount some exploit in the company of others, if the listeners were not to lose prestige, they, too, had to claim the attention of the assembled Rom. Each initiated his own talk to show that he, too, had something to add!

If as far as the Gypsies were concerned, no Rom should boss another around, the question of leadership became particularly acute in relation to the *gaźo* authorities, since they traditionally assumed that Gypsy communities had leaders—known in Hungarian as *vajda*. In some communities where there was a *gaźo* resource that could be monopolized by one man, such figures did emerge—as in rural communities where the cooperative farm had a need for occasional Gypsy labor in large numbers. In Harangos there were no such resources and no *vajda*. Even so, officials' preference for dealing with such figureheads meant that policemen, council officers, and even representatives of national governments sought out *vajda*s when trying to deal with the Harangos Gypsies collectively.[15] One day when a local council representative came to visit the Third Class and was greeted by a large group of frustrated Gypsies, he immediately stated that he was unwilling to deal with so many people at once, and he asked to speak to the *vajda*. One old man claimed to be such, but before so much as a word had been exchanged, his own son stood up and ridiculed him as a drunken illiterate. No one came to the old man's defense; after all, the Romany term for *vajda* was *mujalo*, "informer."

Identity Built in the Present

For most cultures the language of kinship focuses attention on the transmission, the perpetuation, and the transformation of identity across generations. Although the Gypsies could not entirely transcend a concern with these processes, their use of the image of brotherhood to conceive of their most important communal relations was expressive of a rather special cultural construction. For them, identity was neither primordial nor essential, though it was no less deeply felt for that.

As we try to think our way into this, the peasants of Hungary provide a helpfully familiar contrast. For the head of a peasant household, a *gazda*, one image of a "well-spent life" was the successful transfer to one of his children of the patrimony he himself had inherited. In so doing, he was handing on much more than material wealth; he was passing into the future the family's name and an identity embodied in the family house.

For the Rom, essential aspects of one's identity did not derive from the past but were learned for oneself in conjunction with one's contemporaries, so the whole question of inheritance was construed differently. I was often surprised when I asked about the sites of previous houses and who had built them to discover that my Gypsy informants had completely forgotten. Even when Gypsy parents left wealth behind, this was not passed onto their children but consumed at the funeral and on their graves.

As non-Gypsies, we tend to have an idea of the Gypsy social world as being supremely closed to outsiders. In Harangos I initially accepted this stereotypical view. I often saw *gažos* who had dealings with the Rom and were keen to find out something about the Gypsies. The Rom played with these casual inquirers, seekers of some exotic tidbit of information with which to titillate their friends, and kept them "out" by ruses, half-lies, and misinformation. In other cases, however, as I discovered, the Rom had no trouble admitting that it was possible to be born a *gažo* and become a Rom. Among the Rom of Harangos and nearby villages, there were several such people. One of these was famous among the Rom as the biggest horse dealer in a ring of markets around Budapest. I never heard it suggested that because of their non-Gypsy ancestry, these people were somehow less Rom than anyone else. Their children were also fully accepted as Gypsies. So when I discovered that one entire extended family in the Third Class was descended from a Jewish grandmother, I was the only person interested in the story. No one seemed to remember the circumstances.

This idea, that one could become a Gypsy by living with the Rom and learning from them, was expressed in the way Gypsies talked in Romany of Gypsy culture as *romanes*, a term that also meant the language Romany. Acquiring one was akin to acquiring the other. Indeed, when I asked Gypsies how one might become a Rom, the answer, as often as not, was "if you learn to speak Romany" (*te sitjos te des duma romanes*; literally, "if you learn to give speech in the Rom way"). Knowing Romany shaped identity because of the relationships this involved one in, and so here the two meanings of *romanes*, as language and culture, became one: It was by relating as an equal with other Rom that one established one's shared identity.

The point was that the Rom idea of reproduction was not so much rooted in an ideology of descent and inheritance of character as in an ideology of nurture and shared social activity. I said previously that the Rom commonly addressed each other as boys and girls, as if they lived in a world without parents. This impression was reinforced by the frequent use of the attribute *čoro*, "orphan" (and also poor) to describe the Rom. It was as if the relations that these parentless "children" sustained with each other, not some primordial or even historical event, determined their identity. Sharing activity, food, dress, language, was thus a form of continuous nurture of one another, a constant reinvention of being. For this reason, it seems to me, the Rom were fiercely insistent that Rom stepparents love their acquired children exactly as their own.[16]

The masking of a person's past behind his or her present, achieved identity was also reflected in the names that individual Gypsies acquired.

A Rom's name was not a fixed marker of an identity that existed outside a network of relations, as our names are. Our surnames attach us to a patriline that exists independently of us; our forenames, at least in Protestant countries, most often predicate a unique individual personality that is thought to exist prior to and beyond our relations with others. Rom names were more like our nicknames, acquired as a marker, and often a comic one, of a place in a network of relations. Thus, a Rom may have had several names at any one time in his life. He would have had a "Magyar forename" *(ungriko anav)* that *gaźo* colleagues used and that Gypsies who did not work with him probably did not know. He had an official (state) Hungarian surname, which might have been his father's or mother's, depending on the legal state of their union at the time of his birth. Then, apart from the name given to him by his Rom godparents, he may have had names associated with particular habits or features at certain times. As a young person's reputation developed, so did these names; a man or a woman could have had, in effect, a different name in each village or settlement where he or she had lived.[17]

Such ideas also determined the way that other types of shared Gypsy identity were conceived. In some contexts all people who accepted the *gaźo* definition of them as *Cigány* might be included in the group of "Gypsies"; more commonly all people who called themselves Rom would be "in." At lower "levels" there were categories of identity generically called *nemzeto*s, a term that the Rom translated into Hungarian as *nép*, "the people." *Nemzeto*s were not really groups in any sense, but the term referred to a concept used to loosely define differences of style among bands of Gypsies who did things together.[18] In all these cases, a person shared identity with others as a result of joint activity, and the whole idea of descent was trivialized. When I asked why some *nemzeto*s were named after particular men, people were either not interested or could not remember. For the Gypsies, the past was truly another country. It is appropriate to think of these *nemzeto*s as brotherhoods (groups of Gypsies who shared activity together), and when at Christmas or Easter men talked about their whole *nemzeto* gathering, they were invariably expecting to see the men they called their brothers.[19]

Alternative Images of Sociality: Nonbrotherly Relations

The idea of a community of brothers depended upon the Rom playing down, and in effect ignoring, in their public rhetoric at least, the relationships men had with women as sisters. Although it was relatively easy to suppress this relation, since it was the basis of no significant social action, marriage was a different matter. Although young couples did not immediately form a new household, marriage laid the basis for their founding the basic social unit in which the Rom lived: the nuclear household. Marriage posed, however, a number of fundamental problems for the idea that the key social relations were brotherly. First, if only by allying each brother with a potentially different set of in-laws, marriage differentiated a united group of brothers. Second, marriage could mean that men who had previously treated each other as brothers now related as "brothers-in-law" (*šogoro*). Third, if marital relations were repeated between a group of brothers and a group of sisters, they could be construed as creating a distinct and potentially closed circle of intermarrying families, an endogamous group within the wider endogamous circle of the Rom. Fourth, to behave *romanes* was to suppress and ignore all these ideological problems. I take them in reverse order.

Because a high proportion of first marriages (most of which were arranged) ended in divorce as a result of the incompatibility of the spouses, many adults in the Third Class had been married more than once. In several families I knew, a man was then married to a woman who had been the wife of a near neighbor in the past. Given the ideology of *romanes*, the men could have seen themselves as in some sense "sharing" or "exchanging" these women. But this was not something that the Rom wished to consider at all. To the contrary, the whole topic was taboo, and divorced women told me that they made strenuous efforts to avoid their former parents-in-law and spouses. Among the men concerned, no mention was ever made of the woman who linked them.

The Rom insisted that, though Rom should marry Rom, it was not *romanes* to "marry close," especially not to marry first cousins.[20] In fact, in the recent past at least, marriage among first cousins had become a common practice, though one that no one liked to talk about. What remained completely taboo was to swap sisters, and people seemed amazed when I told them that there are peoples who do just this, exchange their daughters. Although I knew several cases in which two or more brothers married a group of sisters, in these alliances women only "went" (*žal*) one way. And in the kinship data I collected for some thirty families covering at least three generations, in most cases I found no evidence of a reversal of direction in succeeding generations. Most people spontaneously just said that this was not the Rom custom, but one man offered a more general explanation, one confirmed afterward by others. He told me that the same rule applied as between co-godparents (*kirvos*). If I "go to you" (*žav tuke*) as *kirvo*, then I cannot ask you to "come" to me as *kirvo* to one of my children. What was enjoined, therefore, was some form of extended exchange, and the possibility of a restricted "closure" of the marriage circle between two groups of families was denied.

In the Romany spoken in Harangos, there was no term such as the English "in-laws" for affines in general. Whereas in Parisian Romany it is possible (however rare) to refer to all a child's spouse's relatives as "our relatives by marriage" (*amare xanamika*),[21] Harangos Rom did not speak this way. Indeed, although in principle the parents of married children could have referred to each other as *xanamik*, the term was avoided, and in most cases I was made to feel that I had committed an embarrassing, if minor, faux pas when I used it. This was even true in those cases in which two brothers had married two sisters. Instead, what people tended to do was to treat affinal relations as relevant only to the individuals directly linked by a marriage, the husband/wife and parents-in-law. Thus, at a funeral I once heard a man called Šošoj refer to another as "our brother-in-law" (*šogoro*)—this was his actual father's brother's daughter's husband—but moments later a "brother" of Šošoj ostentatiously talked of Šošoj's *šogoro*, thereby restating the affinal relation as a personal one between two men, sidelining it for everyone else, and "allowing" them to continue addressing each other as brother. On other occasions when a man referred to another as our brother-in-law, although the usage was polite, it was also a way of distancing the individual, putting him outside and beyond the circle of brothers.[22]

If marriage's potential to create a closed group of intermarrying brothers was effectively suppressed, there remained the problem that marriage inevitably created brothers-in-law out of men who most often had previously treated each other as brothers. A clue to the "solution" adopted by the Gypsies can be found in the betrothal ceremony. More than any other time, it would then have been possible to conceive of the Gypsy social universe as divided into two groups linked by the coming marriage. The initial gesture of the ceremony was the journey of a group of men from the house of the groom to the house of the bride, carrying a bottle of hard spirits with unopened red rosehip buds wrapped around it. The "request" (*mangaljipe*, or *mangimo*), however, made clear that marriage occurred within the circle of brothers and reestablished those brotherly relations. For a start, when the groom's party arrived, elaborately polite devices were adopted to conceal the real intentions as if the men had just come to celebrate their brother, to be with him and enjoy his company. Only very much later and with great trepidation was the question put concerning the girl.

This is how a girl's hand was finally asked for in Csóka one Saturday evening in early summer 1985. The groom's father addressed the bride's father:

> I find you with God, my darling brother! Are you pleased that I have looked for you and found you? I have come far. I didn't rest until I arrived. But my

sheep's tracks, my sheep's tracks, they lead from there, from my house to this house. Brother! My sheep is here with you. You have to give her back. Whatever you have to say, whatever you demand for her, I am willing, my brother, to collect my sheep from your care. Because she is the one! She is mine. Well, all right, you looked after her; you protected her; you defended her from everything here. Be lucky, my brother! And if she has something to say . . . or if she doesn't, if she is here or not . . .

And the father of the bride replied: "She is here, your sheep. Be lucky! Be lucky! Let them live long!"[23]

The image of the lost sheep being retrieved is a common element of traditional Hungarian wedding ceremonies, but the Rom seemed to have given the formulaic speeches a special significance. Here the idea of marriage as an exchange of a woman between two families was replaced by an image of a man retrieving a person held in trust for him by his brother. Sometimes men agreed when their children were still toddlers to marry them in the future, and in these instances the imagery of the speech must have been especially evocative. But there was always a sense in which children were raised for the good of the Gypsies as a whole, were in a sense shared as a common resource by all the Rom, and so this kind of speech touched on a more general experience. Once the speech was made and the request accepted, the men return to their partying and the creation of brotherly sentiment by sharing a drink and a song together.

The suppression of the idea of marriage as an exchange continued after marriage in the representation of the relationships established between individuals and families as a result of the alliance.[24] Of all inter-Gypsy relations, the affinal relationship was perhaps the one most tinged with hierarchical elements because, unlike any other transfer between the Gypsies, when a family "gave its daughter" (*das amara śa*) to another family, the transaction could not be reversed. Swapping clothes, trinkets, and horses might be what made men brothers, but not swapping daughters. As a result, children-in-law in particular were expected to show respect, distance, and stiff, formal behavior to their parents-in-law quite unlike the relaxed relations children had with their own parents.

However, although the relationship was categorically hierarchical and unidirectional, the Rom in Harangos seemed to make much effort to deny or avoid these implications of affinity. In some contexts, such as paying a formal visit to a sick relative in hospital, the situation required that a man address his wife's brother as *šogoro* (brother-in-law), but there was always some ambivalence about this, even in cases in which the term was being used only to qualify the relationship between two individuals. On several occasions I noticed men addressing their brothers-in-law respectfully (both sister's husband and wife's brother) as *šogoro* but then being called

Relatives of the groom dance outside the bride's house. (I. Németh)

phral in return. In those contexts in which affinity had to be recognized for respect to be paid, it seemed as if that affinity was then immediately "put away" so that the brotherly nature of male relations could be reestablished. Even in intergenerational relations, a man might have referred to a son-in-law as such (*muro žamutro*), but the moral connotations of the term were so hierarchical that the man would have refrained from using it in address or even within earshot of his son-in-law, since it suggested that the son-in-law had married in and therefore that his own natal household lacked the resources to help the young couple. Indeed, I found that men who had close relations with their parents-in-law affectionately, and reciprocally, replaced the affinal terms by consanguineal ones. Son-in-law became son or brother.

As one might expect, the situation for a daughter-in-law was more complex, since her subordination as a woman was reinforced by the respect she owed her affines. In her presence, her parents-in-law might talk of her as "our daughter-in-law" (*amari bori*). But because of the general egalitarianism of Rom relationships, this relation of a woman with her parents-in-law was openly acknowledged to be fraught with difficulties. I was very struck one morning when I saw a relatively poor and unprestigious woman crossing the railway tracks into the town. Behind her, just

The bride cries as she is taken out of her mother's home. (I. Németh)

as a wife walks behind her husband, came her *bori*—a woman who had married without any formal ceremonial request or wedding. The appearance of the elder woman was thereby transformed; she had acquired a new status and substance. In the house her *bori* performed most of the domestic labor and was on constant duty to her husband's family. As a result, within six weeks of moving there, she had persuaded her husband to return to her parents' village, where she could evade the onerous task of tiptoeing around her husband's parents. There were some economic and social advantages to this move for the husband, but if he had not gone with her, she might have left anyway; he could not have made her stay against her will. From then on she only had to present the proper behavior of the *bori* on the occasional, quasi-ceremonial visit.

Finally, I come to the idea that for a group of brothers the act of marriage inevitably divided and distinguished. What was at stake here has been summed up by Patrick Williams writing about the Parisian Rom: "Marriage is that which separates: for the spouses it is a process of individualisation; it is also that which regroups: for the children it is the marriage of their parents which determines their identity."[25] In Harangos it was really only at marriage that young Gypsies began to leave the domestic realm and establish a distinct persona on the public stage. Marriage led to children, and through these a man began to establish ceremonial relations with others in his own right. For most young men, the first feast/celebration he might host was the one at which he invited another to be godfather to his child. For a woman, too, it was only when established in her own home with her own children that she acquired a persona distinct from that of her natal or marital family. Marriage was therefore the start of a process of individualization for the persons concerned.

But marriage also founded a new group, a new domestic unit that would make its own way in the world, establishing relations with its own *gaźos* and building its own reputation among the Rom.[26] Whatever the rhetorical stress on brotherhood, this basic fact of life could not be denied: The Rom were not a celibate monkhood; they reproduced their communities by natural means, in families. Although the Rom were largely oblivious to their past and their ancestry, they were concerned with the durability of their way of life, and their children were the guarantor of this. The problem seemed to be that marriage, by establishing independent households, created a challenge to their way of life by laying the basis for differentiation of the brothers. The conflict was reinforced because, whereas sharing was an expression of the ideology of brotherhood, accumulation for one's family and children was the appropriate goal of domestic life. One man's comments were typical: "I want to take my children further. I work so they can live better, to progress into something better. I don't want to be the last one in the line." Indeed, more effort probably went into creating and enriching one's house than into anything else.

Given my account of the way in which the Rom could demand assistance from each other as part of the ethic of *romanes,* when someone accumulated wealth, there had to be a legitimate means for refusing the demands of kin and neighbors. One important means for doing so came with children. A common feature of Gypsy rhetoric illustrates this point. When I first went to live with the Gypsies, I was often infuriated when, if I refused a request to help someone, that person would not just take my "no" for a definitive answer. In such cases I got myself into circles of request and refusal, each time the request being put anew by a different person, who, it was believed, might win me over. Once, however, almost without thinking, in an argument over a lift to a distant village that I had been asked to give to a visiting Rom, I added, "Let my son die [that is, if I am lying]; I can't go." I had almost unconsciously been imitating the style of argument of my hosts, but suddenly I found that the ground of the argument had shifted; I had now provided firm reason for refusal. Now my "children" came to my defense. "Michael's put a curse on himself" (*armaja das*), the Rom chorused. If it had been only my "will" in question, I could not finally have rejected a demand to help a brother, but by upping the stakes and cursing, I had put my will beyond question. So in a world where everyone was supposed to be open to the needs of others, and where one's standing in a community depended, in part, on generosity, children provided a legitimate reason for denying one's brotherly obligations. Buttressed by verbal forms that altered the implications of what one was saying, a refusal to help no longer carried the implication that one was rejecting the idea of helping in general.[27]

Breaking Down the House

This discussion of affinity and the problematic role of the marital relation in the *romanes* way throws a rather new light on the brotherly practice of sharing. One might almost say that, if the Rom lived in a state of siege in relation to the *gažos*, the Rom household stood in a similar relation to the brothers. In this light, *romanes* represented a desire to render permeable the walls of the household and to suggest that Gypsies should be open to one another independently of their household ties, even though those ties, most of the time, were as strong, if not stronger, than those between the brothers. Thus, for instance, we saw that the passage of food between houses and the avoidance of a fixed mealtime denied the idea of an exclusive, private house. The same symbolic intention underlay the custom by which Gypsy yards were left open or did not have gates at all, while every Magyar house in the Third Class was kept secure behind a locked iron gate. Nor did a Gypsy ever lock her front door when there were members of the family in the settlement. At almost any time of night or day, unless one saw a towel hung over the door as a sign that someone was washing, one might enter a house without any preparatory greeting or warning. Rarely did I see a Gypsy make another feel that an unexpected visit fell at an inconvenient time. Even arriving with a party of men after midnight on one occasion, our host was out of bed, offering drinks and coffee in a matter of minutes and making us feel that he would be happy to talk with us throughout the rest of the night.

However, if men and women wished to treat their homes as places that could be opened out to the Rom, they also knew that for men this was always fraught with difficulty, since most often in a group there was one person who, thanks to previous ill-feeling, was unwilling to enter a particular house. As a result, the winter months were a period of enforced isolation. Then Gypsies gathered briefly at either end of the day around small fires lit in several corners of the settlement, exchanged the bare essentials of gossip and news before returning to their own private affairs in the shelter of their homes. Each family remained cooped up in its own house waiting to be visited, rarely daring to initiate such a reciprocal process. Apart from a *mulatšago*, there were few occasions for a person's practical attention to be turned outward away from the problems of his or her particular family. Then suddenly when the spring sun finally appeared, within hours Gypsy women were moving their kitchen stoves out of doors, and men were optimistically stripping to the waist as if casting off a veil of claustrophobia and hastening the coming of the period of openness and renewed gregariousness on neutral soil.

One particularly arresting form of these attempts to balance the demands of the domestic with those of the brotherhood pertained to the care of children. Concern for children's welfare meant that, although adults rarely had a right to interfere in one another's business, if a Rom hit a child, others did intervene; in this case autonomy gave way to other aspects of *romanes*. In other ways too the Gypsies seemed to be constructing an image of the community as a unity by "sharing" the children. Adults sought petty forms of assistance from other people's children in the settlement. A neighbor's child, even if one was not on particularly good terms with that child's parents, might be sent to the shop or asked to guard the sleeping baby almost as easily as one's own child would. As children grew older, they were encouraged to spend time with other members of their extended family, as if they were being shared out among their relatives, returning home when they wished. In one case a woman had given all her children by her first marriage to her mother to look after. She insisted that this was not the wish of her second husband but of her mother. It was acknowledged, of course, that most children were emotionally attached to their parents, but for that very reason, I believe, adults sometimes teasingly "kidnapped" children, persuading them to come off secretly on a trip for a few hours as if to remind them that their commitment to their parents and their home was not absolute. In such ritualized games, Gypsies played on the ambivalent ties of children to their households and to the wider network of relatives.

This assault on the household affected the use of petty cash. It was primarily the duty of the woman as wife or mother to ensure that the needs of the household were met, but women would boast of their ability to get by without having spent much and without having asked their husband for money. Many women were proud of the way they kept their family's pigs without ever having to go to the agricultural supplies shop to buy commercial fodder. By refusing to pay for rail tickets on the way to garbage dumps or the market fees while selling thread, as well as by establishing relations in the town market with *gažo* traders who then sold the women produce cheaply, they tried to save cash.

The difference between men's and women's practice was especially marked immediately following payday. Then the women could be seen trying to take care of the provision of the home for the next month, while the men went out drinking and celebrating with their relatives, freely, almost ostentatiously consuming their funds to visit distant relatives in taxis that the men paid *gaźos* to drive.

The most dramatic form of this conspicuously unthrifty consumption was card-playing, an activity that was normally tied to paydays. On Fridays, after receiving wages, groups of men would gather in one of the bars in the town and drink away the early part of the evening until suitable card-playing partners turned up. Most often these were Romungros or *gaźos*, but occasionally the Rom played against each other. On such evenings older men were often invited to come drinking, but with the exception of two elderly men who still worked in factories, the senior members of the party all used to return home before the younger, working men, often really quite drunk by then, went off to gambling sessions that went on all night or even longer.

Normally men played in informal teams. In them one man actually played the cards against a Romungro, while the rest of the men laid their bets on their fellow Rom. The Romungros played likewise. The game was always "Twenty-one," and the pack was shuffled every time so that the outcome rested on chance, not on memory and calculation of odds. At each deal "Reds" (100-forint notes) were thrown by each party into the space between the men. As the night progressed, more beer was drunk, the bets expanded, and "Greens" (1,000-forint notes) were played. When playing in a large space, the men might keep their cash in piles beside them, which rose or decreased with their luck. The games went on until all the money of one side had been won by the other side or at least until it appeared that this was the case.

In the talk and practice of gambling, one of the things that was stressed was the brute quantity, as physical object, of red and green money. It seems to me that as this dry, paper money slipped from one side of the game to the other, quite independently of the will or skill of the players, the men were enacting the symbolic annihilation of that part of the person that had gone into making that money in wage labor. Factory work was dominated by the alien intentionality and other-directedness of the *gaźo* bosses, and the money that derived from it bore these marks. The money that came from the haphazard game of gambling was free of the taint of labor, liberated from its demeaning "past." Losing could therefore be nearly as acceptable as winning and certainly preferable to not joining the game at all. Men who by midnight had doubled their money did not give up and go home satisfied; they played on until one side or the other was drained. It was quite extraordinary to me, observing working men who had lost huge sums of money (maybe four times a month's salary) preparing to enter the game the following month.[28]

In light of the role of the Rom household as the locus of accumulation, the meaning of gambling did not just derive from its opposition to wage labor. It also stood in some contexts against saving and caring for the family. This was made explicit in a song that the Rom sang in which a man lost not only his coat but also his family—his wife left him temporarily because, as someone once explained to me, the "hero" sold the duvets of his children's beds.

Eladom a bőr kabátom:	I'll sell my leather coat:
Visszaszerzem a családom.	I'll get back my family today.
Aj aj devla so te kerav?	Oy, oy God, what should I do?
Panź, šo šela kaj te rodav?	Five, six hundred: where will I find it?
Panź, šo šela kaj te rodav?	Five, six hundred: where will I find it?
Taj vi pav le le phralentsa.	And I'll drink it with the brothers.
Taj vi pav le le phralentsa.	And I'll drink it with the brothers.
Taj le laśe šogorentsa.	And with the good brothers-in-law.
Mindjar aba me te merav	Right away let me die [if I lie]!
De panź, šo šela naj but love!	But five, six hundred isn't money![29]

The hero thinks (in Hungarian) to regain his family by selling the symbol of his status, the leather coat of the horse dealer, but his contrition does not last long, and so he sings in Romany that if he gets the cash, he will drink it with his brothers. Finally he points out, as if outraged at his ill-fortune, that what he wants adds up to so very little; how absurd it is that he cannot lay hands on it. Through the motifs in such songs, people could tell the stories of their lives. My host was not the only man who told me that he had taken the duvets of his children's beds to sell them— only to win them back, with much else besides, when he had returned to the game.

A similar opposition of gambling and the household took shape in the heavily standardized accounts that older men, grandparents, gave me of the occasion when they had finally abandoned card-playing.[30] For each of them, there had been a night when they had lost 60,000 forints (a "formulaic price" that reflected the cost, in 1985, of the best horses). Then they had lost so much that they had had to call for more money to be brought from their home. The money arrived in their wives' head scarves, and still they lost. That was the end of their dealing in cards. In this story, to sustain the activity of the gambler, money had to be brought from the household, from the wife, who sent it in the piece of her clothing that was particularly representative of her "true Gypsy" nature,[31] in a form that reminded the man of his ties to his "true" wife. The opposition and potential conflict between two forms of consumption were here openly acknowledged.

The process of dividing the consumption of wealth into that associated with the household and that associated with brotherly activities was given lexical expression in Romany in a fashion that linked these paired opposites to *gažo* and Gypsy values, respectively. In the Romany spoken in Harangos, countless Hungarian terms were calqued, but the Hungarian term for money, *forint*, was taboo. Instead, a number of euphemisms were in common use so that, in effect, *gažo* forints were turned, for example, into Gypsy *pengős* (the old Hungarian currency that had been destroyed in the world's worst-ever hyperinflation of 1945–1946) or *rup*, "silver."

Although Gypsy women were often given the role of dealing with money in its forint aspect (that is, spending it in shops on necessities or placing it in the bank), they were also involved in a lexical and practical denial that money divided the Gypsies from each other. I saw young men who had run out of money during the month after payday simply grab small sums out of the front of the apron of female relatives. One such youth, who had no money simply because he had not taken a job that month, grabbed 60 forints one day from his impoverished, widowed aunt. She expressed neither surprise nor hostility toward him. "He needs it," she told me after he had left. "Let him have it." Just as a woman would give her last few forints to her husband to gamble, so this woman was showing her transcendence of her potential as the unbrotherly hoarder of money, a role linked to her involvement in sustaining the private household of which she was the mother.

That Gypsy money, in the formally sanctioned discourse, was a means to a higher end than personal accumulation was also illustrated by rhetorical gestures adopted by the men. I was sometimes asked to take pictures of groups of brothers, with one man fanning out his money to show how much he had and how much he was willing to share. In singing, too, men would often hold out wads of banknotes as they sang how, to a true Gypsy, spending "500, 600 is not much money." They brought this money out less to show off their wealth than to show that it was not hidden in a bank away from the claims and demands of the brothers.[32] But to my mind, most moving of all was the custom adopted when someone was being frustrated by the petty preoccupations of another. On such occasions a man might tear up or throw in the fire several thousand-forint notes (each worth a real equivalent of nearly $200) to show, for example, that his desire to visit his brother at 3:00 A.M. was more important than the price charged by a *gažo* taxi driver, or than the goodwill of the recalcitrant chauffeur-anthropologist. Others would try to stop the man and remove his cash until his temper cooled. Far from losing respect for this "loss of control," as I saw it, he showed that one was dealing with a man for whom the brothers and their good mood came before all else.

But in the end, these ritualized gestures were for the high moments of life when men agonistically displayed their adherence to *romanes* on a public stage. These displays represented only a temporary and partial victory for the demands of communal life, the brothers, over those of the households. Just as the Rom tried at times to close their doors on their importuning neighbors and save a bit of money for the future, so they dreamed of "getting out," leaving and trying to find a place for themselves and their families in the world of the *gaźos*, away from all those demanding relatives. In the next chapter I tell the story of two such attempts. But first I wish to offer a final word on the resilience of the Gypsy community.

The Nature of Community and the Means of Resistance

The persistence of Gypsy communities may, it seems to me, be due in large part to their inherently flexible form—the fact that there was "nothing there" for the state to get its hands on. Rom communal life was not "objectivized" in offices of religious or secular leadership, regular meetings, or other institutionalized social forms. Brotherhood had no tangible, corporate form. A Gypsy family might live alone in a village or alongside several hundred other families; it made little difference. So long as there was a group of Rom with whom family members interacted when they did meet, the family was part of a community. No particular emphasis was put by the Rom on the bare fact of where they lived. I remember being amazed when I talked to the people in the Third Class about the possibility that their almost idyllic settlement might be flattened to make room for a new factory. I had thought that they might complain to the ministry in Budapest, but their attitude was much more relaxed: If they lost their homes, they would move elsewhere. These Gypsies were in no sense "nomads," but a "place of their own" was not in the end a place at all; rather, it was the always fragile realization of an intangible quality of life together.[33]

5

BREAKING OUT

IN CHAPTER 4 I SHOWED HOW THE ROM of Harangos had to deal with the inescapable contradiction that derived from their living in a community of households while representing crucial social relations as brotherly. Marriage provided two challenges to this way of thinking about Gypsy identity: It suggested an ideological alternative to the idea that social relations should be conceived as brotherly, and it founded households inside the doors of which the demands of the brothers could come to seem unreasonable and importuning. I examined one "solution" to the contradiction: a systematic attempt to restrict the claims of the household. In this chapter I consider another resolution: attempts to limit the claims of the brothers, if not actually sever ties altogether.

The two stories I tell in this chapter each carry two messages. First, they show that there were pressures within the Rom community itself pushing people out of it. Second, they suggest that as a result there were always people to whom an assimilationist policy might appeal. So before considering the outside world into which the Rom were supposed to assimilate, I present here the story of two families whose circumstances made them potential candidates for absorption into the non-Gypsy world.

"If Only We Lived Alone"

During my time in the Third Class, I lost count of the discussions I had with men and women about their dreams of "getting away" and finding a home in a village where there would not be "all those Gypsies" (*e but rom*) around them. In these conversations the Rom often returned to one image of the problems of living in a community: the disadvantages of sticking, that is, slaughtering, a pig when living among Gypsies. In Hungary, as in many parts of Eastern Europe, the pre-Christmas pig kill

73

was a major event in the calendar of rural families. A pig raised in a family's sty on slops from its own kitchen would be more or less ceremonially slaughtered by the men of the house. Every last bit of the animal would find some use, and much of the meat would be smoked or turned into sausages so that the pig fed the family throughout the lean months to follow. Although nearly all the Gypsy families in the Third Class bought and raised piglets, during the time I lived there none stuck a pig. Morga, the wife of Zeleno whom we met in Chapter 2, explained:

> We won't slaughter our pigs ourselves because, as you know, we've got a big extended family [*nemzeto*]. We'd have to give everyone meat, so what would remain for us? Instead, we'll deliver our pigs to the slaughterhouse and take the money. But if we lived in our own village, if our family ate on its own, then we would slaughter. But here lots of people live on this settlement, and one has to give each other meat. Why are the Gypsies like this? God knows why! We're not like the peasants . . . who wouldn't give their own neighbor a morsel of food. We give to other Gypsies, have to give to them. You see the Gypsies aren't mean. They have a good heart for each other; they offer each other food when they go to each other's houses, when they drink. You ask if it is sometimes hard to live like this? Yes, we always have to give meat away, and when someone slaughters their pigs for themselves, some people get cross, and then we'll fight. That is why my husband and I sell ours to the state.

Morga had a good heart for her neighbors, but however generous, she was also not stupid. Eight months' hard work feeding four pigs and a fair investment of cash for feed and vet's fees could not just be thrown away in a potlatch of collective consumption. How much easier it would have been, Morga and other people told me, if they had been able to kill a pig and store it for later use "like the Hungarians."[1]

To understand Morga's commentary on her predicament, we have to know something about Gypsy uses of money. Morga said that it was by turning pigs into cash that she and her husband protected their wealth from their neighbors. The point was that paper money, the tabooed forint, unlike hay or food, could be hidden and then accumulated or transformed into wealth that could less easily be shared. When Gypsy men wished to save money, they might hastily lend it to a reliable relative, but it was safer still to give the money to their wives, who kept it in a purse under their aprons, making it hard for others to get at. While I worked in the settlement, a common solution after payday was to give money to Judit Szegő to hide over the weekend. In this way a husband's relatives could honestly be told that there was no money in the house to be loaned—if the money had been there, the man could not have honorably refused a brother who came in need. Best of all, however, was to give the money to the *gaźo*s in the bank, where the money, in a fixed-term account, was safe from relatives.

Turning wealth into cash thus offered one way to resolve the problem posed by the conflict between the ethics of sharing and those of accumulation. There was, however, a more drastic solution to the conflict between brotherhood and family: to hide oneself among the *gaźo*s, *to* leave the ghetto behind.

Šošoj and Čaja: Getting Rich on One's Own

Šošoj and his wife, Čaja, were in 1984 clearly the richest Rom in the Third Class. People talked in awe of how he had 100,000 forints in his ordinary bank account at a time when an average salary was less than 6,000 forints. In 1977 Šošoj and Čaja had bought a house in the Third Class for 106,000 forints in cash, knocked down the existing house, and set about building a new one. They completed their new home in three months without even needing the low-interest saving's bank loan every other family depended upon. Whereas ordinary Gypsies' lives were ruled by the arrival of the monthly pension or the wage packet, Šošoj and Čaja seemed to have money on tap. The woman who collected the quarterly electricity bills in the Third Class used to come round on payday to ensure she was paid by the poorer Gypsies. Čaja and Thulo's wife, whose house I described in Chapter 3, were the only two who could have paid at any time. Šošoj often had the finest horses in the settlement, and when he did not have a perfect pair of matching horses, he was on the lookout for this peculiarly pleasing combination.

Of all the men in the Third Class, Šošoj was the man who commanded the immediate respect of outsiders, including myself. He could be ludicrously demanding—when after a period of especially close involvement with his affairs, I refused to privilege him over a member of another family to whom I was previously committed, I found myself almost excommunicated by his entourage. However trying personally, he was capable of making "things" happen with amazing rapidity. And more often than with any other man, one would hear people mutter behind his back, after his deals, that he seemed to have had another striking piece of luck.

Šošoj's and Čaja's home, the finest in the settlement, was a huge two-winged house with an open verandah and a concrete-floored stable ample enough for four horses, as many cows, and a few dozen chickens. A large summer kitchen stood at the edge of their land. Sitting out under their orchard of apricot trees and eating the ripe fruits in late June with one of their five daughters, I could understand why the Third Class was said to be "a little bit of heaven."

There were disputes about the origins of this family's wealth, but all concurred that their decision to live alone in a village for the first twenty years of their marriage had been fundamental. Šošoj, the third of six children, had been orphaned in March 1944 when their father was murdered by another Rom. He told me that his personal tragedy had not made him any poorer than his fellow Rom; no one had had "anything" at that time. But when his mother died some ten years later, Šošoj's father's brother, who had by then moved to the Third Class, took him and his younger brothers in for the next few years. Without parents, none of the elder boys had formal marriages, and none was able to provide a home for a wife. In 1957 Šošoj succeeded in asking for and obtaining the hand of another poor Gypsy, Čaja, whose own father was in prison for murder and whose mother had died some years previously. Čaja had no choice but to accept Šošoj, since she and her younger brother needed the protection of somebody.

Perhaps as much from necessity as from choice, Šošoj moved to Čaja's natal village of Dongó, where he easily obtained a residence permit, something that might have been more difficult the other way round, since the Harangos town council did not readily give residence permits to incoming Gypsies.[2] There were two other advantages to this move. Being "the only Gypsy in the village" meant that Šošoj was able to prosper without either providing for needy relatives or running the gauntlet of public hostility. As he kept animals, Šošoj had to have some means to feed them, and when he lived in Dongó, he was able to do as his peasant neighbors did: buy hay cheaply during summer for the year ahead. In a community of Gypsies, he would have found his stocks rapidly depleted as one needy relative after another came to beg for assistance. Nor did he have to conceal from anyone the names and addresses of his peasant business partners. In general, the Rom assumed that any goodwill a *gažo* might display was a limited good, and to establish relations, a Rom would have to persuade *gažos* that he was different from the mass of Gypsies. In Dongó Šošoj could "keep his own *gažos* to himself." Finally, since there were no other *Cigány* around, Šošoj's family had a monopoly on the kind of jobs that the Gypsies performed for the *gažos* and could always hope for special treatment, thereby evading the tendency of the Magyars to "lump all the Gypsies together."

The experience of Šošoj's wife's "brother," Thulo, the man who first invited me to attend his daughter's wedding, shows the kind of problem they had circumvented. Poor old Thulo in Harangos was in constant trouble with "his" *gažos*. In 1984, for example, Thulo had been forewarned that potato fields nearby were to be opened up to gleaners on a

certain day. He went off on his own, returning with a cart brimming over with potatoes. The next day the whole of the Third Class set off in the morning to the same fields. Most of them shared carts, though some enterprising street cleaners came out pushing the huge rubbish bins they used in their work to bring back the potatoes. During the gleaning, some people apparently stole melons from an adjacent field, and an altercation took place between the Gypsies and the workers of the cooperative farm. Thulo, who had stayed at home that day, took the news very badly, knowing that he would be blamed for these Gypsies' bad behavior and that unless he could disassociate himself from them the following year, he would not be privileged with early information.

Šošoj himself attributed his wealth to his horses; Čaja, to her scrap dealing. But, above all, it was their ability to sustain close relations with *gažos*, ordinary peasants and officials alike, that had enabled them to grow rich. The core of Šošoj's economy was his involvement with the private farmers of his region, the collectivized farms, and the state exporting agencies. To begin as a trader at all, however, Šošoj had had to sort out his work papers, since throughout the socialist period all citizens had to have a "legitimate" source of income, which meant, in effect, salaried employment in a state concern.[3] At a certain cost, rumored to have been 30,000 forints, Šošoj had managed to have a weak leg diagnosed and get pensioned off as more than 60 percent unfit for work. Whereas other men of his age were a little wary on market day if the police started checking papers to see that Gypsy horse owners had a registered workplace and were not "living from trade," Šošoj was always aboveboard.

By establishing relations with officials of collective farms, Šošoj obtained contracts with state purchasing concerns. In particular, he was paid to provide horses for export to Dutch and Italian horse-meat producers. Many other Gypsies participated on a small scale in this business, but Šošoj once or twice a year would hand over up to eight or ten horses—a scale of delivery that involved him in extensive trawls throughout the Hungarian countryside for suitable horses. This was a risky business as big profits depended on finding horses at the last moment and so avoiding the costs of keeping them in stable.[4] Šošoj was in fact so good at this that he also used his father-in-law's name to provide horses in the county where his old village, Dongó, lay, using the old man's "official" residence there. And all this he achieved without attracting the eye of the socialist tax collector.

Constantly in contact with *gažos* in a range of economic niches, Šošoj and Čaja were well placed to discover the latest "maneuvers," to use the subsidies provided by the socialist state. In 1985 this involved keeping cows. Over several years the number of peasants raising cows in Hungary had declined, largely, it was reported, because peasant women had refused to perform the heavy physical labor associated with milking. To reverse this trend, subsidies had been introduced. In principle these subsidies were for people who kept cows for long periods, but since officials were unlikely to check, Šošoj was able to swap and sell his cows as often as it suited him. When he and his wife did have a milk cow, rather than go through the bother of delivering the relatively small quantity of milk, they used it for their own and their daughter's pigs.

If living alone had proved so profitable, why had Čaja and Šošoj moved back to the Third Class in 1977, twenty years after he had left? Although motivated partly by Čaja's desire not to be left alone in Dongó while Šošoj was in prison, the deeper reason lay in their inability to find a "place of their own" among the *gažos*. They had failed in two senses. First, they had not found *gažo* husbands for their five daughters (they had no sons), and second, they had been unable to convert their wealth into an equivalent social standing among the "peasants." But there was also a practical reason: Having once established themselves as wealthy Gypsies, they were now able to manipulate "the system" and acquire "protection" (*protekció*) wherever they went, even in a town with as many Gypsies as Harangos had.[5]

So after Šošoj's imprisonment in 1977 for horse rustling on collective farms, Čaja used her position as sole breadwinner for her remaining children as a bargaining tool with the Harangos council to obtain a residence permit and then an "official permit" (*ipar engedély*) to act as scrap merchant with the exclusive right to remove scrap from the municipal dump. Čaja's achievement in being granted this permit was especially impressive in that, being irregular (*alkalmi*) and not strictly regulated, this was precisely the kind of economic activity from which Gypsies were supposed to be excluded as part of the assimilationist policy. But as Čaja boasted, "I've got a permit . . . so the police can't say anything to me."

Čaja's close and somewhat privileged relation with the town authorities protected her family at a number of crucial moments over the next few years. For instance, all house construction had in principle been forbidden at the Third Class since the early 1960s, when the site was set aside for industrial development. But when Šošoj and Čaja built their house, they escaped paying a fine for doing so, since they had "arranged" matters. Likewise, shortly after the young boy Malats was removed from his parents for failing to attend school,[6] the woman who arranged this legalized kidnapping told me that Čaja's family was one of the best Gypsy families in the town, though she knew full well that Čaja's thirteen-year-old daughter had never once set foot in school. Indeed, throughout the council offices I heard nothing but fine words about this family: "You must remember," I would be told in relation to them, "not to put all the Gypsies under one hat."

Even though Šošoj and Čaja's wealth had enabled them to move back to Harangos without suffering the kind of indignity that was Thulo's fate, it did not explain why they chose to come back and live among the Rom rather than in the town proper. For Čaja, it was her daughters who drew her. Although she and her husband had lived in Dongó, established good neighborly relations with the peasants, and sent their children to school with local children, when it came to marrying off these (five) daughters, there were no willing Magyars—none would take a Gypsy girl. Čaja and Šošoj might have married their daughters to poor Gypsy men willing to become in-living sons-in-law (*žamutros*), but by 1977 all of the girls had married some of the most eligible Gypsy men in Harangos and moved to their husbands' homes. To each of the daughters' families, Čaja and Šošoj provided help. He introduced his sons-in-law to the horse trade and in two cases provided much of the money for a new house. Čaja saw herself in this way: "I give some to one daughter and some to the other. That is how my daughters have made their big houses. They get their wages, and they spend them. But I hold things together. I give them money to eat so they can earn for themselves. I help them all." To hold things together, Čaja had to be in their midst. Moreover, as she told me one day while driving back from a visit to Dongó, when their last daughter had left home, they had felt lonely "out there" and wanted to be surrounded by their family again. Their firstborn had just remarried—this time to her younger sister's husband's elder brother—and Čaja had offered to take on the children from the first marriage. Čaja was an indefatigable promoter of her family's welfare, and so only a few months after losing her last daughter to marriage, she adopted three grandchildren to "begin" with them what she had already done for her own children.

If it was her ambitious dreams for her daughters that had brought Čaja back, it was the brothers who had drawn Šošoj, or, rather, the possibility that he might find a distinctive place among them. In the village of Magyars, he had undoubtedly had good business relations with many men; he would often boast of his relations with important *gažos*, with "big peasants . . . big gentlemen . . . big comrades," as he put it, with typical disdain for the niceties of *gažo* social distinctions. But among them his status remained that of an outsider, a *Cigány*. This point was brought home forcefully to me when we went together to buy hay from the collective farm at a village a few kilometers from the settlement in the heart of the Harangos viticulture belt. It was late spring, fodder was in short supply across the country, and Šošoj had come to ask a favor: to buy enough fodder to tide him over until the new grass came up. Often enough on such trips, one dealt with a junior official in charge of the feed supply. On this occasion the head of the farm, "the doctor," was there and, overhearing Šošoj's booming voice, announced that he would see us personally. But before we had set foot inside the office, his secretary roughly told us, as she would have addressed any common Gypsy, to wait outside the door. When the doctor had finished his business, he came out and brusquely told Šošoj that he should have bought his fodder the previous year when it was cheap. Why was it, the doctor wondered aloud, that the Gypsies all kept horses, and yet none either grew or bought enough fodder to keep their animals through the winter? And in any case, how could Šošoj expect a favor from the very farm that his son-in-law had only the previous week cheated in a horse deal? If we had been in the back of a peasant's yard, Šošoj's voice would have risen in righteous indignation at this slur on his family. But abuse and vitriol, however sweet, would have done Šošoj no good here. He was dealing here with a "big, educated man," as he put it to me afterward, and I felt that he had lost his footing. The tough and severe dealer whom I had so often seen harrying a peasant until his defenses were worn down had, as if by magic, been metamorphosed into a little man, a supplicant excusing his demands on "the good doctor's time," quietly accepting the doctor's admonitions as any poorer Gypsy might have done.[7]

Within the world of the Gypsies, Šošoj was a "king" (*kraj*), a man above the others in so many respects. This position allowed him to remain more or less aloof from the kinds of trivial squabbles that marred settlement life. If Šošoj did intervene in a dispute, his voice carried the authority consequent on his elevation from daily dispute. As long as he stayed in the settlement, he could seem a truly grand figure. There, and among the marginalized peasants of Communist Hungary, as I saw him wheel and deal and make others respond, it was easy to forget how limited were the contexts in which he had this elevated status. Out in the world of real power, the grandeur of the greatest Gypsy dealer was mercilessly unmasked. Ultimately, it was this inability to turn wealth into prestige among the non-Gypsies, an inability to avoid the kind of humiliation all other *Cigány* suffered, that had driven Šošoj back into the arms of his brothers.

But even in the Third Class, the status of Šošoj and Čaja was not secure, since it was never wholly clear whether they belonged. To the other Rom with whom he had grown up, Šošoj had become rich, while they had remained poor. Šošoj was therefore axiomatically a stingy person. In a community where more than half of the families had difficulty reaching the end of the month without falling into debt, the thought that Šošoj and his family looked down on the other families provoked these latter families to pour scorn on such riches. Whenever Šošoj was seen to renege on some apparently easily fulfilled obligation, people would comment to me how this showed that "money does not make the man." By getting rich, he and Čaja had left the other Rom behind. But the suggestion was that he and his family had also begun to abandon the Gypsy way. It was said, behind his back by envious relatives, that he had found his wealth not by trading with powerful *gaźos* but by cleaning out the toilets of the peasants in Dongó and surrounding villages. Certainly this was one of the best-paid jobs in rural Hungary at the time, but the intended meaning was that Šošoj and Čaja had paid dearly for their wealth; they had polluted themselves forever and so rendered themselves as low as the *gaźos*.

Another common form of backbiting concerned the supposedly abnormal sexual division of labor in their household. Čaja and Šošoj worked their "farm," as others mockingly called it, as a team. Although horse matters were in principle the exclusive affair of men, and most men would not consider consulting their wives on the details of a particular deal, there were relatively few occasions on which I or other drivers took Šošoj off alone searching for a horse. Čaja was always at his side. And although Šošoj always did all the public dealing, he would invariably seek Čaja's opinion about a trade. Čaja might try in public to represent their respective roles in a fashion more typical of other Gypsies: She used an unstabled nag for her scrap work, letting Šošoj alone drive out their finer horses, and she talked of herself providing for the daily necessities, attributing the spectacular, one-shot profits to her husband.[8] But others nonetheless asked who was the man (*rom*) and who the woman (*romni*) in their household: If Čaja needed to go to the horse market, then it followed that she was the *rom*, and if she was the man, then Šošoj must be her *romni*. Did Šošoj, I was once asked rhetorically, ever go to a celebration on his own? No, he always went accompanied by his *romni*. I pointed out that Čaja kept one of the cleanest (*vuźi*) houses in the settlement, but a man snapped back that she herself stank (*khandel*). If one had once waded waist deep in "shit," one could never remove the smell, he concluded.

This hostility to their wealth and distinction, the constant demands on their generosity, and disputes with their poorer neighbors finally drove Šošoj and Čaja in 1987 to seek once again a home among the *gaźos*, this time in the center of Harangos itself. They did so, however, with great difficulty, since the seller was keen not to pass on his property to a Gypsy. There were by then three rich Gypsy families in the town center, and their wealthy Magyar neighbors made no bones about their intention to make the incomers feel unwelcome. Unable to find peace there, Šošoj and Čaja returned in 1989 to the Third Class, only to leave again in 1991, this time to a house just beyond the edge of the settlement between the Gypsies and the main road. There, half in and half out, in a kind of no-man's-land, they seemed to have found a place of their own.

Čoro and Luludji's Story: Upwardly Mobile Gypsies

Getting away was an option not only in the repertoire of rich Gypsies but also in that of relatively poor ones. For them, however, it was less the demands of needy relatives than the absence of decent housing that was the most pressing problem. Most ordinary Gypsies were too poor and lacked the *protekció* they needed to buy a home away from a settlement with their own resources. But the interests of such people could at times be aligned with those of Communist authorities who saw their goal as prizing Gypsy families away from "Gypsy concentrations." Official rhetoric represented Gypsy settlements as "breeding grounds" for the Gypsy mentality, as places from which elevation to a "civilized" standard of life was impossible.[9] To break up these settlements and disperse the Gypsies, the state kept a lookout for families that showed themselves capable of diverging from the Gypsy norm. As a family on a settlement began to keep a good work record, build itself a slightly better than average house, and accumulate domestic goods, it was to be given the chance to assimilate "up" into the Hungarian population by being offered a council flat in a "better," that is to say, Magyar, area of town. In Harangos itself a recent head of the Housing Department had been well known among disgruntled Magyars for having attempted to speed up the process of assimilation by encouraging the dispersal of Gypsy families from their settlements to council flats among Magyar families.

However, the coalition of interest did not stretch far, and Gypsy families faced great difficulties in taking this road "out." On the one hand, Gypsy neighbors saw the departure of relatives as a threat to the future of their communities. Anxious to maintain their way of life, they would not let their relatives go without a struggle. On the other hand, officialdom, no less than ordinary Magyar opinion, was none too keen on an "uncontrolled" or rapid influx of Gypsies into town. Most single Gypsy women, separated as a result of divorce, imprisonment, or death of a husband, had chosen to move to council housing with their children instead of remaining in the ambit of their parents or parents-in-law. Likewise, there were some newly married couples who wished to avoid residential commitment to either side of the marriage and chose to live in state accommodation or were too poor to buy a plot of land and build their own home. But most of these Gypsies had been resettled in one of the state-defined ghettos in a non-Gypsy area of town. Two of my friends were, however, more fortunate.

On the face of it, Čoro's and Luludji's marriage was a typical Gypsy union. With their two young children, they lived in two small rooms adjacent to his parents' house. He had a job in a local factory but kept horses and pigs in his parents' yard. She stayed at home "helping the old people." If anything marked them out from other Gypsies, it was their shared desire to "do something better" for their children, not to be "the last one in the line," as Čoro used to say. In Luludji these high aspirations were forthrightly expressed in a desire to win the approval of respectable, that is, non-Gypsy, society; indeed, this was how I came to know her, since she had been keen to build a relationship with the musicologist who introduced me to the Third Class. She often used to point out to me how, in little ways, she did things "just like the Magyars." Once I gave her and her children a lift to her parents' home village, though she knew that other Rom would be shocked at the idea of a woman going "alone" with a man in his car. On that journey, as she mused about such matters, she complained to me that as a Gypsy she could never do anything "enjoyable," that is, *gažo*-like, such as having a family holiday on Lake Balaton.

Čoro and Luludji refused to acquiesce in what other less ambitious people might have seen as their fate. It was such an attitude that had led in the first place to their marriage, which, unlike that of many other Gypsies, had been a love alliance. They had known each other since they were young children, his father and her mother being siblings. They had not, however, been planned for each other, partly because first-cousin marriage was frowned upon.[10] Luludji had been an excellent pupil in her school and had been encouraged by her non-Gypsy teachers to study further with an eye toward teaching Gypsy children herself. Since this would, in effect, have removed her from her family, her parents had firmly opposed the idea. They saw their only salvation in marrying her quickly to the local boy to whom she had long been promised. She, however, was horrified. Although he was two years her elder, he had been a weak pupil, and she had often spent mornings helping him with his work and correcting it in class. Luludji would not consider marrying a boy whom she had long treated as a younger sibling, not a man to whom she could look up. Čoro meanwhile had recently divorced the woman "from across the road" to whom his parents had married him at age fifteen. Hearing that Luludji's hand had already been formally demanded, Čoro sent a message to her workplace telling her to meet him at the bus stop in her village the next afternoon. They fled together from there, hiding for five days in his elder brother's home in another part of Harangos. To avoid rekindling fury among her parents' neighbors, Čoro and Luludji moved permanently to his parents' plot of land in Harangos.

Although immediately after they married they lived in the back room of his parents' house, Čoro and Luludji had a strong desire to achieve greater independence and to keep up with those of their brothers who were building fine homes for their families. Čoro was not especially well-off, so there was no question of building one of the two-story houses that richer Gypsies were dreaming about at this time, but he did not want to get stuck, as two of his elder brothers had, with huge loans to buy an old house in the Third Class and then have no money for building something smarter and more modern. So he began to boast about plans to move out of the settlement in order to "move up."

Like many other Gypsies, Čoro and Luludji saw in the official assimilationist policy some positive elements, particularly the suggestion that people should stop being *Cigány*. Living in a place such as the Third Class, which was visibly a Gypsy settlement, made it hard to avoid feeling looked down on, for, as Luludji told me, "when the peasants come up to town and look across the railway line and see that *Cigány* live here, they don't want to come over. They are scared to cross over the line because we are *Cigány*. If someone is ill here, the ambulance will only come as far as the tracks when there is a lot of mud. It won't come in for the *Cigány*."[11] If they left the Third Class, they would get a better home and maybe stop being seen as *Cigány*.

Čoro and Luludji came into the highly competitive resettlement game at a fortunate moment in that the Harangos council was under pressure from county and national levels to improve its treatment of Gypsies.[12] So when Čoro and Luludji asked for council assistance to be rehoused in the early 1980s, they were put on the waiting list for a proper "all-mod-cons" (*összkomfortos*) flat in a modern housing estate. After four years their application was accepted, and the long process that could lead to resettlement "among the Hungarians" began.

Council officials, like most Magyars, were hearty believers in the (mythical) stories of Gypsies who had been moved directly from a settlement into all-mod-cons flats, only to install a pig in a bath or burn the parquet flooring as firewood in winter. To prevent such "outrages," a selection process had been instigated in which the Gypsies were first sent to the barrack houses known as the Chicken Plot, where they could "accustom themselves" to "modern" life. Only if they proved themselves capable of maintaining "civilized" (*művelt*) standards there would they be allowed to ascend the next rung up the ladder into a housing estate. Most of the Gypsies living in the Chicken Plot had never been allowed to make this move, but for Čoro and Luludji a small one-bedroom flat in the ghetto was the only gateway out of the housing trap.

While they lived there, they were the object of regular and quite thorough "controls" from the Housing Department. In Communist Hungary there were no social service departments or social workers, but the spirit of the Harangos Housing Department's officers was similar. Apart from checking the regularity of rent and other monthly payments, they also inspected Čoro and Luludji's living conditions. Health Department workers assessed the cleanliness of the bedroom, kitchen, and toilet. Others came round to check whether the family was throwing rubbish out of the back window onto the wasteland between the rows of houses. Maintaining a clean house when there was a constant stream of visitors who traipsed the ubiquitous mud found on such a settlement through the kitchen was a Sisyphean task, but Luludji reckoned that she could get her family through all these tests. The children's behavior and manners were taken into consideration as well, so Luludji forbade them to play with other children in the settlement.

Čoro and Luludji had to persuade the *gaźo* officials that they were "a different class of Gypsy," ready to abandon the Gypsy way of life. They both knew that in trying to convince the *gaźo*s of this, while also keeping up relations with their family and other Rom, they were walking a tightrope. One day Luludji told me a story to show the difficulties of sustaining a balance between the two ways of life.

It was always hard for Gypsies to get prestige jobs that allowed access to goods in short supply in the socialist economy, but at the end of the 1970s Luludji had nonetheless managed to be appointed to the kitchens of Harangos's prestige hotel, the Balaton. This was a hotel in which only the richest Gypsy in the town might have dared to set foot. So Luludji's was a double achievement, since she was also the only Gypsy in town allowed to handle food served to Magyars. She was, she said, "the one they didn't dislike." She worked there until her second pregnancy, when she took extended maternity leave (three years at that time), but after this she had found herself brusquely turned out of the hotel's back door. Luludji explained what had happened: "I was off sick on maternity leave, having had my last child. At that time we desperately needed money. All the other Gypsies had horses and pigs, and we didn't want them to say that we didn't have anything at all. And so I said to Čoro, 'Look, let's buy ten pigs for ourselves. And we'll put them down at the slaughterhouse, collecting 40,000 forints from that. And then we can buy a horse.' And so, Michael, I used to go collecting bread from the rubbish bins to feed the pigs."

Luludji, like other women, had ambivalent feelings about this activity. It provided an ideal form of wealth, but the women were always keen not to be seen by Magyars whom they otherwise knew while out with sacks and digging sticks. They also had to put up with a regular barrage of hostile jibes from Magyar passersby asking them if they were ashamed of themselves. Although the local vet admitted privately that feeding pigs this way carried no serious health risks, the council was officially opposed to such "scavenging" (*kukázás*), and every so often I would see the public health inspector hiding in a car trying to catch Gypsy women and fine them for "unsanitary activities." So Luludji was engaged in an occupation along with fifty or more other women in Harangos.

Unfortunately for her,

> when my maternity leave had run out, I went back to my old workplace. And my boss told me "I can't possibly take you back into the Balaton hotel, where they cook food and you offer it to the guests." He couldn't take me into his workplace because he had seen me digging around in the rubbish bins. I told him, this director, "It is quite impossible that you saw me doing that. I have a sister, and no doubt you mixed me up with her." So the boss told me, "I didn't confuse you with anybody. I would recognize you, Luludji, from a hundred kilometers away." So, my friend, when I heard that he had seen me in the rubbish bins, I didn't want to force him to take me back. He gave me back my work book there and then. I was so ashamed of myself that, out of my shame, I couldn't even see the door to walk out of the room. Then a paper was sent out to me saying that they had cut my employment off and that I would never be able to work there again, since I go around digging in rubbish bins.

In 1984 Luludji chose to refrain from this or any other kind of scavenging in order to protect her image among those who might effect the housing transfer. But in doing so, she damaged her image among her sister Gypsy women, who saw in her behavior the same standoffishness and "big-headedness" that characterized non-Gypsy behavior.

Čoro, too, had his problems. He had had a more or less constant work record for the previous ten years as a machine operator in a parquet flooring factory and had even been awarded a prize as an "outstanding worker" (*kiváló dolgozó*) in the work competition between socialist labor brigades. He had the framed certificate of this prize hanging in a prominent position in the kitchen. Although there were times when Čoro took two weeks of sick leave, his and Luludji's commitment to increasing their wealth kept these "lapses" to a minimum. Indeed, some time later when I worked with Čoro in his factory, I noticed that of the Gypsy men, he was the most attentive to the small details of factory work, which impressed the supervisors. He was willing to return to work on time, he did not take short breaks from the machine when there was a delay on the line, and he even called others to order when they were slacking. He was the managers' "new model" Gypsy worker.

But, unlike Luludji, while living in the Chicken Plot, Čoro tried to keep his hand in the Gypsy economy, too. Forbidden to keep farm animals beside his barrack flat, since it was located in the residential central area of Harangos, and all the while insisting officially that he and Luludji had left behind the "life of the settlement" for good, Čoro kept animals, notably horses and pigs, in his father's sheds. Having these animals both necessitated and enabled his continued commitment to the Gypsy economy in the sense of trying to make a living without engaging in what the local peasants classified as "productive labor" (*termelő munka*). With his horse Čoro went out gleaning for grapes, melons, tomatoes, and potatoes for the family, but his action did not fit with the council's idea of the settled lifestyle appropriate to a resident of a housing estate. Čoro therefore kept quiet about these activities.

Since one of Čoro and Luludji's aims in getting out of the Third Class was to cease being treated as *Cigány*, they had to get a flat in a Hungarian stairwell on a housing estate that was not becoming a new Gypsy ghetto. They were also motivated by the consideration that if later they came to sell this flat on the private market, they would get a better price than if they were in a block with other Gypsy families. So even in the Chicken Plot Luludji asked not to be put in a row with other "bad" Gypsy families. She then carefully cultivated her *gažo* neighbors so that when officials checked up on their suitability to be given a flat among Magyars, supportive comments would be made.[13]

Just as Šošoj and Čaja were attacked for leaving the Rom behind economically, Čoro and Luludji had left themselves open to the accusation that they were leaving their brothers behind morally. Luludji used to boast about her friends among the *gažo* neighbors and how they were willing to enter her home and not that of any other Gypsy. She would tell other Gypsies about her close relations with *gažo* researchers, such as my colleagues from Budapest, or how she and Čoro had married for love, "like the Magyars." She and her husband seemed to be threatening their ties with the Rom even more effectively than Šošoj and Čaja had done.

And even more than the rich couple, they were pressured by Čoro's family to hold them to the Gypsy way. Čoro and Luludji both knew that, if their occasional windfall money (as when he got a share of the great grape-gleaning bonanza) was kept at home, it would be frittered away. Čoro would be persuaded to go and gamble, or one of his brothers would come and ask to borrow money, and he would feel obliged to help. To be saved, the money had to be invested. For Luludji, the solution was to buy small home improvements, a new cupboard, decorative glasses for the cabinet, a new wall-to-wall poster. Čoro's eyes were set more on the kind of consumption that established a man's prestige, his horses. "Look, Michael," Luludji told me one day, discussing Čoro's possible purchase of a horse with his father, "I'm not going to allow him to spend that money. To me what's important is the house. Once we've made our house . . . we can have a horse or not. *I'm* not interested in horses. It's only Čoro who is interested." For Luludji, what counted was home improvements of the sort that would make her future guests gasp in amazement. "When a Gypsy comes into my house, they are going to be amazed at the kind of house we live in," she added.[14]

If they had lived alone, Luludji and Čoro might well have been able to resolve such conflicting goals. After all, it was Čoro as much as Luludji who insisted on me taking a whole roll of pictures of him and his family in his clean room with all his wife's luxurious furniture on display in the background. But from the point of view of Čoro's family, in diverting family resources into home decoration, Luludji was turning Čoro's mind, blinding him to his brothers and their needs. When Čoro won 10,000 forints at cards, just before he left the Third Class, Luludji put this aside for carpets in her new home. Later, I noticed her mother-in-law refer to them as "Luludji's carpets." Even more pointedly, her mother-in-law and brother-in-law told me that, if Čoro had kept two "beetle-black" foals until they were older, instead of building Luludji a clean room next to his parent's house, he would have received "several hundred thousand forints." "And you see where he is now? No house, no money, and stuck in the Chicken Plot," concluded his envious brother.

Luludji's minor sins were a matter of her supposedly profligate expenditure. Potent though this line of criticism was, it had its limits in suggesting that Luludji was leading Čoro away from *romanes*, since Luludji could always argue that her house's style of decoration, the sumptuousness and excess she managed to create, provided a fitting proof of the success of her family in living according to the Gypsy way. She could further reason that thanks to her efforts, Čoro could provide an even more fitting place to welcome his brothers to celebrate. So a more productive line of attack for Čoro's anxious brothers and their wives was to focus upon her "greedy" (*bokhalo*) character. There was a suggestion here that Luludji did not feed her husband properly, just as in the past it had been said that she had not fed her parents-in-law's pigs as much as her own, when they had shared a sty. This was bad enough for a Rom wife, since it implied that both her femininity and her sense of kinship were sorely lacking, in a fashion reminiscent of the *gaźos*. But it was the sexual overtones of being "greedy" and "hungry" that were really damaging to her reputation.

At a trivial level, Čoro's children were often teased that their father was thin because of their mother's sexual "hunger." But there was also a more vicious commentary among the adults on her sexual standards. The signs of a presumedly uncontrolled appetite were visible, it was said, in her occasional appearance in public with her hair hanging loose and her "scarf' (*dikhlo*), which ought to have covered her hair, hanging round her neck.

She had even been seen in town without an "apron" (*ketrintsa*). In both these ways she was behaving like a non-Gypsy woman and in a fashion for which, as she herself told me, she would have been beaten by her parents-in-law as a newly wed girl.

Most serious, however, were persistent accusations by her in-laws that Luludji was having an adulterous affair with a leading Gypsy in another town. This man was married to another well-educated Gypsy woman, but it was known that he was fed up with this marriage. Before he separated rumors started spreading that Luludji and he were in contact. The "truth," as far as I could ever tell, was that this man had indeed on a number of occasions looked at Luludji at the market but had never received the slightest encouragement. Once they had bumped into each other, and he had suggested that they run off together, but Luludji had laughed at him. Since there was no such thing as a private encounter on the Harangos market square, rumors started straightaway, and soon enough the man's wife wrote a letter to him, in Luludji's name, saying that they ought to go off together immediately. When they bumped into each other again, the man said that he was very happy to go off, though not right away. Luludji was amazed and so got to hear of the false letter. Perhaps because he thought Luludji had been play-acting when they had last met, the man decided to write a letter to her saying the whole idea was no good. He then thought better and put the letter in the stove. Unfortunately, the paper did not burn, and when the wife found it later in the day, she went straight round to Čoro at work and told him "the whole story." Luludji was beaten by Čoro within an inch of her life, but she went to church and took an "oath" (*colax*) on the life of her children that nothing had ever happened between her and this man.

Despite this, the wound would not close. At the end of February 1985, the man in question finally left his wife, who was thus provoked to speak to Čoro once again. Čoro telephoned his mother at the factory beside the Third Class where the Rom were able to receive urgent calls, and a few moments later she was seen, white and shaking, setting out to the Chicken Plot to send her daughter-in-law back to her own parents. Fortunately, perhaps, Luludji was not at home, and her mother-in-law left. The atmosphere in Čoro's mother's house later that day was vile, as a lynching mood was worked up. A regular visitor who had been absent for several weeks turned up and sunk his venom into Luludji's reputation. Everyone who came around talked about how they had all known the rumors but "just hadn't said anything" to Čoro earlier. Only a few days before, Čoro had apparently threatened to fight with a man who had claimed to have seen Luludji with the other man. Now all the shreds of evidence against Luludji were put together, and Čoro was silent: Her irregular working hours were construed as evidence that she was making up time for the hours missing when she was presumed to have been with her lover. When she had worked in the hotel, she had worn "freshly washed clothes" every day—to please her lover (a man who, incidentally, unlike most Gypsies, would have been served in the hotel). Her sister-in-law added: "I don't know what to say. She didn't pity Čoro nor her children, she didn't pity anyone, . . . or, rather, she took pity on every man who came her way." Later on, the same woman commented to me with barely concealed schadenfreude that Luludji had always thought she was "more civilized than us, but all the same she ends up like this."

I saw Luludji a few days later. She had aged years since I had last visited. Čoro, too, looked completely exhausted. That she had got drunk one day and sung that her life was at an end had been taken as the conclusive proof of her guilt. Now, she explained to me, she could do nothing right. If she drank, it was to cover her sorrow at losing her lover; if she refused to drink, it was for the same reason; if she dressed properly, it was to please her lover; if she let herself go, it was because she knew there was no hope. One evening that week, Čoro had come home and found her curling her hair with tongs. He flew into a rage, asking if she was thinking of putting herself in for the beauty contest, and threatened to scorch her with the tongs. Luludji felt that Čoro could neither love nor trust her now. At this point she told me that Čoro would kill her—what other option did he have? He was the laughingstock of the whole community. Little children could be overheard joking that if a man "had" Luludji, Čoro just turned his back. This was also what Čoro's mother feared—that he would end up in prison, fully aware of what he was doing but determined to regain his and his brothers' honor.

In the end Luludji's mother, Čoro's aunt, turned up and with the support of Čoro's brother who lived in her house used her position as intermediary in the family to calm matters down somewhat, pouring scorn on the lewd suggestions concerning her daughter.[15] As a result, three weeks later not a soul mentioned the affair, and when a boy teased Luludji's son about his mother's "many husbands," other children made him eat his words and admit that his own had "probably had twenty as well." Only a few weeks later, at Easter, did I notice the reluctance with which one of Čoro's brothers greeted him and refused to extend his greetings to the other members of the house. Twice again before I left Harangos, the sore burst, and its poison spread in the family. Miraculously, Luludji and Čoro held together.

At the beginning of 1986 when I left Harangos, Čoro and Luludji were expecting to receive an offer of a three-bedroom, fully modernized flat in a stairwell otherwise occupied entirely by Magyar families. This was the beginning of their dream. Čoro had begun to float the idea that they might take advantage of the council's new privatization program and return the flat to the council, thus receiving a large payment in lieu of tenancy rights. With 160,000 forints or so, they would be able to purchase a plot of land and build an ideal home. Where they would do so was a moot point—shortly after moving to the Chicken Plot, Luludji told me that she would never consider moving back to the Third Class, having just left behind the mud, the mess, and the envious relatives.

But Čoro's father and mother were there, and as the last son of six children, he was the one they leaned on most heavily. Apart from the moments of greatest crisis with the in-laws, when Luludji came round she would often tidy up a little or cook for her mother-in-law. Most days Čoro would pass by on his way to or from work to help his father with the animals. Moreover, if they returned to the Third Class, they would no longer feel "lonely" (*korkoro*), as they had in the Chicken Plot and as they feared they always might among Magyars. Luludji, too, would be able to work as there would be no problem with child care. Whether Čoro would burn his Gypsy boats and try to start a life among the *gażo*s or whether he would return to the Third Class and risk beginning all over again seemed unclear. After all that had happened, the decision was not going to be easy.

The Rejection of Differentiation

At this point I leave the story of this particular family. The problems that family members faced vis-à-vis other Rom when trying to leave a settlement were a function of the way the Rom rejected any form of differentiation, as discussed in Chapter 4. In a state of siege the social implications of inequalities among households were always divisive: Difference, specificity, and individuality could all be interpreted as an attempt to stand apart from and above the Gypsies, to cultivate privileged relations with the *gażo*s, and to leave other Gypsies behind.

The contradictions that Čoro and Luludji found themselves in were not, however, solely a consequence of the way in which the Rom were treated by the non-Gypsies. These contradictions also arose from within the values of *romanes*, with its conflict among the egalitarian ethic of similarity, the pressure to level differences, and the libertarian ethic of autonomy. The ideology of autonomy inherent in the Gypsy construction of brotherhood and the denial of any external authority meant that people's individuality, as well as their personal abilities, was celebrated. Men and women were said to have "manias," personal whims or manners of doing things, which, far from being thought troublesome or disruptive of social integration, were expressly indulged.

However, the other side of this indulgence was that a friendship between two men might blossom for a few weeks, during which they seemed to spend every moment of the day together, but then they argued, one felt that the other had been disrespectful, and they were not seen again in each other's company.[16] Because people were inevitably unique and individual, the achievement of equality required a continual reassertion of commitment to the Gypsy way. So long as all the Gypsies did the same, looked the same, and ate the same food, they appeared as equals. By demanding of each other regular and public proof of continued brotherly feeling and intent, the Rom thereby tried to preserve their community. And, as I argued in Chapter 4, all these issues acquired much greater resonance than they might otherwise have had because of the construction of Gypsy identity as something that could be acquired *and could therefore also be lost.* It was not enough to be born to a Gypsy family—one had to continually reaffirm this identity by participating in activity together, by doing things in a similar manner, by actively displaying one's continuing attachment to the Gypsy way of doing things.

I have treated in detail the economic aspects of this constant effort to level, showing how, while I lived in the Third Class, I felt I was watching a continual oscillation between an image of the Gypsies selflessly helping each other and an image of them mercilessly counting the cost of their relatives' demands. But there are still a few words to be said about the moral aspect of the conflict I am discussing.

At times the combination of radical individuality and egalitarian hypersensitivity to (often imagined) insult became thoroughly disruptive. At the main feasts of the annual cycle, the Rom expected to attend celebrations with each other in houses in the settlement. But though all the brothers in a family ought to have come together, this rarely happened, since no one man in the community formed a natural focus for all the Gypsy men to gather around. It could seem then as if their wives and their homes were the obstacle, for each family living in its home, with food cooked by its wife or mother, became a competing focus for a gathering. To bring together a group of these almost petulant men was a near-impossible task, since someone always seemed to feel insulted by the presence of someone else. Moreover, to go to someone else's house and participate in his *mulatšago* might seem like an acceptance of inferior status, especially if the host on this occasion would not reciprocate on another. As in all matters of brotherly interaction, the agonistic performance of status made brotherly solidarity look like a cloth that unraveled as fast as it was woven.

But if the conflicts between men were an inherent consequence of the contradictory motivations implicit in the Gypsy way, this does not mean that they were recognized as such. In Čoro and Luludji's unhappy battles, an outsider might well see a classic conflict over a man's loyalty and resources. In this his kin were pitted against his wife, but the main *visible* struggle took place between daughter-in-law and mother-in-law. So what was really a disagreement between men as brothers over symbolic and material resources was masked or hidden.[17] Because the threats to the brotherhood, by, for example, a family leaving the community could always be blamed on and fought out with a man's wife, the ideology of brotherhood remained intact and unchallenged.

There is a final point. The radical restriction of differentiation led inevitably to a situation in which the Gypsies were either "in" or "out" of the ghetto. I learned this the hard way when I moved to the Third Class and found myself encouraged to dress, walk, and talk like the Rom, to make myself an indistinguishable member of their parties. I was encouraged to grow a mustache; Judit Szegő was told to wear aprons and scarves and not to wear trousers. It was as if no halfway position could be contemplated, just as there was no category of affines. In the language of kinship, affinity can provide a kind of halfway house between those people with whom one shares identity and those with whom one has nothing in common, that is, strangers. In the context of the state of siege, it was not surprising that the Gypsies rejected the possibility that there could be a group of people "in between." The brotherhood demanded total commitment.

The example of the Romungros who had over the previous one hundred years tried to assimilate into Magyar society was, paradoxically, an ever-present instance of this Manichaean logic to the Rom. So despised were the Romungros that the very term *muzsikus* (musician), which was one of their own qualifying ethnonyms, was used in Romany as a general term for two-faced behavior. These "sellouts," who used their Gypsiness when it suited them (as musicians) but denied it when it did not (when they might be associated with the even more despised Romany-speaking Gypsies), were in a sense worse than the *gaźo*s. That they constituted living proof of the possibility of some form of mediation with *gaźo* culture made their denigration all the more vitriolic. They were despised by the Rom as no other group was and in their poverty held up as living proof of the idiocy of trying to build bridges between the Rom and the *gaźo*s.

The rejection of all forms of mediation did not occur just at this level of denigrating another group of Gypsies. In relation to each other, too, the Rom practiced what they preached, as I discovered. I thought I had known one family very well until one day I visited the family and found a young woman whom I took to be a *gaźo* visitor—at least I presumed she was *gaźo*, since she refused to sit down while she talked. Only after she left did I discover that she was a daughter of the family who had married a *gaźo*, refused to invite her family to the wedding, and gone to live with his people. She had cut all contact with her family at that point and so had effectively ceased to be a Rom because she had abandoned *romanes*. She had died a social death, and her name was never mentioned by her kin.

Part Two

BEYOND THE GHETTO

6

MAKING WORKERS OUT OF GYPSIES

ONCE BEFORE, AT THE END OF THE EIGHTEENTH CENTURY, the absolutist rulers of the Austro-Hungarian Empire tried to assimilate the Gypsy population. Then they planned to remove children from their families and put the Gypsies to work as "new peasants." But the policy had foundered on the intransigence of local nobles who needed and respected the skills and services that Gypsies already provided. Then for a century and a half the Gypsies remained a nuisance to be tolerated and contained. But with Communist rule they were again to be subject to an assimilationist policy. The skills and services of the Gypsies were an anathema to the Communists, who believed that "productive labor" alone was the truly moral source of income. "Gypsy work" looked like "social parasitism" to the new, puritanical rulers and would have to be halted. Although the Gypsies were hardly capitalists on any scale of reckoning, like them they lived off the labor of others—at least when they could—and like them were to be subjected to the rigorous discipline of "socialist labor."

Assimilation as Proletarianization

When in the late 1950s the Hungarian Communist Party debated the means to be employed in "resolving the Gypsy question," its theoreticians were divided as to the relative importance to be given to each of four aspects of the campaign: schooling, housing, employment, and propaganda against anti-Gypsy feeling among non-Gypsies. Whereas Labor Ministry officials, supported by an ethnologist, suggested that the campaign should rest on "combating prejudice in the Magyar population," as

97

TABLE 6.1   *Length of Employment of Gypsies in Hungary (percentage)*

Employment	1960	1968	1971	1979
Permanent (1 year)	33	40	50	85
Occasional	32	60	35	15
None	35		15	

well as ensuring the education of young Gypsies, a party bureaucrat, Sándor Vendégh, had the last word: The core of the campaign was to be the integration of all Gypsies into the socialist labor force.[1] For a generation afterward, the idea that proletarianization would be tantamount to assimilation provided the basic building block of the Gypsy policy.

When I first went to Hungary, it seemed, on paper at least, that the authorities had been remarkably successful in this respect. In 1964 only one in six Gypsy men in Harangos was employed in the socialist sector; by 1983 nine out of ten men were in full-time, state-sector work. And even though there was a shortage of suitable, light, daytime jobs for Gypsy women, one in five had found work. As far as officials were concerned, the back of Gypsy "work-dodging" had been broken. Although the Gypsies might originally have been legally coerced into factory work, many continued to do it, and others came to join them (see Table 6.1).

The Gypsy policy's success in getting the Rom into the wage labor market was more than statistical. When I talked to Gypsies, in some contexts at least, it did seem that work and the act of laboring had been given a new centrality and value in their lives. The comment of one Rom woman was entirely typical: "We all work now. Some time ago no one worked at all. We went from place to place, getting by. The Gypsies were so poor that when a horse died, the men had to pull the cart with their bare hands. Nowadays if you don't work, you are nothing." The Rom did acknowledge wage labor as the source of the fundamental improvement in their living standards over the previous twenty years. For the vast majority of these Gypsies, the first week after payday was a period of abundance, although followed by three increasingly barren weeks. In that first week fresh coffee and fruit brandy could be found in every home, and all the luxury purchases of the month were made (see Table 6.2). Payday determined the whole cycle of communal life, fixing the dates of weddings, christenings, and other celebrations because it was only on the first Saturday of the month that men would have the funds to travel to a celebration with cash enough to participate.

And yet matters were not so simple. Even though the Rom agreed that working had transformed their lives, this in itself did not mean that Communist policy had succeeded. The official equation of proletarianization with assimilation depended in practice on the Gypsies adopting a highly particular moral attitude toward labor and abandoning their

TABLE 6.2 *Distribution of Consumer Goods Among Gypsies and Hungarians, by Household*

	1977		1983	
	Gypsies near Harangos	*All Hungarians*	*Gypsies near Harangos*	*All Hungarians*
Radio	65	122	78	144
Television	69	88	90	106
Washing machine	65	83	87	97
Refrigerator	17	78	48	97
Bicycle	47	114	57	n/a
Motorbike	8	24	15	26
Car	1	16	4	32

habit of "living day by day or sponging off society."[2] How far did the Gypsies adopt this new ethic, and insofar as they did not, to what extent was their attitude an unintended consequence of the very system, the socialist factory, that was supposed to change their understanding and representation of labor?

"The Living, Form-giving Fire"

In the nineteenth century, socialist theory and literature had picked up and enriched an old Judeo-Christian idea of labor as creation, as the purest form of expressive human activity modeled on the original act: God bringing into being what had not existed before.[3] Marx had elaborated this folk discourse to make labor "the living, form-giving fire."[4] He had also insisted on a new, social view of labor as an activity through which people could experience their interconnectedness and mutual dependence.[5]

The Communist societies of Eastern Europe were predicated in theory on the suppression of the capitalist "alienation" and distortion of the "essence" of labor. Communists believed that the capitalist treatment of labor power as a simple commodity to be bought and sold like any other could be transcended. Work would no longer be based on a private contract between employer and employee but would instead become a service that constituted one as a full member of society and provided social status. People had a duty to work, and society was obliged to provide employment for them.[6] In official rhetoric, Hungary was a "working society" (*dolgozó társadalom*), and the people were a "working people"(*dolgozó nép*) who belonged to society less as "citizens" (*polgár*) than as productive workers.[7] Manual work was thus talked of (mostly by intellectuals, of course!) as having the moral and uplifting qualities more likely associated with unalienated mental or artistic effort.

The woman in the foreground has abandoned her scarf and apron—marks of gypsy identity—worn by her companion. (Courtesy Néprajzi Muzeum, MTI)

Although for most Hungarians this ideology had little direct practical importance after the 1950s, this was not so for the Gypsies, since the assimilationist policy was framed in terms of this ideology.[8] As a result, Communist officials stressed four elements in the process of "raising the Gypsies' level of civilization" and turning them into "socialist workers." First, by working for a wage, they would achieve a new self-respect as members of the (nominally) dominant social class. Second, the practice of steady, regular work in continual employment would provide values that could be transferred to other aspects of their lives. Third, by working in teams, the Gypsies would experience the disciplining "effect of the collective" and gradually grow out of their childish, antisocial, individualist traits. Fourth, if they were engaged in productive tasks, they would learn to relish the pleasures and rewards of labor in their fullest form. Socialist labor would thus raise them out of their childlike attachment to the sudden and spectacular returns of dealing and the profligate, carefree consumption that went with that lifestyle. This last point was especially important because of Marx's argument that it was work alone that created economic value. Most forms of large-scale private capitalized production, trade, and marketing were discouraged, if not totally forbidden, in Hungary, and the Gypsies' income—"rents," that is, profits attributable to the use of capital goods, or "entrepreneurial profits"—were classed as forms of exploitation of labor.

The Parquet Flooring Factory

There were several factories around Harangos that specialized in the employment of Gypsy laborers—mostly places where there was a disproportionate need for unskilled labor in filthy jobs. But one in particular played a crucial role in the life of the Third Class, the parquet flooring factory. The Parketta, as the factory was known, was the offspring of a number of local forestry enterprises that decided in 1968 to find a use for poorquality woods they were unable to export. Over the next two decades, the Parketta was well served by a number of managers who maintained excellent relations with the regional authorities. According to a senior manager who talked to me in 1988, these contacts first and foremost allowed the factory a remarkably liberal wages fund and therefore a quite unusual degree of flexibility as to the way wages were paid. As a result, the Parketta had been able to build a stable and committed workforce and achieve a program of investment that included the purchase of West German machines to replace old and poor-quality Russian ones. By the mid-1980s, the factory had become one of Harangos's success stories, subsidizing its loss-making parent companies and incurring the wrath of the retail sector for not sufficiently supplying the domestic market to relieve the shortage of wooden flooring.

Although the factory had been built in part by Gypsy laborers, the managers tried for many years to employ only local Magyars. Then in the mid-1970s a new wood-preparation section was opened to ensure the factory's independence from its fickle parent companies, which tended to export all their best-quality wood onto the world market. The establishment of a saw shop as part of this, where raw tree planks would be trimmed and cut down to shape, necessitated the employment of the Gypsies, since, by 1975, they were the only source of unskilled labor left in Harangos. The Gypsies, like all other unskilled workers in Hungary, were, however, notorious "wandering birds"—that is, "job hoppers" in search of higher wages or simply a change of atmosphere. Since the whole point of the saw shop was to ensure a regular supply of prepared wood, it was essential to guarantee the shop's labor force.

In fact, the first wave of Gypsies was sent to work there as work-release convicts, thanks to a connection that a manager had established with the police. But this was no long-term solution. Skilled workers could be kept in one factory by the acquisition of firm-specific skills that would not be rewarded elsewhere, but to win a stable group of unskilled Gypsies, the Parketta had to offer firm-specific benefits. In Harangos this meant providing extremely advantageous loans to buy plots of land and construct houses. Shortly after starting work, a man might receive 80,000 forints, virtually interest-free, to buy and reconstruct a house. After ten years of service and then again a few years later, the factory reduced the capital owed on these loans by 10,000 forints. With such inducements, the Parketta had attracted a large group of Gypsy workers by the mid-1980s, all of whom were resident in the Third Class or in one of the two other settlements where Gypsies had been able to buy their own homes.

The factory was also successful in other ways. Magyars and Gypsies were employed alongside each other in mixed brigades, a situation which was relatively rare in Harangos. Most local factory reports complained about the way the Gypsies "didn't fit in," "offended the basic values of the other workers," and were therefore "best kept in their own brigades." At the Parketta the conditions had, by contrast, been established for the full implementation of Communist policy. The Gypsies were permanently employed in productive labor in mixed brigades. By 1986 some 92.3 percent of the Gypsy employees had worked there for more than one year.[9] Two years later I returned to Harangos to work alongside these Rom and discover how people who had worked for up to fifteen years day in day out in the same place had been affected by the work-based ethic being offered to them by the paternalist state and factory managers.

The saw shop was a large area at the front edge of the factory with huge sliding doors that could be opened in the summer to circulate air or closed in winter to keep the air warm. The task of the brigade was to reduce long planks of rough wood to meter-long sticks to be turned elsewhere into fencing or parquet flooring. One group worked around a machine known as the *inga*. This sliced the wood horizontally into three or more pieces, which were then passed on to a group at a second machine. There the short planks were cut vertically into three or more sticks, their width determined by whatever work was in hand at the main part of the factory.

It was a noisy, feebly ventilated environment filled with airborne sawdust. Bottles of soda water were provided for the workers (drinking helped the workers to swallow the sawdust in their mouths!). The work

On the production line at the parquet flooring factory Gypsies drink soda water to better swallow the sawdust they inhale.

was tedious and highly repetitive but for the most part not particularly demanding. The noise of the machines prevented conversation, and so workers went into trance, their faces wearing the same vacant expression of mindless half-concentration required to repeat and repeat and repeat the motions of the job.

To a large extent, the rate of work was set by the machines. In particular, the second set of vertical saws could be forced to go faster only at the cost of damaging them, and so saw speeds were set by the foreman. Sometimes, however, to relieve the tedium, workers played games. On the first day of my second week, I was at the end of the *inga* team. Of the three positions around the *inga*, this was the worst, since here a worker was totally at the mercy of the machine and the men at the other end. That afternoon my Magyar colleagues, Jóska and Feri bácsi (Uncle Feri), suddenly doubled my workload by sending through planks of wood two at a time, one on top of the other. Within moments I found myself leaping about, trying to remove the larger amount of waste now generated, as well as the heavy planks of wood, before the next lot was propelled down the rollers. Now if I made an overly slow movement of the hand, my fingers would be crushed between the blocks of wood; a moment's inattention and the wood would jam, flinging a freestanding iron table onto me.

At four o'clock Jóska and I swapped jobs. Now it was my turn to load the wood down. The two Gypsies on the other machine encouraged me in Romany to "let him have it," and away we went. To bring down two planks of wood at a time from the stack meant juggling the planks so as to have two of equal length. Working like this was more dangerous and physically more demanding but much more satisfying. At last I was in charge of some aspect of the process; I was forcing the machine, not letting it force me; and at the other end was old Jóska suffering as I had an hour earlier, while my Gypsy friends encouraged me with calls (in Romany) to "let the *gaźo* do the work!" And, of course, there were the stacks of wood piling up, the stacks that would ensure we would make our 120 percent productivity norm. Although at this time we were just enjoying taking a little control over our time and labor, later in the week when the *inga* had been down a number of hours and we were under pressure to make up for lost time, we played this game for more burning economic reasons. In general, one could get through a stack of wood in an hour. But forcing wood through two at a time, however much this strained the pendulum device and increased downtime, we could increase our rate by 30 percent.

Redemption Through Labor?

Communist theorizing, rooted as it was in the naturalistic and positivist interpretations of Marx developed by Karl Kautsky and Lenin, assumed that proletarianization would have relatively predictable effects.[10] But what were these effects in reality? To answer this question, I break it down into a number of smaller elements. First, how far had the Gypsies in the Parketta been encouraged to appreciate sober, regular work and "rational calculation"? It was hard to imagine that the organized chaos of life in the Parketta gave anyone a sense of order. Partly this was an unavoidable effect of the outmoded and badly maintained technology found throughout the socialist bloc. There were days in the Parketta when, despite the machinery imported from Western Europe, it seemed we would never get going properly. When everyone and everything were working, we became accustomed to a certain pace that, once set, we kept to mindlessly. On bad days when the machine whined to a halt for the fifth time in an hour, everyone dropped what he was doing, and the workshop would be empty in a matter of seconds. Sometimes, when things went really wrong, we were moved off the West German machines and back onto the old Russian ones. These, however, undermined all desire to work at all. Here we were reduced to getting by as best we could, trying not to fall too desperately behind. But even slamming planks through two at a time and pushing the machine to its physical limits and beyond, we were still slipping 25 percent behind our normal output. When all the accounts were made up at the end of six months, workers could rush the production process, increasing their output enough to make up for earlier slack periods when machine failure or employee absences kept the workshop's output targets from being met.[11] The conclusion seemed unavoidable: Because of the nature of the socialist production line, the ability to rush and forget technical specifications was more important at these times than love of a job well done.

Second, had the Gypsies given up their attachment to the hustler's mentality and come to see the wage as the "just price" of labor? In reality, and quite contrary to the expectations of the officials, it was the very skills of the wheeler-dealer, which the Gypsies used in their ideologically illegitimate trading activities, that were also needed for success in the world of the socialist factory or farm. The Gypsies saw, as did other Hungarians both urban and rural, that personal ties with one's bosses, not hard work itself, ensured access to good jobs and a good position in the internal, firm division of labor. Because of the way socialist production lines were organized, the labor force tended to be split between a core group of (mostly skilled) workers who kept production going, who redesigned jobs when the machines broke down or the standard materials were unavailable, and a peripheral group of workers who simply did what they were told. The core workers were better rewarded by the factory managers who were dependent on them. The qualities required of such core workers included an ability to get on well with the bosses and with workers in charge of key areas of the factory such as the stores.[12] Even outside this core group, an ability to curry favors from the bosses and foremen allowed one access to a regular and high salary. It was thus not through ability or diligence as a worker that one could hope to achieve a position of influence in the socialist production line.

In the Parketta I saw this principle operate when constant interruptions had reduced output to less than 120 percent of the norm and basic wages were threatened. In such crisis conditions the truly self-subverting nature of the socialist work process became apparent, since it was only by bargaining with the foreman as to the rate at which he counted any particular day's work that one's salary could be maintained.[13]

The consequences of this situation for the representation of labor, and for the wage as the just price of a certain quantity of effort, were far-reaching. At first I had been surprised by the inability of anyone in the saw shop to explain in detail how wages were calculated. Only gradually did I realize that, since everything was negotiable, it was better if there was no clear and fixed rules regarding productivity and rates of pay. Workers were quite aware that the rate one was paid reflected "how close one sat to the fire," that is, how much one could persuade the foreman of one's indispensability to his production team.[14] By threatening to leave, workers could achieve small wage rises, often less in the form of basic wages than in access to overtime, premiums, or other forms of recompense. Gypsies who came in on the occasional Communist Saturdays told me they did so to ensure that they participated in a forthcoming wage increase. One Gypsy woman told me that whenever the machines broke down, she always found some task to occupy her and thus secured a premium payment every half year, which she kept secret from her colleagues, Magyar and Gypsy alike.

Payday was, for these reasons, more like the Hungarian state lottery than the factory managers were ready to admit. Luck and the ability to hustle a deal, intensify one's effort on short notice, and work in a situation where one could not calculate the final outcome—capacities with which the Gypsies were perhaps peculiarly well endowed—were as crucial to making a living in the socialist sector as the ability to work carefully and consistently.

Third, what was the supposed "influence of the collective" on what the Communists thought was the normal state of affairs among Gypsies: atomized, competitive, and noncooperative relations in a population fragmented and socially differentiated by industrialization? In fact, as we have seen, and despite all the internal contradictions of a community based on brotherhood, Gypsy communal life had continued to thrive despite the effects of industrialization and without the help of nannying *gaźos*. By contrast, even though the Rom worked beside the Magyars, the solidarity that resulted from this shared experience in the Parketta was extremely fragile; mutual tolerance might have been a better characterization of the relationship. The Gypsies insisted that their *gaźo* colleagues at the Parketta were "good" or "easy" (*laśo*), but relations between the two groups remained minimal. My impression was always that the Gypsies were much more interested in and attentive to *gaźo* behavior and thought than vice versa, no doubt because they had to be. Conversely, the Gypsies did not encourage *gaźo* interest, happily leaving their colleagues in ignorance of the most basic facts of Gypsy life.[15]

The division of the two groups was most dramatically expressed every time there was a meal break and the workers separated. The Magyars either went to the canteen or ate sandwiches beside their machines; the Gypsies from all over the factory (sometimes joined by one Magyar woman) gathered outside and shared their food. The sharing of food, the re-creation of commensality in the brief pauses between sessions, and the use of Romany at these times marked the Gypsies as a distinct group.[16] These were moments in which the unstated, but ever-present, divisions in the workshop between "them" and "us" could not be hidden. At times I was embarrassed by such an explicit recognition of the "ethnic" divide, as when I found myself working in a mixed team and being encouraged by my Gypsy friends to carry on a conversation in Romany to exclude our Magyar colleagues. Being in some senses in between the two groups, I found myself at moments of crisis or dispute called on by both to reject the behavior of the other.

Fourth, and here we reach the most basic point of all, how far had the Gypsies become "proud to be workers"? It would be impossible to give a quantified answer to this question in terms of some imaginary ratio by which I might contrast the "satisfaction" of the Gypsy and that of the non-Gypsy workers. As I have already said, in some contexts the Rom were well aware that receiving regular wages had changed their whole way of life for the better. But this does not truly answer the question. The Rom also talked of work as "suffering" (*briga*) and complained that it was "heavy" or "oppressive" (*phari*), not "light" or "good."

One way of transcending the difficulty may be to consider qualitatively the attitude to the job while on it. The eldest Magyar man in "my" brigade, Feri bácsi, had what I would call a work aesthetic, that is, a certain pleasure in a job well done and completed. When I was put to work with Feri bácsi, the Gypsies warned me that he was *bužanglo*, which in normal parlance meant "cunning." He certainly had a loud curse, but cunning he was not. What made Feri *bužanglo* as far as the Gypsies were concerned was the way he pushed to get one to work harder in keeping with his plans to earn more money at work. He was thus not *njugotto*, that is, calm and tolerant of other people's needs, nor did he understand the spirit of those who dreamed of "lighter" things to do. From Feri bácsi's point of view, of course, the Gypsies' *njugotto* disposition was just another form of work-dodging. The Gypsies called out to me over and again, "Slowly, don't hurry" (*Lokes, na sidjar*). Feri bácsi, for his part, bellowed in Hungarian above the screech of the saw exactly the opposite advice, "Push it now!" (*Nyomja már!*). On payday a lighter mood was noticeable among the Gypsies, and at 1:30 two of the men suggested that we stop work altogether. Whatever he really felt, Feri bácsi acted as if this was the last thing on his mind.

Again, whereas I, with encouragement from my Gypsy protectors, would allow a pile of rubbish to accumulate on the floor around me and then would clear it up during the occasional pause, Feri bácsi and his Magyar mate regularly lectured me on the desirability of keeping my "end" clean, of managing to work without being "flustered" (*kapkodás*). Such questions of style were of no economic significance; they did not affect our output, but they did set Feri bácsi apart from the majority of the Gypsies and fed the simmering conflict in the brigade.

The Gypsy rejection of the idea of work as an end in itself had more important consequences, too. From the point of view of the Gypsy workers, although the use of the *inga* required a certain judgment, it also offered the easiest job in the workshop: sitting and pushing buttons. As such they felt that it should be circulated among the workers.[17] The management, however, objected for two reasons. First, the *inga* was the most expensive and delicate piece of machinery in the shop, and forcing too much wood through could rapidly ruin it. Second, accuracy on the *inga* could save or lose the factory many millions of forints.[18] Although it would have been possible to train the Gypsies to use the *inga,* once the threat of firings could be exercised by the management, which occurred in 1986, the *inga* was declared a no-go area for all but the official operator.

It is important in these matters to disentangle representation from practice. There were work-conscious Gypsies and slack Magyars. In fact, the highest-paid worker in the factory was a Gypsy with total earnings of over 15,000 a month, two and a half times greater than most of his colleagues. As a result, criticism did sometimes flow from the Gypsies to the Magyars. It is also true that differences in work aesthetic were observable among the Gypsies themselves. On days when Čoro was absent, another young Gypsy was brought over to do his job. Every ten minutes or so, this man would leave the workshop and take a breath of fresh air for half a minute. The result was that, whereas Čoro was often found waiting for the *inga* workers to deliver wood to him, now a great pile of wood built up over the eight-hour shift beside his machine. Again, whereas Čoro would take his saws to be oiled before the end of a break, delaying the start-up by only a minute, his stand-in would take the whole break and then go off to lubricate the saws. The other Rom told me, on his behalf, that work "stank" (*khandel*), that is, revolted this man. One could hardly say that such attitudes seriously affected the efficiency of the brigade in the short term, but they did contribute to an ethic that viewed work as something to be reduced to a minimum and in appearance, if not in fact, avoided.

Another source of pride might have been the receipt of the monthly wage, providing, as it does for many recipients the world over, the means to an independent life. Perhaps because of this, when the Gypsies talked with the Magyars or otherwise presented themselves to the outside world, they were happy to adopt the rhetoric of the socialist state, waxing lyrical about their long work records. But at the same time, no one was under any illusion that working for a wage in a factory was an ideal state of affairs. On the day that I left the Parketta, my female colleagues told me that now I would be able to tell people in my own country "how much we suffer for these little wages." Luludji, for her part, just laughed at me and asked how I would feel if I had to imagine all my life stretching out before me in a factory like the Parketta.

In explaining why wage labor had such a limited impact on the Rom's idea of the good life, it is crucial to understand what one might call the "external" roots of their ambivalence to the wage: an attitude widespread throughout Hungary toward the first and second economy, according to which, earnings from the first, the state sector, could always be made to seem less desirable than those from the second, the private sector.[19]

In part that attitude was a matter of low pay in the state sector. As one expert said, for the majority of working people it was "virtually impossible to live reasonably well on the official wage of a single, full-time job in the first economy."[20] A common saying put it more pithily: "I'm too busy working to earn any money." To some extent this disdain for the socialist wage was borne out by the statistics: At the level of the whole economy, when one included tips and other forms of unrecorded payment, earnings from second-economy activities probably amounted to two-thirds of wages paid by the state.[21] Everyone, Magyar and Gypsy alike, knew that *when it could be found*, self-employment in the second economy was more lucrative than labor in a socialist factory. All the wealthy Gypsy families in the town were engaged in horse raising, broom selling, and other commercial second-economy activities. It was these families who lived in large houses in the center of the town, drove their own cars, and had the widest range of contacts with the Magyars.[22]

Even with the Parketta the Rom experienced the ascendancy of the private ethos over the state sector ethos. One of the benefits of working there was the gift of 120 kilograms of scrap wood. Since the Magyar workers lived in modern housing projects with central heating, they took a small cash benefit instead. The Rom took the wood, using some for heating but, like good entrepreneurs, took the rest on their horse carts around local villages to sell to the peasants. They made more money doing this than the Magyars received at the factory instead of their wood.[23]

However, the operative words here are "when work could be found," since the second economy did not offer work to support everyone all the time, any more than the first economy provided good wages. For most families, therefore, some balance had to be found between employment in each sector. Indeed for the Gypsies in particular, because of the non-wage benefits offered by the first economy, which included low interest home loans and agricultural loans for animals available only to those in the socialist sector, there was a huge premium on at least one member of a household maintaining a regular job. In other words for them, as for most ordinary Hungarians, the relation between the first and second economy was, objectively speaking, one of symbiosis.

Nonetheless, and here the failure of the socialist state is laid fully bare, despite the Gypsies' experience of the links between the two sectors of the economy, they too held the widespread idea that the informal economy was the "real" one, the source of innovation and social dynamism. So great was the ideological hegemony of the "private" sector among the population that the very word "private" (*maszek*) had, by 1985, become in some circles a generalized term of praise. Thus one could exclaim "*maszek* good" to mean "truly excellent"!

The "unreality" of the state sector was reinforced by the very generosity that underlay it. During my original research I had been surprised by certain men's willingness to take whole periods of time off work. The secret of their freedom, I later discovered, was the extremely charitable state sickness payment system. As a basic principle of socialist welfare, it had been decided that members of a worker's family should not be penalized for his or her illness. Thus at that time sickness payments covered 75 percent of full pay, it having been estimated that 25 percent of a salary went to work-related expenses. For many individuals the loss was not so great as to make the time at work worthwhile. Thus in 1985 Čoro took two weeks' sick leave and another man deliberately burned his arm with hydrochloric acid, receiving three-months' sick leave as a result. In 1988 the incentive to take sick leave had become even greater, since payment was then on a seven-day basis. For workers who had a five-day week, that meant on paper that they could earn more at home than at work! Zeleno thus made up a mixture of freshly cut chamomile and salt to simulate a burn, for which he received three weeks' sick leave. At the Parketta, recognizing the risks of the new situation, the foreman had managed to introduce an alternate means of paying the part of the wage known as the "flexible wage," so that workers with sick leave lost out.

Nothing had therefore persuaded the Gypsies to place the value of "consistent work" above their more basic commitments. For a while at the Parketta, I was puzzled that all the Gypsies referred to the 2 to 10 P.M. shift as the worse of the two shifts, since everyone also said that after 6 P.M. the time went quicker as night began to fall. But gradually I realized that with the afternoon shift, one's day was completely determined and limited by one's having to go to work after lunch. At least with the morning shift, one could play with the rest of the day as one wished.[24] The resistance among the Gypsies to submitting their lives to the alien logic of the workplace meant that, much to the chagrin of the foreman and management, important events in communal life, such as the arrival of a relative released from prison, the departure of another to military service, or a death, could call the workers away to fulfill their social duties. On days like that, unless the foreman diverted labor from other parts of the factory, the primary wood production could be brought to a virtual standstill.

In all these ways, then, the experience of work provided little reason for the Gypsies to adopt the socialist ideology of labor. The Rom's rejection of Communist ideology was, however, determined not simply by their raw experience of socialist production lines. Rom ideas about the Magyars provided the context in which the Gypsies made sense of and rejected Communist policy, and it is to these ideas that I next turn.

7

GAŹOS, PEASANTS, COMMUNISTS, AND GYPSIES

In our country the government and the party have decided that everyone must have a registered workplace, that everyone will get their wages from their workplace. It is said that what these people do [Gypsy women scavenging for discarded industrial produce] is "usury"; they practice "usury" with these goods.

—*Manual laborer at municipal garbage dump, March 1988*

THE ILLUSION OF THE ALL-POWERFUL STATE was the form of false consciousness peculiar to Communist societies.[1] It was an illusion shared by apparatchiks as much as the objects of their policies. In this chapter I show just how illusory such beliefs were. We see how the state not only failed to redefine the terms of "the Gypsy problem" but also created a new and greater "problem" in its place. In these pages we reach the heart of the story—at least as far as the non-Gypsies are concerned. The Communist Party thought that in offering assimilation to Hungary's Gypsies, it was making an unprecedented approach to the "Gypsy question" or at least doing so in an entirely novel fashion. The Communists presented themselves as offering radical social transformation by creating a clean break with the past. But from the Gypsies' point of view, the official approach to their problems was shaped by ideas inherited lock, stock, and barrel from the past.

Cigány

The Communists' theory of Gypsy assimilation was based on their understanding of how people acquire their ideas. Class society, so the the-

112

ory went, induced a kind of false consciousness in which people's ideas and identities did not directly reflect their experience of the world. The task of the Communists was therefore to lift this veil of mystification so as to allow people to see their "real interests" and liberate the human essence.[2] Because of the blurring effect of ideology, only a profound rupture in social life would enable the "scientifically derived" formulas for the good socialist life to be imposed on a people. The theory of "revolution" was that such an upheaval did just that: wipe the mental slate clean.

But the specific Communist theory of Gypsy consciousness differed slightly from the general model. According to their analysis of the Gypsies, they lost their place in the social division of labor decades previously and seemed not to have a coherent social organization or culture. They even lacked those social features on which a national or ethnic identity was built (different groups of Gypsies, for example, appeared not to acknowledge identity with one another). Perhaps the fact that some of them had a distinct identity as Gypsies was a feature of a kind of tribal consciousness, but most elements of their lifestyle were interpreted as pragmatic responses to poverty.[3] They were quite simply "lumpen proletarians," a class Marx had defined as "thieves and criminals of all kinds, living on the crumbs of society, people without a definite trade, vagabonds, people without a hearth or home."[4] Nothing had to be done to wipe their mental slate clean, since there was nothing on it in the first place. Well-intentioned social reformers could put the instructions for "living as proper Hungarians" on a blank board that was just waiting to be filled.[5]

Ironically, however, in relation to the Gypsies it was the Communists who had not wiped clean their mental slate. When they prepared their policy, they took as their definition of "Gypsy" the Hungarian folk term "Cigány." But as an ethnographer of a village in eastern Hungary explained, in Hungarian, "adjectives coined from Cigány are frequently used by a self-identified Magyar to condemn someone else's behavior, appearance or life style."[6] She added, "The ultimate assertion of low rank or lack of rank [*rangtalanság*] is to accuse a villager of Cigány ancestry."[7] Another writer, this time discussing a village very near Harangos, listed the typical stereotypes attributed to the Cigány: "laziness, begging, stealing, spending and consuming in the present without regard to future needs, dirtiness, promiscuity, prolific reproduction, eating rotten meat and two-facedness."[8] In ordinary Hungarian, the term *cigányság* ("the Gypsies collectively") when used to describe behavior also meant "deceit," and the verb *cigánykodni* ("to carry on like a Gypsy") was used for any behavior that was loud, rowdy, two-faced, or involved flattery. In other words, what the Communists had done was assimilate a prejudicial folk representation to their own Marxist notion of the lumpen proletariat to suggest that once the Gypsies had adopted a "proletarian" way of life, they would cease being Cigány and become Magyar. The term "Cigány" would therefore lose any present-day referent.[9]

Gažo

But there was also another realm of semantics that the state never bothered to consider: that contained in Romany. In this there were simply no terms that corresponded exactly to Cigány and Magyar.

Soon after I arrived in Harangos, the Gypsy man who had taken me into his family asked me the Hungarian word for Rom. Naively, I replied, "*Cigány*," only to be corrected. "No! Rom means human [*ember*]." My translation was mistaken. As Luludji told me, the Magyars looked down on the Rom because "they say we are *Cigány*." On a level deeper, the opposite of Rom was not Magyar but *gažo*, a term used for the non-Gypsies but among other things also meaning "stupid" and "ignorant" of the way to lead a good life.

The semantic gap between these two terms was so great that a Gypsy could assert that he would like to stop being *Cigány*, while having no intention of ceasing to be Rom. I well remember Thulo and his wife telling me proudly that in twenty years' time there would be no *Cigány* left at all. A week earlier they had complained bitterly that the *gažo* teachers would not teach in Romany because they looked down on the Rom children. On the first occasion this man was talking about the attitudes of the *gažo* authorities; on the second, about his basic identity and desire that his children grow up as Rom, speaking *romanes*.[10]

In 1960 the leading Romany-speaking Hungarian ethnographer told the Communist Party that "the essence of the Gypsy question is that there is no Gypsy question. . . . The Gypsies [*Cigány*] want to dissolve into the Hungarian population, they want to become Hungarian citizens with full rights." But he was moving among slippery categories, as he must have known.[11] The party, just like ordinary Hungarians, did not know.

The official approach to the Rom was based, in part, on the mistaken assumption that *Cigány* identity was a product of the Gypsies' exclusion from presocialist society. It was thought that as a result of their marginal position, they had got used to living one day at a time because they had no better way to get by. The reality was that, although often residentially separated, economically marginal, excluded from the social life of the village, and denied kinship ties with most peasants, the Gypsies in Hungarian villages had been in more or less constant contact with the Magyar population through working for better-off peasants.[12] Through such contacts, the Gypsies were certainly familiar with the dominant

Tent of a Vlach Rom family, 1909. The well-dressed couple may have been ethnographers. The police would have been there to protect them from the "dangerous" Gypsies. (Courtesy Néprajzi Muzeum, photo by J. Sagi)

ethics of peasant Magyars, summed up for the Rom in the idea of the *gaźo*. Similarly, if they had not retained their identity as Rom and not become poor, landless laborers before, it was in part because they rejected what non-Gypsy society stood for.

Most anthropologists and sociologists who have studied the Gypsies have noted the opposition of Rom to *gaźo* and explored some aspects of the notion of the non-Gypsy while retaining the accepted translation of *gaźo* as "non-Gypsy."[13] The Hungarian Rom were, however, more specific and glossed the term into Hungarian as "peasant" (*paraszt*)—thereby using basic aspects of peasant identity to talk metaphorically about all non-Gypsies. One method of understanding the way the Rom thought about *gaźo*s is to examine peasant life. That has the added advantage of leading to a deeper sense of what it meant to be a "nonpeasant," or Rom. Since I had little direct experience of non-Gypsy families, I use the classic studies by two native ethnographers, Edit Fél and Tamás Hofer, who described the social life of the village of Átány, only one hour by horse cart from Harangos.[14]

It may seem perverse to turn to a study of a village in Hungary in the 1950s where the dominant ethos was not that of the capitalist farmer, landless laborer, or socialist collective farm member, but that of the independent household farmer. However, ethnographers who have worked in diverse regions of modern Hungary all report the preservation and reproduction of important elements of this peasant culture through to the 1980s. Despite collectivization and the partial industrialization of agriculture, in most regions of Hungary one could still talk of a "peasantry" at that time as opposed to a rural proletariat working in a "roofless factory."[15] The Rom idea that the gaźo were peasants thus retained an actual significance.

The title of Fél and Hofer's study, Proper Peasants (Rendes paraszt), was taken from the Átány villagers' own lips, and it perfectly captures the prescriptive, moral sense of their use of the word "peasant."[16] It is a sense the Gypsies took on and to which they gave new resonance. The elite gazdas (heads of landholding households), who made up the group of proper peasants, accounted for only 20 percent of the population in 1935 and less than 15 percent in 1949. But despite their minority position, they set the tone of village life, were "at the center of society," and provided the values by which most others judged themselves. They were not, however, seen as a class separate from and above the other peasants; rather, they represented an ideal toward which less successful farming families strove.

Peasants Who Are Masters of Themselves

The foundation of the entire "proper" peasant way of life was the idea of the household as a physical entity and a social group.[17] Ideally, this was a self-sustaining unit of production and consumption based on the transmission of a landed estate through time. In part, this continuity was a matter of the physical preservation of a house with attached land and in part a matter of the conservation of a name and descent line. When peasants built a house, they placed inside its "first corner" a bottle that contained the date of construction, the name of the first owner, and sometimes some major (historic or cataclysmic) event of that year.[18] The rightful place of the gazda was at the main table of the house in this corner, in a highly concrete and personal relation with a social and familial past.[19]

The ideal household rested on a sexual and generational division of labor, with a male leader as the owner and proprietor of the family estate. The men went out to work on the land, often spending much of their time in the outlying garden area of the "village" (kert), but this was especially true of the young men—the gazda might spend more time at home. Living mostly out in the "garden," the young men were said to lead "irresponsible" lives as bachelors, stealing even from their own fathers in order to fund their partying in the inn.[20] Whereas all the men were oriented toward the fields, women were focused on the "house" (*ház*).[21] Girls in better-off families were, if possible, kept at home or otherwise were given light work in the vineyards and at haying.[22] In all families a wife's effort was represented as providing the transient goods necessary for daily consumption rather than being used as a basis for the capital used to extend the "house." If women were recognized as participating in the achievement of the family's autonomy, it was through enabling the men's outside activities.[23] Later, if land was given to a girl in dowry, this would be taken from purchased, rather than ancestral, land.

The material support of the ideal household was provided by possession of 8–11 hectares of land, an area that could sustain a "good" (that is, sufficiently numerous) family.[24] The "living soil" of the farm was treated with an appropriate veneration: True peasants "ought to love the earth, not only to work it."[25] When men were out farming, they were said to be "out on the *határ*," a term poorly translated as "boundary." Its sense derived originally from the verb *hatni*, "to impress, affect, influence," which itself gave rise to a series of terms dealing with power and efficacity. The *határ* of the village was the area on which villagers exercised and imposed their "personhood" by the nature and manner of their productive activities—it was a tract of delimited land at the edge of which property and other rights faded. The peasants' link with this land was unashamedly mystical—to swear with one's own soil in one's boots was a guarantee of one's honesty, and the "maintenance and declaration of a correct *határ* was a moral duty, divinely sanctioned."[26] Villagers wanted to be buried within the *határ* of their own village, and those who could not, such as men who died in war, had their personal possessions symbolically interred at home.[27]

If owning land meant one need not labor for someone else, it was labor performed on this land that made the man a peasant and not a capitalist farmer. Labor, for the proper peasant, was the source of all value—labor conceived as "self-denying, careful and efficient work."[28] The peasants talked of the pleasures of those months of the year spent toiling out in the fields, and at such times it was thought worthy to be the first person out of the village in the morning.[29]

Manual effort had to be not just physically demanding but also prolonged and regular to make a proper peasant of a man. Such a work ethic merged naturally into a work aesthetic in which careful, efficient, orderly work was esteemed. Disorderly people who left grain lying in the yard, stored it in their outbuildings rather than near the house, or left their animals uncleaned were looked down upon. As Fél and Hofer said, "For proper peasants, agriculture and work were an art, beyond the practical utility and profit involved. Following the rules of this 'art' gave one security and pride and gained him the esteem of the community."[30] It was an art that one learned in one's father's stable, playing hide-and-seek under the belly of the horse at the age of four or five and harnessing the team at the age of eight. The relationship with horses was crucial: To be a proper peasant, one had to know how to use horses and not cattle in one's agricultural work; oxen made up the shoddy teams used on manorial estates.

The spirit of the people is perhaps most simply evoked in the following nursery rhyme on the letter *D* for *Dolgos*, which means "assiduous" or just "having things to do":

Dolgos gondos szorgalmas légy.	Be active, careful, and industrious.
Minden munkát jó kedvvel tégy.	Perform every task willingly.
Amit véghez kell vinned ma	What you have to do today
Sose halaszd azt holnapra	Never put off until tomorrow.
Minden gonoszság kezdete	All wickedness begins
A henyélés szeretete.	With a liking for idleness.[31]

The ethic of labor for self-sufficiency, naturally enough, determined the attitude toward expenditure. The wealth produced by working was not to be consumed—this would have been the negation of production—but, through self-denial, to be saved. If the proper peasant accumulated money by selling surplus produce of his own, he ought to have used this to buy more land.[32] Villagers admiringly recalled a man who "dared not eat his fill in his whole life" and people who grew rich by taking their wealth "out of their bellies."[33] In such a culture, to dress scruffily day by day was a mark not of poverty but of scrupulous thrift.[34]

The ideas linking these concepts for the proper peasant were summed up by the ethnographers, revealing the ideological connection of land, labor, morality, time, and religion: "The land he cultivated was inherited from his ancestors; to keep and work it with care and responsibility was his moral duty to his precursors and successors, and also to the fatherland and God, since the end product of his labors was bread, the basic subsistence food and the material of the Lord's Supper."[35]

Disorderly Persons

The people who lived in a village were linked to one another in various ways because they lived off one *határ*. All villagers, but no one else, had free access to the natural produce of this land, such as chamomile or unharvested grains for gleaning.[36] But it was the *ownership* of land, rather than residence in the village, that provided the symbolic basis of community. Many villagers, farmhands, for instance, who worked the land were excluded from full participation in the moral community because they did not count as being "of the soil" (*földes*, that is, landowners) and "aboriginal."[37] Neither craftsmen nor herdsmen, both of which lived inside the village, often for long periods, were fully integrated, since they did not own land there.[38] These were not people of the soil any more than the Gypsies were.

From the proper (the Hungarian term also means orderly) peasants' point of view, theirs was an estimable way of life, one that sustained the whole nation of Magyars.[39] Of those in the village who did not live as they did, there were two groups. One was composed of outlying "homestead" (*tanya*) dwellers, poor peasants, and servants who aspired to the status of "born peasant." Then there were the Gypsies and Jews (and, to some extent, craftsmen) who owned no land and appeared to have no aspiration for it. In the final analysis, these were people who did not "produce" or "work" and so belonged to a different moral universe. Since they could not even create the means of their own sustenance (especially in the symbolically important form of wheat for bread), they were always "dependent" on others, on the shop. Living in a sense without proper households, these people were considered inherently licentious; they lacked the self-control that came from the weight of ancestral tradition, the need to conserve the inheritance and the esteem of the family name.[40]

This rejection of the Gypsy and Jew also reflected an ambivalence toward capitalist, or at least market-based, forms of income. In these, people engaged in "games of chance" that demanded "bold and shrewd action," thought to be alien to the customary manner of rural farming. Whereas the herdsman avoided working with the help of his whip, and other craftsmen changed the form of materials that they themselves had not "produced," the Gypsy (like the poor peasant turned horse dealer) made his living effortlessly by crookery and horse trading. And just as diligence induced prudence for the peasant, so for the Jew and Gypsy "gambling" on the market was thought to foster a carefree spirit. As an earlier ethnographer, evoking the spirit of peasant morality, put it, "Easily earned money naturally goes with a rash life-style."[41] In a village like Átány the sudden affluence of a neighbor was "viewed with suspicion." Stories were told of immoral people using sorcery to find treasures in the ground or to bewitch other villagers' cows to obtain their milk by proxy.[42]

Such attitudes hardly encouraged the peasants to seek a rapprochement with the capitalist spirit. Their feelings were summed up by the foremost sociologist of rural Hungary in these terms:

The peasant doesn't take any advantage of the bourgeois benefit of property by living off the annuity. He simply enjoys owning it. It is possible that an industrial worker lives better; it is possible that someone who rents land produces much better. Nonetheless the landed owner considers himself far above those people because he has land. What the peasant really desires above all in life is to be in full control of his land, not to be subject to any outside interference, disturbance or supervision, and to be able to dispose of his produce without any fixed obligations.[43]

Because of this disposition, from within the walls of the peasant court-yard all relations with the outside seemed to threaten the autonomy of the family and its leader, the *gazda*. In principle, families would avoid borrowing from their neighbors. Peasants said that everyone strove not to have to exchange with others, though they recognized that this goal was unrealizable.[44] But they did avoid borrowing key productive tools and had fixed "exchange rates" for all other items. The very idea of an ill-defined and therefore open-ended debt, with the long-term binding re-lationship such a debt might imply in village society, was thus anathe-matized.

Even more important than avoiding dependence on one's neighbors was retaining one's independence from the economic institutions by which the outside world reached into Átány. A true peasant produced enough food to avoid recourse to the shop, which would drain his cash, and never bought "either a piece of fodder or a grain of cereal" in all his life. Corn, especially in the form of flour, the direct constituent of bread, was never sold if this could be avoided.[45] The idea that food bought on the market, especially bread, was less filling than that produced by one's own labor was one way this symbolic alienation from the market was underlined.

It cannot be stressed too strongly, however, that to a large extent the re-jection of the capitalist market by proper peasants was rhetorical. Átány had been thoroughly integrated into the national cash economy since at least the eighteenth century; and the integration of land into the money market in the second half of the nineteenth century affected this village as much as the rest of Hungary. Bankruptcy became common in the late nineteenth century, and many peasants were ruined by the collapse in wheat prices in the 1880s as cheap American grain flooded the European markets.[46] Fél and Hofer's account sticks so very close to the proper peas-ants' own account of themselves that it perhaps does not give full weight to the fact that many of the *gazdas* of 1950 had obtained their land through mortgages secured from banks after World War I—loans that hy-perinflation then reduced to trifling sums.[47] Peter Bell, writing twenty years later about the same historical process, was more cynical:

Despite the pride of many *nagygazda*s [big farmers] in their farming skills and knowledge . . . most of them or their direct ancestors did not acquire their large holdings through wise management or cultivation of smaller holdings. Some large holdings were purchased with funds earned through working in America or through large-scale horse breeding and trading. Fortuitous inflation after both world wars helped others. . . . Farming one's own land was not the common way of achieving *nagygazda* status.[48]

Poor and middling peasants had also been obliged to purchase land on mortgage, for which they needed financial resources. Often they had raised their initial cash through horse dealing.[49] In brief, whatever the ideology of autonomy, the capitalist agricultural product market was the source of much of proper peasant wealth.

The rhetorical nature of the proper peasant attitude can be seen in the way that these peasants organized their own marketing. In general, the woman went to market and sold the produce of her labor.[50] She used the money thus acquired not for subsistence goods but for her children's supplementary needs, such as clothes and her son's payments to the Gypsy musicians in the local tavern.[51] In this way, too, peasant households displaced or denied the reality of their dependence on and involvement with the market. It is also hard not to see in the social organization of the village as a whole a similar symbolic defense of the values of autonomy, independence, and self-reliance in the face of increased subordination in the "real" world. The village was divided into two "ends," the lower one of which was reputedly more "aboriginal." Both ends were ideally self-sufficient, with their own garden areas, craftsmen, shops, wells, herdsmen, pastures, and even cemeteries. As a result, peasants from each half tended not to have to meet each other in their daily business.[52] Right in the middle of the symmetrical village, and thus at the heart of the village land, was the church, where the people of the two ends met once a week, each entering through their own door. On the basis of a virtually nominal difference between newcomers and aboriginals, a division had thus been constructed within which each half of the village could live out, in ritualized form, a self-sufficiency in relation to the other that neither could easily achieve in its relation to the outside world.

Fél and Hofer had conducted their fieldwork in the early 1950s, but throughout the socialist period the independent peasant ethic continued to be transformed (and not abandoned) as an alternative to that propagated by those in power. Socialist agricultural policy rendered the traditional peasant way of life nonviable; the market in land was closed. And yet when a team from the Hungarian Academy of Sciences studied the north Hungarian village of Varsány in the 1970s, the team found that the worker-peasants had reconstructed the idea of autonomy around posses-

Cleaning the streets for the gaźos. *(Courtesy Néprajzi Muzeum, photo by V. Bozzi)*

sion of their labor. Although on collective land they might adopt the attitude of the former manorial serfs, and "reap as if on an estate" (i.e., carelessly), on their own household plots it was reported that "diligence has become a value in itself. The use to which it is put is less important. People who constantly toil are valued more than those who make money by finding shortcuts in their work."[53] In this way the worker-peasants of socialist Hungary created a lifestyle that contrasted with that of the lazy, "do-nothing" (*dologtalan*) bureaucrats, the Communist Party bosses, and people right at the other end of the social spectrum, the Gypsies.

Communists and Gaźos

It seems logical to suggest that, if the Communists were to have persuaded the Rom to become Magyars, they would have had to avoid repeating the behavior of the Gypsies' traditional "other," the *gaźos*. At the outset of Communist rule, however, a bad example had been set: Gypsy agricultural day laborers had been almost wholly excluded from land reform, while their Magyar counterparts had been some of the prime beneficiaries.[54] From the Rom point of view, it seemed that, despite the way the Red Army had saved Rom lives by repelling the Nazis just as deportations of Gypsies were beginning, the new distribution of privilege in the country was going to be the same as the old.

Indeed, twenty years later the core of the Gypsy assimilation policy pitted Rom against *gaźo* exactly as in the past. From the songs sung by Rom in prewar Hungary, we know that the Gypsies then defined themselves as "sons of the market" (*foroske śave*), but it was precisely this identity as traders, with its suggestion—to Communist ears—of usurious exploitation by a middleman, that the Communists hoped to abolish by setting the Gypsies to work. So when the Gypsies were drawn into the socialist labor force, they were being offered the same option as in the past: elevation through laboring for others.

The attitude of the local Communist councils to the Gypsies' second-economy activities also reproduced *gaźo*-peasant hostility to their way of doing things. The authorities could have interpreted Gypsy involvement in the second economy in the same way as they did that of many other Hungarian citizens: a necessity forced on them by socialist circumstances. Instead, it was seen as the thoroughly reprehensible perpetuation of their age-old adherence to casual and irregular work.

Back in 1960 the Communist official charged with producing a coherent policy, Sándor Vendégh, had written that "those kinds of work that do not allow the disciplinary effect of the collective to come into play, or those kinds of work that demand traveling, deliveries to other places, or collection of raw materials, do not prove to be good [for the Gypsies]. In this kind of work the Gypsies . . . evade surveillance . . . and are sometimes connected to criminal activities, or a return to the scavenging [*élősködő*] way of life."[55] Vendégh was only generalizing a principle, enunciated in an earlier study, that, even though craft labor (such as blacksmithing or music making) was not in and of itself socially objectionable, when such labor shifted into "wheeling and dealing" (*kupeckedés*), its social character changed into a form of exploitation of another's labor. Since the trader was creating no new value, he had to be living off the value that others had produced—"practicing usury" (*üzérkednek*). Thus, a Gypsy offering to mend a peasant's fence might be performing a useful function, but if during his work he noticed, say, a machine in the yard and offered to buy it (in order later to sell it at a profit), this would reveal his tendency to "avoid respectable jobs and sponge off society."

In both Communist and popular discussions of Gypsy economic activity, the term "usury" cropped up, revealing both the continuity between official Marxism and folk discourse and, surely, their roots in very much older European, Christian ideas about time and money.[56] In a talk I had in 1988 with one of the men in charge of the council's Works Department (which dealt with rubbish and scrap disposal), I saw how Communist hostility to trade had merged over the years with other current ideas. "The Gypsies do come and rummage about among the scrap," I was told,

> but it would be much better and healthier if they worked like everybody else in proper, tied-down workplaces where they get their monthly wages and try to live from that. . . . You see, this is part of their lifestyle; they don't seem able to live without this sort of thing. Doing things like this arises from their nature as Gypsies. . . . You know, they are sort of free spirits, free temperaments. It's absolutely obvious that they cannot escape from their own nature. . . . They are a fundamentally different type of human being.

Gypsies such as Čaja were fully aware of their barely legitimate position with jobs that were "occasional" and unsupervised. At times she would try to justify her activities in terms that would appeal to the authorities. In a filmed interview Čaja told me that hers was "even harder work than in the factory. . . . All day long from six in the morning up to midday or two o'clock I am here. I'm on my feet all day; I don't sit down at all. Just like someone who goes to work in a factory." But that was for the most part rhetorical camouflage.[57]

Čaja was very well protected in all kinds of ways, but other Gypsies found themselves at the rough end of council efforts—of a more or less symbolic nature—to bring their "disorderly" (*rendetlen*) lifestyle to an end. In 1974 a Harangos council regulation attempted to restrict the ownership of horses in the town to cart drivers and home-based craftsmen. People who lived from keeping and trading in horses, that is, the Gypsies, were forbidden to own the animals. As a result, many of the Gypsies' horses were confiscated in 1976. No compensation was paid for the animals on the grounds that the owners had paid no animal tax for many years. The next council report attempted to provide some ideological justification for this act of expropriation, noting that the Gypsies still sought work in "unrestrictive areas" such as scrap collection and animal husbandry and, furthermore, that "both of these carry the danger that they may become antisocial. Horse carts are one of the implements of criminal acts and encourage vagrancy; keeping animals, in the absence of land, can be just the same [by leading to theft of fodder], apart from being a health and environmental hazard."

The incident ended badly for the authorities, who had to stable the horses with a local cooperative farm and keep them there at great expense until they were sent for slaughter. The income from this by no means met the expenses, and the experiment (in trying "to break the Gypsies from their horses," as one Rom man put it) was not tried again.

In this case we can see particularly clearly that council policy, like Communist policy more generally, was based on a complete misunderstanding of the Gypsies' situation. The Gypsies who suffered most from the expropriation were those Third Class families whose members worked at the Parketta, a factory that had one of the most stable Gypsy workforces in the town. Objectively speaking, the factory and they were symbiotically linked because the Gypsies lived on a settlement where they could keep animals, the socialist wage enabled them to enter the second economy, and this encouraged them to remain at the Parketta. Bank loans had become too small by the mid-1980s for a Gypsy to buy or build a house, and so he needed his own funds to supplement any loan. The fact that residents of the Third Class were able to keep pigs at home meant that they had some basic capital that made the purchase of a house or rebuilding feasible. In other words, it was precisely those Gypsies who appeared to display the "scavenging," "nomadic" mentality (i.e., in reality those with second-economy possibilities) who were in a position to make use of the benefits of permanent socialist wage labor in one factory. The Gypsies living in slums could not use the socialist wage in such a productive fashion and therefore in some ways looked more like Gypsies "on the road to assimilation," while in reality they were slipping further and further into poverty.

From the point of view of Magyar officials, there appeared to be a willful duplicity on the Rom's part. A man might be an "assimilated" worker (*dolgozó*) in the daytime and a "nonassimilated" Gypsy (*Cigány*) in the evening. Frustrated that the policy was apparently not working, the authorities resorted with increasing frequency to "administrative" repression. Thus, from the Rom's perspective, the final consequence of the application of the Gypsy policy—which had aimed first and foremost at ensuring an evenhanded treatment of Gypsies and Magyars—was the application of one standard to the Magyars and another to the Gypsies. From the Rom's point of view, the Communists were just *gaźos* in disguise.

From Civilizing to Discriminating

Although the Rom's use of the term *gaźo* partly reflected the number of "rural people/peasants" they had dealings with, it was not primarily a descriptive term in that teachers, lawyers, council bureaucrats, and colleagues at work were all called "peasants." Although someone who hauled goods by horse cart, for instance, might insist that he was no "peasant man" (*parasztember*), the Rom held to their own intuition that this is just what he was. In calling these people "peasants," the Rom were bringing to the fore and naming that aspect of their relationship with the non-Gypsies that was most salient.

It had been through the substitution of peasantlike anti-Gypsy prejudice for an original leftist critique of Magyar chauvinism that Communists came to behave like the *gaźos* of old. The 1961 policy, whatever its culturally assimilationist bent, did promise an end to systematic discrimination against the Gypsies. In 1957 Labor Ministry officials had been appalled to find a certain János Kolompár of the town of Gyula who had "changed his name [a typical Gypsy surname] by deed-poll to János Kőri so his daughter's life at school would not be ruined."[58] Vendégh likewise reported with outrage the case of a Stakhanovite Gypsy who had been turned back at the gates of eight factories because of the color of his skin.[59] These Communists were clearly shocked at what they had discovered during their research in the country, but in practice, as in so many other areas of social policy, once Communist theory was applied, it almost always lost out to local knowledge or adapted itself in a surprisingly plastic fashion to the contours of popular consciousness.[60]

To some extent at the outset of the assimilation campaign, the Communists were aware of the dangers involved in adapting the policy "to local conditions"—a euphemism for watering it down—and the 1961 policy found a place for a campaign against Magyar prejudice. But precisely because the policy had been framed in terms of assimilating the *Cigány*, the campaign against prejudice was soon dropped: Who, after all, would defend the *Cigány* way of life? It was therefore not long before the intention of the policy was inverted and it was being said that, if there was a "Gypsy problem," it was caused not by Magyar prejudice but by some people behaving in a Gypsy manner.[61]

The seeds of this change were in fact sown at the first stage of policy implementation, when it was adapted to "the local context." In the very first Harangos council document to treat the question, the local Gypsies were blamed for their own poverty: "The families with many children who sponge their existence from unknown sources think of the do-nothing life as a Gypsy *virtus*. They behave impudently and aggressively demand their imagined rights: assistance for their children, improvements for their homes [crumbling hovels built on flood land]. Because of this, we have to put up a continual struggle against them."[62]

Nearly twenty-five years later, a manager of one of the more important factories in Harangos summed up in a single phrase the essence of official thought: "I have never felt any prejudice against the Gypsies," he told me. "I think of them all as people [*emberek*] until, that is, they reveal themselves to be Gypsies [*cigányok*]." Comrade Kiss was proud of his attitude, which he felt expressed his progressive and tolerant approach to his numerous Gypsy employees. In practice, then, it was up to the Gypsies to persuade the Magyars that they were worthy of being treated as people by proving that they were not *Cigány*.[63]

Giving the Gypsies Homes

It was a characteristic of official campaigns in Eastern Europe that a decision of principle by the party might take three to five years to work itself down into a governmental policy. So in the case of the Gypsies, many years were spent in evaluating aspects of the Gypsy problem, drawing up proposals, revising them, and devising bureaucratic structures to implement them. In Harangos a series of reports was produced strictly for appearance's sake to simulate activity. The central government in Budapest had implemented none of the Gypsy policy until 1968, and in Harangos nothing was formally initiated until 1977.[64] Then the council's hand was forced by the arrival of a dynamic Gypsy Affairs secretary to the regional capital. This woman was determined to see some form of policy initiative, especially for rehousing the inhabitants of the Gypsy settlements.

For the most part in Hungary, housing policy had involved the transfer of Gypsies from their old mud-brick houses to new "reduced-value" (Cs) settlements. Although officially presented as a triumph of social engineering, Cs houses, as the Gypsies knew, were not normally dispersed among Magyar dwellings but congregated on the edge of villages, just as the ghettos of the past had been. It has to be said that this consequence of the housing policy was not really in the control of the bureaucrats. Faced with the possibility of a Gypsy "invasion," Magyar landowners in the villages into which Gypsies were to be moved had raised their prices to prevent potential Cs builders from moving in.

But the bureaucrats were responsible for other features of the Cs disaster. In the original building plans, there was often no prescribed expenditure for infrastructural support, and so there were entire new Cs settlements of Gypsies with no roads, schools, shops, or other amenities. Since the installation of electricity lines had not been planned either, only those families that had the resources to pay privately ended up with electricity in their new homes. Thus, the state had replaced "primitive," but functioning, settlements, which had a certain social order of their own, with modern slums built in row upon row of identical, low-cost, low-comfort, low-quality, and unresellable properties.[65]

In Harangos, because the policy of rehousing the Gypsies was implemented so late, the Rom evaded the most destructive effects of resettlement. But the Third Class provides an example of the kind of problem Communist policy fell into even when it seemed to be more tolerant. The relative enrichment of most Gypsy families there during the previous twenty years meant that by 1985, out of thirty properties, some twenty-two were owned by Gypsies. In summer 1985 three Rom families competed to buy one Magyar's property, and the remaining Magyar-owned houses would undoubtedly have been snapped up if their owners had been willing to sell for a reasonable price.

Although these Gypsies were buying good-quality houses, the Harangos town council viewed these developments with ambivalence, if not hostility. The council was under orders to prevent renewed residential segregation, and yet the Gypsies seemed keen to build their homes on land they owned (just like most other Hungarian citizens). The council therefore played a double game. On the one hand, it provided loans for Gypsies to buy houses; on the other, it refused to lift the building ban in the Third Class, which had been introduced in 1960 with the ostensible aim of attracting resources to construct a porcelain factory next to the railway line. The council also kept the Third Class on the list of "settlements that don't meet acceptable standards." What all this meant in practice was that the Gypsies had considerable difficulty securing building loans to construct houses in the style they desired. This situation did not, however, prove an insurmountable obstacle to the resourceful Gypsies. Families would typically knock down three walls of an old mud-brick house, "repair" a large two-story modern house around the old remains, and then pay the fine for having built illegally!

In the past, Magyar villagers had been proud to declare that they lived in villages where "there were neither Gypsies nor Jews nor beggars"; elderly Harangos Rom had themselves suffered evictions from neighboring villages.[66] The Communists had aimed at altering this kind of ethnic chauvinism by dispersing Gypsies among Magyars but had met resistance from both camps. After the Communists failed to improve the Gypsies' living conditions and in many ways worsened them, it is not surprising that the Rom saw the new authorities as only marginally different from the peasants of old who had driven them from their villages.

Education

Another aim of policy was to raise the educational level of Gypsy children, but here, too, prejudice and discrimination soon replaced reform. Instead of seeking to work with the Gypsies and find ways of building on their own experience, the schools tried to "fight the influence of the family." As an official explained, "If we want the Gypsies to become equal members of our society of workers . . . we will have to reduce to a minimum the regressive influence of the family circumstances that encourage the preservation of their traditions." What this meant in practice was, as a 1977 Harangos report put it with characteristic bluntness, "if we were to take the category of 'child at risk' strictly, almost all of the young Gypsy children living on settlements should be taken into care."[67] This was thought to be not altogether a bad solution, since, as a report eight years later explained, "this is also a means of assimilating the Gypsies."[68]

In official dealings with Gypsy families, the midwife was given a special role to play, since she could approach the Gypsies directly through their children.[69] I became acquainted with one such health worker, who showed me an extended study she had written as a result of several years' contact with Gypsies in the Harangos area. In this she singled out the "psychic and mental characteristics" of the Gypsies for discussion. Linking published work with the widely held Magyar representation of Gypsies as children who had failed to "grow up," she observed that "among them instincts, rather than consciousness, determines their actions, and the preconditions of rational argument are still largely waiting to be created. . . . Their actions are carried out on the first impulse that takes them; in a given situation they act without weighing it up and considering." As a result, "they only live for today. . . . In hunting for happiness they seek to satisfy immediately their bodily and physical needs. . . . Their thought is hindered by the poverty of their language . . . [and] . . . in their adjustment to the world the decisive role is played by their sensory organs. The Gypsies even call themselves nature's children."[70] Given their low cultural and intellectual levels, it "had to be recognized" that they were "incapable of grasping a problem in its entirety."

It would be quite wrong to imagine that this woman's opinions reflected an unusually anti-Gypsy attitude. On the contrary, the tone of her text was considerably warmer and more sympathetic than that of many official publications. And in its fundamental assumptions, this document captured the essence of the paternalist, socialist state's perspective on the Gypsies: The Gypsies were not capable of looking after their own affairs, and they carried with them a nomadic lifestyle brought from ancient India.

On a national scale, the Communist Party oscillated between allowing the formation of Gypsy classes (in 1968) and later discouraging the separation of children into de facto ethnic groups. The latter policy, of course, conceded the very principle that the party was set upon denying, namely, that the Gypsies constituted a distinct people rather than a fragment of a social class. In Harangos, after attempts were made in 1976 and again in 1977 to bring the Gypsy children into normal classes, a new reserve area was found for the Gypsy children: the School for the Educationally Subnormal, where one-quarter of the Gypsy children in Harangos went in 1985.[71]

Beyond the local arrangements in individual towns, the Ministry of Education did untold damage to the prospects of all Gypsy children by circulating the numerous publications of amateur ethnographer József Vekerdi and his colleagues. These legitimized the widely held assumption that *romanes* was not a real language and that therefore Gypsy children came to school with a poor vocabulary and weak conceptual abilities.[72] Since the party had also gone out of its way to reject the use of *romanes* in schools both in 1961 and 1974, the door had effectively been shut on using one of the most obvious skills that could have given Gypsy children a sense of belonging at school. Vekerdi's idea that Gypsy culture was but a collection of character traits acquired passively from other peoples on the Gypsies' travels, and that the Gypsy way of life was basically a series of absences (of productive activity, formal authority, life-cycle rituals), further blinded teachers to any of the children's potential.[73]

Although the staff of Harangos's school admitted privately that the bulk of these children were not "educationally subnormal," the practice of ghettoization remained in force, a fact that was well recognized by the Gypsy children, who referred to the school as "The Gypsy School" (*a cigány iskola*) or else as "The Fool's School" (*a bolond iskola*). Indeed, only the threat of being removed from their homes and placed in state care for nonattendance ensured that children spent any time in this institution.

At the end of the day, the sole aspect of the Gypsy education policy that the Harangos council could be proud of was the rise in the number of adults completing their basic primary schooling. But there was a downside even to this: They were acquiring their eighth-grade passes in order to qualify for driving lessons, that is, to pursue more of the "unsupervised" activities that the other hand of officialdom was trying to terminate.[74]

Cleaning Up the Gypsies

There is one final area of public policy in which the council adopted a characteristically "peasant" (*gaźo*) approach: their attitude to the Gypsies' public health. In Hungarian one of the most common epithets associated with the word "*Cigány*" was "dirty" (*piszkos*). But I still found it surprising to hear local government officials, who had on their own admission never been in a Gypsy house, talking to me of the infernal stink they imagined there, the ubiquitous dirt, the lice in the Gypsies' hair. I was often asked how I could stand to live amid all this presumed filth. These opinions informed council policy to the extent that until 1983 the Public Health Department (Köjál) twice every summer organized a "disinfection" of the Gypsies on settlements in the town. This little "action" involved the surprise, early morning encirclement of a settlement by police supported by conscripted soldiers and council officers. Men and women were then passed separately through a program of hair washing, hot showers, and delicing. The Magyars in the settlement were excused from the ordeal.

Whatever the reaction of the Gypsies at the time—and several of the younger men told me that they had fled the settlement—these events were remembered with some bitterness. I was asked rhetorically if the council knew that there were showers at people's place of work. Older people told me of the shame they had felt washing in public. Working men told me that the letters they had been given to explain their absence from work would have made them the laughingstock of the Magyars at the workplace. Rather than hand these letters in, the men had risked getting fired for absenteeism.

The council attached some importance to this particular form of collective humiliation, which breached both the privacy and cleanliness customs of the Gypsies. In the annual report for 1979, the council noted that the "disinfection of 231 persons" was one of the few things that "really achieved something." Ironically, although 30,000 forints had been found for this spectacular, anticarnival festival of order, the council's annual report admitted that "despite several resolutions, the building of a public toilet at the Duranda settlement still has not been done."[75] And six years later, council officials were still citing plans to build a porcelain factory as the reason for refusing to pipe water to houses in the Third Class.

Gypsies, Peasants, and Communists

Quite contrary to all official intentions, throughout the time that the Hungarian Communist Party pursued its Gypsy policy, popular hostility toward the Gypsies grew. Ordinary Magyars saw local councils "diverting" resources toward this "deviant" minority, and the less the policy changed anything, the more officials and citizens alike felt that money was being thrown away. A taxi driver I met in October 1985 explained why he would not take me home to the Third Class: "I hate the Gypsies. I don't think I've ever met a single reasonable one. You know what I say, I'd gather them all together, take them out on the square, and shoot them. They are in charge here now; they wander through the town as though

Living from trade was illegal without a special permit. At a market, police check the work documents of Gypsy traders.

they ruled it; they parade like kings. Not one of them, *not one* works. They live from handouts and theft. And then they build these big houses from their wheeling and dealing with horses." At one point during a visit to the council offices, I suggested, while trying to make polite conversation about the Gypsies, that under socialism "conditions had improved," and I was rather taken aback when the officer I was chatting with leaned over the table and said with real venom, "Yes, indeed, *for them and how very much!*" What was really needed, he felt, were drastic measures to curb the Gypsies' freedom, to put an end to their position "beyond the law."

Behind all this anger lay a curious perception among ordinary Hungarians that the Communists themselves were, in effect, people with a Gypsy mentality. Unlike a diligent Magyar person with "things to do," the Communist officials had "nothing to do/make" but spent their time calculating which way the wind was blowing and orienting themselves accordingly to benefit from policy changes. Moreover, as we saw in relation to the factory, the Communists had brought into being a social system in which bargaining, negotiation, and use of one's personal connections were essential at all moments and levels of social life, from the definition of one's job,[76] to promotion, to the taxes one paid on second incomes. Again, Bell's ethnography of neighboring "Lapos" provides striking evidence of the way this thinking worked. One villager told Bell that the Gypsies were taking over the village, while another made a slightly more poignant point, claiming that "now the people [Magyars] are Gypsy."[77] By this he meant that in the socialist world, the way to get by was through "carrying on like a Gypsy" (*cigánykodás*). Bell defined this as "worming oneself into the good graces of the leadership through ingratiation, two-facedness, betraying fellow workers, flattery, holding back complaints, granting sexual favours, or, expressed metaphorically 'licking upward and spitting (or kicking) downward.'"[78] Of the people who ran the village's cooperative farm it was said, "They don't do any work; they just order people around," and members of the farm believed that job allocation and access to privileges depended on "standing close to the fire."[79] Whatever the real situation (and Bell showed that a new, strict cooperative chairman replacing a corrupt one altered behavior without upsetting the ideological stereotypes), it was thought that in this world it was not a person's labor that advanced him but his contacts. Despite official rhetoric, work and its product had less value now than in the capitalist past. Instead, the Communist hustlers at the top of the social pile seemed to be disproportionately helping the Gypsy hustlers at the bottom of society.[80] As the collective farm doctor put it, while ticking off Šošoj about his fodder problems: "The Gypsies are the only free people left in this country. You don't have to work. . . . You move around as you wish." Turning to me, the doctor added, "You've chosen your subject well—you know, this is the land of the Gypsies!"[81]

From the Rom's point of view, the exact opposite seemed to be the case. As the father of the family I lived with never ceased telling me, the Communists were merely old-fashioned peasants, *gaźos* rewritten. In the prewar years, the *csendőr* (police; literally, keeper of peace) had demanded to see the "passes" (*passzus*) permitting the Gypsies to travel to market; in the new world the *rendőr* (police; literally, keeper of order) demanded proof of "regular income." But to the old man it was all the same: The *gaźo* authorities all looked down on the Rom and tried to prevent them from carrying on their "Gypsy work." The Communists had, despite their rhetoric, reproduced residential segregation and treated the Rom as uncivilized barbarians in schools and health institutions. And while Magyar involvement in the second economy was encouraged by council officers, when Gypsies tried to negotiate better economic conditions for themselves, they were treated as unruly hustlers and legal obstacles were placed in their way.[82]

In this hall of distorting mirrors, where nothing was what it was made out to be, the choice of how to live was inevitably a troublesome matter, as Gypsy families well knew. In the next and final chapter of this part, I return to Čoro's and Luludji's dilemma: to live with the brothers or to seek a way out.

8

STAYING GYPSY IN A WORLD OF GAŻOS

I LEFT THE STORY OF ČORO'S AND LULUDJI'S progress just as they had been transferred to "proper housing," in a stairwell with Magyars, on a well-serviced block of flats. They had fulfilled all the conditions for full council housing, having proved to doubting council officials their willingness to leave the Gypsy way of life behind them. Were they going to take the next step and abandon their community?

"My Heart Was Cut in Two"

Whereas moving to the Chicken Plot had been only a small step away from their old life, the move into a Magyar stairwell looked like the beginning of a decisive shift in relation to their family and community. One council officer, with a little personal experience of life in the Chicken Plot, told me that she thought Čoro and Luludji would find the break from the intense communal life difficult. But the social advantages of assimilation were so self-apparent to her that she never doubted that they would continue the journey, however painful, toward full social integration with their Magyar neighbors.

To some extent Luludji and Čoro shared these hopes. Luludji put it this way: "We wanted to live another kind of life . . . because we were aware that there is a different way of living. The only thing the other Gypsies know about is the rotten old world of the past. That awful old world. When we lived in the housing development, among the peasants, I took off my Gypsy clothes, my scarf, my apron. I even gave up walking around with a sack [*gono*] on my back—so the peasants wouldn't know that we were Gypsies." This last gesture, giving up the sack, was tantamount to resigning her activity as a Gypsy woman, since carrying a sack was the public sign of her scavenging, and it was this that ideologically defined a Gypsy woman's economic activity to *gaźo* and Rom alike.

The new life among the Magyars was hard: "Only peasants lived there. I think they were scared of us because we were Gypsies. At first they thought that a family of poor, dirty Gypsies was moving in, with lots and lots of children. But when they came to our house and looked in, they saw that we are a different kind of Gypsy, different from the majority." Luludji was then shocked and discouraged to find that, despite her efforts, the neighbors "still thought that we'd take up the parquet flooring and burn it, then that we'd let the bath flood, that I'd leave the water running!"

Isolated among people who profoundly mistrusted them, Luludji and Čoro nonetheless held out for over a year. "After a while some people began to be friendly with us. But still they wouldn't come into our house. They would greet us in the street. But most people were still scared of us because we were Gypsies." Then in summer 1987 they decided to burn the boats of integration and return to the Third Class. Luludji, who had so long wanted to lead a more petty bourgeois lifestyle, conceded: "I didn't really feel well there. I was always on my own; Čoro would go off to work, and the children would go to school, and I was always bored. In fact, much of my time I spent in the Third Class. I felt much better out in the settlement." When she visited her in-laws, she said: "My heart was cut in two when I saw the Gypsy women sitting by the fire in the evening as we left them there. I felt so alone." But it was through their children that Čoro and Luludji most felt the contradictions of their situation: "The children didn't like that home. When we lived there, we'd go back to visit the old people. We would say to the children, 'Come back with us.' I'd call them, but they'd say: 'Ah! We're not going back with you. Where do you want to take us? Back to that prison? Why do you want to keep us locked up in that house? All we can see there are the four walls.'" Luludji did not say so on tape, but their children were not welcome among the Magyar children, and the other Gypsy children in the development came from poor Romungro families, not ones with whom the socially aspirant Luludji wished her children to associate.

At first the return to the Third Class was troubled. "I really hated leaving the council house because we had hot water in the winter and there's so much mud in the Third Class. I really missed [literally, pitied] that house, but since then things have come into place in all kinds of ways, and now [one year later] I can't say I miss the old council house."

Čoro and Luludji's position in the Third Class had been transformed by the fact that they had been able to sell their rights in the council house back to the state. With the profit from this, they were able to buy their own house for the first time and, to other Rom, represent their earlier departure from the settlement as a highly successful ploy. They thus bought out the previous, somewhat debauched *gaźo* neighbors of Čoro's parents. The building apparently stank, and Luludji spent many an hour bleaching and disinfecting the rooms, but by midsummer the redecoration was completed, and Čoro and Luludji moved back, fifteen yards away from where they had set out three years earlier. Luludji next found a job in the kitchen of the local food warehouse. Having been thrown off the hotel's lists for her scavenging, she relished the "privilege" of being allowed to work in the food chain again. Čoro continued at the parquet factory and began to rebuild their new home, adding a verandah and two new clean room areas, and like other wealthier residents of the settlement, he was soon talking of installing a shower and washing area.

If the Communists' assimilation program had had any chance of working, it was the Gypsies who attempted to leave their communities that the authorities had to win over. In Šošoj's and Čaja's case, though there was never any intention on their part to sever all relations with the Rom, the fact that they felt isolated and rejected in Dongó meant that their experience there only confirmed their desire to remain Rom. Their only other option would have been to follow the Romungros up the blind alley of quasi-assimilation. So more than these prosperous Rom, Čoro and Luludji represented precisely the sort of Gypsies at whom the Communist campaign was aimed. Indeed, in conversations I had with employees of the council, Mr. and Mrs. G. Kolompár, as they were known on official papers, were often cited as model Gypsies. György Kolompár's records showed that he had an unbroken work history and that he had even been nominated as an "outstanding worker" in the Socialist Labor Competition in his factory. Just as the official theory predicted, it seemed that as a result of his experience of integration into the proletariat, he had seen the value of accepting Magyar values and full integration into Magyar society; moving into a housing development dominated by Magyar families was the logical consequence. These council officers took comfort from the thought that Čoro and Luludji would soon cease to wear distinguishable Gypsy clothes for their day-to-day wear. They would speak more and more Hungarian at home and would ensure that their children completed more than the minimum schooling. Their Gypsy culture (dress, songs, and so on) would become a folklore, a colorful reminder of the past. From Monday to Friday and on the occasional Communist Saturday, they would be workers like any Magyar, but on Sundays and holidays they would relive their past and become Gypsies again for a day, rather as Hungarian youths spend their weekend evenings beating out the dances of their peasant ancestors on the floors of the urban dance halls. But the authorized version of "modernization" was not to be.

The fact that these "willing Gypsies" had turned their backs on assimilation shows how deeply Communist policy had failed. Luludji and her family returned to a settlement where new building was forbidden on pain of substantial fines, where there was no running water, and where the stigma of living as a Cigány clung to the entire family. And although Luludji was soon happy with the home that Čoro had built for her, she remained ashamed to tell people away from the settlement where she lived. Moreover, she did not even have the comfort and prestige of a couple like Šošoj and Čaja as compensation. Despite the enormous economic and social hardship associated with this choice, Čoro and Luludji had remained persuaded that living as Rom offered them, and their children, a more viable way of life than did assimilating among the *gażos*.

The Real and the Imaginary

In assessing Čoro's and Luludji's decision, one should not forget that there has always been movement away from the Gypsy communities, that there have always been individuals and groups that have left the Gypsy way behind, just as there has at times been an opposite movement. But in the past two hundred years, if only to improve their material conditions and evade persecution, over two-thirds of all the Gypsies have given up or attempted to give up the Gypsy way, as the decline in the use of Romany suggests. These pressures, which had operated on the Romungros, continued throughout the Communist period, and in some contexts almost all Gypsies would express a wish to get out of the ghetto. The authors of a 1986 report on Gypsies living in the county around Harangos stated that, of four hundred families asked if they wanted to continue living in a Gypsy settlement, only eight had said "yes."[1]

The following published account of life on a poorer settlement in the 1960s makes clear one of the main reasons for this movement:

> We slept on straw on the floor, covering ourselves with coats. In the winter we built a stove out of mud bricks. Our hut must have been five by four meters large, with eight of us living in it. Our only piece of furniture was a planked bed. Us children weren't even allowed to sit on it, since it was kept for important guests. Only my father earned money. He worked in the forest. He'd walk eighteen kilometers a day to bring back a bit more for the hungry mouths. My mother went hawking and begging in the neighboring villages. Sometimes when she was lucky, she found temporary work. We never once lived well. . . . There was no point regretting the passing of this life. Lots of us thought like this at the time. In 1973 they began to wind up the settlement. Together with my wife we decided we were going to lead a life more fit for human beings. That's how it began.[2]

Undeniably, Čoro and Luludji were driven to leave the settlement in part by the difficulty of living without running water, tarmac roads, and other conveniences. But in some respects they were pushed out of Gypsy society by contradictions inherent in the Rom way of life. There were the contradictions I explored in Chapter 5 between the ethic of brotherly sharing and that of the household. But there were other conflicts concerning the viability of what one might call the whole Rom project. In the celebrations of the men, in their talk after markets, in the rhetoric of everyday life, the Romany-speaking Gypsies of Harangos defined themselves as people who did not produce but who made their living through their wit, their speech, their ability to hustle, their Gypsy work. But they were unable to survive by this alone and were thoroughly dependent on the wages earned in factories, where they were engaged, however peripherally, in productive processes. Without the labor of production, most Gypsy families in the Third Class would have lived in heartrending poverty. Some would have starved.

Another ethnographer of the Gypsies has said that "a massive extension of waged labor could herald the death of the Rom as a separate people from the *gažos*."[3] Given the Rom's economic ethic this would seem, a priori, to make sense. But in Hungary, and the rest of Eastern Europe, the Gypsies became proletarians and yet stayed Rom. It remains to be explained how they surmounted this contradiction: How they worked as laborers but imagined themselves as living from *romani butji*.

When Čoro and Luludji were faced with accepting their "objective" conditions and becoming workers living among other workers as Magyars or, alternatively, returning to the "imaginary" world of their family and community, they hesitated, but only briefly. They were not alone in this choice. In the years of my fieldwork and afterward, houses that were sold in the Third Class always had competing Gypsy buyers— to live there was, in a sense, a privilege compared to the lot of those Gypsies who lived in the Chicken Plot or similar settlements.

In the next and final part of the book, I show how the Rom sustained an image of a viable life. In particular, I argue that in certain carefully defined contexts their dependence on the *gažos* was symbolically reworked as autonomy, and domination by the Magyars was reversed so that it was the Rom who seemed to hold power. Or, put most abstractly, production and reproduction were symbolically denied so that the Rom could live from their unique sort of work.

Part Three

THE REINVENTION OF THE WORLD

9

SONS OF THE MARKET

We deal with horses; it's in our hair. I grew up with horses, and I simply couldn't live without them. I'm completely used to having them by me, although, as you know, they don't work for us. We keep the horses rather than the horses keeping us. We could put the money to other uses, for instance, to buy the children what they need. But, you see, with horses it's like, if one hasn't got them, others say, "Let God strike him down; he's just like a poor Romungro who hasn't got anything." That's why I have horses. Not just me but the Rom in general. We go to the markets, we sell and we buy, we swap: We know how to do it.

Šošoj

THROUGHOUT THE PERIOD OF FIFTEEN MONTHS when I first lived in the Third Class I remained almost oblivious to much of the world I have described in Part 2 of this book: the school, the hospital, the social services department. Most odd, though, is the fact that I managed to ignore the world of the factory, though I knew that all my friends spent their days laboring. My own attitude, it seems to me now, reflected the concerns of the Rom. They might have complained as they walked past my front door in the morning that they were going off to "suffer" again in the factory, but little other reference was made to this crucial part of their lives. The world that obsessed me and captivated my attention was that which the Rom wanted to show me: the world of horses and their owners.

The Rom talked of few things with such passion as their horses. Of all the Gypsies' trading activities, it was buying and selling horses that were most prototypically "Gypsy work." Whenever I visited Rom I was soon taken by the men to inspect and photograph their horses, with the men

141

of the household standing around and the young boys set up on the back of a new purchase. When I visited again I would be asked whether the horse had grown larger, its hair shinier, and its manner more alert in the time it had been in this man's hands. Horses were intimately associated with their owner's persona, so only tiny children and the innocent anthropologist were allowed to tease men that their horses were not "quite perfect."

But—and this is the paradox that I try to explain in this chapter—as the Rom would admit in their calmer moments, it was they who kept the horses rather than vice versa. From a strictly economic point of view, keeping horses was bad business. And yet the trade in horses was celebrated not as a hobby but as the best means of making money. Why?

The traditional explanation for the Gypsies' passionate involvement with these animals is pragmatic: Gypsies travel; therefore they keep horses and celebrate this symbol of their freedom.[1] But the Hungarian Rom have not traveled for forty years and associate their nomadic past with miserable poverty. So that is unlikely to explain their emotional investment. Nonetheless, part of the answer is certainly historical.

In Magyar village life, as in many other parts of Europe, the horse had a special importance as an animal of traction, as well as of gentlemanly distinction, an importance it still had in the 1980s. In the past those who worked with horses invariably had higher status in a village than those who plowed with cattle and oxen, since these latter animals were the reserve of the lowly manorial servants. It was said that anyone could learn to plow with cattle or oxen, but it was only a true or "proper" peasant who could use horses. Successful peasants told Fél and Hofer that "one could recognize a genuine born peasant by his bearing when driving through the village—by the way he held the whip in his hand," and the sheer snob value of being a successful horse-keeper meant that Fél and Hofer had to fill twenty-seven pages of notes with the details of whip etiquette alone![2] The horse's unique place in the peasants' moral economy was institutionalized in the custom of the *gazda* "inheriting a certain breed of horse from his father and bequeathing the same to his children," a practice marked by the branding of such animals with a family sign.[3] These animals were not put into the markets where poorer families were forced to take their animals each year. If the Rom found a way to dominate the peasants in dealing with horses, they would have achieved a particularly rich symbolic victory over their adversaries.[4]

Horses, Men, and Rom

While living in the Third Class, one could not help but notice the special, elevated place of horses (*grast*) in Gypsy life. Day in and day out men planned deals involving horses, going in the most minute detail through every gesture of the deal. Before every proud horse owner stood the possibility of a Big Deal, one really earth-shattering break that would bring a huge profit, as in the weekly lotto in which all the Rom participated. But there was also something else about horses beyond their potential for making money. As Zeleno put it to me: "You can't ride cows. Horses go like *this* [and he made a graceful gesture with his hand]; they make one's good mood [*voja*]; they know how to move. You can't bridle up a cow. Nor can you sing about cows. It's only in Hungarian songs that you find them singing about cows!"

Although at any one time only one-third of all households was keeping a horse, and in 1985 only half the men of the Third Class bought a horse, the ideal of trading in horses was strong for all the Rom I knew, with two exceptions: One was known as the *gaźo*, and the other had another line of trade. The Rom valued dealing in horses to the extent that this activity, unlike most others, could justify the absence of a man from the key Rom social event, their celebrations. I once took a man away from such a gathering to inquire about a horse for sale. On the way back, he took me on a detour past a municipal garbage dump to search for plastic sheeting, but before we returned to the party, he made me swear that I would not tell anyone where we had just been—he was, he said, "ashamed" (*laźavman*) of having stayed away for this sort of scavenging.

Once a Gypsy man had bought a horse, it was understood that this was his most important possession. For a while Čoro's brother did not have a stable and kept his foal at the neighboring house of his brother-in-law.[5] But Čoro said that he could not sleep properly without his filly at his side, that she was "like a child to him," and so he rebuilt the side of his house to allow her space beside his bedroom.

Although men would relinquish a horse at the drop of a coin or two, it was an unspeakable humiliation to be forced to sell or to lose one's horse. Čoro's father, Kannji, had bought a horse on delayed payment from Čepi, a poor old man who lived on the other side of the Third Class. When Kannji was unable to make the final payment, Čepi announced that he would have to demand the return of the horse if his money was not forthcoming. That afternoon I happened to be going to the village of Csóka, where Kannji's wealthiest son lived with his wife and her family, and I was commissioned to tell the young man that his father was "about to lose his horse." The effect was dramatic. Both the son and his father-in-law immediately offered to produce the 3,000 forints that were needed to pay off Čepi. For similar reasons when one morning a man's horse died a sudden and unexpected death, all the Rom of the Third Class paid a visit to his home to commiserate, including members of two normally hostile families. If cows or pigs had died, no one would have bothered.[6]

If a horse could stand for its owner, this was partly because horses were seen as the closest of all animals to their human masters. Sitting one evening with an old man on the meadow outside his house, we watched another man's horse find its way back to its yard from grazing and then enter its stable. Old Mošulo chuckled and pointed out to me that it went home "like a person" (*sar ekh manuš*). Comments about the intelligence and good sense of horses were so common that I gave up noting them. Horses were the cleanest animals and would refuse to lie in their dung. They would drink only the purest water direct from the standing tap in the middle of the settlement and eat the cleanest fodder. They were, as the Rom said approvingly, "fussy" (*kenješo*). It was hard not to hear in this praise of their favorite animal a celebration of themselves. Horses were peculiarly sensitive to the human world. They were the only animals apart from humans that could see the human dead, and disturbances in the stables around midnight were taken as a sign of a ghostly visit. This was one reason for keeping horses in "pairs," or with a "friend" (*amal*), as it was put in Romany, since they would then not be scared. Horses with black markings were also aware when a Gypsy died elsewhere and in this case would come to a sudden halt on the road. If a white animal stopped, this was because it had actually seen ghosts in front of it on the road.

In these ways horses contrasted to "cows" (*gurumni*), which many Rom also kept at various times of the year. Cows were unbothered by cleanliness, willing to eat dusty fodder, happy to wallow in their own feces, and, above all, incapable of the kind of empathetic relation with humans that horses were said to have. "The thing about cows," Šošoj said, "is that you can breed them and can sell one within five weeks of birth." Somehow, and despite the obvious financial benefits of keeping cows, this made them less interesting to the Rom. Being the cleanest and best of all animals, horses were allowed into the houses of poorer Gypsies, at least. Whereas the "dirty" cats that slept in the lofts were not allowed so much as through the porch, two poor men quite happily converted their larders into temporary stables for their horses.

Considering this symbolic association of horses and Rom, we could answer the question as to why Gypsies dealt in horses by saying that it was a marker of the Gypsies' status as a distinct ethnic group and that therefore financial considerations did not count. This was certainly true. But this line of reasoning locks us into a closed analytical circle and only paraphrases Gypsy symbolism at its simplest level without revealing any of the specific pleasures for the Gypsies of dealing in horses, as opposed to any other object. For instance, this reasoning fails to explain why the Rom bought and sold horses rather than keeping them and breeding them. If instead we think about what the Rom actually *did* with horses, we can get beyond the sterile opposition of "economic interest" and "culture." Through acting on horses, the Rom acted on the world, tried to shape it and their relations with the *gažos,* as well as relations among themselves. But what was it about their activity on the market that made dealing in horses so pleasurable? How did the Rom relate to each other and to non-Rom as a result of having horses?

Market Society

Each "market" (*foro*) could be seen as a temporary microcosm of a social world based on commodity exchange. At first sight it seemed as if each individual faced the others as an autonomous actor making his own decisions and deals to maximize his advantage. But if one stepped outside the framework of the individual deal and looked at the whole day's trading, it became immediately obvious that the market as a whole had rhythms, shifts of atmosphere, and activity that could not have been the result of hundreds of entirely separate and autonomous decisions by all those individuals. There was, it seems, an extraordinary social order underlying the individual acts of all those people. As if acknowledging the inherently social nature of the market, the Rom preferred to work together in teams. By doing so, the Rom contributed more than anyone to the spectacular fluxes in activity that characterized market days. There were moments of chaotic activity—when boys driving horses scattered spectators with their warning cries and crowds formed and closed in on dealers who slapped hands, shouted, and then sometimes passed money—and also sudden calms when there was no focus for anyone's attention, the crowd dissipated, and each individual moved off in his own direction. It was said then that "the market's standing still" (*áll a vásár*).

There were various important distinctions operating at the fairs. Pigs, cattle, and horses all had their own area of the field, and dealings in the former two were concluded quickly with little fuss or bargaining. Invariably, these sections of the market were empty long before the horse area even began to clear. Apart from livestock, there was always a "stalled market" (*kirakodo*) of manufactured goods and "fast-food stands" (*laci konyhák*), at that time mostly run by Romungro families.

Exchanges between Gypsy and Magyar or between Rom and Rom, which could be categorically described as "sales" and "swaps," respectively, also tended to be grouped toward the beginning and end of the day. Between these two moments there was a lull. In the last hours of the day before the police cleared the Rom from the square, on most occasions there were crowds of Gypsy men circling between the bars and the field trying, even at the last moment before the horses were led back onto the trucks, to set up a deal with each other over their remaining horses. More than once I saw trucks return and a man leading a horse back down off the truck to try concluding an exchange in the closing minutes of the market.

The Rom behaved in all horse trading with a theatrical and flamboyant air, regardless of whom they were dealing with. Whereas the Rom seemed thoroughly at home on the market, absorbed and passionate in their dealings, the peasants, who commonly adopted a bored, phlegmatic manner, very often appeared ill at ease with the rhetorical displays of their adversaries. Among the self-styled "sons of the market" (*foroske śave*), there were noticeable personalities who attracted the attention of much greater crowds on the field than others, men who seemed to occupy center stage, while other lesser men dealt in the wings beside their carts. It is by following around two such leading players that I want to begin exploring the nature of the market process. To observe Zeleno and Šošoj is to open the door on the whole world of Gypsy trade with horses, a world rather different from our familiar "reality" of buyers, sellers, prices, profits, and losses.

However, before moving to the market field, I want to say a word about the place of these markets in the Hungarian economy. After being all but eliminated in the darkest period of Stalinist terror in the 1950s, the animal trade had slowly revived, and by the time I attended the livestock fairs in 1984–1985, they were impressive affairs easily filling the whole market field. At a large market in the center of the country in May, there were four hundred or more horses for sale.[7] The one big change from an earlier time was in the position of the Gypsies, who by the mid-1980s seemed in virtual control of the movement of horses in Hungary. At the markets I attended, never less than one-half and often as many as two-thirds of the animals brought to the fairs came with the Gypsies. Only twenty years earlier, according to local veterinary doctors, only a few of the horses brought to market in the Harangos area, at least, were in Gypsy hands. Then Gypsy men would come to market and throw their money together at the start of day when they could buy a horse cheap. Later in the day, it would make them a small profit. The social distance traversed by the Rom in a generation seems all the greater in that the relative value of horses had not, as far as I could tell, dropped in the intervening period. The continued importance of household plots, alongside other undercapitalized forms of private agricultural production, and increased private hauling in rural areas meant that demand had remained high. In the standardized terms by which elderly Magyar peasants reckoned horse-price inflation, the traditional 2 hectoliters of wine that had been the equivalent of a top-quality horse remained the accurate figure in 1985.[8] It is time now to visit one of these markets where the Rom and peasants "came up for air," to use Braudel's image, from the dank, "hidden abode" of production.[9]

A Day at the Market

I was awakened at 4 A.M. to set off with my passengers to what promised to be one of the biggest markets of the year, at Nagykőrös in the heart of the Hungarian plain. The horses would travel in front of us in a truck that had belonged to the now-defunct animal hospital at Eger. A friendly young Magyar who trained foals for riding schools drove the ambulance and helped pack the horses onto it. At the market he used his time to find potential customers for himself. Since five or six horses could be packed into the truck, costs were kept low for the Rom at 300 to 500 forints per round trip and 100 more each to the car driver.

Even in June the air was still cold as we waited in the dark for the horses to be loaded—a tense moment as one slip on the steep ramp might break a horse's leg. I had been asked to keep space in my car for two single women, my brother's wife, who needed to sell thread in order to pay for a lawyer to defend her imprisoned son, and a relative of hers with other business. But just as we were about to leave, two old Gypsy men from the far end of town appeared. They had heard I might have space, and since they were going to buy horses and not "merely sell thread," the two women were brusquely turned out of the car to follow by train. Their muttered complaints were silenced by one of my new passengers cursing "the market whores" (*vásári kurva*). As we drove off, he continued in his outraged tone about these women, who pretended they were at the market to sell thread but, he imagined, spent the afternoon giving themselves to the available men.

It was an odd-looking party that stepped out of my car at the first open bar we found on the way. Šošoj was dressed in his smart, circa 1940s militia leather coat; his brother-in-law Zeleno, in a suit; and the two older men, in polished leather boots, breeches, and checked jackets cut in the "English" style. Each of the men had newly combed and twirled his bushy mustache and wore a hat to suit his style. Šošoj and Zeleno wore identical light-blue straw trilbies with a dashing feather, while the older men had more somber felt homburgs decorated with a thick green ribbon. Čaja, who was traveling ahead in the ambulance, had respectfully covered her head with a scarf tied, as always in public, under the chin. For display, Pati, one of the older men, had his stick, which later in the day he would use to beat the ground in outrage as his offers were refused. At my insistence, he put his whip in the boot for our general protection.

Our journey was slow, since the men insisted on traveling directly behind the horse van "in case anything should happen." Nightmare scenarios of the back door breaking open and the horses leaping or falling from the moving van were cited to justify what seemed to me paranoia. We arrived at the market late enough to have to leave the ambulance in a long line of trucks waiting to unload their cargoes down the specially constructed ramp. By this time local peasants and Rom were arriving on their horse carts. The Rom were often accompanied by five or six young men standing crowded behind the driver's board, an imposing sight.

As the dawn mists lifted and overnight tents were being folded up, the market slowly came to life. Gypsy women with business of their own selling nylon thread, rubber gloves, mats, or even fake Rolex watches set up their sales spot near the stalled section of the market beside some poor peasant men who were selling bric-a-brac on blankets at their feet. Those few women who had come with no business of their own went off with their daughters to find relatives. They would then gather at the back of a horse cart or truck, keeping out of the way of their menfolk while the dealing went on.

It was still a few hours before the cries and shouts of the dealers would ring through the air, so Šošoj and Zeleno wandered slowly around the market to see what was being "done." At this stage they looked mostly at horses held by the *gaźos*. Šošoj and Zeleno looked at horses as objects of exchange, so the major constraint was their range of contacts and knowledge of different markets. In the hilly areas of northern Hungary, for instance, heavy and powerful horses were needed by the *gaźos*.

Although later in the day when the Rom dealt among themselves, the horses were handled almost as religious fetishes, for the first few hours of trade during which the Gypsies tried to deal with peasants, the horses were treated simply as commodities, conceived of as stores of monetary value and so measurable in that abstract symbol of human relations, the price. There were, however, several stages of dealing to be gone through before the precise fixing of a simple numerical figure could be achieved.

While circling round the market, Šošoj and Zeleno met a relative from the village of Csóka, and amid greetings to each other for "a lucky day," they were called away to drink at one of the bars beside the fast-food stalls. Two or three "halfs," that is, 5 centiliters, of one of the fruit brandies were put away, but all the men restrained themselves, knowing full well that more than one bad deal had been made at market while drunk. At the bar the Gypsy men heard what other people had brought to market, what they were "doing" (*kerel*). Šošoj announced that he was at last selling his pair of dapple gray cart horses. Zeleno was looking for a replacement for a horse he had just put to slaughter. Šošoj's wife's relative, Dinka, who had just then arrived, joined Šošoj on a renewed tour of the market. Later they might "help" each other out more actively by swapping their own animals, but for the time being they simply accompanied each other.

A while later Zeleno, by now alone, found a slightly diminutive horse he was interested in. Its owner was away, but under another peasant's

Čerbo (center), dressed for battle, cajoles a peasant (right) into buying one of his horses. (D. Lan)

eye Zeleno began his inspection. Starting with the mouth and legs, he thoroughly checked the horse for signs of disease or other damage. This was a task that demanded considerable knowledge, a good eye, and patience. The first thing to know about a horse was its age, since this helped determine the uses to which the animal could be put and thus the potential market for it.[10] As the old Hungarian and English saying "Don't look a gift horse in the mouth" suggests, it was by the teeth of a horse (their number and condition) that its age and therefore value were determined. Mastering this art was a source of pride to the Rom—I was often told that there was not a single *gažo* who could reliably tell a horse's age—and sometimes they inspected horses just for fun before checking the accuracy of their estimate with the owner. On this occasion Zeleno was in no doubt: This mare was just turning seven. He moved on to her legs, her most important asset. Feeling the front ones by the side of the tendons, and both at the ankle and higher up the back legs, he checked for "swellings" (*pók*), the telltale sign that the horse had been overused, possibly fatally.

By this point the owner, a peasant from a village south of Nagykőrös, had returned, and Zeleno gestured, suggesting that the horse was no doubt completely wild. As if on cue, the owner protested that his wife

Gypsy women selling the peasants nylon thread to tie up vines. The thread was scavenged from an industrial waste dump.

and daughter walked around the horse's legs and fed her. He insisted on lifting the leg and then held it with ease in his arm to display how gently one could handle his foal. As he said, reverting to the seller's habitual rhetoric, "This is all that really counts" (*csak ez számít*). Zeleno said that he knew this sort of horse, quipping "it keeps its kick for when you're shoeing it."

On this occasion Zeleno was spared the jousting over claims for the animal's temperament, strength, and eating habits. He was also serious about buying this horse, it seemed, for having walked the horse round a little to watch the movement of its legs, he asked if the horse could be "tested" (in Hungarian, *kiprobálja*; in Romany, *zumavel la*). The "trial," in which a horse was made to drag a cart with chain or rope tied around its wheels to brake it, was the real test of the strength and stamina of a horse. Transporters in Hungary might well carry 2,000 kilograms, or more, over mud tracks, and so the trial was no idle display. Quite frequently, other Rom betted on the trial, the challenger calling out in Hungarian, "He won't do it," deliberately upping the ante.

There were no conventions as to when bargaining began, and offers might be made or demanded at any time. Once a Gypsy approached a peasant and asked him what his "last price" on a particular animal would be. "You haven't heard the first yet!" replied the peasant. "Ah, but we know what that would be!" came back the Gypsy, pointing out that a price asked in this fashion was a price in the abstract and bore little relation to the figure arrived at during a serious request. Sometimes sellers would refuse to answer requests for a price "in general terms," saying, "You'll see when it comes to it." No one liked to make the first move, and both Zeleno and the peasant demanded that the other "name a price" (*mondjon egy árat*). Zeleno waited stubbornly. "I've got money" (*pénz van*), he said slightly cheekily, patting his hand on his pocket as if to prove it.

To open the bargaining was to initiate the risky process of evaluation, which was always also a self-evaluation. If after two or three assertions of "first price" neither party had "moved," the deal reached stalemate and the men separated, cursing each other for lack of serious intent. Making an offer or request demanded a dramatic gesture: The seller might take the hand of the buyer in his left hand and slap his own hand into it, saying, "Give me 45" (45,000 forints). Then pulling his hand back in a grand upward loop opening out over his head and ending back at waist level with his palm up, he waited for the return "cut" (*śinel*). As Zeleno put it to me one day: "We like to strike our hands. For us, this makes trade. . . . It warms our ears!" As each slap rang out, the onlookers knew that here money might be made. This theatrical gesture was repeated by each side throughout the bargaining. In this way Zeleno's seller asked for a respectable 40,000. Zeleno would not pay that and said he doubted anyone else would. He offered 32 and was met with a sneering "Let me hear a serious price," but Zeleno was off without looking back. Sometimes such brusque manners spelled the end of an exchange, but this day Zeleno's rough patience paid off.

Šošoj, meanwhile, was having no luck with his cart horses. A week earlier he had nearly sold them to the local forestry company, but like other agricultural companies, it was mechanizing and was hesitant about taking on two such classically massive animals. At Nagykőrös, however, no one seemed to have the financial resources to make an offer that would even scrape Šošoj's minimum. Just as I turned up, I saw him lightly stroke a man's palm with his fingertips and turn his own hand, palm up, waiting for a return. "Say something," he said (*mondjon valamit*), but to no avail. His son-in-law, Lapoś, then turned up and tied his horse to the side of the ambulance, where he could leave it under Čaja's watchful eye. Zeleno had also returned and, mentioning the animal he had seen, took a small party of Rom back with him to initiate another round of dealing. First, however, they went to the bar to talk some more, while Zeleno showed Šošoj the horse from a distance.

It was not until after 10:30, four hours after we had arrived and after several more rounds of drinks had been consumed, with a consequent heating up of the atmosphere, that the second round of Zeleno's bargaining began. When he now approached the peasant, accompanied this time by several relatives and myself, a crowd of onlookers gathered to watch. In the contest that was market dealing, both parties knew there was a premium on displaying wit, on keeping up good relations with the other, on always appearing the more generous party while never quite dropping the hint of fierceness and even aggression toward the other. Men who were not willing to perform in such situations could never feel at home on the market, like certain non-Gypsies I knew who used the market as a place to find interesting horses and then visited the sellers at home, to deal personally out of the public eye.

Zeleno had slightly offended the would-be seller earlier by walking off, but Šošoj took up the case, reminding the peasant that he had come to market to sell a horse, not to take it home, and here he had a "real buyer" (*komoly vevő*). Twice the peasant refused to move from 38, and Zeleno's helpers teased the peasant that he did not really want to sell. Zeleno was now saying that 36 was his "last price," adding, "You'll never find a buyer like me." He cursed in Romany, for the sake of his Gypsy helpers, on his very life that he would not "put" any more on the mare, but then the peasant took 1,000 off the price, and Zeleno paused. Šošoj took him aside and whispered something, and when Zeleno came back, he lifted a thin wad of green notes from his back pocket and began to count. First he counted into the hand of the Hungarian, and then the seller counted out again into his market neighbor's hand. Šošoj was passed 500 by Zeleno as his "fee," and the deal was completed. As the horse was unbridled, Zeleno asked for the handling rope with toggle (*kötő kötél*) to lead the horse. The peasant refused at first but conceded when his "market neighbor" told him this was "a very old custom." Knowing that this kind of meanness was so very typical of Gypsy-Magyar relations, I wondered if the seller was just being spiteful.

Once the horse was tied, Zeleno joined his helpers at the bar for a "drink to bless the deal." Occasionally when the Rom bought from a peasant, or more likely from a wagoner whom they knew well, buyer and seller would share this drink, the receiver of money normally buying the round, but on this occasion it was the group of Rom who drank alone. The two old men who had come with us in the morning came over and wished Zeleno luck with his new horse. Šošoj meanwhile had started complaining that without a horse cart to show off his animals, his had been a wasted day.

Some peasants were now beginning to leave the market, but not the Rom, and so I wandered off to observe some of the other dealers at work.

There in the middle of the market, in a long alley of trucks, the great Gypsy dealer Čerbo, from Budapest, was at work. Čerbo's presence dominated most markets he attended. He and his son performed a double act, one wearing down the other party by bellowing and haranguing and then the other stepping in as a figure of quiet reason. For a while, somewhat to the puzzlement of the Rom, Čerbo had been "running" a horse without any obvious buyer in view. Then a short while later, a large peasant showed some interest. Čerbo, it now became clear, had been playing drunk in order to encourage a buyer hopeful of a pushover deal. Carrying on this performance, Čerbo physically manhandled his potential customer, thrusting him at the animal, and then bellowed at his son to "drive" the horse. The young man turned the horse in the small crowd, whipping up a panic, and in so doing reinforced the sense that he and his father were scarcely in control of themselves. When the buyer wavered, Čerbo did not leave him to ponder but demanded to know what his problem was. He announced to the world in general that if anyone could find fault with this horse, he would hand it over free. Still frustrated by the recalcitrant peasant, he refused to sell the animal at all to that man and called out to someone else about another animal, attempting to humiliate the would-be buyer in front of the crowd. It was an odd thing about horse markets that everyone liked a deal. That was what the crowd was standing around waiting for, and so in all these ways Čerbo put pressure on the buyer to make a move, not to let the deal fall through, not to seem to be the one who failed to bring it off. Notwithstanding all this effort, Čerbo's bluff was called, and on this occasion the deal fell through.

The Economics of Horse Dealing

Although the horse had a central importance in Gypsy culture, the economic benefits of horse keeping for the average trader were, to say the least, dubious. A commonplace of male Gypsy rhetoric was that the Rom "live from horses" (*trajij anda lende*), but it was hardly an accurate representation of most men's experience, as Šošoj's quote at the beginning of this chapter suggests. The difficulties most Gypsy men had in making any money at all from horses had two sources. First, it was hard to organize one's entry to the market at the right time, since saving money was never easy for people who lived so close to poverty. Second, even after buying an animal and despite enormous knowledge of horses and skill as traders, most Rom were in a relatively disadvantaged position as dealers in a highly structured market.

Perhaps the strongest evidence of the weak entry position of most Rom is that in 1985, though more than half the adult men in the Third Class

Gypsy women labor to fatten pigs, which their husbands sell to support their horse deals.

had owned a horse at one time or other, most managed to launch their dealing for that year only by using money they had originally earned in wage labor in factories. In other words, horse trading was not self-sustaining; either men did not have any money left from their last horse sale, or they were having to supplement this with other nonhorse income. Šošoj, Thulo, and two other men living in the Third Class were the only exceptions. Most commonly, a man would have invested some part of his wages in raising piglets. Six fattened pigs, bought originally for 500 forints apiece, could be sold six or nine months later for as much as 30,000 forints. This pig money and the better part of another month's wages provided the means to acquire a horse of at least average quality.

However, even this way of raising the cash was not a risk-free business. It is true that pig sales were assured and that prices were fixed, but because the pigs that were available in Hungary were a "fast-breed" variety that grew best on commercial fodder, these selectively bred animals fared poorly in the rough conditions most Gypsy families kept them in. Čoro's father, Kannji, again provides a good case study. In October he had bought six growing pigs for 8,000 forints with an agricultural loan from the National Savings Bank. He had also purchased seven bags of feed for 4,500 forints. After that his wife had taken care of fattening the pigs using bread she scavenged in the rubbish bins of the town. Ideally, Kannji would have kept his pigs until the end of February or March, when they would have weighed in over 110 kilos each and brought him a total of some 28,000 forints, but at the beginning of January the demands of his family intervened. Čoro's younger brother, Urban, had a contract to deliver nine pigs to the state slaughterhouse, which he was in danger of reneging on, since he had only one large sow in his sties and three weeks until delivery. If he reneged, he would have to pay a penalty. Urban argued to his skeptical father that, since pig prices had risen after Christmas, by selling now he was doing better than he would have done only a month earlier. This argument was, of course, irrelevant, since Kannji had planned to keep his pigs until spring, but neither Kannji nor his wife wanted to sound mean by refusing to help their son. They were also swayed by the thought that an early delivery date would mean that they could avoid the risk of keeping pigs through the worst of the winter in a flimsy wooden sty. The likelihood of at least one pig dying at this time was high. Kannji's pigs, it was true, were somewhat too small to be accepted at the slaughterhouse, but Urban knew the man at the weighing bridge and insisted that the pigs would be accepted. The bigger ones would "help the little ones go through" by keeping the average weight within the margins of acceptability. In fact Urban's friend at the slaughterhouse wound up having to add 30 kilograms to the recorded total weight of the seven smallest animals to let them through at all.

Trapped though Kannji was in his family's pig-delivery problems, he was at least fortunate in being partially able to organize his entry into the horse trade. When Urban sold the animals, he earned 6,000 less than he might have done had he been able to wait, but he still had a lump sum of nearly 22,000. Other men who had not kept pigs, or whose animals had all died, had to entrust themselves to even riskier ventures, such as playing Twenty-one against the Romungros after payday. Some of these had strokes of luck. One man won some 14,000 forints at cards one weekend in January and was able to buy an old horse with the proceeds. Another man was paid compensation as a result of a *kris* verdict and used the money to buy two top-quality animals. Two other young men joined their brothers-in-law and bought a horse with them before each traded up to acquire their own animals. Another was reduced to getting money from the National Savings Bank to buy pigs and then illegally buying a ropey old horse with his loan. I expressed some anxiety about this tactic, since the bank officials could come and inspect the "pigs," but he explained that, even if they did come out to the Third Class—not a likely event—he would borrow a few pigs for a few days from the neighbors and find witnesses to swear that the others had died.

Having each managed to buy a horse, these men were now faced with a new problem, which was expensive to resolve: feeding the animals, especially through the final lean winter months. For a peasant owner who used his horse profitably, either for hauling building materials for his neighbors during the summer house-building season or as a traction animal on his own household plot, the cost of food was part of the business of keeping a horse. But a Rom bought horses to sell them and kept them in his stable from dawn until dusk, so for him the cost of fodder could be offset only against the profit at the sale. It is true that horse prices were slightly higher in April than in October, but this difference was not great enough to cover the expenses.

And even if a man had money, fodder was not always easily available. From September through April, Gypsy men made regular trips to neighboring villages in search of fodder at the right price, roughly 300 forints per 100 kilos. In summer, although a man might spend half a day searching for well-priced fodder, he was at least guaranteed some choice. Then men bought 10 hundredweight or so at 280 forints per unit. By November trade in fodder was a seller's market, as many bitterly disputed deals attested. Four months later a man was lucky to find any fodder at all that a horse would consider eating. Once I saw a man reduced to feeding his horses bread scavenged by his wife. Several other times men told me that they had decided to sell a horse in order to avoid this kind of crisis.

As a result of such problems, during March I spent whole days driving throughout the countryside with party after party of Rom hopeful of finding a few hundredweight of fodder to see them through the next few weeks. Individual peasant farmers could afford to be choosy about their sales, and the vast bulk of fodder that came into the Third Class was bought from the peasant households of a few neighboring villages. Although in principle cooperative farms often had a surplus at this time of year, a Gypsy never had an easy time buying from them even when, as I once saw, a Magyar man came along and pretended to be the buyer. Some Rom, partly for the pleasure of getting back at the cooperative farms, and partly in desperation when they could not find or afford fodder, went on nighttime raids of the ill-guarded cooperative supplies, but the risks in this game were high fines that well outstripped potential gains. Knowledge of these regular thefts also, of course, only increased the hostility of the cooperative farm managers to potential Gypsy buyers.

It was not just the difficulty the Rom had entering and remaining in the horse market that put most of them in a structurally disadvantaged position. Because of scarce resources, the average Gypsy was restricted to buying horses at the cheap end of the market, animals that were therefore all the harder to dispose of and on which profit margins were at best minimal.[11] Often the potential profit when the animal was sold back to a *gaźo* was so small that if a Rom sold to a Rom, there was nothing to "split"—both men could not "make their little bit of profit" by splitting it. Some slightly more successful men invested larger sums in a single animal with a "condition" that would cure with time, thus enabling a profit to be realized for the risk of keeping it.[12] For other men trapped with an animal at the bottom of the market, putting it to slaughter for sale as meat on the international market was a common solution.[13] Even this, however, did not provide an assured income. One man bought a horse in April for 15,000 hoping to sell her for meat. In early June it suddenly appeared that there might not be such a sale until October, and so this man was stuck with a horse he could not resell. His dealings seemed over for the summer. In the end the buyers, who were known collectively as "the Italians," turned up to buy in early July, but he received only 14,600 forints as his horse was put in the third and lowest price class.

In the cold light of "the morning after," once costs had been weighed against incomes, a calculation that few, if any, Rom engaged in, it seems that the comedy, excitement, and euphoria of the market disguised the fact that, for most Rom, dealing in horses was a means to lose, not to win, money. It is true, of course, that there was the example of the Šošojs and the Thulos to inspire other men. Early on in the year I lived there, Thulo bought a horse for his brother-in-law and three days later resold it for him, making 11,000 forints' profit. This same man bought four ruined horses from the Gödöllő cooperative farm at 40 forints per kilo and put them to slaughter two months later at 55 forints per kilo, making some 20,000 forints' profit. Having more money in the first place, these men were able to buy horses at a better stage of development and then place them with the kind of buyers who would pay for the looks and "style" of a well-bred and carefully tended animal. But the other Rom were not completely naive about the reasons for Thulo's and Šošoj's successes: They knew that these men profited from privileged and protected relations with state firms. In the Appendix, I show how over nearly a year of horse dealing, one more typical man I knew managed to make a mere 7,000 forints' profit on what, given his poverty, was a pretty spectacular cash flow. So the question remains: If these Rom could only dream of dealing like a Šošoj, what alternative motives persuaded these perfectly sensible men to continue in this draining trade?

The Pure Dealer, or Middleman

The peasant came to market to buy or sell an animal he needed in his work. One could hear peasants teasing Gypsy dealers, "If I buy a horse, I'll keep it for thirteen years, not swap it away in two weeks' time." As far as the peasants were concerned, the way that the Gypsies "circulated" (*forgat*) their horses expressed their freedom from the constraints of normal society. Whereas a peasant intended to buy a horse with an eye to the long term, Gypsy dealers (*kupec*) could pick up any piece of living flesh if they could turn it around fast enough. Or as a Rom said: "It's not good to keep a horse for too long. You never know what trouble might come. . . . In general, if his luck comes to him, a man says, 'Let the animal go!'" Sometimes the dealer had to actually buy a horse before being able to pass it on, but often he was able to earn money as a "broker" (*cincár*) or "intermediary" (*közvetítő*).

This role of middleman offered special attractions to the Rom, since it expressed the essence of their position on the market. What was at stake here struck me one morning at a dull and listless market that had been made somewhat worse by the unwanted attention of the local police, who were unusually active checking people's papers to ensure that all the dealers had registered workplaces. Midmorning, as tempers were rising in frustration, a very smooth, professional-looking Gypsy *cincár* set up the first action of the day in a duel of a deal with another Rom on behalf of a peasant buyer. It took ten minutes of terrible cursing and shouting and a tough trial on the horse for the *cincár* to get an agreement. As he did and the money passed hands, he called for the drink to bless the deal and strode out through the crowd, drawing it along behind him, knowing that he was the center of attention and even admiration, knowing also that everyone wanted to know for whom he had bought the horse and how much he had earned for his speech in this deal. Within fifteen minutes of this deal being struck, three more trades that had been stalled all morning were made. The market had at last revived.

It may seem odd that here a Rom *cincár* appeared to help a *gaźo* do business, but the art of the *cincár* was to get horses and money moving in any way possible. Having collected a fee from both parties, this man was not criticized for exploiting his brother but praised instead for taking all the men to the bar and calling for drinks. By setting in motion the first deal of the day—that is, adding to the velocity of dealing as a whole—and then behaving so morally with his profit, the *cincár* had in fact performed two services for his brothers.

To some extent this was a role that even the peasants could acknowledge. Although the *cincár* was the despised *kupec*—of whom an indigenous ethnographer once wrote, "For this no more is needed than a large voice and a good whip"[14]—he was also the man who, in Hungarian terminology, "sanctifies" (*szentesít*) or "blesses" (*áldja*) the deal. In return for his services, he was given "the cost of the holy water" (*a keresztvíz árát*) or "the drink to bless the deal" (*áldomás*).

Dealers as Managers of Men

Despite media coverage of insider dealing and market fixing in Western markets, there is still a strong tendency to think of "true" markets as

"If a man hasn't got horses, others say 'let God strike him down'."

places where individuals come to satisfy purely *economic* needs and where prices are set by mechanical laws of supply and demand. Because markets in Western academic discourse have been constructed as purely economic institutions, theories of "rational calculation" have been developed to explain behavior there. According to these widely accepted models of economic behavior, the generation of a flow of goods and the determination of their prices rest on an impersonal mechanism, a balance of supply and demand. There is always an optimal course of action for market agents that can be determined by calculation, using their present state of knowledge. Action on a market is therefore to be explained by Lionel Robbins's model of allocation of known scarce resources to given ends.

For economic man to react rationally to the world is to accept the given conditions in which we live, to fit like a cog into a machine of moving parts, the motor of which is quite invisible to us and far beyond our manipulation.

Now the Gypsies, despite being at the very bottom of the Hungarian social pile, indeed perhaps precisely because they had no claim on the system whatsoever, did not conceive of their relationship to horse markets in the passive, accepting way called for by rational calculation. Gypsy models of trade and price-setting included the dealers' agency over the terms of trade and potency over their exchange partners. From the perspective of "rational" calculation and allocation, the Gypsies' attempt to take the market into their own hands may appear irrational. But for them, everything happened as if prices were the result of the game of bargaining. Market behavior was constructed as an attempt to alter the terms of trade, to back one's hunches, to grasp imaginatively possibilities unforeseen by others, and then to persuade and coerce one's exchange partners to see the world as one saw it oneself.

The Rom were encouraged to take this active role in forming prices, I suggest, because for them the market was as much a political as an economic forum. It was an arena where the relations between groups of people could be redefined through the definition or evaluation of the objects being exchanged. In this arena the role of the *cincár* was to organize, persuade, or manipulate others into participating in these doubly risky exchanges, into doing business with each other. His business was managing people. Now managing a peasant in full view of a large public was a pleasure very dear to the Rom (both as actors and observers), and, I suggest, it was in order to enjoy the pleasure of creating a deal, as much as for any remuneration, that the Rom played the role of *cincár*.

To sustain their position as the "bosses" of the market, the Rom attempted to establish their potency over the *gaźo*s in a number of media. The apparently anachronistic dress of many Rom dealers suggested one idiom in which they imagined their relations with the *gaźo* peasant, as if they were richer landowners or members of the gentry who did not "labor" to live. By dressing as gentry, the Rom adopted the uniform of a social class whose life had been spent "managing" servants and laborers. The Hungarian ethnographers Fél and Hofer described how peasants talked of the nobility as if "it was in their blood to manage the affairs of the community. There was the manly spirit [*virtus*] of nobles in them. A gentleman was more excellent in his speech; he could express himself better."[15] In dress, the Rom laid symbolic claim to this potency. In 1985 the real masters of the peasants were the chairmen of the cooperative farms, and so, keeping abreast of the times, some of the younger Gypsy dealers had started coming to market in the green coats beloved of farm bureaucrats, together with briefcases (empty, needless to add!) by their side.[16]

Čerbo dressed up for the market in a large butcher's apron and used a two-meter-long herdsman's whip. He was a man whom almost everyone liked and admired, if for no other reason than that he made the market interesting, with his great voice, his endless cries, and his performances. This element of playacting provides a clue to his popularity: His behavior suggested that the market was a game where the normal rules of life, which the Rom knew was no game, were suspended.[17]

But it was in "speech" (*vorba*) that the Gypsy dealers realized their power. As one man put it to me: "I need to have speech. If I don't have that, then I can't do anything. You see, most people don't have this. . . . You have to talk someone into buying a horse. You have to talk the horse up [literally, beside it] so someone will buy it. You have to take a person's hand to make them do business—otherwise they won't come together. People can't talk to each other from a distance, not at all." Another man likened his activity to mine as an "interpreter," bringing together two parties that could not understand each other. "You talk two or three words, and the fee just comes to you. If you don't talk, you won't get the fee."

This is not to say that brokering was a straightforward business. When I asked Zeleno why he was such a good dealer, he replied: "Well, because I am aggressive. If you're not aggressive, you couldn't lift the fee. It's with strength that you can lift someone else's hand. You know, one wants to sell, another to buy. Then the *cincár* brings them together, and they don't mind paying 500 or 600 forints or 1,000—neither of the parties minds that." Partly because Rom men believed there was a need for their "help" to make a deal work, and partly just to enjoy themselves, they were quite surprisingly persistent in their arguments and would rarely take a refusal from a peasant as final. Generally the peasants were treated in a brusque, familiar, though not offensive, fashion, addressed with the formal Hungarian *maga* forms that established respect and distance, yet at the same time these *gaźos* were not left in peace to "make up their own minds."

The curses that the Rom used in dealing were another verbal device in which they enjoyed their potency. More than just colorful and amusing turns of speech, curses were a type of formalized speech that restricted the ability of the listener to challenge the information he was being given. As I argued in Chapter 4 in relation to my own difficulties with requests for help, there was no saying "no" to a curse. So in using them, the Rom tried to turn words from means of expression into means of coercion, to enact the power of words.

After successfully completing a deal, a Rom *cincár* was tangibly excited. He behaved then as if he had pulled off a remarkable coup; he held himself differently and exuded an energy and a confidence that he normally lacked. On one occasion a young man hurtled through three deals, five horses, and several tens of thousands of forints in cash in the space of half an hour. During those minutes, the Rom in question was frantic, bursting with energy, determined to push his luck as far as he could. After the market, he was the talk of the men in his settlement.

Through speech, the Rom said, "we make money turn around, turn around and come to us," and they emphasized the ease with which this might be done as a dealer "rotated" goods between customers. Explaining their trade, Rom men would customarily use a gesture in which the fingers of one hand were lightly touched into the palm of the other at right angles and then their position rapidly reversed, suggesting an exchange of items between one hand and another. The lightness of touch and rapidity with which the hands swapped places seemed to embody the mesmerizing speed, ease, and efficiency of the dealer rotating goods between customers.

What the Rom had done, in effect, was to treat the market as an arena where glory might be achieved by the performance of heroic feats that turned the tables of hierarchy and power within which they lived. In this sense the Rom had held onto or reinvented an original and fuller meaning of the idea of "commerce" as the animated intercourse between persons.[18] According to Albert Hirschman, a historian of ideas, until the eighteenth century the passion for glory and the heroism it engendered had provided the model of both statecraft and economic activity. From that time on, for level-headed capitalists, it was to be the tamed "passion," that of "calm" accumulation, and the sober calculation of "interest" that would provide a model of a balanced social orientation.[19] This puritanical ethic had clearly been rejected by the Rom. Hence, the paradox I posited at the beginning of this chapter could be largely ignored by them.

But there is another reason that questions about the profitability of horse dealing are in a sense ill formed. Since the Rom behaved as if dealing were a form of gambling in which success was determined by "luck," they always lived in hope that money would come to them. For this reason, a successful deal for many men was one that allowed them to buy another horse and try their "luck" again rather than one that produced an absolute profit.[20] By putting their money in horses, and moving these around in time and space, traders appeared to make money produce more of itself and so appeared to lead "the easy life" that the peasants so despised.[21]

The Rom attitude to "profit" here becomes clearer if we recall the discussion in Chapter 4 on the tabooing of the Hungarian term *forint*. When talking with each other, the Rom used alternative terms for "money." Rather as we distinguish various social forms of money with terms such as "rent," "income," and "interest," by which we define the social relation in which money is made and used, so in a less structured way the Rom used their terms to keep distinct the diverse uses of money. Forints came from work and were part of exchanges with the *gaźos* in shops, banks, and so on. The Rom when among themselves used the terms "Red ones" (100 forints), "Green ones" (1,000 forints) and "new ones" (*neve*, money in general).

When, however, after the horse markets the men gathered and sang about their exploits, their money had become "silver" (*rup*). Because the money obtained in trade had been won from the *gaźo* in the game of dealing, it provided a source for creating brotherhood among the Gypsies.[22] Wage labor money, Hungarian forints, carried with it the alien intentionality of the non-Gypsy work provider, the state, according to whose ethic money was to be saved, accumulated, and wisely spent on civilizing one's living conditions and that of one's family. As free-flowing silver, which came without effort, money sustained the Rom by allowing the men to celebrate and make their "good mood" (*voja*) with the "true brothers."

Even if no profit was actually made on any one deal, so long as the Gypsy trader concluded the deal by calling for a drink with his brothers, he showed that he had made a profit from Gypsy work, since by definition (tautologically), it was only such money, "Gypsy money" as it were, that the Rom were willing to spend in *mulatšago*. Thus, however little profit was made, a deal might always seem "good" simply because it was made: The proof of the dealing lay in the drinking!

10

A Passion for Dealing

From Dependence to Autonomy Through Luck

Although Hungarian peasants and Gypsies each imagined the other as the antithesis of itself, both had to deal with a similar predicament: They lived in a society in which status as a full human being was based on the achievement of autonomy, independence, and self-mastery, but both lacked the means to do so. The peasants defined autonomy as avoidance of all exchange. Instead they engaged in production on their own land, if possible, or simply with their own bodies. The Gypsies took refuge in the option the peasants had rejected and strove for independence through trade and exchange. Dealing with horses enabled the Rom to act as "masters of themselves," as agents of their destiny in their relations with each other and with the *gaźo*s.

But the position of the Gypsies in Hungarian society was too weak to allow them any straightforward self-representation as masters of the world or masters of the horses that they moved around the market. Just as peasant *gazda*s had historically been forced into dependence on the very forces they wished to distance themselves from—markets and the banks that gave loans to buy land—so the Rom, being dependent on the *gaźo*s even for the production of horses, were forced to rely on the very people they wished to distance themselves from. In consequence, the process by which the Gypsies constructed an image of glorious independence, that is, the Gypsy work discussed in Chapter 2, became somewhat convoluted.

I argued then that one way the Gypsies tried to circumvent this problem of dependence was through the category of Gypsy horses, with whom the Rom created an image of absolute autonomy from the peasants. In the normal run of things, with *gaźo* horses a Rom dealer took an

164

already trained animal and shuffled it around between *gažo* buyers. But with Gypsy horses, the Rom, by refusing to exchange the very animals that they owned outright, came nearly full circle and met the proper peasant on his own ground of self-sufficiency through ownership. When a Rom did, metaphorically, brand an animal as "Rom," he used it to represent exchanges in which, paradoxically, nothing was really given by the Gypsies. However, the Gypsy horse that really never passed over to the *gažos* was more a mythological than a real creature, good for thinking, but hard to realize.

A second, more common way by which the Rom reimagined their relation with the peasant dealers was through a rhetoric of "luck" (*baxt*). Unlike the rare Romany horse, luck was something found in all dealing. Luck for the Rom was something that inhered in the game of dealing and more particularly adhered to them when they played with a *gažo*, confronting him and persuading him to part with his wealth or to give a horse for less than its value.

Baxt, which, following Gypsy practice, I have translated as "luck," is a complicated concept, especially because it does not exactly correspond to our notion of luck.[1] If a man was *baxtalo*, then wealth came to him, but he was also "intensely happy" (glossed into Hungarian as *boldog*), had many sons, and was probably fat.[2] As luck, efficacy, prosperity, and happiness, *baxt* was one of the constitutive qualities of the Gypsies, just as diligence was of the peasants. Although the Rom might have explained a man's failed deals in terms of his lack of luck, it was nevertheless the very nature of the Gypsies to be lucky. So long as a man was a true Rom, he would be, as a result of his sociomoral comportment, *baxtalo*, "lucky." *Baxt*, therefore, in contrast to our idea of luck as a differentiator, did not distinguish one Rom from another. Although the concept of windfall gain links our usage and that of the Gypsies, *baxt* only partly overlaps with our own idea of chance. We associate luck with coincidence, which we think of as self-evidently uncertain and trivial, but for the Rom luck was the consequence of righteous behavior. So it posed no logical problem for the Gypsies to define their identity as lucky.[3]

Like any symbol, the notion of luck allowed the Rom to play several games at one time. First, it opposed them to the dominant work ethic. The ideal deal was one in which they had not "worked" on the horse in the narrow "peasant" sense of the word "work." The peasants put all their emphasis on the physical changes that toil brought about (to both peasant and object) through its sheer materiality. For them, activity was "work" only if it involved punishing, physically exhausting, sweat-expelling, earth-shifting effort. In dealing, the Gypsies struggled for autonomy by making money grow without the steady preparation of the "soil" of their economy. This, then, was one feature of talking of trade in terms of luck—denying the labor involved in their dealings. Like acrobats, dancers, actors, and other artists, the Gypsies spent their effort appearing effortless.

Second, the Gypsies' notion of luck introduced the element of volition into their market rhetoric. Although traders in the volatile futures markets in capitalist economies may use a language of luck as a variation of capitalist images of impersonal, mechanistic models of exchange,[4] for the Rom luck as efficacy, as the successful manipulation of the *gażo* trader, implied a background of conscious action. This was so because the Rom became lucky only by maintaining proper relations with their wives and thereby keeping themselves pure. In other words, when facing "outward" toward the *gażos*, the Gypsies might represent their success as labor-denying "chance luck," but from the inside "success luck" was the result of the Gypsies' will exercised in an area of social life over which they had some control: their relations with their women. Before we can understand this gendered logic a primary question must be asked: Why was it that the Rom imagined luck adhering to them in the game of horse dealing? To answer this, we need to take a slightly more detailed look at the symbolism of horses for the Rom.

Commodities, Women, and *Gażos*

Most traders, by definition, treat the objects in which they deal as commodities, as the material embodiment of monetary wealth. The Rom could always report how much money they "had" in a horse (though the means of assessing this figure varied), and the Gypsies would not have been involved in horse dealing if doing so had not offered them the possibility of making money from the *gażos*. The very impersonality of "the price" and its apparent objectivity allowed the Gypsies to construe horses as depersonalized commodities, abstracted tokens of value ("a 30,000-forint horse") rather than appendages or products of the peasants (a horse with a Hungarian name, such as Jutka or Csibész).

But in relation to these favored animals, there was also a degree of anthropomorphism related to aspects of the markets not explicable in purely economic terms. Horses were always more than mere commodities, products of impersonal, alienable, and alienated labor. If horses raised by the Gypsies were Rom, then all the other horses that passed through their hands were, by implication, non-Gypsy, representatives of the alien *gażo* world. Partly this intimate association of animal with the one who raised it was a feature of the particularly plastic or malleable nature of horses. More than cows, pigs, or other animals, the previous owners of a horse left tangible marks of their influence on the animal. Non-

Only children and the innocent anthropologist dare to question the perfection of a man's horse. (I. Németh)

Gypsy horses were born in *gaźo* stables, named by *gaźos*, and broken and trained by them. They became accustomed and responded to commands in Hungarian. To make money on these horses, the Gypsies had to return them to the *gaźos*. They sat in the Gypsy stables for a few hours, days, or weeks and were then sent back. Horses were thus representatives of the *gaźo* world on which the Gypsies depended. But this was not how they were represented by the Rom.

For the most part, when in Gypsy stables and yards, horses were talked of and treated as if they shared the qualities of Gypsy women rather than those of the *gaźos*.[5] Whereas boys became men through their control of horses, girls became symbolically linked with horses as they turned into women. I have said that horses were the animals most like humans, being clean and intelligent, but when a man drove a horse cart, or if a man desired a horse as a purchase, he behaved and talked as if he were dealing with a symbolic form of human femininity. This symbolic play worked both ways: Not only were horses treated as women, but also girls and women were likened to horses.

In the search for a horse, "mares" (*khuri*) were considered the perfect purchase. Stallions (uncastrated males) (*grast*) were said to be impractical for traction purposes, and I never saw one pass through a Gypsy's hands. In any case, studs had to be licensed, and the only ones in Harangos were in *gaźo* stables. There were always a few geldings (castrated males) being circulated on the market. These were strong but controllable working animals. However, whenever any of them showed any sign of sexuality (a dangling penis, for instance), Gypsy men were quick to comment that they did not like the look of the animal,[6] and when inspecting geldings, Gypsies would invariably comment, "It's a shame it's not a mare." When I pushed for some explanation of this preference, I was told that since a mare could produce a foal each year, it offered the owner a source of revenue. However, the Rom themselves rarely made use of their mares' fertility, preferring to sell pregnant mares to the *gaźos*, who would pay an extra price for the expected offspring. Although this supplementary profit undoubtedly influenced Gypsy preferences, there was also an aesthetic element: After all, only the "fine and easy foals" (*e láse khure*) appeared in the lyric songs of Gypsy men.

The mare in a Gypsy stable provided a means to elaborate an imagery likening the bodies of horses and women. When she was first brought home, the boys in the house would commonly plait her mane all the way down one side. When I went to a wedding on a cart behind a large white mare, the owner took his wife's two smartest "scarves" (*dikhlos*) and tied one on each side of the mare's head. When we arrived at the wedding, his wife took one of the *dikhlos* off and put it on her own head.

Just as a woman did not cut her hair until a first-degree relative died, it was said that the tail of the horse should never be cut. A woman's hair was associated with her fertility and was kept completely covered inside her scarf. Mares cover their sexual organs with their hair, and I was often warned not to touch or stroke the tail—a sensitive horse might well kick me. Since horsehair was particularly suitable for violin bows and so was much in demand among the Romungro musicians, who themselves did not keep horses, a rich source of conflict was provided. When one such "despicable" Romungro asked a man for a few hairs from his horse's tail, the Rom threatened to lay the Romungro out on the spot. "Aren't you ashamed of yourself," the Rom called out after him. When the Rom told me about this "dirty Romungro," he talked of his horse in such an intimate way that I felt his reaction would have been similar if his daughter's or wife's honor had been insulted.[7]

If horses were treated as women, it was also true that girls were likened to horses. One afternoon as Čoro watched his daughters skip through the garden, I heard him call out to them affectionately, "Little foals" (*tsinne khure*). In children's games, too, I often used to see girls cantering around the settlement in a harness held by little boys. Such associations could also be found in riddles such as the following: "What has two noses, four eyes, four mouths, and six legs?" "A woman on a horse!"[8] Men would in jest sometimes make other metaphorical connections. Once my son began to approach his first birthday, Gypsy women started questioning his mother to see if she was pregnant again. After a few months of listening to her denials, the husband of a good friend teased her that I "ought to get myself into the cart in one" (*be kéne fogni egyesbe*), to "ride" a cart with only one horse (Judit) drawing it.[9]

Such talk of women as if they were mares, though done in jest, was complimentary. One afternoon I sat with an aging Gypsy as we watched his neighbor return home with her shopping. He admired her body; "made for a stallion," he said, and then went on to develop the association of her body with that of a mare. Elsewhere, a beautiful film star was "worth thirty horses." Sometimes the sexuality of the two could become confused. In this way it was said that a woman should keep away from uncastrated horses, since she could "drive a stallion crazy" (*diljarel*) by her smell.[10] Women, too, might use the way horses were treated as a model for explaining the way people behave toward one another. When I once asked a woman where she had lived after she married, she explained that she had obeyed the Gypsy custom in which "the wife follows her husband like a man his horse."

While Zeleno was celebrating the name day of the wife of one of his singing partners, he told a "story" (*paramiča*) to entertain and honor his companions.[11] It was a tale of a man (one learned at the punch line that it was the teller himself) who had one day seen such a fine horse, a mare so perfect that his wish to acquire any other horse left him at once. The horse's owner was proud of his possession and would not sell no matter what price was offered. He assured himself that there were no other buyers with precedence over himself, and he waited. For months he sought to persuade the mare's owner, but in vain. Finally, in despair, the man slipped the horse's halter and ran away with her. Finishing his story, he explained: "And she's been at my side ever since. She's in the kitchen now." The "horse" was, of course, his much-adored wife.

On another occasion I heard a story about a king who had a horse and a wife so faithful that the cunning Gypsy hero was tempted to remove both from the king.[12] By a sly device he did so, and the story concluded with the punning moral "You see, there is neither a woman nor a horse that you can't break" (*nincs olyan ló amit nem lehet betörni, nincs olyan nő amit nem lehet megtörni*).

On one occasion in Gypsy social life, the substitutability of horses and women was realized in practice. If a young wife left her husband before producing offspring, the groom's parents had the right to demand compensation from her parents for the loss. This compensation was normally awarded at a *kris*, but in principle the boy's parents had the right to remove a horse of the girl's father without asking. If, as was normally the case, they refrained from doing so, the sum paid was formally referred to as "the price of a horse."

These symbolic associations influenced the way that the Gypsies traded horses as if the search for a horse were a search for a woman/wife. On the way to market, men would joke that they were going to swap their wives. When a horse was for sale, the Rom behaved rather as if, lacking an owner, it was a woman without a man: Every man thought he could "have a go" (*zumavel*). So if one day I took a man out from the settlement to buy a horse, other men would come around and reserve a trip with me later in the day should the first bidder fail. My landlord, not wishing to be outdone, would then consider aloud if he should go himself, whether he had had any intention of buying a horse at that time or not![13] After failing in such efforts, men would tell me that they were pleased at least to have tested their luck; this way they would not spend hours wondering whether they could have had the horse if only they had tried. The suggestion that men's success in horse dealing was linked to their sexual potency was not one that the Gypsies shied away from, as indicated by the drunken cries of one very rich old dealer to a less fortunate Gypsy trader at the end of a successful market day: "Your cock's no good; it's my cock that's good."

In this hunting of horses, what struck me was the style of Rom behavior: the way that each man thought that he would be able to bring a unique and personal quality to the dealing that would swing it in his favor. It was the same sort of self-confidence that young Gypsy boys displayed when they suggested to me that all they had to do was indicate their desire to a *gažo* girl at a disco, and they would have her for the night.

Horses were "available," as *gažo* women were believed to be and Gypsy women were feared to be. Horses were also, like women, unpredictable and fickle and at the slightest provocation might slip out of control. Although Gypsy men almost always impressed me as being extremely competent in their treatment of horses, they had a concern for them bordering on the neurotic. In the settlement, even in the middle of summer, men would keep their animals tied inside the stables all day long, barely letting them see the light of day, let alone exercise around the meadow. When I asked why they kept their horses cooped up, I was told, "One never knows what might happen with a horse," meaning that one could never be sure that given half a chance, it would not "go crazy" and try to break free.[14]

Once a week in the Third Class, a horse did just that. But for all the regularity and predictability of such events, they still unleashed outright panic in any bystanders. One day a horse tethered outside my window tore its ropes and charged off through the yard, leaving its paired horse trapped in the trough that it had wrenched from the trees where they had been sheltered. The group of women who were in the courtyard began to wail and scream, presuming that the trapped horse, and with it many thousands of forints' investment, were lost. Keeping to the far side of the yard, they sent me off to call for experienced men to come and help, two of whom quickly managed to haul the thrashing animal out by its tail. There were a few tense moments, but it was the cries of the women more than the thrashing of the horses that created the drama.

At markets, where the men were already playing with fire in so many ways, the unpredictability of horses was deliberately cultivated as bystanders tried to provoke horses while they were being "driven" by young men. It took strength and confidence for the boys to guide as much as 700 kilograms of thundering animal through a crowd at a fast trot, and their task was made all the more difficult by men who cracked their whips at the horse's hind legs to see if the animal would buck. Very rarely did a horse break free, but when one did, the crowd scattered amid screams from the women and shouts of "whoa" from the men. It made me wonder if the women were not screaming at an image of chaotic, animal femininity.[15]

In Gypsy discussions, the tameness of the horse seemed to be related to the extent to which the animal was sexed. Thus, the owner of a horse, if he trusted it, would sometimes climb under its hind legs below its genitals, or if it was a mare, lift up her tail and press his back against her sex and anus. All but the most calm horses would react violently to either of these gestures, in the latter case spraying urine over the owner and viciously trying to kick him. Just as the Rom (men and women) said that a man who never beat his wife was, in effect, allowing her to become a whore, so the men seemed to beat their animals to remind them who was in control. Having provoked a degree of waywardness in the animal, the men would attack it again with a fairly brutal beating. They were also, of course, in this way beating the *gaźo* in the horse, since Gypsy horses were, in principle, never hit.

Sometimes such metaphorical relations between the order of animals and that of people were transformed into a metonymic assimilation, the behavior of one part of the equation directly affecting the other. Thus, the ease with which a man controlled a horse was acknowledged to depend on several factors, notably the way it had been treated by previous owners, but one explanation given for a change of temperament in a horse was that the owner did not control his wife. Čoro, for instance, once bought a horse that was said at the time to be the best horse in the Third Class: a tall, sleek mare "with features as fine as a woman's," according to his elder brother. Within a few months of the purchase, Jutka, as she was called, had become dangerously wild and was all but unsellable. Behind Čoro's back, opinion was unanimous that his loss of control over Jutka was directly attributable to his wife's supposed adultery. More than once I heard it suggested that Čoro keep Jutka now to kick his wife, for "one false thing will recognize another."

Luck and the Negation of Production

I have suggested here that the Gypsies masked the fact that horses came from the *gaźos* by symbolically setting horses apart from their producers, either by turning them into pure commodities, bearers of a "price," or, by an alternative symbolism, representing them as "women." And just as the *gaźo* producer was separated from his product, so the role of Gypsy women in producing the money that enabled the purchase of horses (by keeping pigs) was also symbolically devalued. For the Rom, it seemed that they could be successful with their horses only if they kept them in an arena apart from that associated with non-Gypsies and Gypsy women. I said in Chapter 4 that when it came to selling pigs, women were kept out of the moment of exchange; their labor had not given them control over the income. But their removal from the horse business was even more formalized. The Rom (men and women) articulated two reasons for this exclusion. First, women were said to be, and insisted themselves that they were, incapable of controlling a horse, though everyone "knew" that any seven-year-old boy could control a tame horse. In the absence of any other assistance, a wife or mother might have helped get a recalcitrant horse into or out of its stable, but despite my renowned incompetence, if I was around, the Rom preferred to ask me.[16]

Second, any involvement, any comment by a woman while her husband was dealing could spoil his luck. And just as a good wife walked behind her husband's back and not in front of him, so as she went about her ordinary business, she would pass behind any horse parked with a cart. Although the wives of many dealers came to market either to do their own dealing or to meet with relatives, prior to market a man was supposed to avoid sleeping with his wife. Many Gypsy men preferred to spend the night before a market on the market field, as if wishing, just prior to dealing, to disassociate themselves from the house and all its female aspects. In the kind of formalized exhortations that the Rom made on these subjects, I was told that if a Gypsy woman placed her skirt near her husband's head the night before a market, he would have no luck. Since all successful dealing relied on powerful and persuasive speech, it was his head, appropriately enough, that was protected by the taboo; and to say that a man's head was "cursed" (literally, eaten) was to say he "had lost his luck."

The exceptions to these taboos help reveal their logic. Older women, grandmothers beyond the age of reproduction, were not forced away from horse dealing; and one unmarried woman who, alone among all Gypsy women, wore trousers in public and had no intention of getting married or having children handled her father's horses, I was told, "like a man." If these women did not harm a man's luck, the implication seems clear that it was the association of other women with the processes of biological reproduction that rendered them dangerous to the men.

Remaining Rom involved a determination, in the face of greatly hostile odds, to live by Gypsy work, to survive without production—it was luck that allowed the Rom to achieve this feat and that expressed their achievement of remaining true to themselves and being able to live "well" and "lightly" (*lašes*). Horse dealing provided one way in which the Gypsies appeared to live without the weight of labor, but for the Rom to be lucky, their activities in this sphere had to be distinguished from all forms of production. In some way the biological fertility of the Gypsy women threatened this symbolic separation. Why this should have been so will only become clearer after the deeper examination of Rom ideas about reproduction in Chapter 12.

Trade and the Construction of Society

We are now, however, in a position to understand the final, and most passionate, stage of the Rom's dealings with horses: the swaps the Rom carried out with each other. As the intensity of Gypsy-peasant deals decreased around midday, the Gypsies turned their full attention to each other's animals, starting up a second-order game with the horses not as commodities but as token women. During the main part of the day, the dealings with peasants were tortuous and complicated affairs, but the shouting matches that the Rom now locked themselves into surpassed anything that had come before. Of course, it was in part to seek out fresh chances with new partners that the Gypsies were around at the end of every market, when there had not been a peasant in sight for an hour or more, locked in fierce shouting matches with each other. Having brought a horse to market, many Rom dealers believed that it was better to swap it away, in the hope of better luck with a new horse, than take it home again. But the swaps also had a social aspect that reinforced their desirability, for through them the Rom had a chance to enjoy, renew, or even extend brotherly relations among a wide group of men. Nor were these swaps of secondary importance in the day's activity. Indeed, since it was only at this time that the Gypsies set the terms of exchange and were in full control of the market-event, these inter-Rom exchanges had at least as great a significance as the financially more important sales to the gažos.[17]

Inter-Rom transactions were distinguished from those with the *gažos* in a number of ways. As commodities, objects with a price, horses appeared to be things with a social life; it was a 50,000-forint horse that drove the men to deal. Of course, price always expresses a social and political relationship, a distribution of economic social and cultural capital between different people, but it does so in an alienated, apparently mechanical, and objective form. In inter-Rom trading, it was as "women" that horses drove their traders to action.

In keeping with this altered symbolism, the Rom, it was said, "have to tell each other everything about a horse; they have to speak openly about it because otherwise the other Rom would bring it back. You can lie to the peasants but not to the Gypsies." Much of the inter-Gypsy trade was carried out between men who were intimately involved with each other as relatives and friends, and in these cases there was an understanding that the deal ought to be governed by the logic of the "swap." In most cases it was inevitable that money passed hands as it was rare to find two horses of precisely equal value.[18] What the ideology of swap emphasized was that neither Rom should seem to profit from the other.[19] Often during such deals, I would hear men exclaim in outrage at some particularly high demand "I'm not a Romungro! I'm a Rom, too" or offer a price as "15, in the Gypsy way." Paradoxically, because the deals were considered for the sake of good social relations, after such a deal either party might renege on it and reclaim his money or his horse if he was provoked to reevaluate the "value" (economic or social) of the deal. While the Rom were dealing, they might swear that they would not do so, but they retained the right nonetheless. Once I even saw a man remove a horse from the truck after it was loaded because its buyer had just insulted him.

In these deals the ideology according to which the Rom, even complete "stranger Gypsies" (*strejina rom*), should help each other was put to the test in a very public manner. This was particularly so at two extremes of the social continuum. I was told that it was not fair to ask a brother for a horse for he was in no position to refuse the request, and by and large this understanding was honored.[20] At the other extreme, deals with Gypsies at the edge of one's social universe—in particular, those with whom there had been feuding relations in the past—were also dangerously tricky. The relation of trust that existed between "brothers" who made feasts together did not exist with "stranger" Gypsies, so dealing with them was not part of any other moral relation.[21] So for different reasons at both ends of the Rom social continuum, men said that they did not "dare to ask" for a horse.

Moreover, the equalization of horse for horse and the willingness to confer one's own horse on another Rom—never to be taken lightly—were all the more arduous in these two circumstances. As with the little swaps of clothing and personal possessions, the swap implied the substitutability of the partners to the deal. When the means of conversion of two men into brothers were a pair of boots or a watch, little was at stake, but when the means were the horse of a man, his pride and chief symbol of his status as a Rom, the process of equalization was fraught with emotion. The assessment of horses was, as we have seen, a highly complex and risky business, and ironically, only the sale of the horse to a peasant at a later date revealed whether a Rom had been right in his appraisal of the worth of an animal.[22]

Because a man's status as a trader and as a brother was also being evaluated, the Rom tended to stand by an animal and did not willingly admit its faults. Yet part of dealing was giving in, accepting, compromising and doing so toward someone who was asserting with great force and in full view of many Gypsies the righteousness of his position. So even more than in deals between Gypsies and *gažos*, trades among themselves were laced with ultimatums backed by desperate curses. Despite the fact that these curses were supposed to demonstrate the finality of the latest offer, that offer had to be changed. If one side "gave," so should the other. To refuse to reciprocate was to reject serious dealing—and worse. It would be said that the man did not really want to do business, that he lacked "respect" (*patjiv*). From all this stemmed the extraordinary hoo-ha and palaver of the dealing—exaggerated as well by the regular trips to the bar that the men made throughout the day.

Earlier in the day the Rom dealers ordered the *gaźos* around—working in a team, they tried to disorient the *gaźos* and coerce them into deals. When the Room were among themselves, the gestures of the "manager of men" reappeared as the Rom tried to persuade each other to trade. But nothing was more likely to inflame a Rom than to be bossed around by another one who, in trying to sell or swap, was claiming to be acting as a brother. Often a third party, like the *cincár* of Gypsy-peasant deals, was needed to intervene and take over. Uttering some terrible curse, he allowed one side to give in not to the other but to himself. On some occasions horses were swapped in this fashion through two intermediaries, one for each real party, since neither was willing to deal directly with the other.

At Nagykőrös one Sunday in 1988, I recorded such a deal in which Zeleno and Šošoj acted as *cincár*s on behalf of the buyer. Although the seller of the horse spoke for himself, the "buyer" was himself only an intermediary, acting on behalf of an undeclared other. It was claimed afterward that the man behind the scenes was the real brother of the seller, and this certainly would have accounted for the need for a disguise. The men had established their willingness to deal by spending twenty minutes at the bar, together with a large crowd of followers all buying each other beer. When they returned to the field, members of the crowd "interfered" (*vorbil andre*), and I have kept some of their distracting voices in the following transcript. The horse in question was a two-year-old filly with plenty of potential to develop but blighted by "a small drawback": She would not allow herself to be bridled up. The concluding phase of this comically convoluted dealing began with the owner again admitting the horse's fault. The seller was asking 45, and the buyer trying for under 40—the owner's original purchase price. Almost every interjection was shouted at the top of the voice. Among much else, note the underhand way prices change, without anyone stating so openly.[23]

Seller:	I'd sell it for 60,000 if only it would go in the cart.
Buyer:	We're leaving. Remain with God!
Seller:	Hey, where are you running to? Let's make business! Don't be like that! Put something on her, too! . . . Look, I paid 40,000 for her.
Buyer:	Aha, but you're crazy!

Zeleno (to buyer): Be pleased that he's allowed something off the price at all.

Buyer: I'm not paying more than 39. . . . But I won't bring it back.

Seller: What? How could you bring it back anyway? I told you what its fault is. (To the crowd) Why on earth would he bring it back? You'd not bring it back? I'll give it to you on credit!

Zeleno: Don't speak so much now.

Šošoj (to Zeleno): Let's cut between [intervene and mediate], and then it will be sold.

Buyer: I wouldn't give you more even if you want it. . . . Forty, I said. (Pointing at his brother) Let him buy my coffin right now if I give any more! Forty, I said.

Seller: OK, then. Let God give him luck! He won't give more than that. Fine! Let's leave it here, even though it's only farthings in question. Shouldn't he put 2,000 or 5,000 on his original price? I've allowed that much out of mine, and he still won't take it.

Zeleno (to buyer): You know, even if you have to put it to slaughter, you still won't lose money. If nobody else will buy it, I will.

Seller (to buyer): Look, either pay the price, or I'm going home! Please, but quickly.

Buyer: Don't you want to sell? Don't you want to sell? Let my son die, and me, too!

Zeleno (to buyer): Stop your talk!

Buyer: What are you talking about?

Seller: Let me die if I sell it for less than 42! Let me have no more horses if I do so!

Buyer: Let me die if I don't give you four 10s for it.

Seller: Go on, put your wages together then!

Buyer: Where would you get 45 for it?

Seller: I could get over 45, if . . .

Voice:	Give him 41!
Buyer:	A round 40 and it's good. . . . I deal in dollars here! Just pick up your money, and it's yours. Let them [the *cincárs*] pay you if you won't take it from me!
Voice:	He'll get 45 from somebody.
Seller:	Shall I give it for 42? Let's see if he could pay that off. . . . It's nothing more to me.
Zeleno (to seller):	Sell it or you'll take it to six more markets, let them bury me!
Buyer:	How much should I offer? Let me hear you speak!
Voice:	45!
Zeleno:	Don't interfere!
Buyer:	I've said already, let them bury me. Pick up your 41!
Zeleno:	I fuck your dead relatives! His skin alone would go for that. The skin's worth more than that!
Buyer:	I'll just buy his skin then, that's all . . . for 41.
Zeleno:	Cut at 42!
Seller:	I won't give her for 42.
Šošoj:	Hey there, Gypsies don't carry on like that! There'll be a fight. . . . You can't behave like this![24]
Zeleno:	Mary, take me from you! Collect your money! I fuck your dead relatives!
Buyer:	OK, then. Fine. I'll give you that much more, if that's what you want [i.e., 42,000].
Seller:	Bring your money!
Buyer:	Be lucky with your money!
Seller:	Be lucky with your horse!

[Pause while the money is counted out twice]

Voice:	It can't be true; it cannot be true, boys! Hold it there, boys! Did the boy's own brother really buy it?!
Voice:	For 42! That's a good deal, that is.

Šošoj (to all and sundry):	Now everybody wants to buy, but the boy's bought already.
Voice:	Well, let me die!
Voice:	It's sold, is it then?
Zeleno:	Yes, for 42.

For his "speech" here, and he had worked on both parties earlier during a drink at the bar, persuading them not to leave the market without having "done something," Zeleno received 500 forints; his brother-in-law, 100. The main *cincár* who acted as proxy buyer was said to have received 1,000 for his effort.

By sharing a drink together to conclude the exchange, dealers, including peasants who dealt with Gypsies, stated that the deal was made in good faith. But when the Rom dealt like this among themselves and then drank together, they formally showed that more than just business relations existed between them. By toasting each other, the Rom showed that they were capable of the kind of ideal hospitality demanded by *romanes* and that as Rom, not *gažos*, the aim of dealing was not accumulation of money but the "easy" (*lašes*) sharing of pleasure and sociality with their brothers.

What sense can be made, then, of the swap of horses as metaphorical women to make brothers of Gypsy men? In this fashion Gypsy men claimed that they could live from the *gažos* without becoming one of them because it was possible to convert the *gažo* into the Rom without becoming *gažo* in the process. They had proved this initially in sales by making "silver" with the horses of the *gažos*, silver that subsidized the feasting that sustained brotherhood. But now the Rom would prove this claim by exchanging horses/women among themselves.

In their swaps the Gypsies played on the deeper meanings and possibilities of exchange through a startling appropriation. Using the horses produced by non-Gypsies, the Rom engaged in a utopian fantasy of exchanging and swapping their own women. Only on one occasion in Gypsy social life were real women "swapped," and that was during the dances that accompanied the transfer of a bride from her father's to her father-in-law's family at a wedding. Then in the middle of dancing, men would grab a partner from each other, offering their own former dance partner in exchange.[25] Earlier in the wedding day, the bride in all likelihood would have had pictures taken of herself in full bridal wear standing alone with her father's horses. On no other occasion were Gypsy women photographed in this way, with the animals that came and went from the family's stables, though this was the most flattering way to photograph a man.

In other words, in the dances at weddings real woman were swapped in play, whereas the bride was given in earnest, but, as I argued in Chapter 4, under cover of there being no exchange. It was only in the photograph of the young woman with the horse that the bride and her family acknowledged what so much of the rest of the wedding was designed to obscure: the creation of exchange relations between two families. Given the taboo on sister-exchange marriages, the taboo on acknowledging the passage of wives between different Rom households through serial monogamy, and the suppression of the idea of affinity, the horse swaps at the end of the market day now acquire a rather fuller sense.

In them, horses became a means for representing a form of (male) Gypsy potency and creating a fantasy social order at once appealing, necessary, and terrifying. In these mutual horse dealings, Gypsy men brought into the open what was suppressed in their communal life. It was in relation to horses that the Rom created exchange relations as equals through symbolic women. Here, therefore, "women" could be exchanged in a brotherly fashion. Through horses, the reciprocal exchange of "women" became a means of creating identity, not differentiation. As the men drank more and more and moved into the desired state of *voja*, becoming truer and truer brothers and Rom, they tried to increase the velocity of these swaps to show that they could carry on living as brothers.

Finally, the attraction of the swaps also derived from the fact that because Gypsy women, ideologically speaking at least, were subordinate to and controlled by their fathers and husbands, swapping horses/women was a means of playing out (and thereby reproducing) this desired state of affairs. Through the horses produced by the *gaźos* but treated as Gypsy women, the Rom men appeared to celebrate their control over their women (but in reality were symbolically reproducing it by successfully excluding their wives from the business) and at the same time claimed a vicarious symbolic control over the *gaźos*.

Thus, I found myself on Sunday after Sunday in the middle of a field. On one side stood the *gaźos*, gaping like a baffled audience at the antics of Gypsy men immersed in incomprehensible arguments. On the other side the wives of the Rom looked on, praying that their husbands would not end up stabbing their brothers in the drunken heat and fury of the dealing over tokens that represented the two parties excluded from the exchange: the Gypsy women themselves and the *gaźos*. Only the presence of the Communist police, hostile to the whole spectacle of the Gypsy trader drunkenly playing with his wealth, brought an end to this deep play on the meanings of the world that the Rom lived in by driving the rowdy *Cigány* from the field.

11

BROTHERS IN SONG

WHEN THE GYPSIES DID FINALLY RETIRE from a market field, this was not the end of their day. We have just seen how, during the horse dealing, the Rom tried to create a world apart from that of the *gaźos*. Using key symbols of *gaźo* life, the Rom had established that for the time being they, not the *gaźos*, were the masters of the economic and symbolic orders, and as such they engineered a space for the symbolic production of their own sociality. Now there was one step left by which they might finally seal themselves off from the world: the move into a state of brotherhood by drinking and singing with one another.

In this chapter I consider the most important social context in which Rom song was produced, the *mulatšago*, or "celebration." For the Rom, the point of participating in a *mulatšago* was to make "true speech" to each other. Through this they produced the basis for brotherly solidarity. It was by sharing their Romany speech, what the *gaźos* disparagingly described as *cigányul*, the "Gypsy/lying way of talking," that they would achieve this goal. And if this activity therefore involved a deliberate distancing between theirs and the *gaźos'* view of the world, this was not the only transformation at work. Music making was the aspect of Gypsy culture that had contributed more than any other to non-Gypsies' image of them. But, as the reader might by now expect, the musical activity of the Rom inside their communities was very different from that the Gypsies performed for outsiders. In Hungary the one activity for which the Gypsies acquired social status in the world outside their communities was the production of music. Indeed, the only expression of Rom culture that the Communist authorities allowed and encouraged, through folkloric competitions, was Gypsy song and dance. However, as the Rom saw things, those kind of performances could easily become like the music making of the Romungros, a form of service for the *gaźos*. When the Rom were among themselves, music making had a quite other purpose. And

181

though the Rom were extremely ready and able adopters of new influences and styles from the world outside,[1] they retained their own sense of what it meant to make music together.[2]

For the purposes of my argument here, I discuss only songs sung in one social context: *mulatšago*. It was by joining in *mulatšago*s that men attempted to create a world in which they respected each other and the rivalries and squabbles deriving from the particular, private lives of individuals and their families could be put aside. And it was by enabling the men to do so that Rom women, too, participated in sustaining their community. In Chapters 3 and 4 I demonstrated some of the divisive tendencies inherent in a Rom community. Here I show how, by singing together, the Rom manage to transcend these problems, if only temporarily, and create another image of a viable way of life.[3]

Celebrations

Each Sunday on the way home from market, the Rom men made numerous stops at bars along the way for beer or wine. As their chauffeur, I would urge them to get back home so that I could write up my notes of the day's dealings. But the Rom had other intentions: to delay as long as possible the moment they would have to disperse back to their own families. If the "mood" (*voja*) came to them, the men would tarry long enough to sing with each other and "celebrate" (*mulatij*), performing the same songs as at all the turning points of Gypsy life.

Song was the medium in which the Rom expressed their deepest feelings and attachments. I remember my son's godmother visiting one Saturday morning, and rather than telling me her tearful story, she sang about her misery and the suffering she had to endure. On another occasion, as a special way of honoring a group of researchers, including myself, an elder Rom sang the story of his life.[4] The songs sung by individuals when they were moved to do so were often highly personal laments that, though adopting the stock phrases and turns of other Gypsy songs, recounted particular events in the speaker's life, as the following song, sung in Hungarian, illustrates.

Bočanato mangav.	I ask your forgiveness.
Farkas Zoltánné vagyok.	My name is Mrs. Zoltan Farkas.
Aszondja hogy,	She said,[5]
"Megy a fiam a kocsmába."	"My son went to the bar."
Jaj de Megy az anya a nyomába.	Oh, but his mother will go to misery.
Jaj de Mondtam fiam ne menjél be	Oh, I said, "Don't go there, son,
Mert Nagy verekedés lesz belőle	Because there will only be a fight."

Jaj de Látom fiam igyekezik	Oh, but I see my son struggling,
A magyarokkal verekedik.	Fighting with the Hungarians.
Jaj A magyarokat viszi a mentő.	Jaj^6 They take the Hungarians in the ambulance.
A fiamot meg a rendőr.	It's a policeman who takes my son.
Jaj de Mondtam fiam ne menjél be	Jaj I told you, son, not to enter
Mert Nagy verekedés lesz belőle.	Because I knew there'd be a fight.

This kind of personal narration is not, however, characteristic of the songs performed during the *mulatšago*s, which were the most common context in which song was heard in the Third Class. These celebrations were seen by the Rom as one of their defining features, and when I first went to such a gathering, my Gypsy "mother" told me, "Now you'll see what it is to be a Gypsy." At the *mulatšago*, it was normally only men who were invited, though occasionally an elder woman would participate. The following is an account of one that took place in spring 1985.

Bakro had been called up for national service, and his last day at home had finally come. He would leave on the dawn train next morning, but not before holding a "small *mulatšago*," as he put it. At midday Mari, his wife, roasted two ducks. She cooked a soup as well and a paprika stew using chicken given to her by her mother. Earlier in the morning Bakro had been taken by his brothers to one of the local peasants who sold his wine illegally from his kitchen. There they had plied Bakro with brandy. He had then gone into town and spent a while chatting with men on the market square before returning home, where he spent the rest of the morning, sitting outside his house in one of the ditches, talking with his father-in-law and grandfather. In the afternoon Bakro slept a little to recover his strength for the evening.

By 8:00 P.M. the men from the settlement had started to go over to Bakro's house, where they were ushered straight through the kitchen into the clean room. There, a revived Bakro immediately opened beer for them. Bakro had bought ten crates of beer and several bottles of "fruit brandy" (*ratjija*). Next door a few women had gathered: Bakro's mother-in-law and some friends of Bakro's wife. These were women who were on good terms with Mari and whose husbands were also among Bakro's guests. Mari had waited until many men were present to bring in the, now cold, food, which she left in the middle of the carpet among the men. Bakro called the men to go and eat and went to join them, each man squatting on his haunches around the bowl. Having eaten, Bakro called Mari back in to remove the mess.

An hour later a car drew up outside bringing a party from Csóka, including Bakro's godfather and co-godparent, as well as two other relatives. Bakro was very careful to show his gratitude to these men, who had come unexpectedly to show their support at this difficult moment. He called for the food to be brought back and sat down beside them. Others also adopted respectful forms of address with these men, using kin terms rather than personal names. Several times men would make general comments (sometimes as a compliment to all present, sometimes to Bakro) of the sort "All the brothers are here today," or, to me, "Don't be afraid! We are all brothers here," thus suggesting the ideal of trusting relations.

Bakro's departure *mulatšago* was especially successful in gathering together nearly forty men at one time, including "all" the adult men of the Third Class.[7] For a while after the arrival of the guests from Csóka, disparate conversations carried on, one occasionally attracting the attention of all the men. Then voices would rise as several men tried to join in, until the cacophony overwhelmed the attempt to talk together. Failing to reach agreement on whom to listen to and with reconciliatory salutations of "Be lucky," the men fell back into conversation with those nearest to them.

Then without warning, Bakro's godfather called out across the floor of the room to his godson and the assembled in general: "Be lucky, boys! I beg for your permission to make you a speech!" (*T'aven baxtale šavale. Engedelmo mangav te phenav tumenge ekh vorba!*), and Bakro replied, "Say your speech!" (*Phen tji vorba!*). Others chipped in "Ready!" (*kész*, that is, their permission was ready). Most people stopped talking, and those who continued did so in subdued tones. Duduš then started in on a story with a moral about how to survive as a Gypsy alone in the world of *gažos*. But he did not get far before somebody interrupted him to query his version of the story. Duduš ignored the interruption, but the silence had been broken. Some commented to others on the justness or otherwise of the interruption, and others took up the conversations they had left off. Duduš, angered now, raised his voice and called out more greetings. Finally, failing to win attention, he pulled out his knife, brandishing it threateningly in the air, and made fearsome carving gestures as he shouted about the men's lack of "respect" (*patjiv*). Several people now came to his defense, saying that the "old Rom" ought to be allowed to complete his story for it was a good, Romany story. But this defense was in vain. Duduš would not now begin again unless those around begged him, and it was clear that no one was going to do so.

A moment later Čoro's father, Kannji, using the same formula as Duduš, asked permission to speak. But instead of telling a story, he began to sing "his" song: a collection of formulas on the theme of parting in which he imagined his son speaking to him:

T'aven baxtale śavale!	<u>Be lucky, boys! I beg for</u>
Engedelmo mangav te phenav	<u>Your permission to make a</u>
Tumenge jekh čači vorba!	<u>True speech to you.</u>
Devlesa mukhav tut	I leave you with God.
De Phuro Kannje, Devla!	<u>Oh,</u> old Kannji, oh, God!
De Mange si te žavtar	<u>Oh,</u> I have to go now.
De Vod' kamav vodj niči.	<u>Oh,</u> if I want to, if I don't.
De Dur drom si te žav me	<u>Oh,</u> there's a long road I've to take.
De Khatar muro nepo.	<u>Oh,</u> away from my people.

Several men in the room joined in the singing, and the song went on for a few minutes. Every other verse was a variation on the first and was introduced by the first singer calling out, "Once again!" (*inke jekhvar!*). As they finished, the singers called, "Be lucky and healthy!" (*T'aven baxtale taj saste!*). Immediately afterward another man, Bakro's son's godfather, asked for permission and began a song. This singer took up the theme of the first one and sung as if Bakro were speaking.

Apol žavtar mange, mamo	<u>Then</u> I'm leaving now, Mother.
De lungone dromentsa	<u>Oh,</u> on the long roads.
O de lungone dromentsa	<u>Oh,</u> on the long roads
Ke bajpo [?]/entsa.	<u>For</u> . . . troubles [?].[8]
Apol Devlesa mukhav tut,	<u>Then</u> I leave you with God,
Phrala thaj Romale	Brother and Rom!
Phenel, "Mange si te žavtar,	<u>He says,</u> "I have to go now,
Ke Vodj kamav vodj niči."	If I want to, if I don't."
"Či kamav te žav, mamo	"I don't want to go, Mother,
De khatar muro nepo,	Away from my people.
Na rov!	<u>Don't cry!</u>
Khatar o dadoro.	Away from my father.
Khatar i dejori."	Away from my mother."
"Kana palpale reslan, kirve,	<u>"When you get back, Kirvo,</u>[9]
Atun phenesa godo:	<u>Then you'll say this:</u>
'Devlesa rakhav tumen	'I find you with God,
Muro dad taj muri	My father and my

Dej-tej-ej-ej-or-i	Mo-o-o-other
Jaj ke dad thaj phrala''' [?]	<u>Jaj my dad, and my brother.</u>''' [?].
"Či dikhlem tumen jaj,	"I didn't see you, jaj,
Ke avilas tumaro	<u>But</u> now your son
Šavo de na jaaaj."	Has come, jaaaj."
Apol "Fiam t'aves sasto!"	<u>Then</u> "My son, be healthy!"
T'aven baxtale savora žene!	<u>May everyone be lucky!</u>
T'aves baxtalo!	<u>Be lucky!</u>

For an hour or so one song followed another with more or less enthusiastic participation. Every other song referred to parting, and one version or another of the songs just mentioned was sung several times. But not every performance went as smoothly as these two. Many more resembled Duduš's attempt to tell his story, with the singer getting no further than the first line or two of his song and having to give up as conversations continued around him.

Although such disruption of the singing was mostly accepted as inevitable, interference from the women was treated less fatalistically. At one point the noise from the kitchen became so loud that it caused some men to shout out to the women to be quiet because "he's making his speech" (*čit! Phenel peski vorba!*). The women fell silent. However, even among the men, every so often the mood to sing waned for a while and the hum of conversation rose again. This rhythmic alternation of bouts of song and conversation punctuated by drinks, and rounds of coffee sent in from the kitchen, continued throughout the night.

Around 11:30 the Magyar "taxi" driver from Csóka began to demand that his party return home. Bakro himself went to speak with the man, and with a small payment the chauffeur was persuaded to stay a bit longer. After midnight bottles of brandy were opened and offered around in small glasses. Finally at 1:00 A.M. the guests left with their now very angry driver, pleading that they had to work the next day. Shortly after they left, the *mulatšago* nearly broke up when an argument between two men revived a long-standing feud. But despite the flight of several people worried about a fight, many men remained. At dawn Bakro boarded the train, waved off by most of the inhabitants of the settlement, some of them in tears. A large party accompanied Bakro to the gates of the barracks, drinking and singing on the way.

To see what is at stake for the Rom in these events, I want to look at the conventions that govern behavior in them. Men said that they attended the *mulatšago* "to show respect" to the man and the family that organized it. Whereas in daily life only men of equivalent economic standing tended to cooperate, in the *mulatšago* a man's status rested on the quality of his involvement with the celebration, not on his wealth. In Chapter 3 I described the home of one of the poorest Gypsies in the Third Class, Żunga. This man and his family rarely participated in the everyday shared activities of settlement life. And yet at a *mulatšago* one Christmas, when Żunga announced that he had to leave the party early in the evening, the whole company, including some very rich and prestigious Gypsies, prevented his exit. They said that they could not bear to spend the night without his fine voice, without his jokes and wit. The pauper was, for the duration of the *mulatšago*, the toast of all the Gypsies.

The *mulatšago* involved, in effect, the exaggeration and formalization of the basic ethos of *romanes:* the segregation of men and women, the principle of hospitality, and, above all, the display of "respect" (*patjiv*) to other Gypsies. Shame-purity taboos, such as that on a woman walking in front of a man while he was eating, which were only rarely observed from day to day, became de rigeur in *mulatšago*, and in this context, as in horse dealing, men felt it appropriate to say how much better they felt when there were no women around. Ideally, a *mulatšago* lasted all night, as if symbolically to deny or at least distance the brothers from their cohabitation with their wives in households. Gypsy women appeared, by and large, to accept this division of labor; indeed, they positively asserted their keenness for their men to carry on their *mulatšago*s. In this context I felt that their comments sometimes had an unusual note of deference and even reverence. They said things like "The men like it this way; that is why we do it," or explaining why something must not happen, they said, "The men do not like it." It was as if at these moments the men were in the center of society, that what they were doing was fundamental to being Rom and must not be spoiled by the domestic business of women.

For a *mulatšago*, huge quantities of food were cooked, way beyond what could be eaten by the guests. Specifically "Gypsy food" (*romano xaben*) was preferred, including "unleavened bread" (*boxoli*) and "stuffed cabbage" (*šax*). Sometimes, especially in the evening, if it was agreed that no one was hungry, a chorus of "When I drink, I don't like to eat" went around the room. But if the celebrants were "in the mood"—I can think of no better way to describe the haphazard manner in which such an alignment of desire took place—then they would all eat together. In that case there was no question of sitting around and making feeble excuses about having eaten already. More important, however, than eating together was the communal drinking of alcohol, without which the *mulatšago* was inconceivable. The significance of alcohol lay partly in its associations within Magyar peasant culture. It was hardly surprising that the Rom should have felt themselves most Gypsylike when under the influence of alcohol's antiproductive spirit. But the Rom also said that alcohol gave people health and strength by warming the body and strengthening the blood. Water, by contrast, cooled the body and was not to be mixed with beer or wine for fear of causing nausea.[10]

Just as eating was turned into a communal act, so the men all drank the same type of alcohol on any one occasion.[11] Each time a man raised a bottle or glass, he made a toast, for example, "May God give us health and luck" (*Baxt, sastipe te del amen o Del*), which was taken up and drunk to by all. Ideally, no one drank between these toasts. In part, men toasted by way of acknowledging the moral aspect of drinking in transforming their mood so that they became more willing to participate in the *mulatšago*. By drinking, men passed into the state they called *voja*, which was the desired state for *mulatšago*. Therefore, a successful *mulatšago* demanded the participation of all the men present and the (partial) submission of each individual to the collective will, the integration of his acts with the rhythm of the group. If a man did not want to drink, or he wanted to drink his own sort of alcohol in his own time, he did not go to a *mulatšago*.[12]

Likewise, sharing one's speech was also in a sense compulsory. If someone withdrew into himself, another would soon call out: "My brother, what's the matter? Where's your big voice?" A right to respect, to "beautiful respect" (*e šukar patjiv*), was the complement of this duty. Everything was supposed to be done to create the impression of a united group of perfect brothers. As they talked and sang, the men sat crammed on top of each other as if willfully playing down the separation between self and other. It was also quite common for one man to strike another playfully but forcefully. These blows were never returned. It seemed to me as if these, too, were gestures against the very fact of difference among the brothers.

The most impressive and important aspect of the *mulatšago* was, however, the formalization of speech. The Rom said that in the *mulatšago* men talked "in a refined, light manner" (*finoman, lašes*). First and foremost this meant that the Rom spoke in *romanes*, not in *gažikanes*, "the way of speaking of the *gažos*," and men who tried to address the company in Hungarian were told off roundly. Speaking finely also meant that attention was paid to the use of elaborately polite greetings.[13] But beyond matters of courtesy, the very register of talk shifted from "chat" or "ordinary conversation" (*duma*) to "speech" (*vorba*) and, more particularly, "true speech" (*čači vorba*). The *vorba* might have been a tale, a joke, a riddle, or, most commonly, a song. The sharp distinction that we make between speech and song did not exist for the Rom. But if a man called out, "I beg permission from everyone that you may forgive me if I offer you a true speech," the odds were that he would then begin to sing.

Everyday Gypsy social life was a fractious affair. The equality of brothers was lived more as a refusal to admit that any man was better than oneself than as a positive ethic. In normal speech there was no oratorical means for one man to silence another other than by raising his voice. One raised voice led to two and so into a spiraling inflation of vocal display. When it came to singing in the *mulatšago*, this problem could in principle be resolved. All *vorba*s were preceded by greetings to the listeners that indicated that the speech was for the benefit of all present, not part of a private conversation—"Be lucky!" and "I find you with God!" were the most common greetings, often with pleas for forgiveness added as well. Asking for permission, begging for excuses, the singer tried to avoid the implication that he was imposing himself on his fellows.

The greeting in the *mulatšago* at the beginning of *vorba* was, in effect, a hidden request for silence, effective precisely because it was disguised and therefore harder to refuse. At worst, people ignored the speaker-singer and carried on talking. But if permission was granted, silence and stillness were supposed to prevail throughout the song. I became aware of the coercive power of these phrases during a *mulatšago* in which a man, after offering greetings, began to sing. A second man interrupted, wishing to make a toast to another guest. The latter began, "Hold it; I find you with God" (*Aš ta; Devlesa arakhav tumen*) but was interrupted by the singer, who directly addressed his interrupter: "You may forgive me [if I continue]" (*Ša-jertos ma*). Another just said, referring to the singer, "He said, 'Be lucky.'" The interrupter withdrew, saying, "Well, that's different, then." His pique, however, was exposed since to apologize, he switched, rather rudely in the Rom's eyes, into Hungarian.

A man who toasted his brothers before singing, at the moment when he broke into the flow of conversations and asked for silence, attempted to shift the level of speech and thus alter the quality of relations among the assembled. He was trying to move out of banal, powerless, daily speech, in which the only way to impress others was to curse, into true speech—the self-evident truth of which ought to have removed any need to force himself on the others. To refuse to listen now was to turn down the relationship implied in song.

The final convention I mention here is the most important and complex. It was said that all Rom songs had to be "true" (*čačo*). This held for songs sung in daily life by men and women, as well as those performed in the *mulatšago*. In one sense when Gypsies sang, they expressed their truest feelings. Thus, Luludji once came to me and asked for a recording I had made of her singing alone to be erased from my tape.

In her song she had sung the stock line "What is my life for when I have no joy?" (*Minek mange kado trajo kana naj man boldogšago?*). Later Čoro had pestered her to know why she felt this way. In vain did she

Gypsy men remain "boys" forever.

plead with him that she had just sung the words for the sake of my recording; the only way to show publicly that she had lied in her song was to ask for the tape to be erased. Just before I left Harangos, the domestic problems experienced by this couple came again to a head, and members of the family for the first time moved to intervene publicly. In a small family *mulatšago*, the husband's elder brother sang about a man who had to leave his wife and children since his wife was a "whore" (*kurvi*). Čoro left the room immediately, as did several other people, embarrassed at the directness of the brother's approach. They were called back moments later to find Čoro outside thrashing himself against the rough stone wall, blood dripping from his self-inflicted wounds. His grief that his plight now had a public form, had become true by being embodied in a song, said much about the power of speech among the Rom.[14]

Slow Songs

The songs sung in the *mulatšago* concerned the stereotypical, ideologically stressed moments of Gypsy life. That is to say, they told of the grief of "orphanhood" or imprisonment, of the pain of Gypsy mothers at partings, of the way the Gypsies responded to misery by transforming the mood of their brothers with drink and song, of deals at the marketplace, of Gypsy wives and their betrayals of their men. The mood of the songs was sorrowful, and men often interjected comments on the "great grief" (*bari briga*) of life. The Gypsies called their songs "slow" (*loki*), a reference to the protracted performance style. This contrasted to the vigorous and energetic mood of the "dance songs" (*khelimaske djilja*) in which contests of male and female dancers were played out.[15] Every so often the songs quite literally seemed to arise out of tears and at their end reduced men to weeping again.

Although men predominated in the *mulatšago* singing, Gypsy women also knew all the songs that cropped up there. Indeed, the women's knowledge of the songs and willingness to sing them when asked to produce "true Gypsy songs" by folklore collectors have been essential in the process of recording Gypsy song. The conditions under which folklorists work (weekend or daytime visits to Gypsy settlements), mean, however, that from the point of view of *mulatšago*, women are "overrepresented" in their recordings. Wives, rather than their husbands, tended to deal with the importuning *gažos* for whom the men were often unwilling to perform. Privately, men and women did sometimes sing together: Some of the best recordings made by musicologists were made with husband and wife teams.[16] But in the course of settlement life, such partnerships rarely found an institutional forum.

I recorded the following song, led by Šošoj's son-in-law, at a small *mulatšago* one Saturday afternoon in the Chicken Plot.[17] A group of men had gathered, pooled their meager resources, and, as was so often the case on these occasions, managed to drink themselves into their *voja* on only a few bottles of beer.

Jaj śavale romale!	Jaj Boys, Gypsies!
Phenav, "Sa pilem e love."	I say, "I've drunk all the money."
Śavale, romale!	Boys, Gypsies!
Jaj te merav,	Jaj, let me die,[18]
Haj love te n'aśen ma.	And I have no money left.
Śavale Romale Jaj	Boys, Gypsies! Jaj!
Phenav "Sa pilem, sa xalem."	I say, "I've drunk, I've eaten it all."
Phralam, mure love Jaj.	My brother, my money, Jaj.
Apol Love te n'aśen ma.	So I have no money.
Phrala Jaaaj.	My brother! Jaaaj.
Apol me sim laśo śavo.	Then I am a fine/light boy.
Koran detehara, phralam Jaj,	In the early morning, my brother, Jaj,
Kaj kirčima rakhes.	You'll find me at the bar.
Śavale, Megalaši kerav he na na Jaj!	Boys! I make a stop there, he na na Jaj!
Apol phrala mang mol, mang mol	Then, brother, ask for wine, for wine
E bute romenge, mama, Jaj.	For the many Rom, oh Mama, Jaj.
Apol dikh kaj dili romni	Now look at my "crazy" wife,
Sa pala ma phirel, phralam Jaj	Always coming after me, my brother! Jaj,
Haj či del ma pača.	And she won't leave me in peace.
E bengaki daki . . . Jaj.	The devil's mother's . . . Jaj.
Haj apol De ma pača kurva	So leave me in peace, whore![19]
Na phir pala mande.	Don't come after me.
De kurva! Jaj!	Hey, whore! Jaj!
Pala ma phiresa,	If you come after me,
Opre potjinesa.	You'll pay.
Apol opre potjinesa.	Then you'll pay up.
Haj apol Sa pilem, sa xalem Jaj.	So I drank all, I ate all.
Savo'mure love Jaj.	All my money, Jaj.
Haj so phendem, mo?	And what did I say, friend?
Apol love te n'aśen ma.	Then I have no money left.
Lajos!	Lajos![20]
V'atunči sim śavo Jaj	Then also I am a man, Jaj.

Haj so phendem, mo?!	And what did I say, friend?
Apol khuren me te tradem	So, my foals, I drive them out.
Šavale, romale Jaj.	Boys, Gypsies, Jaj.
Koran detehara	In the early morning
Po foro te tradav. Jaj,	I drive out to market. Jaj.
Haj bikinav, paruvav,	And I sell, I swap,
E voja te kerav, phrala, Jaj.	To create the *voja*, brother, Jaj.
De régi nóta!	What an old song!
Haj te kerav e voja	And to make the voja,
Phrala e bute romentsa. Jaj.	Brother! With the many Rom. Jaj.
Te bistrav e briga Phrala!	So I forget my worries, brother!
Mo!	Friend!
Haj žavtar 'tunči žavtar	And I go away; I go away
Lumasa, šavale! De Jaj	Into the wide world, boys! Oh, Jaj.
Apol žav ande lumasa	Then I set into the world
Te resav mura gaža. Jaj.	So I look for my wife. Jaj.
T'aven baxtale taj saste!	May you be lucky and healthy!
Te del o Del sastipe taj zor!	May God give you health and strength!

After the first sung greeting ("Brothers, Gypsies!"), the singer, Lapoś, bemoaned his poverty and to emphasize his honesty, cursed himself ("Let me die!"). The other Rom understood that Lapoś had not fed and drunk himself witless at home, alone, in some gargantuan display. Rather, he had been making a *mulatšago* in the company of his brothers, and so the fact that his money had run out revealed just how true a Gypsy he was: a man who would spend his last forint to entertain his brothers, to keep them by his side as long as he could. Hence, Lapoś adopted the phrase "Then, I am a fine/light boy." Whereas for the *gažos*, conspicuous consumption of this form might appear a fruitless waste of scarce resources, for the Rom there was no shame in poverty if it was the result of such socially oriented generosity.

The next motif of Lapoś's song—"in the early morning"—evoked the moment on the way to the horse market when the Rom gathered after the separation of the night, strengthened themselves with a drink of brandy preceded by formal greetings for luck, and took the road through the dawn mists. Images of markets were popular in Gypsy song, and after a digression this theme came up again. The image of the market dealer in this and other songs was of a man free of all compulsions, a continual creator of possibilities, a man at ease in both the *gažo* ("I sell") and the Rom ("I swap") worlds. The image of driving the horses in cart that appears in many songs, "to ride slowly and quietly" (*lokes te trades, taj čendešen*), conjured up the state of grace that derived from the freedom of movement in the air and the sense of power from control of the horses.

Gypsy songs like this emphasized that being at the market was not a purely personal affair, that the display of men there was not simply an assertion of individual autonomy since the socially acceptable aim of dealing was not to get rich but to make the *voja* of the Gypsies. The term *voja* here referred to a state of excitement when the mood, even the urge, to sing with the "true brothers" (*čače phrala*) overcame a Gypsy: a state partly induced by drink, partly by the sense of well-being and security from the outside world that arose in the company of many Gypsies, and partly by success in public display. *Voja* was what we might call "grace" or "exaltation"; it was the ideal state to achieve in the *mulatšago*, for when men had *voja*, they began to sing. It was also a state that the Gypsies wished to prolong without end, if possible, just as the men tried to slow down the return home to "reality" after the market:

Taj Reslem me ke kirčima.	And I reached a bar.
Te Megalaši aba me kerdem.	I made a stop at once.
Apol Mangav me le śavenge	Then I ordered for the boys
Sa śudri bere, śavale!	For them all cold beer, oh, boys!

In another popular Harangos song, one of the sources of disruption of the *voja* of the men was articulated:

Aba detehara.	It's morning already.
Lungo dromesa źas.	We take a long road.
Xutjil andre hajtsál!	Tie them up and *drive!*[21]
Maškar le phralora.	Among the brothers.

Xutjil, phrala, andre!	Tie them up, brother!
Mre khure bik'maske-j.	My colts are for sale.
Mri čori pal' mande-j.	My poor wife is behind me.
Tradav ando foro.	I drive into the market.
Kan'aba kher reslem	When I got home,
Phenel, aba muri romni	She said, my wife, right away,
"So kerdan tu čoro?	"What have you done, pauper?
Kaj śuttan tje khuren?"	Where have you put your foals?"
So phenes tu?	What do you say?[22]

"Na puš mandar, gaźej!	"Don't ask me, gaźi![23]
Bikindem, parudem	I sold, I swapped.
Bikindem, parudem"	I sold, I swapped."
Haj "Me but love andem."	And "I've brought lots of money."

Songs like this, celebrating the men's horse trades, often ended with the man making the *voja* of his brothers, but here it closed after the exchange with his wife. At first the singer tries to silence her—after all, the market is not a woman's business—but then he relents, telling her what she wants to hear: that he has brought home cash. In this way the song reaffirms the contrast between the world of the brothers and that of the households, between contexts where spending and accumulation are, respectively, the goals of dealing. Ideally, in the context of brotherly singing, the Gypsy man deals for his brothers' *voja*, which is created by his spending money without thought. For his wife, however, the cash brought home is good news since this represents the enrichment of the household. In other songs, the wife appears in that familiar, stock form of the nagging wife "always coming after me." Gypsy women as wives could thus represent in these songs a concern with the household that was incompatible with the antiwork ethic of the *voja* of the brothers. By saying that the men are "good" when they spend all their money on their brothers, the songs deny the importance of what the "Gypsy wife" (*romni*) is made to stand for: the house, material reproduction, familial prestige.

In some songs, however, the potential conflict between the world of the home/wife and that of the brothers appeared to be resolved, or at least held in abeyance:

Babam, babam, de babam,	Baby, baby, oh, baby,
De babam, muri gaźi,	<u>Oh,</u> baby, my *gaźi*,
Mukh tu mange pača,	Leave me in peace,
De numa kadi ratji.	<u>Oh,</u> for this one night alone.
Mukh te xav len pav len	Let me eat and drink them[24]
Ke na tusa rodav len	<u>Because</u> it's not with you I found them.
Na tusa rodav len	It's not with you I found them
Ando baro foro.	In the great market.
Či dav pača, de babam	I won't leave you in peace, oh, baby.
De me khuren či tradav.	But I'm not driving my horses.
Kana khuren trado,	When I'll drive my horses,
Či bunjij te merav.	I won't care then if I die.
Kindem le romnjake	I bought the wife
Ekh šukar lolo dikhlo	A beautiful red scarf
Te na mezil čori,	So she doesn't seem poor,
Te mezilpe raji.	So she looks like a lady.
Te mezilpe raji,	So she looks like a lady,
De Romnjengi anglunji, he	<u>Oh,</u> the first of the Gypsy women, <u>Hey,</u>

Romnjengi anglunji,	The first of the Gypsy women,
Baraki luludji.	A flower from the garden.

Šoha na te meren—Janoskam!	Let them never die—<u>my dear Janos!</u>
Le ratjake śave—sostar?	The sons of the night—<u>why?</u>
Kaj birin te trajin,	Those who know how to live,
Pal' penge sanji čunji.	With their fine, thin whips.

The idea of socially beneficial expenditure expressed in these songs became clear to me one night when Thulo, one of those who was most forthright about his desire to "get away from the settlement," tried to sing his favorite song, a Hungarian "popular hit" (*schlager*). The song went as follows:

Hogyha nékem sok pénzem lesz,	If one day I've lots of money,
Felülök a repülöre.	I'll climb aboard an airplane.
Elszállok, mint a fecske	I'll fly off like the swallow
Fel a magas levegőre	Up into the airy heights.
Amerre én járok,	Wherever I go,
Bámul a világ.	The whole world stares.
Irigyel a sok nép,	Many, many envy me,
Aki engem lát.	Whoever get to see me.

Én a sok pénzt nem sajnálom.	I'll spend my bags of money.
Csak te légy a kicsi párom.	Just you be my little bunny.

So ridiculous and deviant was Thulo's taste that he was ridiculed both behind his back and to his face. In fact, in one *mulatšago*, this song was sung to him, and people laughed at the end, something I never saw at any other time. It was neither the obsession with money nor even the tone, so different from the mournful note in Gypsy "speech," that brought on the scorn. What shocked the Rom and seemed ugly to them was that in this song the man spends his money on himself. The whole world stares at him not because of his generosity but because of his accumulated wealth, his "bags of money." If and when he spends these, it will be not on his brothers but greedily on some "floozy."

In these songs we have begun to see one image of the Gypsy women as wife. But women also appeared as "mothers" (*mama*), especially in the context of parting and of dealing with troubled relations with the *gaźo* authorities:

Ke źaltar o śavo,	For the son is going off,
E mamako rakhlo	The son of the mother.

Na rov, mama; na rov.	Don't cry, Mama; don't cry.
Na rov, keservesen.	Don't cry bitterly.
Avri roves, Mama,	You're crying out, Mama,
Tje duj kale jakha.	Your two black eyes
Ke žavtar aba mama,	<u>For</u> I'm going away, Mama,
Haj me aba rovav.	And I'm crying already.
Maj avasa de jaj,	I'll come back later, jaj,
Ande luma bari.	From the great wide world.[25]

Here the Gypsy woman as onetime bearer of children is celebrated. But she is fêted at the moment when her son leaves her, goes out into the world. There were songs of the return of the son to his mother, when he came to make the *voja* of his family:

Uštji opre, Mamo	Get up, Mother!
Phabar e memelj	Burn the candles
Ke kher'avilas, Mamo,	<u>For</u> your dear son, Mother,
Mamo, tjo šavoro!	Mother, has come home!
Andre phirdem, Mamo	I wandered, Mother,
E luma e bari	In the great wide world.
Paro me či rakhlem	I didn't find a partner[26] [for me],
Mamo, la lumake aba!	Mother, in the whole wide world!

But now that the young man was "of the world," his mother could no longer help him, as the following, extremely popular, song shows. The song is in the form of a dialogue between mother and son, in which the son speaks the first six lines and the mother then answers.

"Mura dake Devles,	"My mother's God [a curse],
Pale bajba pelem.	I'm in trouble again.
M'ande pelem mamo,	I've fallen over,
Haj či žanav sostar."	And I don't know why."
"Pale bajba pelem.	"I'm in trouble again.
Le ma avri, mamo."	Get me out, Mama."
"So žanes le Devles.	"God knows if I can.
Naštig lav tut avri"	I can't get you out."
"But si le melale	"There is so much filth [many police].
Naj ma tehetšego."	I don't have the skill."

There were few songs of romantic love among the Rom, no plaints of unrequited passion. As lovers, the women tended to end up being cursed by the men and contrasted unfavorably to the "pure" mother always waiting, always true. One of the central themes of the songs was the threat of betrayal of the man by the woman through her sexual infidelity. This was so shameful for the man that in the stereotypical gesture required in song, he asks for the locus of his sense of shame, his eyes, to be put out. Then he will not be able to see the pitiful regard of his brothers.

Oj dile! Mure dile!	My crazy one! My crazy one![27]
Ke sost' man' muro trajo?	Why do I live?
Haj č'ašav la romnasa.	I'll not stay with my wife.
Haj Mur'romni bużangli-j.	My wife is cunning.
Taj Butendar zumadi	Tried out by many.
Haj Phrala haj romale!	Brother, Gypsies!
Haj żavtar lumasa,	I'll set off in the world,
Taj či trajij la kurvasa	And I'll not live with the whore
Ke muri romni putardi	For my Romni is "opened."
Xal la, Phrala! E pustija!	Brother! Let her rot![28]
O pand andre mur'jakha	Oh, put my eyes out
Te na dikhav le šavoren.	So I won't see the boys.

True Speech

The notion of truth in the *mulatšago* and in formal speech did not correspond exactly with everyday notions of honesty or exactness. When the Rom said that the songs they sang had to be true, they did not mean that any true words would do. The type of situation allowed in Rom song was, in fact, very restricted, and the Rom would refuse to listen to songs that did not fit the canonical pattern of true speech. Once when I was making an informal recording of Gypsy songs and a Rom sang that he would become rich, a woman teasingly called out, "He's always lying," and the singer himself laughed.

Although, as we have seen, there were rich Rom in the Third Class, as elsewhere, in the songs people did not become rich because they always spent their money on their brothers. Likewise, in real life much time and effort went into building up the household, and cooperation between husband and wife was considered the basis of a good marriage. But in the songs, these activities were devalued beside the making of the fraternity. How was it, then, that the Gypsies accepted as truth these biased and limited representations of reality? How was it that Gypsy song came to define, at the high points of social life, what the life of the Rom was like?

Part of the answer lies in the way experience was shaped narratively inside the songs. The words of the songs and the construction of their stories insinuated an interpretation of experience in an especially powerful and unchallengeable form so that the events described came to seem inevitable and the songs seemed self-obviously true. This sense of inevitability was created by the use of a set of fixed points, instances of grief and joy, from which escape was not so much impossible as simply not in question. In most songs performed in the *mulatšago*, there was little narrative intent. Actions in the songs were not presented in a causal context of motivations and constraints; no options were conceded for the "heroes" of the stories. In Gypsy song the motives and conditions of behavior (the life of the Gypsies among the *gažos*) were taken for granted. All that happened was that the endlessly repeated gestures of Rom life, as ideologically defined, were reenacted. In other cultures and their expressive forms, the sensation that the present order of things is fixed and unalterable may be provided by the gods, an explicitly conceptualized fate, or some other force of nature. Among the Rom, this sensation was created in song through the removal of both motive and context of action. Look, for instance, at this song collected by the Csenki brothers in the 1960s:[29]

Avri tradem mure khures	I drove out my colt
Po zeleno baro rito.	Onto the great green field.
Taj phadjilas lesko punro,	It broke its leg,
Mure šukare khuresko.	My beautiful colt's [leg].
Lesko gazda te dikhela	If the owner sees this,
Zeleno zubano šinla,	He'll tear his green coat,
Zeleno zubano šinla,	He'll tear his green coat,
Medjehaza man peila.	He'll throw me in the county house.
Medjehazate bešla	I sat in the county house.
Kaj la robija andr'avla	The prison opened before me
kaj la robija te bešla.	For me to sit inside.
Mure šavoren mukhela.	I left my sons behind.

The events followed each other with the force of fate. Even when there was an apparent gesture against the ineluctable order of the world, the Gypsy could not break out of the vicious circle, as an alternative version of the last two stanzas made clear:

Kana kodi gazda šundas	When its owner got to hear,
Morčuno zobuno śindas	He tore his leather coat.
"Potjin phrala panź-šo šela	"Pay up, brother, 500 to 600,
Te na xal tu e robija."	Or be cursed [literally, eaten] by prison."
"Sar me phrala te potjinav	"What me, brother, I should pay?
Inkább pav le phralentsa	I'll drink it with the brothers,
Le phralentsa, le butentsa,	With the brothers, with the many,
Haj le laśe manušentsa."	And the fine men."

Although his brother warns him to pay the owner of the horse that he has tried out and injured on the market field, the Rom defies his threatened fate. But precisely because of his devotion to his brothers, he will go to prison; that, tragically, is what it takes to be a true Gypsy.

This feeling of ineluctability is part of the reason that the Rom found their songs "believable." But there is another factor I wish to bring out: the nature of songs as aesthetic achievements in the context of their performance. One of the great pleasures, it seemed to me, for the Rom in singing was the way songs came to express individual experience in a collectively appropriable form. We have just seen how, in terms of the definition of "Rom experience," the songs did this. But in their rendition, too, the personal was made communal and vice versa. However, this shared experience had to be constructed and established in each case. Each singer brought something personal to his singing, and because he often brought a particular song to life, it came to be thought of as "his" song. This did not mean that he had rights in the song but that he tended to be associated with it and sang it more than any other song.

Not only was a man associated with one song, but he also would tend to personalize its performance by improvising within it both musically and textually. As a result, the songs did not have an absolutely fixed shape. Indeed, even within one song changes were made within the melody used in one (solo) performance. That one man sang a song in a certain way was reason enough for another man to try it differently and attempt to show that his version was more pleasing. It just did not make sense to a Rom to sing in a given way because another individual had done so before. He felt free to express himself and was determined to show that in song, as in everything else, no one commanded him. Thus, improvisation had a certain virtuoso tone to it, and a Rom improvising into or around a song often drew attention to his personal touches by his facial gestures.

But in the *mulatšago*, there were musical and textual limits to how far a man could diverge from what was commonly accepted as a song.

Individual autonomy had to be restricted to create a world of homogenized men. The brotherly world demanded the participation of all and the submission of every individual to a series of collective gestures, to the rhythm of the group. So just as the men ate and drank in unison, the aim of singing in the *mulatšago* was for everyone to sing at once, almost in one voice. Wholly personal, and therefore unfamiliar, songs did not allow participation and would not be heard through. Major textual or melodic changes or even excessive grace notes would disrupt the choral-like singing.

If, however, a man was willing to submit himself, he could now, by singing, pay respect to his brothers while asking for it in the form of attention or participation. The collective nature of the song's images (formulas), their nonpersonal quality, allowed his individual experience to be partially subsumed in shared images. In the *mulatšago*, one man would begin to sing, and if he was successful in gaining the attention of his brothers, some or all of them would join him in singing; they would "help" (*žutil*) him. Singing together successfully, they integrated individual and communal aspects of song.

However, the balance achieved was always fragile. The personal element of singing, the choice of a song by one man, his unique touches, the centrality and distinction he gained among the assembled Gypsies while he sang, made each proposed performance an uncertain venture. Consequently, many more songs were started than were finished. The cry "What an old song!" which was frequently interjected during singing, was an attempt to minimize the distinctiveness of the performance by pushing the composition of the song into an impersonal, shared past.[30]

The lack of room for individuation also explained, in part, why there were no instrumentalists in the Gypsy *mulatšago*. A musician would have placed himself above the group in a position of distinction. Since the aim of the *mulatšago* for the Rom was to act as brothers to each other, there was no room for the specialist musician. In the *mulatšago*, the initiator of a song could differentiate himself by singing the echolike two syllables at the end of each four (or two) lines of music, but no further. This part was frequently left "unheard" in individual performance but might be added by the initiator of a song in group singing.

Finally, Gypsy singing of the "slow songs" (*loki djili*) in Harangos involved no contrapuntal forms, no polyphony, no form that allowed significant structural individuation of performers. As Alfred Schutz said, in polyphonic music "each voice has its own particular meaning. ... Each represents a series of ... autarchic musical events."[31] This was precisely what the Gypsies I knew tried to avoid. In the near-monody of the *loki djili*, the Gypsies lived in the music in a single, homogeneous dimension.

Song and the Ritualization of Equality

The successful performance of a song was a moment in which the habitual "agonistic egalitarianism" of settlement life—the refusal to admit that any man was a better Gypsy than another—was momentarily replaced by a positive, lived equality.[32] Through singing in the *mulatšago*, the Gypsies transcended the opposition between themselves as individuals and as brothers. They were released from the endless struggle against each other to maintain autonomy and prestige. While singing a song, a man made it "his own," yet at the same time the song seemed to make the man its own. By expressing himself in true speech, the performer revealed himself as a true Rom or true brother.

The Rom felt that they became fully Rom in the performance of the songs, and so what the songs said became especially convincing. In song they could live as "free," specific, individuals and at the same time submit to the rigorous leveling and homogenizing norms of Gypsy society. Because of this, singing together provided an experience of a viable life as a Rom. The brief moment of communitas seemed to be savored in the protracted performance style. During a song, men called out, "Slowly! Don't hurry!" and between lines of song long pauses were left, pauses in which complete quiet was expected, in which the unison of the men, their mutual respect for each other, could be perfectly, peaceably experienced. If all this was achieved, the assembled men would say that the singing that night was "refined" and not "forced" (*erőltetett*). It showed that no one was under pressure to "get his bit in."

In the *mulatšago*, brotherhood was represented as the way to live in a world of *gažos*, and to sustain this vision, the world associated with women as wives was moved to one side. But they were moved aside only momentarily, since Gypsy women were at the heart of much experience and desire outside the *mulatšago*. As a result, the creation of brotherhood in the *mulatšago* was inherently short-lived. In the successful *mulatšago* with which I opened this chapter, a quarrel broke out that could have led to a fight, and at that point some men fled with relief to their homes and their wives. When I arrived at my co-godfather's house after the squabble, he took the opportunity to tell me that he hated going to *mulatšagos* since the men so often quarreled there. He preferred, he said, to be in his own home with his wife, who knew how to give and receive "respect." No one, he told me, could accompany him as she did. But my co-godfather was back at a *mulatšago*, not holed up with his wife, when Bakro returned to the settlement two weeks later.

The Rom said that men became Rom in "speech" (*vorba*). One answer to the question "What does a true Gypsy do?/How can I become a Rom?" was "[if you learn] to speak in a refined way in company." The answer to a common riddle "When is a man happy?" was "in *vorba.*" There was the straight meaning here, but perhaps a joke was also intended: All people, the Rom included, are always "better" in speech than in practice. But by saying this, I do not wish to revive the tired distinction between the "ideal" and the "real," or—to use the sociological jargon—social structure and social action. Speech (including what we distinguish as song) had a significance for the Rom that it does not have for us since it was through speech that the Gypsies represented the reproduction of their society. The special nature of musical communication made this appear all the more real. Talking of musical events, Schutz noted, "They are doubtless meaningful to the actor as well as to the addressee, but this meaning structure is not capable of being expressed in conceptual terms; they are founded upon communication but not primarily upon a semantic system."[33] Music, for Schutz, worked by moving beyond the referential form of constative speech. Thus, the linking of texts with melodies transforms the former and alters their relation to concrete, individual experience. For instance, since each rendering of a melody involves the performers and audience in the same unsummarizable experience that was had on the previous production of that piece, the same entry into the "inner time" of music that can be had only "in" that piece, they experience a special form of "simultaneity" with the "past."[34] The Gypsy notion that the songs were "ancient" thus seems to have some experiential roots in the irreducible nature of musical performance, in which, according to Schutz, one's very experience of time is altered.

The songs said that singing with one's brothers was the most Rom thing to do. But it was not just what they said, or how they said it, but what they did (by being musical acts) that made this assertion convincing. By making music together, by singing in near-monody, the men became most "Gypsylike." What the songs said and what they did were one and the same, and hence the Gypsies became "brothers in" or "sons of" song.

The *mulatšago* was one of those reflexive or constitutive events that anthropologists refer to as rituals.[35] The songs claimed that the Gypsies shared, drank, and sang together, and the songs suggested a stable order in which the Rom stayed poor, wives betrayed, mothers waited, and men remained Rom. The experience of getting people to sing together demonstrated, to me as an outsider at least, that the state of brotherhood had to be accomplished. But to the Rom, since in achieving brotherhood they became full Rom, by singing together they were doing no more than expressing what was in their nature as Rom. What was in fact achieved was presented as given in the order of things, and this was done through the means of song.

12

THE SHAME OF THE BODY

If uncleanness is matter out of place, we must approach it through order. Uncleanness or dirt is that which must not be included if a pattern is to be maintained.

Mary Douglas, Purity and Danger

ONE OF MY CONCERNS THROUGH THIS BOOK has been to explore separations, the distinctions that sustain a particular social order. The Gypsies of Eastern Europe have been pushed to the edges of the national communities in which they belong. In Harangos most Magyar inhabitants of the town did not want the Gypsies to move in among them; they wanted to keep the Gypsies separate. Gypsies, to them, were dirty and defiling. They were what "must not be included if a pattern is to be maintained." And yet, from another point of view, they were part of that pattern; they were a necessary part of the whole process of social reproduction in Hungary. They fulfilled social functions, jobs, and services that others did not want. There was a moral tension in this separation—after all, in some contexts the Gypsies could be seen as not so very different from other poor Magyars—but perhaps partly because of the greater power of the non-Gypsies, it was a tension that most of them could ignore easily enough.

The Rom, too, defined themselves in opposition to the non-Rom, the *gažos,* and separated themselves morally from those who surrounded and dominated them. We have seen them do this in their egalitarian communal ethic, in their attitudes toward time, money, and labor. In this chapter I look at a final separation that the Rom effected: between themselves as "pure," "respectable" people and the "dirty" *gažos.* In one sense there is a continuity here. Just as the Magyars looked at the Gypsies, so the Rom thought of the *gažo* as potentially defiling "matter out of place." But there

204

the similarity ends. Though the Rom discourse on "pollution" and "shame" built on a common southern European ideology, which shaped Magyar ideas as well, in crucial respects the Rom's ideas were distinctive to themselves. Apart from particular notions of bodily shame that were not held by Magyars, the ideology of shame and pollution played a far more important role in Rom than in Magyar life. Even more important, unlike the Magyars, the division of the world that constituted the Rom as a distinct group rebounded on their own sense of self. Whereas the Magyars could shunt out their "dirty work" onto social others, the Rom were not so fortunate. The Rom owned nothing but their bodies and their homes, and there was no social group subordinate to them, so it was within their own daily lives that they effected the separation that enabled them to imagine that it was possible to live as "pure," "honorable" people.

In the anthropological literature, cleanliness beliefs are perhaps the single most commented on feature of Gypsy "culture." All the major ethnographies of the American Rom, those by Carol Miller, Anne Sutherland, and Rena Gropper, discussed concepts of "pollution" (*marimo*) in terms of a division of the Gypsy world into polluted *gažos* and "pure" Rom and of the Gypsy body into "pure" upper and "impure" lower.[1] Judith Okely also analyzed English Traveler-Gypsy ideas of purity, discovering an alternative inner/outer body symbolism.[2] What all these writers focused upon, following Mary Douglas, was the way Rom cleanliness rituals "protect the political and cultural unity of a minority group."[3] In the analysis that follows, I take the same route as my predecessors, but here a concern with the representation of reproduction leads in a new direction. My argument, in a nutshell, is that the Rom, through the symbolic separation of their bodies, denied or masked their involvement in biological, bodily reproduction in favor of a higher form of social reproduction and in so doing obviated (symbolically) the very things—their bodies—that kept them in a state of dependency to the *gažos*.

I begin this chapter by considering Gypsy morality, notably the idea that the Rom were purer and more respectable than the *gažos*. I then consider more basic notions of the life process. Although some of the Rom's ideas may at first seem exotic, it will gradually become clear that they were transformations of ideas that were widely distributed in the world around them.

Dirty Gypsies

In the course of discussing Harangos council policy in Chapter 7, I said that one of the initiatives of which officials were most proud was the biannual "disinfection" of the Gypsy sites. Although these had been discontinued by the time I lived in the town, the spirit that had inspired them continued. During summer 1985, the Public Health Department visited the Third Class to treat the Gypsies' pigsties with fly killer. A mass of small children quickly gathered to watch and pester until the official in charge distracted them with a promise of sweets. He brought out of his van a handful of small boxes and shook one over the children's heads before handing out the others. A little puzzled, I wandered over to see just what he was distributing: not candies at all but a delicing solution. Of course, his random sprinkling of the children had no medicinal worth whatsoever. But as the phobic gesture of a "clean" Magyar trying to dislodge Gypsy "dirt," it worked well enough.

It was especially telling that it was this man who should have been behaving so queerly, for a few years earlier he had been in charge of council policy toward the Gypsies and instrumental in arranging the disinfections; and yet, in what he claimed had been many years of friendly contact with the Rom, he had never once thought that by such gestures he might humiliate his "friends." I do not know for certain why he felt so blasé about the feelings of people on whose goodwill he always counted and sometimes depended, but I think that the reason for his disdain lay in his belief that the Gypsies had neither a sense of honor nor a sense of shame. I once sat in this man's office while he tried to "educate" me about the Gypsies with stories about the strange behavior of Gypsy women, how they flirted with him, how they could be heard cursing like a man in the market square, and how only a few days before he had seen a Gypsy woman "offer herself" to a man buying nylon thread from her.[4] He concluded this catalog of shame with the case of a family whose members, he claimed, had lengthened their middle fingers the better to pickpocket citizens in the Harangos market square. In his eyes these violators of good citizens, like all the other Gypsies, lacked the sense of honor or shame that would have kept a "proper" person at a distance. Given this basic lack—a failing that rendered the Rom somehow less than human—it seemed to him that to assault the Gypsies was less of a violation or not even one at all.[5]

The real irony of the situation was, however, lost on the official: While he saw himself bringing "cleanliness" and "hygiene" to the ignorant Gypsies, who might thereby acquire a civilized sense of shame, they saw him and his sort as dirty, defiling, and, above all, flagrantly lacking in what *they* thought of as a sense of "shame." In fact, a constant source of comment and contemptuous innuendo among the Rom was the way that the *gažos* "were not ashamed of themselves" (*či laženpe*).[6]

Talk of *gažo* moral torpor occurred in several different contexts. Most concerned the treatment of the body, commonly the way the *gažos* lacked any sense of decorum or cleanliness. The Rom considered domestic animals like cats to be unclean and when watching television would shriek with disgust when a *gažo* character in a film picked up a cat and stroked it. Likewise, the Rom considered the *gažo* habit of lying in a bath and thereby "lying in one's own filth" to be revolting. As a result of such habits and a general moral slovenliness, the *gažos* and their houses, according to the Rom, often smelled bad. It was not unusual for Gypsies to hold their noses and make grimaces to one another behind the back of *gažos* when visiting them in their homes. And when charitable *gažos* gave presents of used clothes, these were elaborately disinfected and washed several times.

The Purity of the Rom Body

At the outset of my stay in Harangos and with much previous published work on Rom morality in mind, I asked a young Rom who had given me some help with Romany for advice on how best to integrate into Harangos Gypsy life. He said that he would tell me about "the sort of things that the Gypsies/men (Rom) get most upset about." First he told me never to mix up either the water or the bowls used in clothes washing and dish washing. Gypsy women avoided doing so and ensured that they were seen by others to avoid doing so by washing all eating utensils in the pans in which food had been cooked and by not using dish towels at all, because they might have been washed with clothes. Dishes were left to stand and dry instead. A few weeks later I moved to the Third Class and in the tumult of trying to cope with my new surroundings promptly forgot his advice about towels. I was then surprised to see the dish towels disappear one day from our kitchen and reappear a while later appropriated by our hosts as foot rags! Many months later, despite the fact that I thought I had become accustomed to the Gypsy distinctions, I made another embarrassing blunder. One afternoon while helping Čoro's mother mend a washing machine, I needed to empty the machine and unthinkingly moved for the nearest receptacle to hand, a large water jug. With a look of astonishment and a gasp, the woman rescued the jug from my attempt to pollute it and brought out the clothes-washing bowl from under her bed.

As my young informant had indicated to me, the business of bathing when in the settlement was often rather furtive. People did not "shamelessly" announce to anyone around that they were going off to wash. The Rom washed their face and hands in the morning, ideally before speaking to anyone outside of the immediate family. The soap was then placed out of sight on a shelf away from eating utensils, and the water was thrown out behind the house by a female member of the household. The Romnis (Gypsy women) then put the "clean" face-washing bowl outside their houses as a sign that they were ready to receive visitors. After this, most people did not wash again until before dusk, at most taking a mouthful of water and spitting this into their hands outside the house. If one's hands were greasy from food, they were wiped on a dry cloth.[7]

It appeared, following Miller's and Sutherland's earlier analyses, that underlying the Rom ideas of cleanliness lay an unspoken, nonverbal, but categorical distinction between upper and lower body. The head, especially the mouth, was the most important and pure part of the upper body, exemplified in the way men would kiss each other full on the mouth as a sign of trust and brotherly closeness. In the idea, discussed in the previous chapter, that the head was the seat of a Rom's "luck" (*baxt*) and in the notion that loss of honor was a matter of having "your mouth eaten" (*xalo-j tjo muj*), we find related notions.[8]

The taboo on washing clothes and dishes together ensured that any dirt from the lower body did not contaminate objects that passed into the mouth. It was for the same reason that the Rom avoided baths. Although soap was used for washing one's face and hands, I noticed the that the women who had washed from head to toe appeared to have used washing powder or liquid—as if keen to ensure that none of their dirt remained on the soap that was kept in the kitchen. One evening soon after moving to Harangos, I watched a television drama with Čoro's brother during which a woman slumped into a hot bath. Missing such *gaźo* comforts, I sighed enviously, but my host, who had put his neck out by befriending me since my arrival, turned away grimacing with disgust toward the wall, his hand over his face. Fortunately for the sake of our friendship, we were alone.

The symbolic separation of upper and lower body was not only given expression in washing prohibitions. The very rigid dress sense of Gypsy women, who endeavored always to maintain a sharp line between the upper and lower body, displayed the embeddedness of this distinction in their thought. Again, whereas men of all ages often walked naked to the waist during summer, no man put on "shorts" even in the most sweltering heat. Older women (of fifty or sixty years) also bared themselves from the waist up quite without embarrassment while at home and even outside during the hot weather. Younger women were more circumspect, although mothers breast-fed as they pleased. Women kept small personal items in their bras. Other items of clothing, such as long coats or one-piece dresses, were "shameful," as if denying the division of the body. Trousers, too, were taboo for women, though the wearing of a man's jacket caused no offense, since this respected the upper/lower aesthetic.

The Stench of Pollution

If the Gypsies did not maintain the separation of upper and lower, they were said to have become "dirty" or "polluted" (*melalo* or *marimo*, both of which could be glossed into Hungarian as *piszkos*, or dirty). Confusing upper and lower, for instance, by washing one's face in water used for washing one's genitals would have made one impure.

The most salient sign of an "unclean" house or person was that "it stank" (*khandel*). The Romany term suggested an overpowering and foul smell, the sort of thing that made one's stomach turn. The noun (*khan*) was used to refer to stench from polluted objects, in contrast to the morally neutral sense of the word "smell" (*sung*). For instance, when arguing with a man about a woman in another settlement, I suggested in her defense that, unlike some members of her family, she was a "clean Gypsy woman" (*vuži romni*). He replied that if I thought that, I should go near her and smell the stench (*khan*) rising from between her legs.

Perhaps it was not incidental that the sensation associated with pollution was smell, since in this form an emission of the lower body passed into the upper body through the nose and mouth. In contrast to a Rom or Romni seeing or being seen by a member of the opposite sex in a state of undress, which was shameful, a *khan* was itself bodily polluting: A young man who left a bar we had just entered and threw up on the ground in front of it explained afterward that the room had "stunk like a toilet." Skin markings (such as spots), disabilities, and infertility were all explained—by vindictive neighbors in most cases—as the outcome of polluting behavior.

Because the *gažos* were unaware of the need to keep upper and lower separate, one could always suggest that they were unclean. On moving into houses where the previous tenants had been *gažos*, the Gypsies would bleach to disinfect the place from the ceiling downward. In the Third Class, there were *gažo* houses that the Gypsies avoided entering for this reason. However, the attitudes of the Rom were not always consistent, for there were also *gažo* houses that the Gypsies entered and ate in; and outside the settlement they would willingly eat in most *gažo* restaurants—so long as there was no *khan*.

Purity and the Sense of Shame

Among the Californian Rom, as among the English Gypsies, matters of pollution and purity "are the core of a system of beliefs that give order to the moral universe of the Rom" by separating clean Rom from foul *gažos*.[9] Although there were great resemblances in the cleanliness beliefs of other Gypsy groups and those of the Rom with whom I lived, there were also crucial variations. Perhaps the most important difference was that the concept of impurity among the Kalderaś Rom of Poland, Sweden, and America not only constituted an ethical code but also provided the basis for a legalistic structure within the Rom community according to which "immoral" Rom could be ostracized and effectively excommunicated on the grounds of "impurity." To declare someone impure (*marimo*) was to exclude that person from all contact with anyone who accepted that judgment.[10] In Harangos, even though much behavior only made sense in terms of the upper/lower division of the body and the fear of pollution, because the Rom did not practice ritual exclusion, they told me, "We don't really hold to *marimo* customs anymore." One man explained that "among the Kalderaś a wife would not even serve her husband water by her own hand. She had to cover her hand with her scarf. In 'the old days' (*varekana;* literally, sometime), it was the Kalderaś who were strictest" because of the institutional arrangements around these customs. Such answers to my questions—answers that often also referred to ideas of *marimo* as "superstitions"—reflected, in part, a more general desire to represent Rom culture as "modern."[11] But in equal part they reflected a slightly different cultural emphasis among the Harangos Rom, a focus on shame as much as on impurity.

Whereas questions of purity and pollution did not occupy much of Rom conversation, the opposite was true of the topics of shame and shameful acts. For beyond being impure, the *gaźos* were completely lacking in "shame" (*laźipe*) and "respect" (*patjiv*).[12] At the heart of this idea was one of those "amazing but true facts" about the "foolish non-Gypsies" (*dilo gaźo*): They displayed no embarrassment about their sexuality, fertility, or other bodily functions in public. Thus, the *gaźi* (female *gaźo*) guest of mine who innocently asked out loud to use the toilet was a source of much amused comment among children and less ribald embarrassment among adults—any respectable person, it was thought, would have known to ask more discreetly for advice from a Gypsy woman. On another occasion a young researcher sitting on the grass outside my house had her legs gently pushed together by Luludji when a man walked into the yard—again no Romni over the age of three would needed to be taught such an elementary lesson in demeanor. But even the everyday dress of non-Gypsy women was thought to be shameless and expressive of a sexuality out of control—unlike the *gaźis,* all the Romnis covered their legs to their knees and wore head scarves.

So although much of the academic discussion of Gypsy morality has been cast in terms of purity and impurity, in Hungary this ethic shaded into a concern with shame and honor, idioms that will be recognized by anyone familiar with the ethnographic literature on southern Europe. Since being pure was to be "owed honor" (*patjivalo*) and one became defiled by having no shame, in reality the two codes merged. This was all the more so, since the Rom sense of shame was rooted in the same conception of the person as that which generated the idea of a pure Rom body.

Shame and the Gendered Person

Among the Rom shame was in some respects prototypically associated with women, their bodies, and their sexuality. Thus, although the performance of bodily functions was a source of shame for all the Rom, in public contexts, at least, this was particularly true for the Romnis. At weddings, the one large mixed-sex gathering of the Rom, the men took over the toilet outside the celebrating house, while the women had to discreetly seek out alternative facilities with other relatives, since Gypsy women were not to be seen by a man going toward a toilet.[13] In regard to bathing, where there was always a chance that a member of the opposite sex might appear unexpectedly, Gypsy women found themselves more constrained than men—even young girls just washing their hair went into the clean room and locked the door behind them. Older women would hang a towel over the outside door to indicate that no one was to come in. Whereas men might have avoided washing in front of a respected guest, before their immediate family they seemed to feel no shame, and adolescent boys washed themselves in the kitchen in a fashion that was inconceivable for their sisters.

Even as young children, female Gypsies were expected to display greater shame around their bodily functions than boys. I once recorded Čoro's sister, Maron, explaining the essence of this aspect of the Gypsy way to her eight-year-old daughter:

> My daughter, when you grow older, you mustn't go wandering around without a chaperon. You must never leave your hair out in the open because if your grandmother or grandfather saw you, they would say, "You won't grow into a good Gypsy girl."
>
> You must wear a scarf on your head because the old Gypsies don't like a young girl who goes around without a head scarf. They'll say that you are "trying to look more beautiful." They'll tease you and humiliate you.
>
> Don't put your hair out in front of your scarf because if you do . . . they'll say it is because you are a little whore.
>
> And you are not allowed to talk to boys for a long time. Your brother will beat you up if you do!
>
> [Later she continued:] When you become a big girl, you mustn't wear trousers because the customs of the *gažos* are no good. Nor must you come around me wearing a short skirt . . . or people will say, "She goes around like the *gažis.*"

In covering her lower body with an apron and her hair with a scarf, in not trying to make herself more attractive, and in keeping her eyes to the ground away from Gypsy men, a girl showed that she was willing to appear ashamed of her sexual desirability. A girl's demeanor in front of guests, her embarrassment, and her steadied gaze at the floor were valued qualities in a potential daughter-in-law. Breaches of this etiquette would lead to scandal, as I discovered when I surprised two girls playing with makeup in our house and putting on a small amount of mascara. Immediately on my entry, they scuttled into the clean room, wiped the makeup off their faces, and made me promise that I would never tell anyone what they had been doing. This kind of repression of desire restricted other activities of young girls. I remember a regular twelve-year-old visitor to our house, one of Čaja's granddaughters, showing me one day appalling burn marks in her palm. It emerged that she had been smoking a cigarette when surprised by an elder relative, and rather than allow her "loose" behavior to become public knowledge, she had crushed the burning cigarette in her palm. For similar reasons, other older girls had found it impossible to go to evening classes for driving lessons until one of their mothers started accompanying them—lest it be said that they were "going wandering around" without supervision. They knew too well the consequences of a loss of reputation: the impossibility of finding a respectable husband.

The power of these taboos was all the greater in that divergent *gažo* behavior was the subject of so much conversation in Romany. *Gažo* girls were known to visit the discos of the town and dress up to deliberately attract men's attention. From the Gypsies' point of view, the *gažis'* lack of restraint was a comic, if not grotesque, sign of a promiscuous sexuality. Nowhere was this more obvious than at the open air municipal swimming pool, to which Čoro and his friends would suggest that we go together in the summer months to stare at the shameless and shocking *gažis*.

The Rom occasionally found such entertainment in the Third Class, too, since an unfortunate *gažo* couple who lived there used to provide a public demonstration of the moral level of their sort, at least from the Rom's point of view. Every so often these middle-aged people would get drunk and dance together in their garden, to the huge amusement of the Rom, both children and adults, who, like visitors to the zoo, would gather outside the fence, laugh and stare in amazement at the two "fools" (*dile*), and egg them on to further "debauchery."

To some extent all the *gažos* were assumed to have the potential for such behavior. This sometimes made me pause before inviting guests, since I knew the Rom would test them to see how "shameless" they were. Most of the time the foibles of my guests were a source of amused comment among the Rom, but on one occasion near the end of my stay when a *gaźi* guest drank too much and collapsed, my hosts told me in no uncertain terms, that such women from Budapest were all "professional whores" (*lubnja*) and were to be avoided. As if to make the point explicitly, on the walls of almost all Gypsy houses were pornographic pictures of naked *gaźis*.

If the non-Gypsy women were presented as depraved and out of control, some of the symbolic associations of the Gypsy women, the Romnis, were much more flattering. Notably there was a pervasive association of femininity with sweet-smelling flowers and young women dressed in vibrant reds.[14] All women's aprons, scarves, and, often, dresses sported flowery patterns. The most expensive and desirable aprons were themselves shaped like plastic flowers, since their fringes were "jagged" (*tsakkos*). All the Rom houses were painted inside with roll-on flower patterns, and the "clean room" was hung with vivid plastic flowers. After a death in a house, these were removed and the painted flowers whitewashed out, suggesting that in some way flowers symbolized life for the Rom. Every day the girls who came to draw in our house obsessively designed the same careful floral patterns with "jagged" tips, while their brothers, equally consistently, drew men with horses and carts and houses as seen from the outside. Unmarried Gypsy girls used to make flowers of their own bodies by cutting their hair over their forehead in a "jagged" fringe.

Dance songs about Gypsy women, from which I cite three examples, also articulated this idea. In the first one, flowers stand for life, in contrast to the night, which is the time when the "ghosts" (*mulo*) wander the earth: "*Te na mezis kali ratji. Te mezis luludjengi raji!*" (Don't resemble the black night. Look like the lady of flowers!). In the second, flowers are associated with the daughter-in-law who produces children for the grandparents:[15] "*E luludji loli si. Muri bori šukar si*" (The flowers are red. My daughter-in-law is beautiful). This image also recalled speeches at "betrothals" (*mangimo*) in which the bride-to-be was described as a flower plucked from the garden. Furthermore, during this ceremony the girl's virginity was represented by a scarlet rose-hip fruit that was tied to a bottle of brandy shaped in the form of a naked woman, which was presented to the girl's father. The tightly closed necks of the hip buds, around which grow jagged leaves, symbolized the unpenetrated nature of the girl. The inside of these buds is hairy, but in the ceremony it stood for hair that had not been "seen." In the rare case of a *mangimo* for a previously married woman, a "head scarf" (*dikhlo*; literally, "seen") was tied around the bottle to symbolize her adult sexual status: As long as she had been "unopened" (*te na putardi*), her head hair could be worn openly.

The commonest expression for menstruation was the euphemistic "I have flowers" (*si ma luludji*), and in the dance ditty that follows we see how, through the systematic intertwining of women with images of flowers, female fertility was represented in a bloodless fashion. Water was poured on the flowers so their *dji*, their "life force," did not wither. The symbolic equation might be thus reduced to the statement "As blood is to women, so water is to flowers." And since women were symbolically assimilated to flowers, their fertility could be represented without the mess and shame of blood.

Šor paji pe luludji	Pour water on the flowers
Te na pharrol lako dji.	So their *dji* won't dry up.
Te pharrola lako dji,	If their *dji* dries up,
Č'avel ame šukar bori!	A pretty bride won't come to us!

If my previous argument was that Gypsy women's shame concerned their sexual desirability, in these associations with flowers, we can see that their fertility itself was being represented in a "tidied-up" fashion. To make more sense of these ideas I asked Judit Szegő to conduct a series of interviews with women about the Rom sense of shame.

The Shame of Bodily Life Processes

In discussions with Judit, the Romnis began talking about the root of their shame being their menstrual cycles, but for them this topic could only truly be broached by discussing Rom customs concerning birth, christening, and death. Although they did not say so abstractly, it is hard to avoid the conclusion that it was the whole nature of biological, bodily processes that caused embarrassment and shame.

Thus, it was because of the shame of menstruation that a girl had to wear an "apron" (*ketrintsa*) over her skirt from the onset of puberty.[16] Unlike the skirt under it, the apron was not polluting, and I saw women wipe plates or even cutlery with it. Most school-age girls said they were "sick" (*nasvali*) when they menstruated and did not go to school or other public places for one week after. In fact, the whole topic was so embarrassing that some girls said that they learned about menstruation only from older girls, since their mothers had never mentioned the subject.[17]

Menstruation seemed to stand for the whole process of bodily fertility. Women said that it was because of menstruation that young girls began to be ashamed of displaying their hair in public. And when the Gypsies said that girls ought to cover their hair so as not to attract the attention of boys, it was not only the girl's sexual attractiveness the Gypsies wished to seclude. Head hair was evocative of bodily strength, fertility, and abundance. For instance, when trying to describe a huge crowd of people, a Gypsy would take a bunch of hair at the forelock and say, "They were this many," the uncountability of hair representing a multitude of people. And on Easter Monday when the men sprinkled the hair of all the women of child-bearing age with perfumed water and received eggs in return, the link between women's hair and fecundity was made explicit.[18] Because of such associations, little boys and girls did not have their hair cut at all for fear that doing so would remove their power to grow. Being the sign of the ability to produce numerous offspring, a woman's hair was never worn free but was always kept tied up and out of sight under a scarf of the same flowery design as her apron. If male guests arrived and caught a Romni casually dressed in her kitchen with the scarf at her neck, she would bring it up fully around her head "out of respect."[19]

The treatment of head hair is a good example of the way that the Rom felt shame about the nature of the body as a whole rather than simply its "lower" aspects. Around pregnancy, too, there was a more nuanced symbolism. Whenever a woman was pregnant, she and her husband were supposed to tell everyone they knew—this ensured that any unexpected desire of the pregnant woman would be fulfilled without question and without need for further explanation. So once the Romni's condition was known, no further reference was made to it. At least outside the intimacy of marriage, and probably even there, pregnancy was publicly construed as an "illness," and even to use the adjective "pregnant" (*kamni*) for a woman was not just improper but somehow insulting.[20] Pregnant Gypsy women wore their aprons to obscure their swelling anatomies with such success that a couple of times during my stay with the Rom I was caught unawares when I heard of a birth to a woman in the settlement; more often it took until the sixth or seventh month of pregnancy for me to realize. Women said that they felt very "ugly" (*žungali*) and "shy" (*lažavma*) when they were pregnant, and they refused to be photographed. During pregnancy, a Gypsy woman began to act out the state of pollution that characterized birth itself. As her apron moved slowly upward until, in the last months, it rose well over her waist, the Romni increasingly took on a tubular form in which her "in between" had disappeared and her "upper" and "lower" regions had merged. I learned the hard way that even the moment of birth should remain unmentioned when one day after a young woman had been taken to the hospital, my clumsy questioning was met with stony silence from a large group of Rom, who, I realized after a while, just wished I would cease my inopportune pestering!

As a man, I was not in a position to make my own inquiries about Rom practices, but this is how a fifty-year-old woman recounted to her sister what she had seen as a young woman:[21]

When the baby was being born, they said it was forbidden for the men to come in, even into the yard! Then for three days the girl could not leave the house. She could not go near water. Nowhere. Only inside the house. She was ashamed of herself, the girl.

She wasn't allowed to give any food to her husband. Kneading pasta was forbidden, nor was she allowed to cook. She wasn't to hand anything out from the house.

If another woman entered the house, she took a piece of straw away with her—you know, from the bed—so that she did not take the child's "dream/soul" *(lindra)* with her. Otherwise the child would cry terribly.

And there was no wearing of "trousers" [women's underpants, which were baggy and shaped like long shorts]. She wiped herself with her skirt. She was not allowed to put her clothes out at night but had to keep them under her head.

Well, when the women went to church, when they christened the child, then the mother could move about. Once the baby was six or seven weeks, one could look at him. Until then they let in no one. Especially when he bathed, they allowed absolutely no one in so that the visitors could not take away the little one's "dream" nor "beat him with their eyes."[22]

This description of birth rituals referred to a time when birth normally took place outside the home, not at a hospital, assisted by a Gypsy midwife.[23] Instruments used at birth, such as the knife, were thrown away, and the placenta itself ended up in the dung pile kept away from the house.[24] After the baby was washed, it was then kept on a bed of straw until it was christened so that its soul would remain in it until christening. The mother meanwhile was thoroughly polluted: Placing her bloodied clothes under her head showed her resignation in her unique condition.

Some younger women would insist that this sort of thing was "just superstition," but the "modernizing" Luludji, who had had her first child in 1975, told me that she had refused to come out of her house and see her father-in-law for a week after her first birth, so "ashamed" had she felt. And in the Third Class in 1985, at least until the baby's christening, postpartum women were still forbidden from going near the water source that other Rom used so as not to pollute it.

After birth children were said to be weak, their souls only feebly connected to their bodies, and the main prohibitions were aimed at protecting the attachment of the baby's soul to its body. Once the newborn had been brought back to the house, mirrors were covered up, since, like standing water, they were gateways to the other world. Through these the baby's soul could "distance itself," as Judit discovered when she nearly passed in front of a mirror with our own baby son in her arms. Čoro's sister screamed out and leaped across the room, knocking Judit sideways, to prevent our baby son from seeing himself in the mirror.[25]

In light of the vulnerable nature of the child, the crucial ritual act at this time was the "christening" (*bolimo*), which occurred within three weeks of the birth.[26] Unlike *gažo* baptisms, the Rom version involved the combination of two distinct acts, one with the *gažos* (the women's business) and the other with the Rom (the men's concern).[27] Both these moments of baptism were necessary, but the Rom almost deliberately kept them apart. In the *romano bolimo* mention of the word "priest" (*rasaj*) was strictly taboo and "unlucky"; and no woman entered the room where the men sat. Nor was there any stress on actually having the child present during the men's proceedings. In church the baby was washed with holy water by the priest, who thus removed the impurity of birth. Thanks to the priest's actions, the child's color changed, and she or he became "beautiful" (*šukar*). An added benefit, I was often told to encourage me to christen my own son, was that the baby would cry less once baptized. In the church the Gypsy women asked the attendants for holy water, which they later sprinkled over each other and around their homes, also blessing their relatives for health and "purity." This protected the baby from the spirit of "the Unclean" (*o bivužo*), a spirit who might have gained access to the baby through the places or people she or he had common contact with. No one ever mentioned any theological rationale for christening. Instead, church baptism was a kind of mechanical act that could work or fail. Thus, in Csóka I once came across a sick child who was being christened "for the second time." In fact, the priest had refused to do so, but the Rom had smuggled the child into the christening of another baby. It turned out that originally this child had been christened by the *gaži* wife of a Rom who had then been divorced. As the Rom told me, "The first christening did not work. The first time we christened her the godmother was . . . not one of us, not our sort of person, and the child has been ill ever since."

The Rom baptism was timed to coincide with the church christening but focused on an all-night *mulatšago* at which the father and godfather (appointed some six months earlier at another male-only celebration) celebrated their mutual relations—from this time on they could call each other "*kirvo*," co-godfather. Since all such celebrations were aimed at generating health, strength, and luck for the participants, and since the physical condition of the godparents was believed to have a direct bodily effect on the newborn, the partying indirectly aided the baby as well. This, in a sense, was the beginning of the alternative, social nurturing of the new Rom.

The Body and Soul at Death

The pattern that is emerging here about Rom attitudes toward life processes and reproduction becomes even clearer in relation to the treatment of death. Like the shameful experience of birth, when pollution had to be dumped on the unsuspecting *gažo* priest, at death, too, a similar process of externalization took place. But whereas at birth the soul was secured in its bodily lodging, at death the soul and the body had to be separated so that the body could be securely placed in the ground. Then, and this was the aim of the rites, the dead Rom would not return as a restless "ghost" (*mulo*).

What we think of as the moment of death was for the Rom the cessation of the flow of blood in the body—in other words, of the activity of the *dji*.[28] The *lindra*, which throughout life was more or less well attached to a person, then left the body.[29] It was this socio-physiognomy that informed the death rituals.[30]

When dealing with the death of a person in a community, the Rom obeyed a series of positive injunctions concerning the nonbodily, spiritual aspect of the deceased.[31] Both women and men gathered, in separate groups at the deceased's house, from dusk each day until the funeral, to mourn, sing, and drink until dawn together. At this time the relatives and associates of the deceased engaged in his favorite forms of drinking and his most typical "true speech" (normally particular songs); but jokes would be told if the person had been particularly amusing or stories if he had had a reputation in this field. Later during the burial, at the moments when the *gažo* priest was absent or when he had finished his blessings and the *gažo* grave diggers were filling in the grave, groups of Gypsies sang, this time to the accompaniment of musicians.

At the same time, and parallel to this Rom mourning, the body of the deceased had to be dealt with; but, as at birth, this was done by the *gažo* priest. In the past if a Gypsy had died at home, the hope was that he could be moved outside before giving his last breath so as to release his *lindra*. The house was then immediately sealed and whitewashed "so the dead person will not recognize his house" (*te na pinžarel pesko kher*). The body was then washed by female relatives of the deceased; redressed in finest and most favored clothes; placed in the inner, clean room; covered with a white sheet; surrounded with an uneven number of candles; and arranged with feet facing the door. Straw was then strewn over the floor, coins were placed on the deceased's eyes, and the mouth was stopped. All these were ritualized ways of sealing the body and keeping the soul from returning.[32] By 1985 the basic tasks concerning the body had been happily handed over to the *gažo* officials, but the treatment of the house and the candles remained. It may be that it was because the body was no longer fully "Rom" that the Gypsies, who in any other context were terrified of losing one of their number into the world of the *gažos*, proved surprisingly keen on new hygienic regulations by which the care of corpses was transferred to the alien *gažo* hospital.[33]

When it came to burial, most of the work was handed over to the priest and his assistants. In Gypsy folklore priests were the victims of excessive bodily desire, licentious and uncontrolled sexuality, and unnatural craving for food and drink. Stories of the bizarre consequences of priests' debauchery—giving birth to rabbits or falling into the depth of a latrine and emerging covered with feces—were commonplace in Gypsy tales. Their polluted inner state was, comically as far as the Gypsies were concerned, given public recognition in their "ugly," long black cassocks, an anomalous form of dress designed expressly, one might think, to confirm the worst suspicions of the Rom. A Rom who was going about his business and saw a priest was said to lose his luck, and men attempted to remove this effect by cursing the priest ("May he pass with the night," or "May he pass with menstrual blood") or, another ethnographer reported, by touching their genitals.[34] Although it was the nature of the priest's polluted condition to wallow in his bodily pleasure, when a priest arrived one day at a funeral with an entourage of female cantors, the provocation was too great for some of the more touchy old Rom. Čoro's father even called out in Hungarian, "What kind of priest is this? Calls himself a priest! With a band of whores. Can't he wait?" Although he was silenced by his relatives, aware that the *gažo* onlookers would be appalled at such "disrespect," later these same men and women agreed that they shared the older man's disgust.

It was not just the polluted priest who was given a symbolic role that appeared to be an obstacle to the successful conclusion of the rites. Female relatives of the deceased were also habitually expected to try reviving the corpse by raising it from the coffin or "watering" it with alcohol. They also tried, sometimes with great physical violence, to delay the sealing of the coffin, as well as the placing of the coffin in the ground. Unwashed, with disheveled, uncombed hair, in black clothes, their desire not to surrender the corpse had to be overcome to let the process of death take its course.[35]

Underlying these disruptive forces was their association with biological, reproductive sexuality and the *gažo* aspect of social life. The priest himself was always a *gažo*, just as polluted women were symbolically like *gažos*, since it was the nature of the *gažo* to be polluted.[36] In other words, the whole aspect of death that concerned the body was shunted "out" to be dealt with by *gažos* or those Rom who were in a *gažo*-like state.

After burial, and for one year until the final mass was said, the close family was supposed to behave in some respects as if their bodily condition was linked to that of the deceased. Men did not shave, and women cut their hair off, both acts that made their bodies abnormally "ugly" (*žungalo*). They avoided life-enhancing red colors in their clothes, but most strikingly, singing, drinking, and celebrating, which were enjoined during the wake

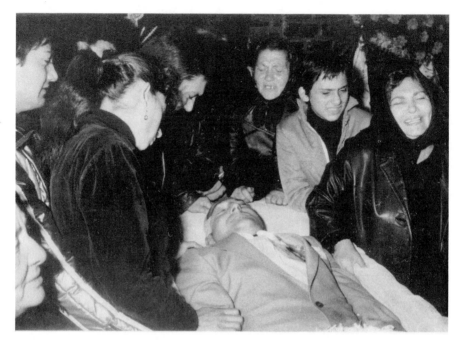

The soul of the dead Gypsy is cared for by his relatives. The polluted body is given to the gaźo priest.

and were always an essential part of Gypsy social life, were now forbidden. Those people most touched by the event of death thus entered a phase when they stopped looking like normal, pure Rom and ceased in some ways to be fully active members of the Gypsy ritual community.

At the end of this period, the corpse was believed to have been reduced to its bones. Then, apart from the masses said in church, a "feast of remembrance" (*pomana*) was held at the house of the deceased, to which only close relatives came. New potatoes, new beans, and new cabbage were cooked and served, signaling the "new" life of the deceased, unattached to his past. Some of this food was placed on the windowsill to be eaten by the dead person, and a candle was placed behind it so that the ghost would not enter the house. The grave might be visited and cleaned, with tobacco and brandy placed in the earth. What was striking about the meal was that the deceased was fed with white, soft vegetables. On this occasion meat on the bone, the one thing that the Gypsies thought of as real food, was replaced by beans, which were the meat substitute of poor Gypsies. The annual custom of giving the first cherries to unknown children "so that our dead can eat" reflected a similar symbolism: a gift of a

The gaźo priest, horrified by the Gypsies' own arrangements, refused to bless the deceased at the "clean room" grave. The rites were performed at a safe distance.

red (but this time watery, not bloody) fleshy food with a hard core, a kind of meat for the dead.

Gypsy Death

I argued in Chapter 4 that the metaphorical definition of Gypsy sociality in terms of brotherhood implied a construction of life in which age, parent-child relations, and indeed the very replacement of one generation by another—that is, reproduction itself—were to a large extent masked ideologically.[37] The brotherhood of the Rom could then emerge as an eternal, unchanging state in contrast to the punctuated, developmental life of the *gaźos'* households. At death, when the biological life cycle erupted into the transcendent existence of the brotherhood, the illusion that one could continue forever as a Gypsy brother, living in a kind of timeless present, was momentarily shattered.[38] So I suggest that Rom rites of death were an attempt to reestablish the conditions in which it seemed possible for a Rom to continue living in a time apart from the *gaźos*. Or, following Maurice Bloch and Jonathan Parry, one might invert the explanatory logic and say that for the Rom death was an occasion when a transcendent social order was constructed, over and above that of the mortal body, the ritual creating the image of the world and not vice versa.[39]

This was achieved, I suggest, by the division of the Gypsy person in two. The Rom thus took a familiar Christian idea and turned it on its head by, in effect, giving the rotting body to the *gaźo* priest to bury, while retaining the soul for ritual treatment themselves.[40] Throughout the wakes I attended, Gypsies sang; they said that this way they "drew out the deceased person's strength" (*tsirdas avri leski zor*). They removed his attachment to this earthly existence so as to allow him to rest firmly in the other world.

As we saw in the previous chapter, during a man's life all the Gypsy songs he sung in public at *mulatšagos* were stereotypically "ancient," but in their rendition by him with reference to his specific life they became personally "true." Singing such a song together with his brothers was socially powerful because it allowed a near-perfect alignment of individual and collective perspectives on Gypsy life and so created an experience of the ideal unity of the brothers.[41] In doing so, singing was also spiritually enabling in the sense that in song men achieved a state of *voja* in which the troubles of the world no longer touched them, in which they became "true brothers" to one another.

At death, songs and forms of speech that had become associated with the individual were taken over, reappropriated by other closely related Gypsies, and began to be deindividualized. By singing at the wake, the mourners showed their "respect," showed that the deceased would not be forgotten and at the same time ensured that he would stay on the other side, not seek to rejoin his brothers in their song on later occasions. Ideally, at the graveside the final act of the mourners (but at this time "strangers" to the deceased and not relatives) was to sing some of these songs while the sons and close family looked on—observing the achieved transfer of

Relatives of the deceased listen to his favorite Gypsy songs performed in the cemetery.

this cultural "capital" back to the wider group and so demonstrating that Gypsy life continued despite the death of this one individual.

In Hungary peasants who attended Gypsy funerals were often amazed, not to say appalled, at the presence of Gypsy children at burials. What the *gaźos* did not realize was that to exclude the children would have been tantamount to admitting that death disrupted the ongoing order of brothers. To the Rom, these were the children whose humanity, whose Rom-ness, they themselves had called into being by the singing at christening and who would go on being nurtured, like all the Rom, parentless "boys" and "girls" alike, in that never-ending fashion that only the Rom knew. The presence of the children indicated that for the Rom one-half of the funeral was simply part of their daily, unchanging, ritual reproduction of Rom personhood and so proved their symbolic victory over long-term, cyclical reproduction through fertility and birth. One year after the burial, when the period of mourning was over, and in stark contrast to Catholic Magyar neighbors, the Gypsy women abandoned the black of mourning. While the peasants continued to acknowledge the deaths of the past in their clothes, the Gypsies recovered their previous state in which the importance of the dead for the living community of Gypsies was denied.

The Modest and the Shameless Body

In the life crisis rituals of birth and death, the Rom represented the process of sustaining life as in some sense "bodiless." Although bodily birth and death, natural reproduction, had to be carried on, these processes were symbolized as *gažo*. Real human, Rom, reproduction was a social affair, a matter of nurture and shared activity. It was through speech and song that the Rom element of life was represented, created, and reproduced. This rejection of the body was also at the heart of the more common celebrations of the brothers when the men drank and sang together. Often on such occasions, when I would leave the room with other men to urinate, I would be reminded that "we" were not like the *gažos*, who would stand up and excuse themselves, thereby letting everyone know that they were going to the toilet. "We, the Rom" (*ame le rom*), knew how to disguise our exit with a request to "have a word in private" with another man.

But as this very example shows, the ideal of a nonbodily existence was impossible to sustain. The Gypsies lived in their bodies, just as the rest of us do. In some form the Rom had to reincorporate bodily existence, if only in a limited and acceptable form. It was striking, for instance, that among a people with such a strong sense of physical modesty Gypsy women breast-fed in public and celebrated the fact that they breast-fed each others' children when necessary. This upper-body, socialized feeding found a place in *romanes*. And there was another separation that allowed an even more significant reintegration of what had been symbolically denied: the separation of sexuality from fertility.

As any Hungarian man who has had any dealings with a Gypsy woman may tell you, my account of Rom modesty and shame provides only half the picture of Rom morality, since there were contexts in which Gypsies, especially Gypsy women, behaved quite "shamelessly." Brazenness, as Judith Okely observed among English Gypsies, though discouraged in inter-Gypsy relations, was valued in dealings with the *gažos*.[42] In part because non-Gypsies did not appear to display shame or restraint in their dress and behavior, Harangos Rom felt no taboo about sexual innuendo with them. Indeed, on almost every occasion when I arrived among unfamiliar Rom who did not know that I spoke Romany, I was subjected to the kind of irreverent sexual banter and teasing reserved for the supposedly uncontrollable, randy *gažos*.[43] Gypsy women, too, turned the tables on the *gažos* in more public contexts. When a man complained to a market dealer that her car mats had holes in them, she quipped, "So do I, and you wouldn't refuse me," and she moved as if to grab her reluctant customer for herself. Judit Szegő was also the subject of occasional unsolicited propositions before men realized that she was "not like other *gaźis*," that she would not willingly "go off into the woods," as one of the men suggested.

Judith Okely suggested that in dealings with the *gaźos*, Gypsy women played on *gaźo* stereotypes of the romantic and sexy Gypsy lover. This they certainly did in Harangos, but in Hungary fantasy representations of sexually available *gaźos* also had a use among the Rom themselves. Despite the cult of "shame," and at first sight in flagrant contradiction to the impression I gave, most Gypsy houses were decorated with semi-pornographic pictures of naked women, which jostled for space with images of the Virgin Mary and family snaps. The sexual pictures seemed intended to make positive statements about carnal desire. Thus, one evening as I sat celebrating a Gypsy woman's name day with a group of men, the talk turned to relations between men and women. At one point one of the louder men in the settlement who was given to making rather self-advertising little speeches pointed to a picture of a nude on the wall and placing his hand over her pubic hair said that this was the most important thing in the world. I had very rarely heard any comment about a Romni's looks or any more direct reference to her sexuality. And yet here was a man in company, and on an occasion when polite conversation was de rigeur, saying that sex was what he lived for. It cannot have been accidental that the picture he had his hand on, like all such images in Gypsy houses, was of a pale-skinned and obviously *gaźi* woman.

Sexual desire was celebrated not only via images of fantasized *gaźi* outsiders. There was also a delighted celebration of young Gypsy children's potential sexuality. When very small children were brought to meet a grandparent, they were often greeted with kisses on their genitals and effusive blessings for their future sexual exploits. For a people so very prudish most of the time, the talk directed at young babies was quite surprisingly unrestrained. The following is an example of Čaja speaking with her grandson: "She will lick his cock. What a diamond! A tulip! I'll lick his cock! Look how beautiful he is, oh, God! Look, what's that?" As she pointed at his genitals she continued: "A little treasure! Oh, my boy! See his eyes staring at [literally, falling into] my arse/vagina! What a beautiful baby! I'll lick his eyes!"44 A regular visitor at our house would bring her year-old daughter and place her next to my son, Gergely, advising him: "You can fuck [literally, file] her now. Go on, Gergely! Kiss her cunt! . . . She'll eat his cock then!"45 When my son was at his godfather's, he was often laid down beside the latter's five-year-old daughter so she could "give him her butt" (*te del les laki bul*).

If sexuality was thus celebrated through joking relations with *gaźos* and baby children, it also found a surreptitious place in relations among adults. Or such is my interpretation of the way Gypsy men and women often addressed each other, affectionately using the terms "my *gaźo*" and "my *gaźi.*" Given the systematic opposition of the Rom to the *gaźos* at the heart of Gypsy culture, it was surprising to find in formal Rom speech, which was categorically defined as "true speech," that men in particular tended to use this form of address for their wives, sometimes substituting the apparently coarser term "my whore" (*kurvi*). Puzzled by this use of the despised outsider to address the closest insider, I asked an old Rom to explain it. To speak in this way was, he said, a way of respecting, or being charming to, one's spouse. An examination of this usage will allow me to close the discussion of the Rom construction of gender and show how gender provided a language and symbolism to mark boundaries not only between men and women but also between all the Rom and the world outside.

The *Gaźi* in the Romni

A *kurvi*'s, that is, a whore's, role is defined by her sexuality, all the more so in that for her clients she has no fertility or reproductive power. Ordinary *gaźi* were, in this sense, like *kurvi* for the Rom. Many Rom men I knew had had *gaźi* lovers, and some had even brought them home for a few days or weeks to live with parents. In the many stories I heard of seductions of non-Gypsy women, the *gaźis* typically relished sex and demanded that it be prolonged. Predictably, men would say that, unlike a Romni, "who will only raise her skirt" and wore normal clothes in bed, a *gaźi* would strip naked for sex.[46] But it was rare indeed for a *gaźi* to become a Romni, since she did not normally bear children for her man. So the *gaźi* was "had," and that was the end to the matter. Like sex imagined with the women in the quasi-pornographic pictures on the wall, and the sexuality of little children, this sex had no social consequences for the Rom.[47]

So it seems that a Rom, by talking of his wife as a metaphorical *gaźi*, could flatter his Romni, admire her as an object of sexual desire, and yet at the same time retain her "really" as a properly shameful Romni and therefore part of the world of the Rom. By representing bodily desire as *gaźo*-like, the Rom both allowed for and neatly compartmentalized it. The same logic worked for Gypsy women. In addressing a spouse as "my *gaźo*," a woman acknowledged her sexual attraction (it was only with *gaźos* that women engaged in public sexual play, as if they were attracted to their client), without appearing to move outside her role as "shameful" wife to a pure Rom.

Two aspects of sexual expression were thus represented openly by the Rom: sex for pleasure's sake and the potential consequence of sexual pleasure, children. It was the whole process by which one led to the other that posed a problem for the Rom. One could see this paradox in the way attitudes toward young married Gypsies changed at the time of pregnancy. Čoro's brother's daughter married a young man just before a Granada television crew arrived to do some filming in 1988. The Rom were keen to treat these "respected" guests well, and so the producer was given his own room next door to the young couple. I was asked to explain to him that the young husband and wife might spend much time in bed together and to ask, politely, whether he minded. Now, in part, this was no doubt a teasing way of playing on Rom ideas about non-Gypsy morality. But over the next few weeks, there was little shame in the circle of regular visitors to the house in admitting that the two were in bed in the middle of the afternoon making love. Just a few months later, when I returned, the young wife was now pregnant. At this time no one joked or talked about her "sleeping" habits—it would have been shameful and disgusting to do so.

But representing sex openly in some contexts was not the end of the matter. In representing sex as *gažo*, the Romnis showed their mastery of this aspect of themselves and demonstrated that they were keeping control of the *gaži* in themselves. By decorating their homes with pornographic pictures, which they placed alongside pictures of themselves, with their children, in Gypsy clothes, as well as images of the Virgin Mary, the Romnis illustrated how different they were from the *gažis*, who let the sexual aspect of existence take over their lives. What Romni, after all, would ever pose for a pornographic photograph? Thus, by participating in the system that tabooed their biological, reproductive fertility, the Romnis showed that they were not like the despised *gažis*.

The Asymmetry of the Sexes

In the course of this kind of fairly abstract symbolic analysis, the reader may have lost the sense that the ritual and symbolism discussed here really made a difference to the way Gypsy men and women lived. On the night of a birth, the father of the child, at least if he was born a son, went celebrating and drank heavily with his brothers, feasting the arrival of a new Rom. But there was no such public celebration for the mother, who was secluded in the hospital, ashamed of her person. Her return home from the hospital some days later was greeted with no fanfare.

Likewise, because the alien *gažo* principle was ritually emphasized in the Romni, her status as a full participant in Rom life sometimes seemed ambivalent. Imagined as Romni, often pictured on the wall of her house properly, respectfully dressed in the Gypsy fashion right beside the naked *gaži* flaunting herself, the Gypsy woman was clearly a part of the world of the Rom. But unlike the Virgin Mary, who often sat beside these pictures, the Romni was a sexually reproductive being and could never get wholly beyond an association with polluting procreation—after all, her children, too, were pictured on the wall.[48]

If a woman did not restrain herself in public life (if she kept a "dirty" home, if she had lovers), she revealed her inability to transcend bodily, *gaźo* nature. She became, in effect, a real *gaźi*, the kind of person who went around with her hair loose and exposed, who felt no shame about pregnancy, and who wore baggy, one-piece clothes that positively emphasized her expectant condition. Even though each sex could fall from the Rom way—there was one alcoholic man in the Third Class who was referred to as the *gaźo*, perhaps precisely to emphasize his enslavement to his bodily needs—it was always more plausible to suggest that a woman might be swayed.

Thus, attitudes toward the public expression of male and female sexuality and desire were strikingly asymmetrical. Although there was little public representation of male Gypsy sexual activity, apart from occasional jokes about Gypsy sexual prowess vis-à-vis outsiders, the fact of male sexuality had no negative value, whereas female Gypsy sexual activity could more easily be made to appear socially disruptive. In Chapter 6, in relation to Luludji's reputation I showed how this might happen. Young Gypsy men said they would sleep with women when and as they felt fit; women, by contrast, had to wait until they were married and then have sex only with their husbands. Girls, too, concurred in this, and though they may have had fantasies about non-Gypsy boys, they kept these to themselves. Many parents were supportive of a son's sexual exploits, at least implicitly condoning but sometimes actually encouraging a son in his extramarital affairs. In regard to other men, most Gypsy women accepted resignedly that it was in men's nature to chase after women and to "have a go." Famed male adulterers were never subject to much rumor-mongering. It was, both men and women held, up to the woman in any such situation to resist. As one old woman put it, trying to impress her point regarding her own son's apparently unrestrained philandering, "A man would fuck his own mother if she allowed him." As a result, in cases of suspected adultery, whatever domestic pressure a wife brought to bear on a husband, a public expression of anger was most likely to be directed against the other female party rather than the man, who was not expected to control his desire and whose transgressions were not constructed as threatening the social order. In a couple of cases, a woman went with a daughter and gave a third party a "good beating" to punish the adulterous woman.

Whatever a man may have believed about his own wife, or a woman about herself and her daughters, everyone agreed that the control of other Romnis over their sexuality was fragile. Bouts of intense, jealous suspicion were commonplace, and in some contexts men were inordinately quick to doubt the fidelity of their wives. Čoro's brother's wife, a grandmother of five, then aged fifty-five, once spent half an hour out of her husband's sight at a horse market, thereby provoking him to fly into a rage and demand to know where she had been, who she had "lain" with. Although the accused woman vehemently denied her guilt and privately ridiculed her husband's fantasies, the very same woman reacted quite differently when another woman was involved in a similar dispute and helped publicize damaging stories that the woman concerned had been a "great whore sometime ago."

Beyond the Body

To conclude, it may help to put these strands of argument in the context of anthropological discussion of the social significance of pollution beliefs. Some time ago Sherry Ortner argued that women's association with "nature" and "species life" explained the "pan-cultural devaluation of women."[49] Marilyn Strathern's suggestion that gender can be less a way of talking about men and women than of defining more general "issues of social concern" led others, such as Jill Dubisch, to go beyond a simple association of pollution and gender. Presenting material from rural Greece, Dubisch argued that, if local beliefs represented women as polluting, this was not necessarily a way of talking about women, since such beliefs may "reflect structural and ideological features that transcend gender roles."[50] As it happens, much of the writing on the Rom and the Gypsies had already taken up this line, suggesting that an upper/lower or inner/outer symbolism of the body represented an ethnic division of the world. As the clean Rom was to the dirty *gažo,* so the upper/inner was to the lower/outer body. In this way Gypsy gender rhetoric was seen to embody and "really" be about an ethic of ethnic distinctiveness.[51] Certainly in Harangos the recognition of this division was seen as one of the ways that the Gypsies defined themselves as different from the *gažos,* especially from *gažis* who wore one-piece dresses, bathed in their own filth, and flaunted themselves "unscarved" (*šerangli*) in public.

However, the specifically female shame of girls and women as to the display of their hair, the cleanliness of the apron, and the way in which women seemed more touched by all these taboos cannot, I believe, simply be accounted for as a by-product of the upper/lower body symbolism. The Rom idea of "cleanliness" (*vužipe*) was closely and inherently linked to notions of sexual shame in regard to sexual desire and human fertility. Thus, when I asked for examples of *marimo* (polluting) behavior, I was told stories about "obscene sexual acts" (*baro kurvašago*) instead of about washing customs.

My argument is that for the Hungarian Rom the symbolic associations of shame and purity were closely tied to the specific Gypsy experience of a people who, in its own self-image, lived without "producing" or "re-producing" in the natural world and in some sense tried to live as if without bodies. The representation of femaleness, perhaps because of women's association with the biological cycle of menstruation and child-bearing itself, offered a symbolic means to represent a separation by which the Rom could remain different from the *gažos*. From this per-spective I suggest that the upper/lower distinction was but the ac-knowledgment and tangible representation of the deeper duality be-tween two ways of living in the world: one stuck in the biological time of procreation and the other transcending this with social forms of nur-ture. I have presented evidence throughout this chapter that, I believe, sustains this argument, but let me just mention one final instance. Whereas it was common in rural Eastern Europe for peasants to bury the placenta of a newborn child under their house so as to bind the baby to the home, to its past and future, the Rom disposed of the afterbirth to the *gažos*—the Rom would have as little to do with this aspect of existence as they could. So it is not that "upper" is to Rom as "lower" is to *gažo*, but that what makes people Rom is that they realize to be human, one must divide the body, and what makes others *gažo* is that they do not. From the outside this may look like a familiar ethnic division of the world, but the implication of my analysis is that this is not how the Rom experienced this division.[52]

A parallel can be drawn between the attempt of the Gypsies to repre-sent a social order transcendent of the body and that of the Aghori as-cetics described by Jonathan Parry who live in the cremation grounds of Benares eating carrion from emptied human skulls.[53] To demonstrate their transcendence of the body and death, and their attainment of an ideal, deathless order, these religious specialists paradoxically had to enact a virtual celebration of their own bodily pollution. By their bizarre eating habits they showed that for them these did not matter. The Indian parallel seems to me compelling because, unlike the "pure" Brahmins, who had other castes to perform polluting tasks and enact a polluted state for them, but like the Aghori religious specialists, the Rom had to "internalize" pollution. If the Rom had had the power of the Brahmins, perhaps matters would have been different. Then the *gažos* might have carried all the pollution on their shoulders. But because the Rom were so-cially and economically marginal, they could imagine that they had tran-scended pollution only if "their own" Gypsy women contained and yet repressed this aspect of existence.

So when the Communists found Gypsies scavenging in the bread bins of the town, cadging a battery off a peasant to sell its scrap metal, or trading in horses, the Rom were doing much more than just trying to make a bit of money by "usury." If we return to the question left hanging in Chapter 11 as to why the presence of Gypsy women would have disrupted the men's horse dealing, we can now see that the "luck" of horse dealing, which was, in effect, the ability to get something for nothing and to create value without production, was linked to a symbolism of the body that attempted to establish an unbridgeable divide between its two halves. Horses were ideal for this symbolic task: Bred for the most part by the *gažos*, horses could be represented by the Rom as sustaining Rom life without the taint of biological process.[54] And when the Rom took a *gažo* horse in order to make a Gypsy horse, they sacrificed the mother to cleanse the offspring of the taint of procreation and then made money by asking riddles that celebrated their ability to make horses without mothers.

Thus, it was precisely the mark of women's biological fertility, their menstrual blood, that made them dangerous to the horse dealer because this symbolized the *gažo* way of doing things. Gypsy business belonged to a different order of reality. So, for instance, the bread that the Rom told me was "truly Gypsy" and "the only bread that really fills you"—that is, their *boxoli*—could be baked only by Romnis who were not menstruating. The making of bread in rural Christian Europe was commonly symbolic of the process of natural fertility, an imitation of human fertility.[55] Rom bread, which because it was unleavened, did not rise and swell in imitation of a woman's body, could be made only if the woman was "clean" of the mark of her bodily fertility. In Chapter 10 I said that the Rom could talk of "a woman following her husband like a man his horse." This referred to residence after marriage, but the product of marriage is children, just as the product of men chasing horses is money. In both cases, for the result to be achieved in the Gypsy way, mundane production and reproduction had to be denied. So in their *romani butji,* the Rom were engaged in an effort to prove that it was possible for them to live "without their bodies"—obviating that aspect of their existence that rendered them dependent and dominated by the *gažo* bosses: their labor and their bodies. The Communist assimilators would have had to offer to the Rom a much more profound and rewarding alternative to have persuaded them to surrender this extraordinary vision of the good life.

13

CONCLUSION: MARGINALITY, RESISTANCE, AND IDEOLOGY

It is not true to say that to understand the concepts of the society (in the same way its members do) is to understand the society. Concepts are as liable to mask reality as to reveal it and masking some of it may be part of their function.

Ernest Gellner, "Concepts and Society"

I HAVE WRITTEN THIS BOOK during a dark time for the Gypsies of Europe, especially for those in the former Communist countries. More Gypsies had their houses burned, were expelled from their villages, and were killed in racist attacks between 1989 and 1996 than in all the time that has passed since World War II. I hope I have given some sense of the sources from which the fear of Gypsies arises. But explaining the non-Gypsies' attitudes has not been my prime concern. That has been to explore the world as seen by the Rom. At the outset I asked how it was that the Gypsies, the Rom whom I got to know by living in one of their communities, carried on in the face of their desperate circumstances. In Chapter 2 I rephrased the terms of my problem and asked instead how Gypsies could relocate themselves from the margins of society to the center of humanity and how they thought it was possible to live in an uninterrupted free lunch.

In Part 3 I have argued that the key to understanding the persistence of Rom communities and the Rom way of life lies in the way these Gypsies have been able to take their experience of the world around them and convert or transform it into their own cultural terms, into a specifically Rom sense of what it was to be human. The Rom defined themselves in opposition to the *gaźos*, who were seen as less fully human than the Rom.

232

Sign on door reading, "Please throw the letters—the Gypsies stole the box," Hungary, 1991. (courtesy Néprajzi Muzeum; photog., L. Tóth)

Street gamblers, 1947: The Gypsies still use their luck to make easy money from the "foolish gaźos." (Courtesy Néprajzi Muzeum)

To live with the Rom in a settlement, as an ethnographer, as a child growing up, or as an adult was to listen to a constant assertion of their distinctiveness and moral/cultural superiority over others.[1] One had to become Rom or, for me at least, like a Rom, and then constantly demonstrate one's adherence to this ethic. Since the Rom adhered to a strongly performative model of identity and personhood and lived in a world where they were despised by the non-Rom, establishing a separation between themselves and outsiders/others and then "policing" the boundary were central parts of their cultural activity.

They talked about many features of their life in terms of their contrast with *gaźo* customs. The Rom substituted egalitarian relations and mutual respect within the community (at least among same-sex members of their society) for the hierarchical ones they suffered with the *gaźos* and that the *gaźos* endured with each other. I have described three acts of cultural appropriation and self-assertion: those concerning horses and trading, speech, and ideas about "bodily" shame. In each case the Rom had taken objects, representations, or institutions given in the outside world and representative of that "outside" and inverted the meanings attached to them by the *gažos*. So in Rom culture there were "cultural themes" of the outside world, but shifted in key and tone. The Cigány were said to be "dirty" and "shameless" by the Magyars, but the Rom turned this sense upside down and represented the world in such a way that it was the *gažos* who appeared ridiculously and shamelessly unable to transcend their bodies. The kind of social, spatial, and bodily compartmentalization discussed in Chapters 3 and 12 meant that there was an arena within which the Rom could negate representations of themselves as Cigány that would have tied them as inferiors into hierarchical relations with more powerful outsiders. The *gažos*, both educated linguists such as Jozsef Vekerdi and ordinary citizens of a town such as Harangos, talked of Romany as *cigányul*, "the Cigány way of talking" and imagined it as hardly a language at all, a kind of hodgepodge of terms calqued from other languages in which, at best, the Gypsies could express their "child-like" emotional passions. To these outsiders, the Rom's language represented their impoverished state. But the Rom would never buy that. They lived in their language; it was their culture, the substitute for a territory, as Patrick Williams suggested.[2] It was by transferring that culturally valued form of speech, "true speech," that the Rom represented the preservation of their supreme cultural values. And it was also through their speech that these Rom performed what impressed me as their greatest trick on the world: the conversion of the horses of the *gažos* into a support for the Rom way of life.

The process of conversion was also worked on money earned in the socialist sector. The "silver" of brotherhood had come from forints, money of the Hungarian state. As a result of this symbolic conversion, the Rom could believe that wage labor did not irreparably disrupt their way of life because the money thus acquired, forints, embodied a socially worthless relation with the *gažos*; it led nowhere for members of a Rom community. Payday had its place in a revised Rom calendar, but it only signaled all-night purges in which the forints were remorselessly gambled into the pure cash of the brotherhood of horse traders. Moreover, by talking of forints as *gažo* money, the Rom distanced the private accumulation of wealth from "true Gypsy" behavior. The Rom thus represented an ideal resolution of the problem of accumulation in an open, sharing society. Money got through labor was good, at best, for feeding the household but had to be cleansed by gambling with cards and horses before the Rom could live from it.[3]

The Sources of the Rom Adaptation

It could be argued, and several writers on the Gypsies and Rom have taken this perspective, that the Rom way of life is the product of their adaptation as an ethnic group like any other, a group of "foreigners" who came to Europe in and around the fourteenth century and found a particularly successful niche that enabled their persistence as a distinct population. Thus, Anne Sutherland talked of the American Rom as being the descendants of a people that had "left India approximately 1000 A.D."[4] Czech ethnographer Milena Hűbschmannová, among many others, argued that the Rom's ancestors were Indian Dom and discussed Rom subgroupings as the legacy of Indian *jata* and their purity beliefs, likewise as a "survival."[5] In Eastern Europe today this kind of reasoning finds a ready audience: The kind of parallel that I drew in Chapter 12 between Aghori ascetics and the Rom—to my mind a comparison of the consequences of similar ideological schema—would be taken as a historical explanation of Rom cultural specificity in Hungary. Often this search for origins has been rather haphazard—any Indian, or, more particularly, northern Indian, custom that reminds people of Gypsy behavior is seen as ancestral.[6] Sadly, this kind of explanation is widely seen as "acceptable" and one that encourages "tolerance" of diversity on the principle that "if your ancestors come from elsewhere, you, too, can be different." But despite the attractions of going down this road of least resistance, I have not followed this line of reasoning.

The author of the most recent and scholarly encyclopedic history of Rom groups, Angus Fraser, who himself tends to the Indian historical explanation of Gypsy specificity, pointed out that "it would have taken only about one marriage per hundred on average to be with a non-Gypsy since they left India to bring their present proportion of non-Indic ancestors to over one-half."[7] Judith Okely, working among English Traveler-Gypsies, who in terms of physical anthropology are indistinguishable from the surrounding population, had the insight that it was possible to explain the existence of Gypsies in terms of social differentiation within late feudal and early capitalist societies: Gypsies, she argued, were the landless poor who had refused to become proletarians.[8] In any case, the historical experience of Eastern Europe indicates that the mere existence of foreign origins does not explain the persistence of cultural difference. It has been suggested, for instance, that the Szeklers in Transylvania were originally a non-Magyar group that assimilated into the Magyars.[9] Inside modern Hungary's borders, two major ethnic groups, the Jasgians and the Cumanians, have over the past one thousand years disappeared into the majority population. So if the Hungarian Rom were reproduced as a distinct group, I would argue that it was because of the way they lived inside Hungary.

It may be that the particular way that the Gypsies and Rom have been reproduced was originally conditioned by the cultural, technological, and social baggage brought by those of their ancestors who were foreign.

But in the absence of any substantial historical evidence about the migration of proto-Gypsy populations, I have taken the pragmatic stance and concentrated on the European context in which Gypsies have lived for five hundred years. This is also, I believe, a more disturbing and challenging standpoint: that the Rom adaptation has been made from within our kind of society—the Gypsies are a part of ourselves, a part that we have difficulty acknowledging. Locating the Rom within their Eastern European setting enables us, moreover, to see the profound reasoning in their insistence that everyone else around them is a "peasant." Indeed, the Gypsy and peasant ethics are constituted by a series of structural oppositions, at once economic, social, and moral:

Peasant	*Gypsy*
Land forms the person	No attachment to place
Labor	Dealing
Toil	Talk
Diligence	Cleverness
Production	Circulation
Autonomy through avoidance of exchange	Autonomy through avoidance of labor
Mundane activity	Magic
Thrift	Spendthrift
Familial accumulation	Brotherly sharing
Past weighs on living	Past unimportant

For the Rom, the total social process of the production and circulation of the means of life was reduced to one of its moments—that of circulation—and for the peasants the converse was true. In this perspective the "Gypsy position" can be seen as an elaboration of a sense of peripherality and homelessness. Lacking land and being unable to realize autonomy through labor, the Rom took hold of circulation. In their rejection of the symbolism of production and reproduction, they were pushed into treating identity as "situational,"[10] as existing in changing and mutually constituting relations with each other and the non-Gypsy.

But I have also argued that, despite the dominant essentialism of Magyar images of ethnic identity, in Hungary we found a more relational view, or at least this is how I would interpret the way so many Magyars told me during my research that theirs was now "the land of the Gypsies"; or as Bell's informants claimed, "The people are Cigány now."[11] This kind of rhetorical assertion was the consequence of the productive system and culture of a "people's democracy," within which many Hungarians came to feel homeless and peripheralized in their own society. Party membership was the passport to full participation in society, and so most

Hungarians felt excluded from the social process. In bleak moments it appeared to the Magyars that the "Gypsy way," flattering those in power to cream off some privilege, was becoming the only viable method to "get on."[12]

And, of course, it was not just under the people's democracies that people felt this way. As Eastern Europeans have discovered during the upheaval accompanying their integration into capitalism, in the "free world" it is possible to feel homeless and marginalized. In this sense, then, we live in what one might call "the time of the Gypsies," a period of European history in which "Gypsiness" is continually made possible by the nature of our societies. This is not just a rhetorical trope. In the past 150 years in Ireland, a population of Travelers has arisen from among the landless poor and has developed an indistinguishably "Gypsy" way of life.[13] More recently in Britain, the rise of the New Age Travelers may reflect a similar creative response to a sense of marginality.[14] So it is not so much, to paraphrase Jean-Paul Sartre, that "if there weren't any Gypsies, we would have to invent them" than that even if the *gaźos* assimilated all the Gypsies, "they" would reinvent themselves.

Rom Identity, Ethnicity, and Ideology

Acknowledging the fact that Rom "culture" can best be seen as oppositional to that of the non-Gypsies enables us to place the Rom "adaptation" in a sociologically revealing perspective by comparing them with others who labor for their living without the aid of land or capital. Seen comparatively, the story of the Gypsies might form just one chapter in a much longer European history of conflict and struggle over the meaning and social value to be accorded to "labor." This story may go back at least to the ninth century, when, according to the historian Jacques Le Goff, "for the first time in the history of medieval Christendom" the economic as a mode of activity distinct from others was ideologically acknowledged and given social value by the inclusion of the category of *laboratores* in the tripartite model of the social order.[15] Certainly in the subsequent history of medieval Europe, there were many of the unresolved issues that surfaced in Communist Hungary nearly one millennium later.[16]

Le Goff argued that the Middle Ages saw a reversal of the traditional otherworldly attitude of the church toward "labor." Whereas once it had been defined as a form of condemnation or penitence, from the twelfth century on "a positive theology of labor" took root, so that by A.D. 1200 "the working saint was giving way to the saintly worker."[17] Le Goff also pointed out that at the very point the church was giving way to social pressure for a reevaluation of worldly activity, the rise in trade, credit, and monetary payment/remuneration posed new challenges to this theology. Adapting the older penitential idea of labor as toil, as suffering, the church successfully argued that in these new social relations on markets, payment was justified only if "labor" had been given. Although the modern idea of "an economic task performed for others" (as opposed to toil) existed in practice in the markets that had sprung up, the church was incapable of theorizing the idea of the "economic." But the definition of labor as suffering surely helped determine the fate of this reevaluation of labor, which "never really ceased to be a mark of servility."[18] Centuries later the attempt by the people's democracies to give a new value to labor, to turn everyone into a member of a laboring-but-ruling class, might be seen as perhaps the last outbreak of this frustrated conversation in which, as before, there were groups that refused the glorification of suffering through one's body.[19]

At a purely formal level of the comparison of ideological schema, we could compare the world of the Rom with that of those heretical sects of the Middle Ages, such as the Cathars, that rejected the whole idea of labor. But the really fruitful comparison is with other members of modern industrial societies, others who own nothing but their bodies and sell their labor for a living. The sociological literature on modern European societies is well supplied with studies of the efforts of workers to deal with their position at the bottom of the social pile. From Henry Mayhew's pioneering studies of London's laboring poor, through Harry Braverman's study of deskilling and the degradation of work and Huw Beynon's account of a response to Fordism, to more recent ethnographies of the way workers adapt and transform the work process to give value to it, we can build a sense of the diversity of response within a common cultural setting.[20] In the rather special conditions at Fords U.K. in the late 1960s, Beynon's informants treated the factory as a field of guerrilla war. At the outset the management "thought they could treat us like dirt. . . . We took a hammering. . . . They were robbing us blind up here. They were getting away with murder."[21] By the time Beynon studied the factory, the workers had won a certain tactical freedom, but still the attitude was commonly, "I don't want nothing from this company. . . . If they want to be nasty that suits me. . . . They're just a bunch of crooks and we're going to stop them doing too much thieving."[22] Or as another worker put it, "You're just counted as a number here. Treated like robots."[23] The situation at Fords was extreme. Among skilled workers in factories studied by Miklos Haraszti (in socialist Hungary) and Michael Burawoy (in capitalist America), labor was not completely devalued by the workforce but rather turned into a kind of game.[24] By inventing their own routines with machines and thereby playing with time, workers transformed their experience of labor and gave it new value—to the extent that in Haraszti's case workers, at great risk to themselves, used company time, machinery, and property to make artistic objects or practical tools for their own use, which they then smuggled home with them. This redefinition of working for a wage is also found in the very different setting of a textile factory in the British Midlands. There Sally Westwood showed how low-paid women fought to retain control over their work by, among other things, wearing slippers at work and decorating their machines with personal domestic imagery.[25] They also converted the factory space, attempting "to reinsert their lives, as women and as workers, into the production process."[26] Home was for these women "an experience and a space which offered them some degree of autonomy over their lives and the warmth, support and affection" of their families.[27] Home was also associated with the "one area of excitement which never seemed to wane": the romantic "white wedding" with Mills and Boon brides and gallants.[28] So the reconstruction of the work space as "home" was "a way of switching off, of being elsewhere (at home) when in reality the women were tied to the factory chairs."[29]

Perhaps most telling, however, from the Rom point of view, is Jeremy Tunstall's classic study of Hull fishermen. Here we are told that "the young fisherman can contract out of his inferior position in the class system while at sea. And while ashore he can be king for a day, wearing new suits, riding in taxis, drinking whisky."[30] The labor that the men performed was talked about rhetorically in terms of the manly qualities it required and inspired,[31] but, most interestingly, this labor was also redefined by the skippers as a form of "gambling," a game that was played "not just one night in the week, but ten days and nights in a row."[32] Success in this game depended on the luck of the crew and its leader.[33]

This brings us conveniently back to the Gypsies and Rom, who also labored for a living but redefined the importance of doing so to create a space apart for themselves. The Gypsies living in capitalist societies where self-employment and trade had not been demonized were able to define themselves as people who did not work for a wage. Anne Sutherland reported that the Californian Gypsies, though often reduced to wage labor, considered prolonged employment to be "polluting" (*marimo*).[34] And Okely said that the Travelers told her, "If we Travellers took regular jobs it would spoil us."[35] Through their willingness to chop and change activities, what Thomas Acton and Judith Okely called their "flexibility," they turned casual wage labor into a form of trade in which earnings were less a wage than the lucky fee they managed to lift.[36]

In Hungary, given the more repressive nature of the state and its ideological obsession with making everyone a worker, the Rom retreated. Many of the Gypsies I worked with were relatively uninvolved in their work, but sullenness represented a silent, passive resistance, not the guerrilla war of Fords in the 1960s. Although it was said of one man in the

Parketta that "work *stinks* for him," the symbolic potential of declaring that permanent wage work was "polluting" and un-Gypsy was not taken up by these Rom. The Rom did not anathematize labor in the fashion of the skilled workers whom Haraszti and Burawoy described, nor did they try to domesticate it, as did Needletown's sewing women. Work was simply tolerated and was given little or no value in their lives. So successful were they in masking its importance while not actually in the factory that it was only on my return to England after a field trip of fifteen months that I realized that I had almost no information about what the Rom thought of "work." They simply did not talk about it when they were at home. So long as they did not have to acknowledge it, the Harangos Rom could just about bear working in the parquet flooring or similar factories. They could do this partly because of the nature of the socialist work process, which encouraged everyone to develop a "Gypsy-like" relation with the economy, but also because the Rom were capable of creating an alternative "economic" and social order beyond and outside the factory.

So unlike both Beynon's and Westwood's workers, whose main efforts outside the factory went into sustaining homes in which they realized social value, the Rom took the resources they earned in the sphere of production and bought horses. With these they defined a sphere of action with the *gaźos* that allowed them a much more profound sense of autonomy and self-direction than that afforded most waged workers.

A Sealed Ideology and Its "Open Sesame"

I have paraphrased Rom rhetoric, saying that to be a Rom was to be a different type of human than the *gaźos*.[37] The Rom were the kind of people who engaged in *romani butji*, with all we have seen that to imply concerning labor, kinship, households, social reproduction, and, more generally, time itself. But one of the implications of my account of the Rom's persistence in redefining and reinventing their experience of the non-Gypsy world is that the way the Rom lived was *not circumscribed by what they represented to themselves as lived.* The representation of the Gypsies as "people who lived without labor" was, in effect, an ideological elaboration, a kind of rhetorical distortion and simplification of the complex reality of Gypsy lives.[38] They did not live wholly inside their ideology of exclusive distinctiveness.[39] In fact, to understand them fully, we have to see that they survived by breaching the code of *romanes*, as well as by observing it. From 1965 until 1985, the Rom of Harangos had undergone a de facto proletarianization that happened to correspond with the political program of the Communist Party. Day in and day out, the Rom had to do things that were un-Rom. They negotiated their way, as Rom, through this period of massive social change by a continual process of adjustment that would not have been possible if Rom ideology were so rigid that it shattered the moment the Rom were not able to live wholly within its terms.

And in a sense it was precisely because they had such little control over the world outside the settlement and over the way this impinged on their communal life that so many of their efforts were directed toward the creation of a hermetically sealed identity. Like Tunstall's fishermen, who lived only part of the time at sea, and Westwood's housewives, who had to leave their homes, the Rom also had to abandon the world of *romanes* to survive. Even the high point of men's activities, the horse markets where they forged their sense of freedom, were said to be "no good if there are only Rom there."

A similar point could be made about the peasant ethic and the way it prioritized the moment of production. The peasants, being in a socially more secure position, had been able to shift the ideologically devalued economic "moments" onto outside-others (Jews, Gypsies, and, to some extent, their in-marrying wives who dealt with trade and exchange on a daily basis).[40] Sometimes, however, they could not help the eruption of Gypsy-like behavior within their homes. For instance, it was said that among the youths "there is no man in Átány who did not steal," especially corn from his father (on whose land and for whom he worked).[41] The men stole, not to provide themselves with a productive base for household expansion, but to pay the Gypsy musicians at weekly revels in the village bar, to drink with age-mates and later brawl with the men of the other "end" of the village. But this emergence of Gypsy-like behavior within the peasant household was temporary, for after a year or so of this life the peasant lads went on national service. Ordered, disciplined, and brought into "manhood" thereby, they returned transformed into members of the Hungarian "homeland" (*haza*; the term is cognate with that for household), and as such they were ready to become fully active members of the village *haza*—itself seen as the core and image in miniature of the nation.[42] Then if they were lucky, they were given land to work, took a wife, and began the effort to transmit their wealth to their descendants.

By contrast, consider four ways in which the Rom tried to live within the ideology of Gypsy work. First, in Chapters 3 and 4, I gave a sense of Rom hospitality and the ethic of "sharing." At the time I talked of these both as responses to the state of siege that the Rom lived in and also as consequences of the egalitarianism of *romanes*. But this generosity can also be seen as one of the prime means by which the Rom sustained an image of themselves as living in a world of natural abundance, a world in which the *gaźos* were supposedly so "stupid" that they let the Rom take the cream off the top of the milk. Note, however, that it was by enforcing hospitality *on each other* that the Rom lived out the dream of belonging to a world of natural abundance.[43] Second, I said that on holidays, and even on mornings before work, the men started the day by drinking. It was particularly *romanes* to seek a state of mild intoxication during Rom activities such as horse dealing and *mulatšago*. So in drinking before work, the Rom were denying the "time" of the *gažos*, initiating themselves into their own world. I have only to put it this way, however, for the fragility of their position to be obvious.

Third, wealthier Rom could occasionally use cheap *gažo* laborers to work for them, thus neatly reversing the habitual pattern of dependency. Some wealthy Rom families I knew nearer Budapest—relatives of residents of the Third Class—employed simpleminded and often alcoholic *gažos* as quasi-servants. In this institutional arrangement, the *gažo*, who might well have otherwise ended up in a detention center for work avoidance, was used as a general laborer for tasks that the Rom would rather not have done.[44] The Rom treated these men as good-natured fools—though one Rom argued that he treated "his *gažo* better than the peasants treated their servants" since he gave the men the same food as he ate, not just the remains he had not finished.[45] Through this relation of command and domination of a *gažo*, rich Rom lived out an image of the world in which the *gažos* really did save the Rom the suffering and shame of labor.[46] But given the real status of these men in the outside world and the fact that they provided only ancillary help for their Rom employers, it seemed to me as if they were kept as much for the fantasy they enabled as for their real contribution to the Rom family. And fourth, it surely says more of their own marginal position that the people whom the Rom defined themselves against in order to place themselves at the center of humanity were the "peasants." I have suggested some of the very good reasons, to do with the peasant work ethic, for making them *the* other, but nevertheless this was a social group only one level up the social ladder, only slightly less marginal than the Rom themselves.

To argue, as I have, that sealed ideologies such as *romanes*, or the peasant work ethic, have to deal with parts of the world they ignore or devalue has two consequences. For anyone who wishes the cultural transformation of a Europe divided by ethnic and other deeply felt cultural identities—that are lived in by their "bearers" as absolute and all-encompassing definitions of the self—this perspective offers some hope. These kinds of ideologies are vulnerable to some sorts of challenge and have an "open sesame" with which it would be possible to greet them and in so doing lever them open.[47] The Communist social engineers tried to do just this and bridge the gap between Magyar and Gypsy, but having completely misjudged the Rom adaptation, the Communists were doomed to failure. Perhaps because the Rom were at the edge or bottom of Hungarian society, they had already incorporated and "dealt with" those very aspects of the non-Gypsy world with which the authorities approached them offering social reconciliation. In fact, because of their preconceptions about the Cigány, the Communists never even bothered to discover what the relevant "sesame" might be, who among the Rom might have opened the door to the cave. In any case, the only way they could have done so would have been to follow the advice of their ethnographer Kamill Erdős, whose work they used when it suited them but ignored when it did not. In 1960 he told the party, "The goal is not for us to feel good among the Gypsies, but that they should feel at home in our society. For this to happen we have to become 'a little Gypsy' ourselves."[48]

The second consequence of acknowledging fractures in ideologies of identity is to make us remember that the process of self-definition implied by an ideology such as *romanes* is inherently tortured. The cultural conversions that the Rom engaged in were entirely remarkable. But within Rom society, there existed its opposite, the *gažo*. Just as the Gypsies' bodies were impossibly divided, incorporating the very other that they rejected, so the construction of a sealed Rom identity was always in danger of collapsing on itself. Unable to unite the two halves of the severed whole of social reproduction, the Gypsies could not transcend their condition and stabilize the sense of *voja*.[49]

Their efforts at New Year were typical. This celebration involved the ritual form used for all partings: staying awake all night. By 9:00 in the evening, all families in the Third Class were with other Rom. On this day of the year, uniquely for *mulatšago*, men and women sat together in the same room. They behaved then as they did every other winter's evening when each couple was together at home: They watched television. The only difference was that on this night they drank a little. On the two occasions when I was present, the men and women became noticeably miserable as the evening wore on. One complained that the television programs were no good, and another said that what was good was too short; the feeling spread that no one had anything to say to each other. Before midnight, in a kind of vesperal gloom, a degree of order was created in the room and low tables with mats on them were brought out. Plastic flowers were placed in the middle of the tables, and the Russian champagne that everyone bought for New Year was put beside these. As the clock approached midnight, some of the men counted down to zero, at which point, as the Hungarian national anthem was broadcast from the television and Hungarians all over the country joined in singing, the Rom burst into tears. Sobbing openly or weeping silently, they rose and kissed their closest relatives, their spouses, their parents, and their brothers and sisters. The women cried most, but the misery overwhelmed many men as well.

As the night wore on, women slowly returned to their own homes, but the men began to tour the houses of the settlement with greetings for the new year. At certain homes, more or less randomly, groups of men gathered together in what increasingly resembled normal *mulatšagos*. As the night passed into day, the men struggled to keep their hard-won celebration going, desperate not to let it end. Money would always be found somewhere to call for more wine for the brothers. There would always be another man to call the others to listen to his "beautiful, true speech." And then at some point during the first day of the new year, in several houses in the settlement, the man of the house would begin to break small domestic items. Luludji complained that there had not been one new year when Čoro had not broken all the glasses with which she carefully decorated her glass cabinets. Other men broke bottles, tore up their money, or overturned furniture. In these ways, at the point when they began the year anew, men assaulted the *gažo* lurking among the Rom in their own homes.

Wage labor dominated their years of youth, yet the Rom could give no moral value to the time and effort spent in the factories; there they were treated for the most part by the Magyars with whom they worked as if they were mere representatives of their group, and largely ignored as unique, individual persons. Still, the Rom struggled to understand and derive some pleasure, to make *voja* in their sad and troubled lives. On occasion they purged all the effort of labor in their gambling and risky horse dealing. But how many Rom really felt they were "pure"? How much alcohol did they have to drink to achieve that state of "respect" and *voja* they longed for?

Today, the states of Eastern Europe have abandoned their attempts to force the Gypsies to assimilate. There are Gypsy political parties, newspapers, and even television programs. But there are also new pressures on the Rom. Ironically, the "jobs for all" policies of the old regimes ensured that many more Rom lived out their dream of "Gypsy work" than will be able to in the future. In Harangos the Parketta was bought by a German company, and in 1996 only one Rom from the Third Class still worked there. However, those Gypsies, like the Harangos Rom, who have been able to preserve their identities and communities are, it seems, better placed to deal with the more competitive world of Eastern European capitalism than those who tried to abandon *romanes* totally. Unfortunately, it is this successful adaptation to the new conditions that makes many of their non-Gypsy neighbors so fearful of them.

Like the rest of us, Hungary's Rom are caught in "the storm blowing from paradise" that "irresistibly propels us into the future." In a much-cited commentary on a painting by Paul Klee, the German mystic Communist Walter Benjamin encapsulated the modern intellectual's condition.[50] He imagined an angel of history, with his face turned toward the past, helplessly observing the debris of historical events as it accumulates skyward; he hopes to wake the dead and reunite what human ideology has severed. Benjamin, writing in a messianic Judeo-Christian tradition, believed that "only a redeemed mankind receives the fullness of its past."[51] For him it is as if a millenarian liberation from the weight of the past will enable a simultaneous coming to terms with that past. But the Gypsies offer an alternative image of liberation. For the Gypsies there is no angel of history, nor is there a past to be redeemed. They live with their gaze fixed on a permanent present that is always becoming, a time-less now in which their continued existence as Rom is all that counts. Like the angel, they are being blown in the storm of progress, but unlike the angel, they have no dream of "integration"; they fear the dead will awaken, and they wish that what is whole will be severed. Ultimately, neither angel nor Gypsy can effect his will, but the Gypsies are at least fortunate that the pile of debris that history throws up around them is constantly consigned to the homogeneous, obliterating "sometime ago" (*varekana*) in which they talk of their past. In the end, I believe, that is why the Rom can live so "lightly" and "easily" in a world so full of heaviness and trouble.

GLOSSARY

bácsi	uncle (an affectionate term of address for an older man)
baxt	luck, auspiciousness
barimasko	big-headed, proud, like the Romungros and *gažo*s
bori	daughter-in-law
bužanglo	cunning (negatively or positively)
Cigány	Hungarian term for Gypsy (normally derogatory)
cincár	intermediary, trader, broker
Cs	abbreviation for "reduced value" (cheap housing built mostly for Gypsies)
dilo	foolish
forint	Hungarian currency. In 1986, 45 forints equaled U.S.$1
foro	town, market
gaži	non-Rom woman
gažo	non-Rom man
gazda	head (male, normally) of land-holding peasant household
inga	a mechanical saw operated with a pendulum device
kirvo	co-godparent, as in Spanish *compadrazgo* to whom one is spiritually related through the act of baptism: used reciprocally
kris	judgment; meeting of Rom to resolve dispute between Rom
kupec	trader, middleman (mildly derogatory)
kurvi	whore, literally; but also term of address to women in songs
lašo	good, easy, light; contrasted with "*pharo*," difficult, heavy, un pleasant
lindra	soul, dream
mangimo	celebration to request a bride from another Rom family
mulatšago	celebration
nemzeto	grouping of people who share activity in common, normally relatives; roughly like French Romany *vitsa*
nepo	people, calqued from Hungarian *nép*, used in Romany to refer to relatives
Parketta	the Parquet Flooring Factory
paruvel	"he swaps," the verb, rather than the abstract noun, *paruipe*, is commonly used to mean "swapping"
patjiv	respect
phral	brother
phenj	sister

247

rendes paraszt	Hungarian for "proper peasant": the moral ideal of the good peasant
Rom	Gypsy, human, not *gažo*
Romanes	Romany, the language; *romanes,* in the Gypsy way
romani butji	"Gypsy work": the cunning and wit that allow the Rom to live as they do, to reap without sowing
Romni	Gypsy woman, human female
Romungro	half Rom, half *ungro* (Hungarian). Romany term for the Hungarian-speaking "Hungarian Gypsies"
śav	boy, common description of all Rom men
śej	girl, common description of all Rom women
šogoro	brother-in-law
šukar soba	clean room, or "parlor"; literally "beautiful room," used for decorative display of mirrors and furniture; also for displaying the dead before burial
Third Class	the name of a settlement in Harangos where the dominant majority of residents were Rom. The name comes from a division of lands around the town and has no special social significance.
voja	good mood, exaltation
vorba	speech, especially formal speech in *mulatšago*

APPENDIX

I recorded the deals of one man, Rudi, through most of the year that I lived in Harangos (see Table A.1). Rudi was pensioned from work and received 3,000 forints each month. His wife also earned a little. Note the truly enormous sums that passed through his hands during this period, sixty times his monthly income.

Note, however, the difficulties of calculating profit. Rudi had 10,000 invested in Horse A on February 17. On April 4 he swapped this for C and 3,000, therefore having 7,000 in C. C is then swapped for D and 3,000 that same afternoon. In D Rudi now had 4,000. He therefore had a large potential profit, D being valued at 16,000 among the Rom, which is to say, more on a market. When on April 23, D died, had Rudi lost 4,000 forints, 12,000 forints, or more—say, the 18,000 he might have sold D for at the market? In Table A.1, I calculated his loss at the price other Rom would have paid if buying from Rudi.

By contrast, see Table A.2 for the trades of Lapoś, Šošoj's son-in-law, at Nagykőrös near the end of the season.

250

TABLE A.1 Economic Activity of Harangos Pensioner During Ten Months

Credit In	Transaction	Date	Other Comments	Debit Out
22,000	Sells 6 pigs	JAN 8		6 pigs
	Repays loan for fodder to son	9		3,000
	Repays loan to bank for pig feed			1,000
	Lends nephew money to prevent depletion of funds	16		9,000
3 pigs	Buys from son Gives remaining cash to daughter	17		8,000 1,000
10,000, Horse A	Borrows cash from brother	FEB 17	Owes 9,000	10,000
12,500	Sells pigs	24	Repays loan; 2,500 left	3 pigs 10,000
500 kg fodder		25	1,000 left	1,500
9,000	Receives back loan from Jan 16	MAR 16 A.M.	Has wife bring this money No fodder left	
Old nag (horse B)	Buys from Rom for 13,500	16 P.M.	Still owes 6,000 until end of May	7,500
600 kg fodder		24	Has 700 left after buying fodder	1,800
		26	Fails to trick peasant into buying horse B— broken nail and weak foot	
200	Sells manure to peasant	27	Now has 900	
Filly C 3,000	Swaps horse A; receives cash and new filly	APR 4 A.M.	Value of C put at 12,000	Horse A
Horse D, 3,000	Swaps horse C; receives cash and new horse	P.M.	Pays 1,000 *cincár* fee for deal; value of D put at 16,000 and rising (a good horse)	Horse C, 1,000
Subtotal				
59,700	He also has horses B and D, valued at 29,500 together, so he has a nominal total credit of 88,200		But he still has debt of 6,000 on horse B, leaving a nominal profit of 28,400 from an original sum of 18,000 on Jan 16	**53,800**

(continues)

TABLE A.1 *(continued)*

Credit In	Transaction	Date	Other Comments	Debit Out
Calf 1, 3,000	Does a swap in which Bakro will pay 6,000 supplement, half to be paid next payday (May)	APR 11	Does deal partly to help his nephew Bakro, who needs a horse	Horse B
Horse B	Returns calf and cash to Bakro, who was usingthe horse to cart scrap iron and might be ruining it in the process, without having cleared debt	14	Accused by original seller of B of cheating Bakro and treating him like a *Romungro*; Rudi still not paid for B; Bakro's wife curses Rudi to have no luck with his horses	Bakro's calf, 3,000
13,000	Sells B to another Rom to pay off his debt on the horse	21		Horse B
	Pays off debt	21 eve.		6,000
		23	Horse D dies on road to market (after this disaster Rudi's profit never really recovers)	Horse D, 16,000
Horse C	Recovers original filly C from third party, since vet avers it was sick when bought	24	Gives tip to vet Pays fee to lawyer for threatening letter	500 950
Horse E, Foal F, 2,500	Swaps C at Árokszállás market for near-blind, decrepit mare and 2-month foal plus cash	MAY 7	On return to Third Class immediately offered 13,000 for the E and F, or 6,000 for the foal, F	Horse C
			Lends cash to relatives until 10	6,000
			Contributes to domestic budget	1,450
(10,000)	Sells horse E to Ferko—	8	Due to money out on loan (now 17,000), fails to buy a fine horse going for 22,000 (12 immediately, 10 to be paid next month) at Jászapáti market	

(continues)

252

TABLE A.1 *(continued)*

Credit In	Transaction	Date	Other Comments	Debit Out
1,500	Sells foal for 6,500 to Bakro's son, 5,000 to be paid on 17 (payday)	10		Foal F, (10,000)
			Ferko decides not to buy horse E as too	
6,000	Repays loans from May 7		lame; see May 8	
Calf 2, 5,000	Swaps horse E with Bakro and cash supplement. E, though blind, is now visibly less lame. Bakro needs horse to earn at scrap dealing.	11	The confusion over the lameness seems to derive from two abscesses by the nail that improved after Rudi had bled the horse.	Horse E
Subtotal				
90,700	Rudi is still owed 5,000 from May 10, so he is still up. Rudi claims the calf is worth 6,500 or more		Nominal profit might now be 9,500; note also some money goes to daughter/household.	**87,700**
Horse G	Bought at Pásztó market	12		28,000
3,500	Borrows from neighbor until 18th		Cost of transport home for horse	500
5,000	Borrows from son			
2,800	Bakro produces some of the money owed from 10th; very apologetic Bakro explains he can't pay off remaining 2,200	17	Zeleno offers 14,000 for horse E and foal F together (Rudi could now reclaim them from Bakro), but Rudi prefers to wait for Bakro's cash	
27,000	Hatvan market, sells G	21		Horse G
4,000	Borrows 4,000 from Mošulo to make next trade			
Horse H	Buys horse		Still owes son 5,000 from May 12	31,000
Horse J, 1,000	Swaps Receives 1,000	28		Horse H

(continues)

TABLE A.1   (continued)

Credit In	Transaction	Date	Other Comments	Debit Out
	supplement, then repaid to Mošulo			1,000
700	Bakro repays part of loan; 1,500 still owed	JUNE 7	Begins to clear debt from May 12; rest promised for 25	500
8,000	Sells calf 2	14		Calf 2
9 piglets	Buys from local market			9,500
	One pig falls ill, dies	19		1,050
	Another pig killed for meat before it dies	20		1,050
			Gives fee to vet to inject pigs	300
11,500, Horse K	Swaps horse for a foal, K, plus cash	21	Repays son 5,000 and Mošulo 3,000	Horse J 8,000
	Two more pigs ill and die	JULY 21	Pays vet for visit	220
Meat from pig	Kills pig before it dies; 4 left	27		1,050
5,000	Sells 4 remaining pigs	AUG		4 Piglets
		2	Loans to son	5,000
			Contributes to household expenses	1,000
19,000	At Koka market sells foal K (3,500 profit on this horse)	SEP 6		Horse K
Horse L	Buys horse	13		20,000
5,000, Horse M	Son repays loan Swaps horse, paying supplement	22		Horse L 1,000
3,500 (600) Horse P	Plans to slaughter horse M for expected 26,000, but instead swaps with Gagarin for cash, 200 kg fodder, and working horse for winter	27		Horse M
800 kg fodder		OCT 14		2,400
	Rudi's former horse sold for slaughter by Gagarin for 31,000	26		

(continues)

TABLE A.1 (continued)

Credit In	Transaction	Date	Other Comments	Debit Out
Total				
183,500	Rudi, however, has a horse worth at least 21,000			**(199,270)**
5,230 profit				

TABLE A.2 Economic Activity Šošoj's son-in-law During Ten Days

Credits In	Transaction	Date	Comments	Debits Out
72,000 plus old, heavy, Horse 3	Sells paired mares "tobacco chewer" (bago)	OCT 27 A.M.	Lapoś had 85,000 in these	Horses 1 + 2
2,000, Horse 4, Horse 5 (foal)	Swaps bago for knackers' horse and foal plus cash	P.M.		Horse 3 Transport cost home 1,000
14,000	Sells foal	29		Horse 5
7,000	Sends knacker to slaughter	NOV 6		Horse 4
Total				**(86,000)**
95,000	A net profit of 9,000 forints in ten days			

NOTES

Chapter 1

1. *London Guardian*, April 7, 1993.

2. Guy (1975, pp. 219–220) described the way that the Communists in Czechoslovakia had earlier prevented Slovak Gypsies who worked in the Czech lands from settling there.

3. BBC Monitoring Service, August 16, 1995.

4. Nicolae Gheorghe (personal communication). After the 1991 government-inspired miners' riot in Bucharest, some of the miners and political officers rampaged through the Gypsy quarters in Bucharest.

5. See, for example, Szuhay (1995).

6. See BBC Monitoring Service, December 14, 1995.

7. Romanies Complain to OCSE over Breach of Human Rights, BBC Monitoring Service, December 5, 1995.

8. See Guy (1975, pp. 209–210).

9. Studies by anthropologists have shown how in capitalist countries Gypsies have carved out a niche for themselves through a combination of self-employment and residential mobility. Conflicts with the state have centered on attempts to control the Gypsies' access to land. See Okely (1983); Piasere (1984); and Sutherland (1975). For a historical perspective, see Mayall (1988).

10. See Havas, Kertesi, and Kemény (1995, p. 80).

11. Meanwhile, in Switzerland all Gypsy children were forcibly removed from their parents and adopted by Swiss families. No record was ever kept of their families.

12. See, for example, Bán and Pogány (1957).

13. In Czechoslovakia there was also a campaign against so-called Gypsy nomadism. Guy (1975, pp. 215–218) described how Gypsies were believed to be migrating from Slovakia to the Czech land to find "untied," that is, loosely disciplined, workplaces. In fact their frequent travels were mostly for family visits.

14. Since the term "Hungarian" refers ambiguously to both an ethnic group and citizens of a state, Gypsies thought of themselves as Hungarian in this latter context and would often say, "We're Hungarian . . . Hungarian Gypsies." To mark the difference I use the term "Magyar" for the Hungarian ethnic group.

15. This negative point of view was reinforced among Communist officials in Hungary by reports of a "disproportionate" number of Gypsies participating in the 1956 revolution. See Vendégh (1960, p. 53).

16. Marx and Engels (1996, p. 9).

17. See Weber (1947); and Simmel (1978).

18. Lévi-Strauss (1977, pp. 327–328).

19. I carried out further fieldwork in 1987 and 1988 when I worked alongside the Rom in a local factory.

20. Panaitescu (1941); Vekerdi (1971).

21. See Kemény (1976).

22. See, for instance, the classic study by Cohen (1969).

23. Though Alexander (1992) has a challenging discussion of the nature of price in Indonesian markets.

24. There are no studies of Hungarian, Boyash, or other Eastern European Gypsies with which to compare my evidence and build a broader picture. The only exception, so far, are some short sections of Kaminski's (1980, pp. 196–240) study, based on several extended visits, that deal with the Rom in Slovakia.

25. Williams's (1984) study is a protracted discussion of what the lack of a center means for the Rom/Gypsy culture.

26. See Okely (1983); and Piasere (1984).

Chapter 2

1. Celebrated in a savagely anti-Gypsy book, published in the Communist era when such things were supposed to be forbidden, by Moldova (1988).

2. Many researchers who have worked with Gypsies stress that, unlike people with fixed jobs, and especially unlike those with ordained tasks, Gypsies live, and revel in living, "by their wits." See, for example, Gmelch (1986, pp. 313–314).

3. Other writers on Gypsies have referred to this flexibility of strategy, though they tend to emphasize the "rational" basis of such diversification of activities. See, for example, Acton (1974, pp. 250, 262); Okely (1983, pp. 56–57); and Salo (1981, pp. 77–84).

4. See Williams (1984, pp. 318–322).

5. See Baumann's (1986, pp. 12–32) account of such tales in the United States.

6. Hungarian accounts of the Gypsies tend to devote considerable space to such devious practices, for instance, Domán (1984, pp. 134–137); and Erdős (1959, pp. 1–6).

7. One of my uses to my hosts was as a taxi driver, since in 1984–1985 none of the Rom had cars of their own. This status suited me well as it provided me with a perfectly acceptable reason to attend events that otherwise would have been none of my concern. Indeed, early on when I suggested that I might give someone a lift to a market for free, the man who had taken me into his home gave me a long, hard stare and told me that I was only to drive anyone for money. To do otherwise would have been to suggest, as some men believed, that I was being paid to go with the Rom by someone else. And who else would that have been but the Hungarian police?

8. On occasion it was possible to make money grow directly with no intermediary object since, although private moneylending at interest was illegal in Hungary, it was possible to write contracts that included the interest to be paid as part of the capital extended in credit. I heard on one occasion that rates of 25 percent were being charged for an emergency loan to a *gaźo* in great trouble.

The magic of the Gypsies included their ability to tell fortunes. This practice continued up to the end of the Second World War when the Communists banned fortune-telling. Gropper (1975, pp. 42–44) noted of the American Rom that "the Gypsies themselves are always surprised at the foolish behaviour of their customers" and that "readings to *gažos* are considered entirely fallacious; should the seer believe during a reading that she has really foreseen a future event, she is disturbed; usually she does not reveal her vision to the customer." By looking into the person's fate and future, the Gypsy establishes some sort of moral relation with the *gažo*, but this, I believe, is just what the Gypsies wish to deny and avoid.

9. Hungarian Statistical Handbook (1984); Eger (1984).

10. See Sutherland (1975); Williams (1984); and Piasere (1984).

11. Piasere (1984, p. 137) rightly criticized another author who "wanted at any price to 'rehabilitate' the Gypsies among the non-Gypsies [by] pretending not to have noticed their 'happy indolence.'" Another ethnographer had his academic work, writing about the Rom, reinterpreted by his Rom friends as another form of "living off the *gažos*." Patrick Williams (personal communication).

Chapter 3

1. Grellmann's book was published in English four years later (1787). In reality, the facts are a little obscure, since Wáli never wrote down his own encounter; with Grellmann's book it comes to us at third hand. Malabar at that time could refer to the whole west coast of India, so the students may have been from Goa. Certainly, if they were from the area now known as Malabar, Wáli would not have recognized any Indo-European vocabulary items at all. I am grateful to Chris Fuller for this point.

2. Okely (1983, pp. 8–15).

3. In Stewart (1995) I argue this in greater detail.

4. It was perhaps not entirely accidental that the political opposition to the Communist Party in Hungary took up the Gypsy cause in the 1970s. In the 1980s, these people founded the first, then illegal, charity to help impoverished Gypsy families.

5. Williams (1984, p. 337).

6. Sutherland (1975, p. 290).

7. These pictures were no doubt scavenged by the women of both families at the same time from the industrial garbage dump at Budapest.

8. They were thought of as two groupings by the residents, thanks to the masking of generation in their assessment of kinship. See Chapter 4; and Stewart (1988, pp. 160–169).

9. A little less than half of the thousand Gypsies were not Rom but Romungros (non-Romany-speaking).

10. Many other Gypsies lived among Magyars in what council documents referred to as "Gypsy concentrations" in the oldest blocks of the town.

11. This did not stop some of the Magyars from (illegally) selling wine and spirits to the Rom, often at exorbitant credit rates.

12. See Chapter 11.

13. The incident was observed and noted by Judit Szegő.

14. A forint is the main unit of Hungarian currency. The stolen amount was equivalent to about $22 in 1985.

15. This continued for three years, though only the first year was at full pay.

16. Women participated even in the heaviest work of house building, though the men tended to organize and direct the work.

17. The image of "siege" is from de Heusch (1966). This Belgian ethnographer, who was taken on a tour of Gypsy communities in Eastern Europe by Jan Yoors, a Dutchman who had grown up with the Rom, observed the "many protective measures taken to preserve the integrity of a culture in a state of siege, a culture which wishes to remain impervious to the world outside" (p. 89). My use of the term differs slightly in that I emphasize the way the siege was imposed by the *gažos*.

18. At public events such as the May Day festivities held in the hills above town, the hostility of many Harangos dwellers to the reveling Gypsies was palpable and discomfiting. But this hostility was also a feature of daily life in the bars and restaurants of the town.

19. See Országos Statisztikai Hivatal (1895).

20. Although my evidence is purely anecdotal, I have the impression from occasional conversations that in Hungary for many Romungros the Rom represent "true Gypsies," "real brothers." This is not my experience in Czechoslovakia, where the local equivalents of the Romungros still speak *Romanes* and see the Vlach-dialect-speaking Rom as just another group of Gypsies.

21. See Réger (1990) for examples of their speech recorded in Harangos by Szegő.

22. See Fred Myers's discussion of aboriginal "property" (1986, pp. 153–158).

23. Concomitantly, men also had to accept help offered by other men if they did not want to be called proud or big-headed.

24. See Chapter 11 for further discussion of these matters.

25. This concern with food, the outsider may feel, provides rather slight evidence of a deep commitment to sharing. But consider the fact that as a result of their hospitality early in the month, many Gypsy families were reduced to a diet of bread, potatoes, and onions by the end of the month, and you begin to see the order of their priorities.

26. Thus, two authors stressed the Gypsies' lack of "civilized standards" by pointing out that "on a settlement there is no set meal time. There is no Romany word for each of the meals. . . . They do not have the concept of breakfast and supper." Mészáros and Vekerdi (1978, p. 22).

27. Those non-Gypsies who did eat with the Rom were much praised, and this fact was always cited if these non-Gypsies' standing was somehow in question.

Chapter 4

1. Although it would be a confusion of idiom to talk of Rom families having a "head," those women who raised children on their own were, at the ritual moments of Rom life, somewhat marginalized. Groups of men touring a settlement

and offering greetings at Christmas, for instance, would not normally go to a house where no man was living. This at times even applied to "true" brothers of the women in question.

2. There was a noticeable difference between public and private behavior. When others were not around, women did not have to engage in formal, respectful behavior toward their husbands, though in domestic arguments one way for a man to gain the upper hand was to demand that they should. Compare Sutherland's (1975, p. 266) report of the American Rom: "In private a woman may step over her husband's clothes . . . but she would be very ashamed to do this in public."

3. There are obvious similarities between this and Melanesian ethnography. See Strathern (1978, pp. 186–191); and Josephides (1985).

4. The fact that the dispute took place between women allowed the men, and the representation of brotherly relations between them and their houses, to carry on as if little had happened.

5. Okely (1975) explored the contradictions and potential that these opened up to Gypsy women.

6. See Williams (1984, p. 324).

7. See the discussion of Šošoj's and Čaja's family division of labor in Chapter 5.

8. Sutherland (1975, p. 71); Gropper (1975, p. 38); and Williams (1984, p. 194) reported exactly the same pattern for other Rom groups.

9. Strathern (1978, p. 173).

10. Because of Rom endogamy, mother's and father's brother were politely addressed using the same term, *Nano*, sometimes *Kako*, "if you want to be on very good terms with him." In some cases people would say they referred to their mother's brother's wife as "aunt" *(bibi)* and in others as "sister-in-law" *(šogorkina)*. One's father's sister's husband could be called "uncle" *(nano)*, or in some contexts, he could be called "brother-in-law." The use depended on one's relation with these people, who in any case would normally be addressed reciprocally as *šej* (girl), *mo* (lad), or *šav* (boy).

11. In Hungarian, Gypsies said these exchanges were *csere*, or "swaps."

12. See also Williams (1984, p. 433) on the constant search for unanimity among the Parisian Rom.

13. See Erdős (1961b) for further details.

14. See also Turnbull (1978); and Marshall (1961).

15. This is also, incidentally, the explanation for the appearance of the various "kings" and "emperors" of the Gypsies in parts of Eastern Europe since 1990, especially in Romania. They are exploiting niches created by *gažo* credulity.

16. And perhaps this, too, explains why these Rom loathed the notion of divorced parents keeping in touch with any children who lived with the other party.

17. Williams's discussion of names (1984, pp. 151–160) was the inspiration for this interpretation. Nicknames, too, protected Rom from identification by *gažo* outsiders, just as their language did. See also Okely (1983, pp. 174–175).

18. In Harangos these names did not refer to social entities of any size. The Hungarian word *nemzet*, which had been calqued, is closer to the French, rather than the Anglo-Saxon, sense of nation. The former may normally imply but does

not subsume the idea of *patrie*, "homeland." The idea of traditional attachment to land or place was absent from the Rom term.

19. As Williams (1984, p. 253) wrote of Parisian Gypsy conceptions, such a word was a name given to the social space in which Gypsies "carry out the gestures which make them Rom," within which they lived together.

20. Marriage to Rom who were socially very distant was also thought to be difficult, since there would be "so much to learn."

21. Patrick Williams (personal communication).

22. See Bloch (1975) for a discussion of the masking of affinity within endogamous groups.

23. *Bivaj* was the Romany term used here. It is used only in this context and in tales to indicate that a marriage had been agreed.

24. At the marriage itself, I was always struck by how the marital couple was hardly visible apart from a ceremonial procession, often in any case poorly attended, from the bride's to the groom's house.

25. Williams (1984, p. 339).

26. Although young couples might have carried on living adjacent to elder relatives for many years, especially if these were grandparents, they normally kept their own hearth and "economy" from early on and certainly after the birth of the first child.

27. See Bloch (1974).

28. I thank Akis Papataxiarchis for his help in understanding this process. My own inability to enjoy the game of gambling as I watched my friends play Twenty-one meant that I only attended a few of these contests. Finding it impossible to take my leisure with a game of moneymaking, I could not bring myself to play; the Rom, of course, did not share my confusion. See Chapter 10 for further discussion.

29. I transcribed this song from the archives of the Hungarian Academy of Sciences' Musicology Department, but related variants were known and sung in Harangos. Unless otherwise indicated, all the songs I discuss in this book were recorded by myself either in *mulatšago* or, to improve the quality of the recording, in arranged sessions.

30. One man who regularly lost most of his income at cards won no respect for his addiction to the game, but his wife, who did not work at all and failed to provide a respectable home, was criticized behind her back in sharper terms. Whereas the man was pitied, she was scorned for turning her back on her responsibilities.

31. See Chapter 12.

32. In the Disappearing World film *Across the Tracks* (1988, dir. J. Blake, Granada Television), one sees a man holding out his money while another jokingly grabs at it as if asserting his brotherly right to take the money.

33. Silverman's comments about Rom in the United States are helpful here: "Nomadism and sedentarism are alternate strategies for negotiating the social and economic niche. The amount of time spent traveling is inconsequential; what is significant is that the option to travel is constantly present" (1988, p. 270). See, too, Houseman's discussion (1994, p. 13) of the "constant circulation" in Gypsy and Rom groups.

Chapter 5

1. In reality, as Chris Hann (personal communication) pointed out to me, Hungarian peasants, too, are under obligation to share some of the meat from their pigs—though not to the extent of the Rom—since they can at least store food.

2. This point was explained to me by a senior member of the Housing Department. The practice was to give "temporary" permits to Gypsies.

3. Exceptions were made by the authorities. Chris Hann (personal communication) told me that in Bács-Kiskun County the regulations were never enforced. In the 1980s a special category was introduced to allow intellectuals and artists to earn money freelance. Needless to say, few thought of allowing Gypsies such a privilege.

4. Likewise, if he had failed to fulfill his contract, he would have had to pay a hefty forfeit.

5. The term came into currency in the last years of the Dual Monarchy (1867–1914) but acquired a fundamental significance to all aspects of public life under the Communist regime.

6. See Chapter 3.

7. This was not false humility from the arsenal of the weak. See Scott (1985).

8. She was, in any case, a grandmother and therefore not subject to the sort of taboos that kept younger women and horses apart.

9. As a report from the county authority to the Political Committee put it: "As far as employment is concerned, we can state that work morale improves every year. However, the settlements and hovels represent a great retardant and regressive force." MSZMP Archives, Budapest, November 24, 1964.

10. Ten years later the attitude of his close relatives to the marriage was still one of plain embarrassment, and they vividly recalled their terror at the thought that the children might have been born deformed. It seemed to other Gypsies that Čoro had married practically from within his own *nemzeto*.

11. Although she was speaking in Romany, each time she used the Hungarian word for Gypsies, not *Rom*.

12. In many parts of the country, large sums had been invested in providing "reduced-value" (in Hungarian, *Csökkent értékű*, or *Cs* for short) flats away from the old settlements to replace the hovels in which many Gypsies had been living. This policy had been sharply criticized by sociologists and journalists during the 1970s for reproducing poor-quality housing and new Gypsy ghettos. See Demszky (1980). Čoro and Luludji's fortune derived from the fact that in Harangos the national Gypsy policy was effectively ignored until the very end of the 1970s.

13. They were fortunate with these neighbors, old couples who were pleased to have friendly company, unlike some other Magyars there who had fenced of the area in front of their houses and kept Alsatian dogs on chains to keep out any Gypsies.

14. In fact, the very next day Čoro did buy the horse in question with his father.

15. That she was also Čoro's father's sister counted for rather little, since her brother had, or at least affected, a low opinion of her.

16. Women's friendships were more stable, perhaps because women were less involved in agonistic display in public.

17. I am following Francis Pine's (1987, pp. 227–229) analysis of Gorale family disputes here.

Chapter 6

1. See Bán and Pogány (1957); and Vendégh (1960).

2. Mezey (1986, p. 240).

3. See Le Goff (1985, p. 61).

4. Marx (1973, p. 361). See also Gurevich (1985).

5. But see Dumont (1976) for a critique of the individualist model behind some of Marx's writings on labor.

6. Swain (1985, p. 6) showed how under actually existing socialism "labour power *has* to be purchased, since all members of society are expected to work; and it cannot be relinquished simply because of inadequate demand or low profitability" (emphasis added). He also showed how these societies were therefore ideologically committed to maintaining full employment.

7. Meaning both "citizen" and "bourgeois," *polgár* was poor currency in socialist Hungary.

8. This intellectual model did inform important institutional arrangements throughout the socialist period. Thus, the Socialist Labor Competitions, which determined financially important bonus payments and politically important relations of workers with their bosses, were measured not just in terms of physical output but also in terms of the extent of the competing brigades' cultural and social activities. In this context, at least, there was no ontological difference between increasing productivity and organizing a party for retired members of a brigade, a collective visit to sick colleagues in the hospital, or even a workplace exhibition. All these acts were equally expressions of sociality.

9. These statistics were in contrast to most other factories in the area. See Stewart (1990) for further details.

10. See Kolakowski (1978, pp. 40–43); and Lichtheim (1961, pp. 244–258).

11. Sometimes, though rarely, things worked the other way around. Thus, at the end of the first half of 1988 the wood stores had a productivity ratio of 125 percent but were paid at 105 percent—the factory, they were told, had run out of funds, and the shortfall would be made up later.

12. See Kemény (1978); Ladó and Tóth (1988, p. 525); Haraszti (1971); and Galasi and Szirácki (1985).

13. The point was that significantly variable rates were paid by the factory for time spent working on different types of wood and on jobs of varying complexity. When it came to calculating payment, the foreman could play on paper with these differentials.

14. Although on paper there were trade unions and everyone was obliged to pay the (minimal) membership fee, wages were set not by collective but by individual bargaining.

15. For example, some maintained fictitious stories of abandonment by a husband in order to qualify for social security payments for single parents. *Gažo* colleagues were not let in on these ruses.

16. The habit of sharing used to surprise the Magyars. I remember one day removing an apple from my "sister's" bag without asking her and noticing the long, amazed stare of the Magyar forewoman and then her smile as she realized the very different morality of the Gypsies.

17. From the interviews I conducted with skilled workers from the main workshop, it seemed that for many years job rotation and equality of pay were maintained for all the core workers who had come when the factory had been founded.

In principle, the *inga* ought to have been operated by a trained, skilled worker. But in the Hungarian skilled labor famine, the Parketta had been unable to attract any and so had had to make do with Feri bácsi's semiskilled labor. Since Feri bácsi was only slightly more skilled than his fellow Gypsies, it seemed to them that they had justification for their demands.

18. Some 50 million forints worth of wood passed through the *inga* each year. Since 20-centimeter pieces were used in the next stage of the production line, if the worker cut pieces at 1.02 meters, this amounted to a 2 percent loss, or 1 million forints a year. But if many went through at 98 centimeters, the losses could have been as much as 18 percent, or 9 million forints.

19. The second economy had flourished despite all the efforts of the Communist Party (especially in the period up to 1968, but continuing afterwards too) to eradicate markets and private economic initiatives. The logic of Communist economic policy can be seen, for instance, in a tendency, most acute in the early 1950s, but felt until the late 1980s, to try to reduce the role of wages in the allocation of labor. In fact wages continued to play a role both to attract workers to factories and to allow them to provision themselves and their families, since the distribution of consumer goods via central allocation was never attempted. Nonetheless, by providing a large range of basic services (public transport, holiday resorts, staple foods including meat) at massively subsidized prices, the central economic management tried to reduce the role of market forces such as wages.

In 1983 there were 5 million active earners in the first economy and the equivalent of 1 million in the second. Total wages earned there amounted to one-third of wages in the state economy, and about one-fifth of GNP was produced there.

20. Marrese (1981, p. 58). The size of Gypsy families made their position worse. Whereas each Magyar earner had to support 0.82 nonearners, each Gypsy earner kept 2.24 people. In Harangos each working Gypsy kept 3.45 others. Kozák (1982, p. 59) and Eger (1984, p. 8).

21. Gábor and Galasi (1985, pp. 130–131).

22. A council report lamented, "There are more and more opportunities for occasional and seasonal work for which they have a particular liking, and which they willingly take on." Report on Gypsy Employment (Harangos Town Cleaning Department, 1985). And as early as 1962, Bács-Kiskun County complained that Gypsy men earned more from casual work making mud bricks than from state employment (Bács-Kiskun County, 1982).

23. The Gypsies were particularly well placed to make use of the second economy. Two Hungarian scholars said that "most individuals who carry on activities in the second economy find a diffuse, unorganised market where even a basic infrastructure is lacking ... the flow of information and the system of market connections are not given to any newcomer, every individual has to organise and establish his own chain of market connections" (Kertesi and Sziráczki 1985, p. 232). By historical specialization the Rom were peculiarly well prepared for the brinkmanship and risk-taking demanded upon entrance into the second economy.

24. This attitude toward the afternoon shift was by no means held only by the Gypsies; so widespread was it that the factory paid a 20 percent supplement to all those who worked both shifts.

Chapter 7

1. See Verdery (1991, pp. 426–428).

2. See Bloch (1983, pp. 95–124) for a discussion of the epistemology.

3. See Bán and Pogány (1957).

4. Marx and Engels (1958, vol. 1, p. 155).

5. Guy (1978); Erdős (1960, 1961b). As this theory came to be applied, the blank board was replaced by animality: What the Gypsies really needed was to be turned into human beings. A Harangos report early on in the campaign commented that the Gypsies "need very much help if they are to find their place in the great human family, if society is to raise them into human beings" (Harangos, 1964, p. 3). See, too, Turnbull's (1966) account of African villagers' attitudes toward Mbuti Pygmies.

6. Szent-Györgyi (1983, p. 193).

7. Ibid., p. 194.

8. Bell (1984, p. 285).

9. There were undoubtedly major changes in official rhetoric over the years, notably in the late 1970s and 1980s when Gypsies were redefined as "an ethnic group with its own specific features." As a result, it became legitimate to suggest that the Gypsies would not "assimilate" but merely "integrate" into Hungarian society. But since the new definitions were adopted without explicitly rejecting and proscribing the old ones, most local councils continued unabashedly to pursue the 1961 assimilationist policy (Báthory 1988, pp. 621–622). In a town such as Harangos, a child might occasionally receive an invitation to join a reading camp, and once a journalist came round from the new bimonthly Romany national newspaper (though he was more interested in investigating my presence than in recording the experiences of the Gypsies), but these developments had little effect on the Rom.

10. Similarly, I heard the Rom criticize the Magyars with whom they were arguing by saying, "You are worse than the Cigány!"

11. Erdős (1960, p. 8).

12. See, for example, Fél and Hofer (1969); and Havas (1982b).

13. See Sutherland (1975); and Okely (1983). Irish Travelers I know in London referred to non-Gypsies as "country people," that is, farmers.

14. Fél and Hofer (1961, 1969).

15. In Hollós and Máday (1983, p. 19). See also Hann's (1980, p. 31) study of a successful Hungarian cooperative village; and Bell's (1984, pp. 160–164) study of "Lapos" just north of the Great Plain, near Átány. The term "peasant" did not always have the derogatory, metaphorical sense found in urban European discourse. Since the end of the eighteenth century and especially during the twentieth century in populist and progressive circles, a much more positive image of peasants emerged as the heart, soul, and moving force of the nation. This meaning, though elaborated by intellectuals, was rooted, in part, in the discourse of the peasants themselves. See Erdei (1941).

16. In relying so heavily on one source, I may be accused of constructing a paradigmatic or ideal-typical "peasant worldview." It is true that there has long been great diversity of social structures in different regions of Hungary. It is also true that the nature of village social life as a process of differentiation cannot be understood with a static idea of the peasant family as if all such families were alike (Pine, 1987). And yet it is possible to see that the way a labor unit, land, and labor are related *at the level of ideas* is reworked over time in farming families of central and eastern Europe within remarkably similar ideological constraints. See, for example, Warriner (1938); Hollós and Máday (1983); Pine (1987); and Lampland (1991).

17. The heading of this section is a translation of the Hungarian term *Maga-ura parasztok*. Although the argument of this section was developed in parallel to, rather than in conjunction with, Lampland (1991, pp. 469–470), we share some of our understandings of the peasant ethic. I have taken the term "self-possession" from her work, as well as some of the historical setting she provided. See also Stewart (1988, pp. 271–290).

18. Fél and Hofer (1969, p. 81).

19. Ibid., p. 113. Átány did not lie in an area where the one-child family system had taken hold as it did in other Magyar areas.

20. Ibid., pp. 127–129.

21. Fél and Hofer (1961, pp. 107, 119, 124).

22. Women from poorer families were somewhat freer and were involved in marketing sackcloth and agricultural produce in neighboring villages. See Pine (1987) for discussion of the relation between wealth, sexual division of labor, and authority in Polish mountain farms.

23. Fél and Hofer (1969, p. 113).

24. Ibid., p. 233. The hectarage represents 15–20 Hungarian "holds," the local unit of land measurement.

25. Ibid., pp. 56–57.

26. Ibid., p. 40.

27. Ibid., p. 301.

28. Ibid., p. 274.

29. The Átány villagers were so proud of their ardor that they claimed to have a reputation for it even among the migrant workers of Budapest, where most people disappeared in the anonymous crowd. Ibid., pp. 58, 348.

30. Ibid., p. 380.

31. Ibid., p. 397. Lampland (1991) discussed the concept of *dolog*.

32. Fél and Hofer (1969, p. 281).

33. Ibid., p. 253.

34. Ibid., p. 274.

35. Ibid., p. 380.

36. Ibid., p. 317.

37. Ibid., p. 230. Strictly speaking, it was not enough to own land to be *földes*, since land ought also to have been inherited. Thus, the "isolated farmstead" (*tanya*) owners near Átány were treated as "eccentrics" and did not qualify as "of the soil" since they had "sneaked in" by purchasing their houses. Ibid., p. 57.

38. Ibid., pp. 244–245.

39. "Proper" (*rendes*) also had connotations of belonging to an established hierarchical order. See Szent-Györgyi (1983) for a discussion of the elaborate ranking systems found in Hungarian villages.

40. Fél and Hofer (1969, p. 115). The lower the status of the family was, the less the rank of the past marked the present members of the family. Herdsmen were thought to have dubious moral standards and to be prone to fritter away their wealth on drink and women. Ibid., pp. 233, 240, 277.

41. Kiss ([1939] 1981, p. 287).

42. Fél and Hofer (1969, p. 249). I came across an amusing story of Gypsies in the later 1890s tricking a peasant in a village just outside of Harangos out of all his money by convincing him they would turn it into gold and then persuading him to remain locked in his home for two days (*Egri Újság* 22, 1892, pp. 173–174). For the peasants, this was the prototype of Gypsy ways of making money.

43. Erdei (1941, pp. 93–94), cited in Lampland (1991, p. 468); but see Hann (1980) for a case of peasants in a "frontier" zone.

44. Fél and Hofer (1969, p. 174).

45. Ibid., p. 48.

46. Ibid., pp. 248, 268–269.

47. See also Bell (1984).

48. Ibid., p. 51.

49. Fél and Hofer (1969, p. 281).

50. Ibid., p. 348.

51. The woman was in some ways an outsider in the family (the trousseau she brought at marriage ideally lasted her all her life, so she never had to absorb her husband's family's wealth to clothe herself). Her labor could therefore be marketed without loss of household reputation or family substance. Ibid., p. 119.

52. There is a hint in the ethnography that a significant number of marriages took place between these two halves of the village. Ibid., pp. 171, 196.

53. Javor (1983, p. 297). See also Martha Lampland's study of the confluence of meanings around the word *dolog* (thing, activity, work). Whereas older villagers retained only a "rivalry in diligence," younger ones adopted an increasingly capitalist orientation to market production. But both continued to realize a personal dignity and social value through their productive work through being *dolgos*. Lampland (1991, p. 466).

54. Csalog (1984, p. 50).

55. Vendégh (1960, p. 46).

56. Le Goff (1985, pp. 29–42).

57. On another occasion Čaja told me: "I could work in a factory, but this is better. I'm not tied to the clock in this job. I get up when I like; I go to bed when I like. . . . Nobody bosses me around. I earn a lot more here than the other Gypsy women. They earn 4,000. I can earn 12,000 in a month. Of course, it's dirty work, but it pays well. What can I do about that? I can make a profit this way. You see, it's like business [*šefta*]. When I'm not in a good mood [*naj man voja*], I collect 1,000 or 1,500, and I come home."

58. Bán and Pogány (1957, p. 23).

59. Vendégh (1960, p. 44).

60. This might be attributed simply to opportunism, of which there are plenty of examples in Communist politics—one thinks of the use of anti-Semitism throughout the Soviet dominion (Fejtő, 1974, pp. 295–299)—or else attributed to the way in which Hungarian communism arose in an intellectual and social vacuum (the internal development of scientific Marxism, on the one hand, and the conditions of émigré life in Stalin's Moscow, on the other) and then shriveled rapidly when exposed to the fresh air.

61. A critical report by István Darabos to the national Political Committee of the Communist Party in 1962 noted that in many areas the 1961 policy had been "interpreted in racial terms" and that "instead of educational work, administrative and police measures have been carried out." MSZMP Archives, Budapest.

62. Harangos, 1964. It is hard not to notice the similarity with nineteenth-century British discussions of the undeserving poor.

63. It might seem that the evidence presented in the last chapter of increasing Gypsy employment runs against this line of reasoning, but in reality, as everyone on the Harangos council knew, this was as much the result of the socialist economy's insatiable labor hunger as the effects of the political campaign to get Gypsies to work. The sources of this hunger lay both at national and enterprise levels. At the former, there were economic pressures to expand production; at the latter, the pressures were political, since enlargement gave the firm's managers greater clout in negotiating their plan with higher-level bureaucrats.

But there was also a particular need for unskilled labor in Hungary, from which the Gypsies in particular benefited; and this was due to a quite unintended quirk of planning. Anti-inflationary wage policies had been designed in terms of each firm's *average wage bill*. To increase skilled workers' pay, so-called cotton wool workers were employed to "dilute" the labor force. In Harangos these were, largely, the Gypsies. See Stewart (1990).

64. According to Demszky (1980, p. 72), the pressure on the Hungarian Communist Party to begin rehousing the Gypsies came from outside of the socialist bloc. "At the beginning of the 1960's a report appeared in *Life* magazine, among the pictures of which was one of a Miskolc city-landscape and a settlement of hovels stretching out behind it. Within a few months, the settlement had been pulled down. This was when the prototype of today's "reduced-value" (*Csökkent értékű*, or *Cs*) settlements came into being."

65. Almost the worst humiliation that the average Gypsy *Cs* house builder had suffered was to see his Magyar work mates constructing fine houses for themselves while the Gypsy, who was often a building worker himself, was being built

a house in a new ghetto without any of the conveniences available to most better-off non-Gypsies on the black market.

The official statistics for this time reveal the increasingly disadvantaged position of the Gypsies. As Demszky (1980, p. 71) showed, of the 1.4 million homes constructed between 1960 and 1980, only 24,000, that is, 1.7 percent, were made for the Gypsies, even though they made up 3.5 percent of the population. Even when one adds the 10,000 homes bought by the Gypsies at this time, they received only 2.4 percent of the total available stock.

66. Bell (1984, p. 284).

67. Harangos, 1977.

68. Harangos, 1985.

69. At this time, while midwives were supposed to encourage ethnic Magyars to give birth, they had exactly the opposite role in relation to the Gypsies, a point that the midwives well understood. Despite the occasional rough encounter with hostile Gypsy men, for the most part these women had good relations with the Gypsy women. It should be said that they also received a special premium for visiting the settlement.

70. Dissertation, author's files. A local doctor told me that the Gypsies' childlike mentality could be seen in the way they decorated their houses with a "jumble of colors," in the passion of arguments that would be forgotten the next day, and in their inability to save their resources from one day to another.

71. In Harangos by 1985, 28.5 percent of the children at the school were Gypsy, though they made up 3 percent of all children (Harangos, 1985). At the national level, even though Gypsy children made up 5 percent of all children in 1974, 40 percent of all children officially registered as "at risk" and 50 percent of the children in homes were Gypsy. At the same time, the Gypsies made up 24 percent of those in special education schools. This figure rose to 36 percent in 1983, that is, 15 percent of all Gypsy children. See Mezey (1986, p. 279).

72. Vekerdi's *A magyarországi cigány nyelvjárások szótára* (The dictionary of Gypsy dialects in Hungary) (1983) reflects his methods most clearly. There Romany words in current usage throughout Hungary (for example, *temnica*/prison, *kris*/tribunal) are marked as obsolete in order to better create the impression of a dying culture and language.

73. Vekerdi (1981); Mészáros and Vekerdi (1978).

74. By 1985 Budapest authorities had become aware, in the words of the chief state official, that the main obstacle to Gypsy education was the influence of officials in the Ministry of Education, "who are full of prejudice about Gypsies." Kozák (1984, p. 33).

75. Harangos (1979).

76. There was, for instance, between 1973 and 1976, a 10 percent reduction in the number of "comfortable" manual jobs, a decline that resulted from bargaining by workers to be reclassified into better-paid "uncomfortable jobs," not from any worsening of work conditions. Kertesi and Sziráczki (1985, p. 227).

77. Bell (1984, pp. 289, 294).

78. Ibid., pp. 253–254.

79. Ibid., pp. 170, 247.

80. See Kenedi (1986) for a more general discussion of the Gypsy stereotype in late socialism.

81. In 1989 a Hungarian opinion poll revealed that the Gypsies were thought to be second only to Communist Party members in the extent of their privileges. Nearly 75 percent of respondents thought that Communist Party members had "many privileges," and 47 percent thought that Gypsies did, too. The next most favored group was reckoned to be small-scale entrepreneurs (27 percent). Miklos Tomka (personal communication).

82. See Havas (1982b, pp. 185–186); and, for instance, the non-Communist Nagy's (1940, p. 73) comments, written before the war, which indicate a very similar attitude to the Gypsies: "There are some Gypsies who do peasant's work . . . it is they who in the end will form the elite of the Tzigans" because the "hardy life of the working peasant . . . imparts self-reliance to whoever lives it."

Chapter 8

1. Eger (1984, p. 13). Of course, this was an official inquiry, and the Gypsies were always prone to use such occasions to curry favor with officials and provide the desired answers.

2. Búzás (1983, p. 104).

3. Piasere (1984, p. 145).

Chapter 9

1. See, for example, de Vaux de Foletier (1983, p. 33).

2. Fél and Hofer (1969, p. 380).

3. Ibid., pp. 281–282.

4. Compare Lawrence (1982), a fascinating study of marginality.

5. At this time he was in dispute with Čoro over the use of their father's stable and had petulantly refused to share it.

6. When a horse died, it was taken to the carrion pit outside the town and burning tires were thrown in so that the "dirty Romungros" would not take the dead horse out of the pit to eat it.

7. Despite a legal ban on holding horses for personal agricultural use that remained in force until 1977, in the more liberal economic atmosphere of Kádárite Hungary many peasants seemed to find ways to keep some horses. See Swain (1985, p. 73). The number of horses owned by peasants rose from a low of 18,000 in 1964, through a high of 56,000 in 1969, to around 40,000 in 1980.

8. See, for example, Hann (1980); Swain (1985); and Domán (1984, p. 124).

9. Braudel (1982, p. 26).

10. A horse from its third until its eighth year was at its prime and would, all things being equal, fetch a stable price during that time. After the age of eight, its price began to fall, though horses were in some cases worked for up to seventeen years.

11. Horses could be grouped roughly according to their prices. Small, old, and cheap "knackers" (bandy-legged, for instance, or broken-winded) could come

under 20,000 forints, as did colts and foals in their first year. Young horses coming into peak condition, as well as larger, older ones on the way down, came in between 20,000 and 35,000. Top-quality mares or geldings in their prime would put a man back between 40,000 and 50,000 forints, more if they came in a pair.

12. The difficulties of poorer men were made worse by the virtual monopoly position of the Gypsies at a nearby village, who had made a specialty of collecting violent horses and putting them to slaughter.

13. Gypsy and Rom groups differed in their attitude to the slaughter of horses for meat, some tabooing it (see Okely, 1983, p. 100), others happily participating in it. When the Harangos Rom put large numbers of horse to slaughter, they organized a kind of metaphorical wake for them, staying up all night before they were sent off on the death trains.

14. Kiss ([1939] 1981, p. 277).

15. Fél and Hofer (1969, p. 280).

16. In the eighteenth century, Grellman (1787, p. 16) noted that the pipes used by the Rom were the long-handled sort that had to be drawn while seated—a favorite of the gentry rather than the laboring classes.

17. Baumann's (1986, pp. 26–27) comment about dog trades—that, although they were lived as play, they were also "always susceptible to being understood as business"—is relevant to these deals as well.

18. Notably (in its original usage) "commerce" involved persons of the opposite sex. It is as if the Rom have substituted the Rom/*gažo* divide for gender.

19. Hirschman (1977, pp. 42–63).

20. I am grateful to Steven Gudeman for pointing this out to me.

21. Nagy (1940, p. 153), too, noted the way that financial considerations were quite irrelevant for the Rom on markets.

22. Lévi-Strauss (1966, p. 32) suggested that, whereas rituals unite what was previously separate, games divide what was originally similar. At the end of dealing, the Rom hoped to have made a profit over the *gažo*s, hoped to have won the "game," and thus in a sense hoped to have separated themselves from the *gažo*s to whom they were otherwise inextricably tied.

Chapter 10

1. The Rom gave the Hungarian term *szerencse*, "*luck*," as one translation.

2. A man with an adulterous wife was "cursed" (literally, eaten) by "misery" (*prikežija*) and loss of luck.

3. Geertz (1960, p. 31) briefly discussed the Indonesian concept of *tjog-tjog*, roughly translated as "coincidence," and showed how for Indonesians coincidence was a sign not of trivia but of *true* value, since it was evidence of events, persons, the universe, "fitting" together.

4. See Smith (1989).

5. Okely (1983, p. 100), too, noticed an ambiguous symbolism of English Traveler-Gypsy horses as Gypsy/*gažo*, male/female.

6. In one case a old man insisted that this was a sign that the horse had caught cold, but other younger men remained unconvinced of the animal's attractiveness.

7. A further, possibly trivial, association was the use of the term "harness" (*kantari*) for a woman's bra.

8. The riddle perhaps makes more sense if one realizes that the normal euphemism for sexual intercourse is "to eat."

9. This kind of teasing about imagined extramarital affairs was quite common among the Rom, men and women. See also the sexual innuendo in the riddle "Between two naked ones, a hairy one." Answer: "A horse between the poles of the cart."

10. See Okely (1983, p. 100) for an exact parallel.

11. *Paramiča* can be both fictional and historical but are always "true"—see the discussion of songs in Chapter 11.

12. In Rom folktales, the Rom hero is often a king, but not here. See, for example, Kovalcsik (1988).

13. While someone was "having a go," no one else might try for it. See also Erdős (1961a, p. 59).

14. Keeping them in a stable, out of the elements, also meant that their hair would have the sleek, well-oiled look that the men loved their horses to show off.

15. See Okely's (1975, pp. 212–213) discussion of English Traveling women's horror at uncontrolled sexuality.

16. In a film I helped to make about these Gypsies, the only scene about which I received complaints afterward was one in which a woman could be seen carrying dung from her husband's stable. She told me that she prayed none of her relatives from other villages would ever get to see this—though, of course, women there as well most likely cleaned the stables.

17. The fact that these exchanges came second in the day merely reflected the power relations of the Rom with the non-Gypsies. I thank Steven Gudeman for pointing this out to me.

18. Compare Baumann's (1986, p. 14) account of dog traders: Although many of the trades are actual sales, "the dynamic of these transactions is the same in all essentials as trading [i.e., swapping], and they are considered to be and labelled trades." Dog trading is "a form of play, a contest of wit and words."

19. Since the goal of all horse trading was in the end to make money from the *gaźos*, a horse swap was a supreme instance of the sort of occasion in which the Gypsies were expected to be open to one another's needs.

20. Two exceptions underlined the general point. The actions of a man who gave a horse to his brother at cost when his brother's wife had been imprisoned was said to be extremely "honorable." On another occasion, when a poor man tried to get a horse from his brother, with a promise to pay a month later, he was refused. Such delayed-payment arrangements were the source of much misery between men and could constitute grounds for refusing a deal.

21. And despite the ideology, the Rom did try to cheat one another, since to put one over on one's equal was sometimes a pleasure greater than tricking the "foolish *gaźo*." Even men who knew each other lied about how much money they had with them. Several times Gypsy men would ask me to keep their money in order to "lend" it to them later during their trading if need be. With a peasant, such maneuvering was considered fair play, but since no one should allow a brother to

borrow from a *gaźo* (myself included) if he could help it, this was a somewhat underhand action in inter-Gypsy dealing.

22. Recognizing the egalitarian ethos of deals with each other, the Gypsies were quite clear that markets where there were no *gaźo*s were no good, as it was no good doing business only with the Gypsies—no "profit" might be made. However, to take an animal to market was to admit to oneself and one's friends that one would like to see the back of it. If there were no *gaźo* buyers left, the Gypsies could deal only with each other.

23. There were numerous whispered comments between the dealers that the tape recorder missed.

24. Šošoj said this because the seller had already suggested "42" as a fair price and now appeared to renege on this offer.

25. There was quite often more than a little tension between groups of young men as this exchanging went on.

Chapter 11

1. See, for example, Kovalcsik (1987).

2. I well remember trying to create the mood of a *mulatšago* for the Granada Disappearing World crew to film. The Rom, who had been so keen to help with all other aspects of the filming, became distanced and vacant and only went through the motions of singing together. They were determined not to let their central act of social reproduction become entertainment for the *gaźo*s.

3. Kertész-Wilkinson (forthcoming) rightly pointed out that a fuller treatment of song could be given if one were to look at other informal contexts in which the Rom sing. It is gratifying to see, however, that her description of formal contexts parallels my own and that she states that "seemingly similar rules [are] to be observed" in the "widely public" and "very personal" context. Since I have no musical training, I have not tried to add a strictly musicological interpretation. For this, see, for example, Kovalcsik (1985); and Hajdu (1958).

4. My ethnomusicologist companion, Katalin Kovalcsik, told me that her raconteur, Mihály Rostás, sang songs to her that he could not sing to anyone else because they breached the shared understandings discussed in this chapter and in Kovalcsik (1991).

5. All underscored passages in the printed song texts were spoken or shouted interjections that in the body of the song either set a context or else just acted to emphasize the words.

6. *Jaj* is an exclamation much used in Hungarian and Romany, like English "Oh!" or more like Yiddish "Oy, Oy!"

7. Of course, not all the men living in the Third Class were in the clean room. Not one of the Magyars had been invited, and even the Hungarian driver of the guests from the other settlement stayed outside in the kitchen with the Gypsy women, where he was offered food.

8. The recording was unintelligible at this point.

9. Kirvo is co-godparent.

10. See Stewart (1992) for a discussion of these ideas at greater length.

11. It was the duty of the host to provide the bulk, if not all, of the drink, and a man would normally spend nearly half a month's earnings on a *mulatšago* like Bakro's.

The goal of uniformity was more critically viewed when the Rom were not celebrating together, and I would sometimes hear men complain that they had had to drink alcohol that they did not like in order not to make a scene.

12. Being on a course of medicine provided the only acceptable excuse for refusing the injunction to partake with the other men. During mourning, men avoided *mulatšago*s.

13. On one occasion a group of men who had traveled all evening to a wedding left within minutes of their arrival after the host had failed even to greet them.

14. On another occasion a song was said to have been the root of a feud that arose after some men had sung about a whore. Another had taken this as a slight on his wife and fought with the singers, though this did not right matters, and when the chance came, his family gave false testimony to the police and put one of the singers behind bars. I believe that more was involved here, but my informant seemed to consider this a sufficient explanation when telling me the story.

15. I very rarely witnessed dancing among the Rom except at weddings and arranged recordings for foreign folklorists.

16. See, or rather hear, Vig (1976).

17. Musically, most of the songs had descending four-line melodies, with a range wider than the octave, in major, as well as minor, keys. They were largely monodic, though in a *mulatšago* they were sung by a group of men and not solo. The rhythm was a variable parlando rubato, following a speechlike pattern, and there were many half-sung interjections (underscored passages in the transcriptions). One notable feature of the "slow songs" was the closing pattern in which the last note of a verse was left hanging listlessly or almost swallowed after a pause. In group singing, this pattern finds a new use.

18. That is, if I am lying to you now.

19. See Chapter 12 for a discussion of such apparently abusive ways of addressing a woman.

20. This is the name of a man who was present.

21. The horse was, of course, Hungarian, or so we can see from the fact that the commands were in this tongue.

22. Another man called this out.

23. The term *gaži* literally means "non-Gypsy woman." See Chapter 12 for an explanation of this puzzling usage.

24. That is, banknotes.

25. This text is from the academy's collection.

26. The literal translation is "pair," as in a matched team of horses.

27. *Dili* was an alternative address for "wife" similar to *gaži*, in that the *gažo*s were all *dilo,* that is, crazy and foolish.

28. Literally, "Let destruction eat her."

29. Csenki and Csenki (1980, p. 73).

30. Most Gypsy songs were thought to be "ancient" (*dulmutano*), though, in fact, many songs appeared and disappeared within a generation or less.

31. Schutz (1964, p. 173).

32. See also Reisman (1974).
33. Schutz (1964, p. 159).
34. Ibid., p. 171.
35. See, for example, Bloch (1986).

Chapter 12

1. Miller (1975); Sutherland (1975, pp. 225–287); Gropper (1975, pp. 90–96). See also Silverman (1981).

2. Okely (1983, pp. 77–104). All these authors were, of course, profoundly indebted to Barth's (1969) discussion of ethnic group boundaries and Douglas's (1966) book on purity conventions.

3. Douglas (1966, p. 124).

4. In this vein, Domán (1984, p. 37) gave an extraordinary, and thoroughly misleading, account of Gypsy life based on impressions he gained as a veterinary doctor in Szarvas, in south-central Hungary. He took at face value, for instance, Gypsy girls' claims that they did not know the father of their children, never wondering if they were not having him on.

5. The symbolic logic seems to be that being honorable is to be "integral" and "untouched." See Campbell (1964, p. 269).

6. The fact that this man was divorced from his first wife and then consorted with a woman "half his age" only increased the Rom's amused disdain for him.

7. Washing oneself was a potentially weakening act. Small children, who in any case were said to lack "strength" (*zor*), were not washed every day. Even adults treated their dirty water as if it contained a vital part of the self, and its disposal was done so as not to open oneself to mystical attack.

8. That these Rom ideas reworked common European concerns can be seen, for example, in a comparison with Dubisch's (1986) discussion of modern Greek pollution beliefs. The Romany word *marimo* ("polluted") is, incidentally, derived from the Greek. Day (1995) also reported that sex workers in London created an upper/lower and inner/outer symbolism of their bodies to divide the world of work from that of other relationships.

See, too, Shakespeare's lines from *King Lear* (4.6.118–130): "Down from the waist they were centaurs, / Though women all above; / But to the girdle do the gods inherit, / Beneath was all the fiends."

9. Sutherland (1975, p. 255).

10. Ibid., pp. 261–264; and Kaminski (1980, pp. 45–48).

11. When Judit Szegő was recording tapes about such "superstitions," she was made to agree to give them solely to a woman colleague of mine at the Academy of Sciences and not to let me, a man, hear them because of the shame they would feel if a man heard them openly discuss these matters.

12. In an article on drinking, I (1992) consider related issues from the point of view of strengthening and weakening bodily substance.

13. However, members of each sex willingly accompanied one another to the toilet.

14. Red was a color associated with luck, health, youth, and strength and was much used to ward off evil spirits and ghosts. Babies were dressed in red if they were ill, and the background of many flower images was red. Older women tended to wear brown and blue, paisley-patterned dresses.

15. One social relationship in which women located a sense of shame was that with their parents-in-law.

16. Since part of the motivation for keeping these taboos was to keep up appearances, most girls actually wore the apron from an early age to display their willingness and readiness to become respectable, adult Romnis.

17. Despite the official representation, girls could be very excited by their first menstruation, and one girl came especially to tell Judit.

18. This is, of course, a very common custom throughout rural Europe.

19. Hair was combed in the early evening and out of sight of the men.

20. See also Erdős (1958, p. 55).

21. Recorded by Judit Szegő.

22. I asked Judit Szegő to record this. "Beat him with eyes" means cast an evil eye, something adults inadvertently did when children stared at them. Adults often spat on children to prevent their *lindra* attaching itself to them. Note also the term "trousers" for pants: The *gażo* custom of women wearing trousers was thought to be revolting and ugly. So here the Romni's hidden trousers showed that she kept such ugliness out of sight.

23. The Rom have made use of the services provided by *gażo* hospitals since at least 1945. It seems that, as Okely (1983, p. 211) argued for English Gypsies, most Romnis were happy to have the foolish *gażis* do the polluting work of delivery for them. However, even today when the ambulance is too slow, there is an old Rom woman in the Third Class who acts as midwife.

24. This dung was removed each spring and autumn by the *gażos*, who (amusingly, given its polluted quality as far as the Rom were concerned) bought it as fertilizer.

25. Afterward I heard that some years previously the young couple who had lived there had lost a child in exactly this way.

26. See also Gropper (1975, p. 129).

27. Men did not have to attend, but some mothers insisted that the godfather come along to the church, too, especially when there was a fear that the godparent's marriage might not be permanent.

28. Related terms are *djilo*, "heart"; *godji*, "mind"; and *djivel*, "live."

29. When we are asleep, the soul may wander, and hence people "dream" (*suno dikhel*). Some Gypsies said that the soul is not in the body at all during sleep, and if the *lindra* does not return, a person dies during sleep.

30. Okely (1983, p. 228) made a pioneering analysis suggesting that for English Gypsies a dead person "has become like a gorgio [*gażo*]—death was equivalent to assimilation" into non-Gypsy society. Piasere (1984, pp. 235–242) later suggested that for Slovenian Rom in Italy the identity of the dead shifted around gradually from being *gażo*-like at first and then being reintegrated into the world of the Gypsy dead. Here I propose a slightly different interpretation, one that incidentally acknowledges the Christian context in which the Gypsies operate.

31. I take as my model the death of a Gypsy man, since men's funerals tended to be larger and more substantial affairs than women's. A respected woman's wake and funeral might, however, have outdone that of a marginal man.

32. Some said that one lights candles to provide light for the deceased on her journey to the other world. In the past, Vlach Gypsies surrounded their newborn babies with candles with the inverse intention. See Wlislocki (1886, p. 362). Candles kept troublesome spirits away, which was also the reason that the Rom lit them in front of saint's statues in church.

33. See Piasere (1984, pp. 237–242) for a very detailed discussion of the long process of dying among the Yugoslav Rom in Italy.

34. See also de Heusch (1966, p. 105).

35. It has not always been Gypsy women who have played this symbolic role. A study of the Rom in the 1930s described sexual games among young Gypsy boys and girls that had a similar ritual function. At the height of their "orgy," elder Rom effected a terrifying revitalization of the corpse—as if to dramatize the idea that sex at this time would create the very antithesis of the Rom's goal, to safely dispose of the body. See Nagy (1940, pp. 12–13).

36. Since the 1970s, when ecclesiastical Romany churches were founded, the leaders have been careful not to call themselves "priests" (*rasaj*) but have instead calqued the Hungarian term for "vicar" as *pasztori*.

37. Indeed, the whole notion of childhood is somewhat curtailed, the aim of upbringing being to create a young autonomous Gypsy as quickly as possible.

38. Among the peasants of Eastern Europe, there is a notion of the good death. See Kligman (1988) for Romania; Pine (1996) for Poland; and Fél and Hofer (1969) for Hungary. The good death comes in old age when a person can prepare for it, and the corpse is then surrounded by those whose future security derived from the person's efforts in the past. From a certain perspective, this kind of death does not threaten oblivion. The Gypsies, however, had no notion of a good death. Every death was construed as a sudden, violent, and utterly unexpected event, even when someone was already ill in hospital. (See also Piasere, 1984, p. 186.) The death of a Rom, ideologically speaking, could not be prepared for. And although grandchildren might lead the "final journey" of the deceased to the grave, this was not in celebration of fulfillment.

Čoro's mother and some other elderly women talked to me one day with incredulity of the *gaźo*s who prepared a place in a grave for a surviving spouse. To these women's astonishment, this custom had also been taken on by one family of rich Gypsies in Harangos who were maintaining a sepulchre. Both were considered victims of a murderous folly, since they invited death by preparing for it.

39. Bloch and Parry (1982, p. 27).

40. I am grateful to Fenella Cannell for pointing my thoughts in this direction.

41. See Stewart (1989).

42. Okely (1975, p. 61).

43. See, too, Okely's (1983, p. 212) account of her own treatment in England. Teasing among men and women was common in the Third Class, and after one christening I heard a young man asked whether he would sleep with his son's godmother. The clever answer, I was led to understand, was to say, "Yes, but as

a godmother [*kirvi*]," that is, not as a lover. To have shared a bed thus would have been no shame.

44. From a recording made by Judit Szegő. Out of context, when transcribing these tapes, women shrieked with embarrassed laughter on hearing such expressions.

45. I have translated using English slang, since these terms in Romany are also commonly terms of abuse, as our terms are.

46. Men denied that they would feel dirty after sex with a *gaźi*, and they laughed when I suggested that a Romni would not want them if she knew they had had sex with a *gaźi*.

47. When the Rom wished to talk about "real" prostitutes, women who were actually here and now and not just potentially promiscuous, they used the Romany term *lubnuj* or the obsolete Hungarian term *bárcás kurva* (licensed prostitute). Licensed prostitute refers to the existence of legalized prostitution in prewar Hungary.

48. Curiously, there were almost no pictures in Rom houses of Christ as an adult.

49. Ortner (1974, p. 73).

50. Dubisch (1986, p. 212).

51. See Sutherland (1975, pp. 258–261). Okely (1983, pp. 80–83, 207) suggested that there were "primary pollution taboos" associated with the symbolic separation of "the secret ethnic self" and that therefore "the pollution associated specifically with women, animals and death . . . follow[s] from this."

Uncleanness and lack of shame in Harangos were by no means only a condition of the *gaźo*s; in fact, rather fewer comments were made about *gaźo* standards of cleanliness than about other Gypsy families whose habits were regularly derided. *Gaźo* habits were taken as given; by contrast, the Gypsies had to continually prove to each other that they were maintaining proper behavior, and there were always some who could be represented as failing in this. Those families in which shameful behavior appeared to be tolerated (from allowing cats and dogs into the house, to permitting a daughter to wander around the town) were the subject of fairly vicious gossip and innuendo.

52. In this sense pollution beliefs here, though not really about women, do indicate a different, though perhaps not a lower, valuation of women. See Dubisch (1986, p. 212). Once gendered differences have been "used" by the Rom to construct other social differences, these then reflect back on the gender distinction.

53. Parry (1982). I am grateful to Maurice Bloch for pointing out the parallel to me. Male Gypsy dress, though formally smart, was often conspicuously dirty or messy to *gaźo* eyes, and I suspect that here, too, the Gypsies were showing to the world that they were not demeaned by this kind of dirt, since they knew that the *gaźo*s were dirty in another, much more profound sense.

54. Cows, which everyone said were good for breeding and kept by many Gypsies at some time or other, were, it will be remembered, socially and culturally marginal.

55. See, for example, Pina-Cabral (1986, p. 44). Fél and Hofer (1969, pp. 84, 121) also offered evidence of a similar symbolism.

Chapter 13

1. See Williams's (1984, pp. 407–413) discussion of the assertion of cohesion through the use of the phrase "we the Rom"; and Piasere's (1984, p. 131) reference to the same idea.

2. Williams (1984, p. 389).

3. See Parry and Bloch (1989) for a discussion of these kinds of separation. More generally, Hall et al. (1977) and Willis (1977) have shaped my thinking about the oppositional incorporation and conversion of "the outside."

4. Sutherland (1975, p. 15).

5. Hűbschmannova (1972, pp. 54–64).

6. For a recent example that provides a typical list, see Fonseca (1995, pp. 106–107). Fonseca was quoting other sources, but her own attitude seems more ambivalent. See also Basham (1967, pp. 514–517), who argued for a specifically Rajasthani origin.

7. Fraser (1993, p. 24).

8. At first sight, this seems to be a position close to the Communist parties of Eastern Europe, which saw the Gypsies as exhibiting a lifestyle. Perhaps the problem is one of cultural meaning: Our ideology of ethnicity binds us to an opposition between "freely chosen" lifestyle and "traditional" ethnic identity. In this postenlightenment age it is, peculiarly, still more acceptable to be different not because one has chosen to be so but because one was "born into that way."

9. See Kosa (1982, pp. 585–586).

10. My inspiration is Leach's (1954, pp. 29–61, 288–292) discussion of Kachin and Shan as identities that, he said, were not attached to "tribal entities" of any scale.

11. Bell (1984, p. 294).

12. In southern Poland Gorale villagers said that one had to "speak/lie like a Gypsy" (*treaba cyganzie*) to deal with the state. Francis Pine (personal communication).

13. See Gmelch (1977).

14. See Lowe and Shaw (1992).

15. Le Goff (1985, p. 57).

16. See also Gurevich (1985); and Little (1978).

17. Le Goff (1985, pp. 111, 114).

18. Ibid., p. 121.

19. Le Goff's (1985) comment that social classes that rose thanks to toil were quick to deny their origins applied as much to socialist Eastern Europe as to preindustrial France. Communist leaders were quick to join hunting associations that retained their aristocratic style to the end. See Pünkősti (1986). The very existence of the laws declaring those who avoided work as "publicly dangerous" (*közveszelyesmunkakerülés*) suggested that the proletarian life had not convinced everyone, and the introduction of compulsory labor for the unemployed in 1986 could only have blackened further the image of manual labor.

20. Mayhew (1963); Braverman (1974); Beynon (1973).

21. Beynon (1973, p. 87).

22. Ibid., p. 111.

23. Ibid., p. 107.
24. Haraszti (1971); Burawoy (1985).
25. Westwood (1984, pp. 46–47).
26. Ibid., p. 21.
27. Ibid., p. 236.
28. Ibid., p. 102.
29. Ibid., p. 22. See also Pollert (1981).
30. Tunstall (1962, p. 117).
31. Ibid., p. 110.
32. Ibid., p. 200.
33. Ibid., p. 166.
34. Sutherland (1975, pp. 72, 89–91).
35. Okely (1983, pp. 53–54).
36. Acton (1974, pp. 250, 262); Okely (1983, pp. 56–60). See also Salo (1981, pp. 77–84).
37. See Piasere (1984, pp. 137–140).
38. From eighteenth-century sources such as Grellman's (1787, p. 32) study, one can see that the Gypsies may always have lived by a combination of wage labor for the propertied and forms of hustling and dealing.
39. If there was a time when the Rom were blacksmiths or musicians or horse dealers to the exclusion of all else, then the ideology of living without incorporating the *gaźo* aspect of life through labor-toil might have represented much of their experience, since these were all forms of illicit or infamous occupation in late-feudal Europe. However, many of the people listed as smiths in the census of 1782 may have also been engaged in other work for peasants, as Grellman's (1787, pp. 32–33) account suggests. Certainly by 1877 it is highly improbable that Harangos supported the forty full-time Rom musicians listed in the census. Self-ascription then may have been no more accurate than now.
40. Fél and Hofer (1969, p. 348).
41. Ibid., p. 198.
42. Ibid., p. 17.
43. I thank Akis Papataxiarchis for pointing this out to me. See Papataxiarchis (n.d.).
44. See also Okely's (1983, p. 62) account of "dossers" or "slaves" among English Traveler-Gypsies.
45. They were, however, fed in a separate room.
46. These men were also subject to almost daily sexual joking by both male and female Rom, having their sexuality discussed in an open and ribald way that no Rom would ever have suffered.
47. I am grateful to an anonymous reader for the image.
48. Erdős (1960, p. 9).
49. See also Sutherland's (1975, p. 289) intuition that the Rom's position "is always a precarious adaptation that is never resolved." The success of Romany evangelical churches with Gypsies across Europe is but one evidence of the potential instability of Gypsy ideology. See Williams (1991).
50. Benjamin (1973, pp. 259–60). He was commenting on *Angelus Novus*.
51. Ibid., p. 256.

BIBLIOGRAPHY

Acton, T. 1974. *Gypsy Politics and Social Change*. London: Routledge and Kegan Paul.

Alexander, P. 1992. What's in a Price: Trade Practices in Peasant (and Other) Markets. In *Contesting Markets: Analyses of Ideology, Discourse, and Practice*, ed. R. Dilley. Edinburgh: Edinburgh University Press.

Bács-Kiskun County. 1982. Beszámoló A Magyarországi Cigány kerdésről, Bács-Kiskun Megye [Annual Report on the Gypsy Question from Bács-Kiskun County], MSZMP (Hungarian Socialist Workers' Party) Archives, Budapest.

Bán, G., and G. Pogány. 1957. *A magyarországi cigány helyzetérol* (On the situation of Hungarian Gypsies). Budapest: Ministry of Labor. Mimeographed.

Barth, F. 1969. Introduction. In *Ethnic Groups and Boundaries*, ed. F. Barth. London: George Allen and Unwin.

Basham, A. 1967. *The Wonder That Was India*. London: Fontana-Collins.

Báthory, J. 1988. A cigányság a politika tükrében (Gypsies in the mirror of politics). *Világosság* 8–9:615–623.

Baumann, R. 1986. *Story, Performance, and Event: Contextual Studies of Oral Narrative*. Cambridge: Cambridge University Press.

Bebesi, K. 1983. Honnan? Hova? (Whence? Whither?). In *Roma: Válogatás a cigányokkal kapcsolatos sajtótermékekből* (Roma: A selection of media treatment of Gypsies), ed. J. Bársony. Pp. 60–64. Budapest: Népművelési Intézet.

Bell, P. 1984. *Peasants in Socialist Transition: Life in a Collectivized Hungarian Village*. Berkeley and Los Angeles: University of California Press.

Benjamin, W. 1973. *Illuminations*. London: Fontana-Collins.

Beynon, H. 1973. *Working for Fords*. London: Allen Lane.

Bloch, M. 1974. Symbol, Song, Dance, and Features of Articulation: Is Religion an Extreme Form of Traditional Authority? *Archives Européennes de Sociologie* 15 (1):55–81.

_____. 1975. Property and the End of Affinity. In *Marxist Analyses and Social Anthropology*, ed. M. Bloch. London: Malaby.

_____. 1983. *Marxism and Anthropology: The History of a Relationship*. Oxford: Clarendon Press.

_____. 1986. *From Blessing to Violence*. Cambridge: Cambridge University Press.

Bloch, M., and J. Parry, eds. 1982. *Death and the Regeneration of Life*. Cambridge: Cambridge University Press.

Braudel, F. 1982. *The Wheels of Commerce*. Vol. 2: *Civilization and Capitalism*. London: Fontana-Collins.

Braverman, H. 1974. *Labor and Monopoly Capital: The Degradation of Work in the Twentieth Century*. New York: Monthly Review Press.

Burawoy, M. 1985. *The Politics of Production:* London: Verso.

Búzás, Gy. 1983. Egy cigány telep felszámolása (Winding up a Gypsy settlement). In *Roma: Válogatás a cigányokkal kapcsolatos sajtótermékekből* (Roma: A selection of the media treatment of Gypsies), ed. J. Bársony. Pp. 103–105. Budapest: Népművelési Intézet.

Campbell, J. 1964. *Honour, Family, and Patronage: A Study of Institutions and Moral Values in a Greek Mountain Community.* Oxford: Oxford University Press.

Cohen, A. 1969. *Custom and Politics in Urban West Africa: A Study of Hausa Migrants in Yoruba Towns.* London: Routledge and Kegan Paul.

Csalog, Z. S. 1984. Jegyzetek a cigányság támogatásának kérdéseiröl (Notes on questions about the support given to Gypsies). *Szociálpolitikai Értesitö* 2:36–79.

Csenki, S., and I. Csenki. 1980. *Cigány népballadák és keservesek* (Gypsy folk songs and laments). Budapest: Gondolat.

Day, S. 1995. What Counts as Rape? Physical Assaults and Broken Contract: Contrasting Images of Rape Among London Sex Workers. In *Sex and Violence: Issues in Representation and Experience*, ed. P. Harvey and P. Gose. London: Routledge.

De Heusch, L. 1966. *A la découverte des Tsiganes: Une expedition de reconnaissance (1961).* Brussels: Editions de L'Institut de Sociologie de L'Université Libre.

De Vaux de Foletier, F. 1983. *Le monde des Tsiganes.* Paris: Berger-Levrault.

Demszky, G. 1980. Cs. (Reduced value). *Kritika* 10:18–21. Reprinted in *Roma, Válogatás a cigányokkal kapcsolatos sajtótermékekből* (Roma: A selection of the media treatment of Gypsies), ed. E. Kalla. Pp. 63–84. Budapest: Népművelési Intézet.

Domán, I. 1984. *A Szarvasi Cigányok* (The Gypsies of Szarvas). Kecskemét, Hungary: Petőfi Nyomda.

Douglas, M. 1966. *Purity and Danger.* London: Routledge and Kegan Paul.

Dubisch, J. 1986. Culture Enters Through the Kitchen: Women, Food, and Social Boundaries in Rural Greece. In *Gender and Power in Rural Greece*, ed. J. Dubisch. Princeton: Princeton University Press.

Dumont, L. 1977. *From Mandeville to Marx: Genesis and Triumph of Economic Ideology.* Chicago: University of Chicago Press.

Eger. 1984. Beszámoló a megyében élő cigánylakosság helyzetéről (Report on the condition of the Gypsies living in the county). Eger, County Archives.

Egri Újság. 1892. A Gyöngyöshalászi arany csinálók (The gold-makers of Gyöngyöshalász). Author anonymous. 3.ik évfolyam (3rd year of pub.), no. 22, May 31, pp. 173–174.

Erdei, F. 1941. *A Magyar paraszttársadalom* (Hungarian peasant society). Budapest: Franklin Társulat.

Erdős, K. 1958. Notes on Pregnancy and Birth Customs Among the Gypsies of Hungary. *Journal of the Gypsy Lore Society* [hereafter, *JGLS*] 27 (pts. 1–2):50–56.

_____. 1959. Gypsy Horse Dealers in Hungary. *JGLS* 16 (pts. 1–2):113–124.

_____. 1960. Le problème Tsigane en Hongrie (The Gypsy Problem in Hungary). *Études Tsiganes* 3:1–10.

_____. 1961a. Jottings on Gypsy Judicature in Hungary. *JGLS* 18 (pt. 3):51–60.

_____. 1961b. Remarque sur le problème Tsigane en Hongrie (Note on the Gypsy Problem in Hungary). *Études Tsiganes* 7:8–13.

Fejtö, F. 1974. *A History of the People's Democracies.* Harmondsworth, England: Penguin.

Fél, E., and T. Hofer. 1961. Az átányai gazdálkodás ágai (The branches of agriculture in Átány). *Néprajzi Közlemények* 6 (2):1–220.

_____. 1969. *Proper Peasants: Traditional Life in a Hungarian Village.* Chicago: Aldine.

Fonseca, I. 1995. *Bury Me Standing.* London: Chatto and Windus.

Forray, K., and A. Hegedűs. 1985. *Az együttélés rejtett szabályai: Egy cigány csoport sikerének mértéke és ázra egy iskolában* (The hidden rules of cohabitation: The degree and cost of a Gypsy group's successes in a school). Budapest: Országos Pedagógiai Intézet.

Fraser, A. 1993. *The Gypsies.* Oxford: Blackwell.

Galasi, P., and G. Sziráczki, eds. 1985. *Labour Market and Second Economy in Hungary.* Frankfurt: Campus Verlag.

Geertz, C. 1960. *The Religion of Java.* Chicago: University of Chicago Press.

Gellner, E. 1973. Concepts and Society. In *Rationality,* ed. B. Wilson. Oxford: Blackwell.

Gmelch, G. 1977. *The Irish Tinkers: The Urbanization of an Itinerant People.* Menlo Park, Calif.: Cummings.

Gmelch, S. 1986. Groups That Don't Want in: Gypsies and Other Artisan, Trader, and Entertainer Minorities. *Annual Review of Anthropology* 15:307–330.

Grass, G. 1992. Losses. *Granta,* no. 42, pp. 99–108.

Grellmann, A. 1787. *A Dissertation on the Gypsies.* Trans. M. Roper. London.

Gropper, R. 1975. *Gypsies in the City: Culture Patterns and Survival.* Princeton: Darwin Press.

Gurevich, V. 1985. *Categories of Medieval Culture.* Trans. G. Campbell. London: Routledge and Kegan Paul.

Guy, W. 1975. Ways of Looking at Rom: The Case of Czechoslovakia. In *Gypsies, Tinkers, and Other Travellers,* ed. F. Rehfisch. London: Academic Press.

_____. 1978. The Attempt of Socialist Czechoslovakia to Assimilate Its Gypsy Population. Ph.D. Thesis. University of Bristol.

Hajdu, A. 1958. Les Tsiganes de Hongrie et Leur Musique. *Études Tsiganes* 1:1–30.

Hall, S., et al. 1977. *Resistance Through Rituals.* London: Hutchinson.

Hann, C. 1980. *Tázlár: A Village in Hungary.* Cambridge: Cambridge University Press.

Harangos. 1964. A Cigánykerdés (The Gypsy question). Report dated July 20.

_____. 1977. Beszámoló a cigány lakosság helyzetéről (Report on the condition of the Gypsies). Művlődési osztaly (Cultural Department). April 14.

_____. 1979. Beszámoló a cigány lakosság helyzetéről (Report on the condition of the Gypsies). Vegrehajtó Bizottság (Executive Committee).

_____. 1985. Beszámoló a cigány lakosság helyzetéről (Report on the condition of the Gypsies). Vegrehajtó Bizottság (Executive Committee). October 24.

Haraszti, M. 1971. *A Worker in a Worker's State.* London: Allen Lane.

Havas, G. 1982a. A Baranya megyei teknővájó cigányok (The Gypsies of Baranya County). In *Cigányok* (Gypsies), ed. M. Andor. Budapest: Művelődési Intézet.

_____. 1982b. Foglalkózásváltási stratégiák különböző cigány közösségekben (Strategies for changing occupations in differing Gypsy communities). In *Cigányok* (Gypsies), ed. M. Andor. Budapest: Művelődési Intézet.

Havas, G., I. Kertesi, and I. Kemény. 1995. The Statistics of Deprivation. *Hungarian Quarterly* 36:67–80.

Hirschman, A. 1977. *The Passions and the Interests: Political Arguments for Capitalism Before Its Triumph*. Princeton: Princeton University Press.

Hollós, M., and B. Máday. 1983. Introduction. In *New Hungarian Peasants: An East-Central European Experience with Collectivization*, ed. M. Hollós and B. Máday. Brooklyn, N.Y.: Brooklyn College Press.

Houseman, M. 1994. Etudes tsiganes et questions d'anthropologie. *Etudes Tsiganes* (special issue) 2:11–18.

Hűbschmannová, M. 1972. What Can Sociology Suggest About the Origin of Roms? *Archiv Orientalni* 40 (pt. 1):51–64.

Hungarian Statistical Handbook. 1984. Budapest: Országos Statisztikai Hivatal.

Javor, K. 1983. Continuity and Change in the Social and Value Systems of a North Hungarian Village. In *New Hungarian Peasants: An East-Central European Experience with Collectivization*, ed. M. Hollós and B. Máday. Brooklyn, N.Y.: Brooklyn College Press.

Josephides, L. 1985. *The Production of Inequality: Gender and Exchange Among the Kewa*. London: Tavistock.

Kaminski, I.-M. 1980. *The State of Ambiguity: Studies of Gypsy Refugees*. Gothenburg, Sweden: Anthropological Research.

Kemény, I. 1976. A magyarországi cigány lakosság (The Gypsy population of Hungary). *Valóság* 1:63–72.

_____. 1978. La chaine dans une usine hongroise. *Actes de la Recherche en Sciences Sociales* (November), 8–12.

Kenedi, J. 1986. Why Is the Gypsy the Scapegoat and Not the Jew? *East European Reporter* 2 (1):11–14.

Kertesi, G., and G. Sziráczki. 1985. Worker Behaviour in the Labour Market. In *Labour Market and Second Economy in Hungary*, ed. P. Galasi and G. Sziráczki. Frankfurt: Campus Verlag.

Kertész-Wilkinson, I. Forthcoming. Song Performance: A Model for Social Interaction Among Vlach Gypsies in Southeastern Hungary. In *New Perspectives on Roma Culture*, ed. T. Acton. Hertford, England: University of Hertfordshire Press.

Kiss, L. [1939] 1981. *A szegény emberek élete* (The life of the poor). Vol. 1. Reprint, Budapest: Gondolat.

Kligman, G. 1988. *The Wedding of the Dead: Ritual, Poetics, and Popular Culture in Transylvania*. Berkeley and Los Angeles: University of California Press.

Kolakowski, L. 1978. *Main Currents of Marxism*. Vol. 2. Oxford: Clarendon Press.

Kósa, L. 1982. Székelyek (The Szeklers). In *Magyar néprajzi lexikon* (Hungarian ethnographical encyclopedia), ed. G. Ortutay. Vol. 3. Budapest: Akadémia.

Kovalcsik, K. 1985. *Vlach Gypsy Folk Songs in Slovakia*. Budapest: MTA Zenetudományi Intézet.

_____. 1987. Popular Dance Music Elements in the Folk Music of Gypsies in Hungary. *Popular Music* 1 (1):45–65.

_____. 1988. Mihály Rostás, a Gypsy story-teller. *Hungarian Gypsy Studies*, no. 5. MTA Néprajzi Kutató Csoport (Hungarian Academy of Sciences' Ethnographic Research Institute).

_____. 1991. Chansons Tsiganes lentes sur les experiences personelles: L'écart entre le chanteur et le groupe (Slow Gypsy Songs About Personal Experiences: The Gap Between the Singer and the Group). *Cahiers de la Litérature Orale*, no. 30, pp. 45–64.

Kozák, I. 1984. A cigány lakosság helyzetének javitása érdekében hozott központi határozatok végrehajtott akadalyozó tényezők (Factors obstructing the implementation of central resolutions aimed at improving the position of the Gypsy population), in *Szocial-Politikai Értesitő*, no. 2, pp. 11–35.

Ladó, M., and A. Tóth. 1988. In the Shadow of the Formal Rules. *Economic and Industrial Democracy* 9 (4):523–533.

Lampland, M. 1991. Pigs, party secretaries, and private lives in Hungary. *American Ethnologist* 18 (3):459–479.

Lawrence, E. 1982. *Rodeo: An Anthropologist Looks at the Wild and the Tame.* Chicago: University of Chicago Press.

Le Goff, J. 1985. *Time, Work, and Culture in the Middle Ages.* Chicago: Goldhammer.

Leach. E. 1954. *Political Systems of Highland Burma.* London: Athlone Press.

Lévi-Strauss, C. 1966. *The Savage Mind.* London: Weidenfield and Nicholoson.

_____. 1977. Race and Culture. In *Structural Anthropology*, ed. C. Lévi-Strauss. Vol 2. 1952. Reprint. London: Allen Lane.

Lichtheim, G. 1961. *Marxism: An Historical and Critical Study.* London: Routledge and Kegan Paul.

Little, L. 1978 *Religious Poverty and the Profit Economy in Medieval Europe.* London: Paul Elek.

Lowe, R., and W. Shaw. 1992. *Travellers: Voices of the New Age Nomads.* London: Fourth Estate.

Marrese, M. 1981. The Evolution of Wage Regulation in Hungary. In *Hungary: A Decade of Economic Reform*, ed. P. Hare, P. Radice, and N. Swain. London: Allen and Unwin.

Marshall, L. 1961. Sharing, Talking, and Giving: Relief of Social Tensions Among !Kung Bushmen. *Africa* 31 (3):231–244.

Marx, K. 1973. *Grundrisse: Contribution to a Critique of Political Economy.* Harmondsworth, England: Penguin.

Marx, K., and Engels, F. 1958. *Selected Works.* Moscow: Progress Publishers.

_____. 1996. *The Communist Manifesto.* London: Phoenix.

Mayall, D. 1988. *Gypsy-Travellers in Nineteenth-century Society.* Cambridge: Cambridge University Press.

Mayhew, H. 1963. Selections from London Labour and the Labouring Poor (1851–1852), ed. E. Thompson. Oxford: World Classics.

Mészáros, Gy., and J. Vekerdi. 1978. *A cigányság a felelmekedés útján* (Gypsies on the road up). Budapest: Hazafias Népfront.

Mezey, B., ed. 1986. *A magyarországi cigánykerdés dokumentumokban, 1422–1985* (The Hungarian Gypsy question through documents, 1422–1985). Budapest: Kossuth.

Miller, C. 1975. American Rom and the Ideology of Defilement. In *Gypsies, Tinkers, and Other Travellers*, ed. F. Rehfisch. London: Academic Press.

Moldova, Gy. 1988. *Bűn az élet* (A life of crime/life is a crime). Budapest: Magvető.

Myers, F. 1986. *Pintupi Country, Pintupi Self: Sentiment, Place and Politics Among Western Desert Aborigines*. Washington: Smithsonian Institution Press.

Nagy, I. 1940. The Gypsies of the Sárrét *JGLS* 19 (pt. 1):1–16; (pt. 2):67–77; (pts. 3–4):152–159.

Okely, J. 1975. Gypsy Women: Models in Conflict. In *Perceiving Women*, ed. S. Ardener. London: Malaby.

———. 1983. *The Traveller-Gypsies*. Cambridge: Cambridge University Press.

Országos Statisztikai Hivatal. 1895. *Magyar statisztikai közlemények, a Magyarországban 1893. január 31.-én végrehajtott cigányösszeirás eredmnyei* (The results of the census carried out in Hungary among Gypsies on 31 Jan. 1893). Budapest: Orsz. Stat. Hiv., Athenaeum.

Ortner, S. 1974. Is Female to Male as Nature Is to Culture? In *Woman, Culture, and Society*, ed. M. Rosaldo and L. Lamphere. Stanford: Stanford University Press.

Ortutay, G. 1982. *Magyar néprajzi lexikon* (Hungarian ethnographical encyclopedia). Vol. 3. Budapest: Akadémia.

Panaitescu, P. 1941. The Gypsies in Wallachia and Moldavia: A Chapter of Economic History. *JGLS* 20 (pt. 2):58–72.

Papataxiarchis, E. N.d. Gambling, Competitive Drinking, and the Configurations of Masculinity in a Greek Aegean Community. Paper presented at a conference on identity, Le Creuseot, France, 1992.

Parry, J. 1982. Sacrificial Death and the Necrophagous Ascetic. In *Death and the Regeneration of Life*, ed. M. Bloch and J. Parry. Cambridge: Cambridge University Press.

Parry, J., and M. Bloch. 1989. Introduction. In *Money and the Morality of Exchange*, ed. J. Parry and M. Bloch. Cambridge: Cambridge University Press.

Piasere, L. 1984. *Mare Roma: Categories humaines et structure sociale: Une contribution a l'ethnologie Tsigane*. Paris. Études et documents balkaniques, no. 6.

Pina-Cabral, J. 1986. *Sons of Adam, Daughters of Eve: The Peasant World-view in the Alto Minho*. Oxford: Oxford University Press.

Pine, F. 1987. Kinship, Marriage, and Social Change in a Polish Highland Village. Ph.D. thesis presented at University of London.

———. 1996. Naming the House and Naming the Land: Kinship and Social Groups in the Polish Highlands. *Journal of the Royal Anthropological Institute* 2 (3):443–460.

Pollert, A. 1981. *Girls, Wives, Factory Lives*. London: Macmillan.

Pünkősti, A. 1986. *Vadat, halat s mi jó falat* (Game, fish, and what good food). Budapest: Szépirodalmi Kiadó.

Réger, Z. 1990. Romani Child-directed Speech and Children's Language Among Gypsies in Hungary. *Language in Society* 20:601–617.

Rehfisch, F., ed. 1975. *Gypsies, Tinkers, and Other Travellers*. London: Academic Press.

Reisman, K. 1974. Contrapuntal Conversations in an Antiguan Village. In *Explorations in the Ethnography of Speaking*, ed. R. Baumann and J. Scherzer. Cambridge: Cambridge University Press.

Salo, M. 1981. Kalderaś Economic Organization. In *The American Kalderaś: Gypsies in the New World*, ed. M. Salo. Hackettstown, N.J.: Centenary College Gypsy Lore Society.

Schutz, A. 1964. Making Music Together: A Study in Social Relationship. In *Collected Works*, ed. A. Brodersen. Vol. 2. The Hague: Martinus Nijhoff.

Scott, J. 1985. *Weapons of the Weak: Everyday Forms of Peasant Resistance*. New Haven: Yale University Press.

Silverman, C. 1981. Pollution and Power: Gypsy Women in America. In *The American Kalderaś: Gypsies in the New World*, ed. M. Salo. Hackettstown, N.J.: Centenary College Gypsy Lore Society.

_____. 1988. Negotiating Gypsiness: Strategies of Ethnicity in the American context. In *Symbols and Situations in Ethnicity*, ed. J. Cicala and S. Stern. Detroit: Wayne State University Press.

Simmel, G. 1978. *The Philosophy of Money*. London: Routledge and Kegan Paul.

Smith, C. 1989. *Auctions: The Social Construction of Value*. London: Harvester Wheatsheaf.

Stewart, M. 1988. Brothers in Song: The Persistence of (Vlach) Gypsy Community and Identity in Socialist Hungary. Ph.D. thesis presented at University of London.

_____. 1989. "True Speech": Song and the Moral Order of a Vlach Gypsy Community in Hungary. *Man* 24:79–102.

_____. 1990. Gypsies, Work, and Civil Society. In *Market Economy and Civil Society in Hungary*, ed. C. Hann. London: Frank Cass.

_____. 1992. I Can't Drink Beer, I've Just Drunk Water: Alcohol, Bodily Substance, and Commensality Among Hungarian Rom. In *Alcohol, Gender, and Culture*, ed. D. Gefou-Madianou. London: Routledge.

_____. 1994. Mauvaises morts, prêtres impurs et le pouvoir récupérateur du chant, les rituels mortuaires chez les Tsiganes de Hongrie. *Terrain* 20:21–36.

_____. 1995. "Identita sostanziale e identita relazionale": Gli Zingari ungheresi sons un gruppo "etnico"? In *Comunita girovaghe, comunita zingare*, ed. L. Piasere. Naples: Liguori.

Strathern, M. 1978. The Achievement of Sex: Paradoxes in Hagen Gender Thinking. In *The Yearbook of Symbolic Anthropology*, ed. E. Schwimmer. London: Hurst.

_____. 1981. Self-interest and the Social Good: Some Implications of Hagen Gender Imagery. In *Sexual Meanings*, ed. S. Ortner and H. Whitehead. Cambridge: Cambridge University Press.

Sutherland, A. 1975. *Gypsies: The Hidden Americans*. London, Tavistock.

Swain, N. 1985. *Collective Farms Which Work?* Cambridge: Cambridge University Press.

Szent-Györgyi, K. 1983. Ranking Categories and Models in Two Villages of Northeastern Hungary. In *New Hungarian Peasants: An East-Central European Experience with Collectivization*, ed. M. Hollós and B. Madáy. Brooklyn, N.Y.: Brooklyn College Press.

Szuhay, P. 1995. Arson on Gypsy Row. *Hungarian Quarterly* 36:81–91.

Tunstall, J. 1962. *The Fishermen.* London: MacGibbon and Kee.

Turnbull, C. 1978. The Politics of Non-aggression. In *Learning Non-aggression: The Experience of Non-literate Societies*, ed. A. Montagu. Oxford: Oxford University Press.

Vekerdi, J. 1971. The Gurvari Gypsy Dialect in Hungary. *Acta Orient. Hung.* XXIV (3:381-389).

_____. 1972. Eltérő vélemények a cigánykerdésben (Divergence of opinion on the Gypsy question). *Forrás* 6:57–61.

_____. 1974. Nemzetiség-e a cigányság? (Are the Gypsies a national minority?). *Napjaink* 10:1.

_____. 1981. Nyelvészeti adalékok a cigányság östörténetéhez (Linguistic data on the ancient history of the Gypsies). *Nyelvtudómányi Közlemények* 81 (2):409–421.

_____. 1983. *A magyarországi cigány nyelvjárások szótára* (The dictionary of Gypsy dialects in Hungary). Pécs, Hungary: Janus Pannonius Tudományegyetem Tanárképzo Kar, Tanulamányok VII.

Vendégh, S. 1960. A Magyarországi Cigány Lakosság között végzendő Munka Időszerü Feladatai (Tasks of the day to be carried out among the Hungarian Gypsy population). *Tajékoztató,* no. 2, pp. 38–55.

Verdery, K. 1991. Theorizing Socialism: A Prologue to the Transition. *American Ethnologist* 18:419–439.

Vig, R. 1976. Sleeve notes to *Gypsy Folk Songs from Hungary.* Budapest: MHV, Hungaroton, SLPX 18028–29. Record.

Warriner, D. 1938. *The Economics of Peasant Farming.* Oxford: Oxford University Press.

Weber, M. 1947. *The Theory of Social and Economic Organization.* New York: Free Press.

Westwood, S. 1984. *All Day, Every Day: Factory and Family in the Making of Women's Lives.* London: Pluto Press.

Williams, P. 1982. The Invisibility of the Kalderash of Paris: Some Aspects of the Economic and Settlement Patterns of the Paris Suburbs. *Urban Anthropology* 11 (3–4):315–345.

_____. 1984. *Marriage Tsigane: Une cérémonie de fiançailles chez les Rom de Paris.* Paris: L'Harmattan, Selaf.

_____. 1991. Le miracle et la necessité: Apropos du développement du pentecôtisme chez les Tsiganes. *Archives de Sciences Sociales des Religions* 73:81–98.

Willis, P. 1977. *Learning to Labour: How Working-class Kids Get Working-class Jobs.* London: Gower.

Wlislocki, H. 1986. Az erdélyi sátoros cigányok keresztelési és temetési szokásai (The christening and burial customs of the Transylvanian tent Gypsies). *Vasárnapi Újság* 23–24:52.

ABOUT THE BOOK AND AUTHOR

UNTIL 1989 IT WAS OFFICIAL COMMUNIST POLICY in eastern Europe to absorb Gypsies into the "ruling" working class. But many Gypsies fought to maintain their separate identity. This book is about the refusal of one group of Gypsies—the Rom—to abandon their way of life and accept assimilation into the majority population. It is a story about the sources of cultural diversity in modern industrial society and about the fear and hatred that such social and cultural difference may give rise to. The core of the book, based on eighteen months of observation of daily life in a Gypsy settlement, describes the cultivation, celebration, and reinvention of cultural difference and diversity by a people deemed by their social superiors to be too stupid and uncivilized to have a "culture" at all.

Michael Stewart received his Ph.D. from the London School of Economics. He has since been a documentary producer with the BBC and is currently a Leverhulme Research Fellow at LSE.

289

INDEX